CW00696390

WORLD ANIMAL DREAMING

REVISED AND EXPANDED EDITION

Interpreting the symbolic language of the world's animals

SCOTT ALEXANDER KING

ILLUSTRATED BY KAREN BRANCHFLOWER

Animal Dreaming
www.animaldreaming.com

Animal Dreaming Publishing
www.animaldreamingpublishing.com

WORLD ANIMAL DREAMING
Revised and Expanded

ANIMAL DREAMING PUBLISHING
PO Box 5203 East Lismore NSW 2480
AUSTRALIA
Phone +61 2 6622 6147

www.AnimalDreamingPublishing.com
www.facebook.com/AnimalDreamingPublishing

Originally published in 2006 by New Holland Australia under the title, 'Animal Messenger',
World Animal Dreaming has been completely revised, redesigned and expanded

First published in 2014
Reprinted in 2018
Copyright text © Scott Alexander King
www.AnimalDreaming.com
Copyright illustrations and cover art © Karen Branchflower

ISBN 978-0-6481820-7-8

All rights reserved. No part of this publication may be reproduced in whole or in part, stored
in a retrievable system, or transmitted in any form or by any means, eletronic, mechanical,
photocopying, recording or otherwise, without written permission of the copyright holder or
publisher.

This book is intended for spiritual and emotional guidance only.
It is not intended to replace medical assistance or treatment.

Designed by Animal Dreaming Publishing
Printed in Australia

I dedicate this book to my wife, Trudy, and our three children,
Rosie, Kaleb and Oskar

In loving memory of Rebecca; Rosie's Angel

Not to hurt our humble brethren (the animals) is our first duty to them,
but to stop there is not enough. We have a higher mission – to be of service
to them whenever they require it. If you have men who will exclude any of
God's creatures from the shelter of compassion and pity, you will have men
who will deal likewise with their fellow men.
Saint Francis of Assisi

Mother to Light
As your Spirit shines bright
From the Hawk in the Sky
The ever watching Eye
And the Deer that leaps
All heart she keeps
Born blood of her in your veins
And cry with her every time it rains

Matthew Barquero

CONTENTS

PREFACE

It is impossible to estimate how many animal species are lost each year to extinction, or how many species remain. Of the five to 15 million species of plants, animals and micro-organisms thought to exist in the world today, only about 1.5 million have been documented. Biologists estimate about 300,000 plant species, between four and eight million insects and perhaps 50,000 vertebrates currently share the planet with us, with about 1,130 mammalian species and 1,194 bird species listed as endangered. Few people know that we are losing species to changes in land use, unsustainable use of natural resources, invasive introduced species, climate change, growth in human population and consumer lifestyle, waste and pollution, urban development and international conflict far quicker than the rate of extinction determined by natural selection. Few realise, for example, that as many as 137 species become extinct every day; 50,000 species every year. Species at risk of becoming extinct are classified as 'endangered'; species with little or no chance of survival if the causal factors are allowed to continue. The word 'extinct' is used to describe a species of which no living members exist.

Decimation of habitat is probably the biggest cause of species loss in the world today. Expansion of agricultural land, logging and overgrazing has contributed greatly to forest loss and degradation. About half of the world's oldest forests have already been lost to habitat destruction, with more disappearing 10 times faster than any form of natural replacement could ever keep up with. Around 17 million hectares of forested land is being cleared each year, threatening the existence of the birds and animals that rely on them. As human populations continue to increase and the natural habitats of the world's animal species continue to shrink, competition for living space and food will continue to pose a problem for man and beast alike.

Global warming is another potentially devastating environmental influence triggering the loss of many vulnerable species every day. Habitat change caused by global warming and the affected species' inability to migrate to new sites, are the biggest cause of species loss under these circumstances. It has been predicted that global warming alone will see the less mobile species in some areas completely wiped out in the near future. It is feared that most of the world's species will not be able to redistribute themselves effectively or quickly enough to survive the changes we are experiencing at present.

Pollution is also beginning to pay its toll with chemicals turning up in the blood and fat reserves of the animals living in some of the world's most pristine and remote environments. Chemicals used in pesticide crop sprays have been found to cause mutations and fertility problems in animals and birds that rely on the oceans and waterways for their survival. It has been predicted that in the not so distant future the Arctic, for example, will be devoid of ice during its summer months. Such an occurrence would not only see Polar Bears suffer immensely (successful hunting of their prey would be made almost impossible) and possibly pushed to the edge of possible extinction, but also all the other animals and people that depend on them for their survival. Polar Bear cubs have been discovered yielding both male and female sex organs, a direct consequence of the increase in pollution now infiltrating the polar North.

People have traded in animals for cash or exchange for centuries, relying on wildlife products for food, shelter, adornment and clothing. Did you know, though, that many of the world's rarest animals (consequently on the verge of extinction) are being bought and sold internationally through a trade in exotic 'pets', while others are being served up in fancy restaurants as illegal 'delicacies'? Demand has escalated exorbitantly over the past 15 years, with Gorilla meat, Bear paws (amputated without anaesthetic) and Shark fins (often sliced off while they are still alive) being served at wedding banquets, birthday feasts and business dinners.

At least a quarter of the world's population today relies on practices endorsed by traditional Chinese medicine. Trade in Chinese medicine is worth billions of dollars to China annually, with demand continuing to grow. Sadly, many traditional practitioners are resisting foreign demand for regulation of their practices to protect endangered species. They see human lives as being more important than those of animals. It is essential that a sustainable or alternative way to practise traditional Chinese medicine be found, and soon. The use of Tiger parts in traditional medicine can be traced back to more than 1,000 years ago in Chinese culture. The practice has, in a word, sanctioned illegal poaching in an attempt to fill demand, pushing the three remaining species of Tiger close to extinction. Of the eight subspecies of Tiger, two stand out as the most famous: the Bengal and the Sumatran. Unfortunately, due to poaching, there are only about 5,000 Bengal Tigers and between 300 and 500 Sumatran Tigers in the wild today. The Indochinese Tiger is limited to only 2,000 wild individuals, the South Chinese (or Amoy) Tiger to about 100, while the Siberian population has approximately only 450 animals left in the wild today. Sadly, the Javan, Balinese and Caspian Tigers have all been lost to extinction over the past 50 years. Today, one Tiger is killed every day to meet the international demand for traditional Chinese medicine. Moon Bears, too, are enslaved and killed for unsubstantiated 'medicinal' reasons. Taken from the wild by 'Bear Farmers' at three months of age (usually at the fatal cost of their mother), Moon Bears are trained as circus after which they are then confined to tiny cages and 'milked' of their bile. Valves are inserted (without anaesthesia) into the gall bladder in order to drain the bile.

Sometimes hollow steel tubes are simply pushed through the animal's abdomen, allowing the bile to drain into strategically placed bowls. Despite a clear and obvious lack of proven medicinal worth, the bile is harvested and sold as a traditional remedy for fever, liver failure and sore eyes, usually in the form of pills and powders, ointments, wines, lozenges, teas, and shampoos. The American Black Bear, Grizzly Bear and Polar Bear are also illegally targeted for their 'medicinally prized' body parts. Rhinoceros horn is also high on the list of most revered ingredients in traditional Chinese medicine. It is believed to hold properties that, when consumed internally as a powder, offer aphrodisiacal outcomes while simultaneously curing impotency, worms, epilepsy, vertigo, fever, stomach ache, convulsions and smallpox.

Some startling facts
- One half of the world's species will be extinct within the next 100 years; one quarter of all known mammals will be extinct within the next 30 years.
- As many as 137 species disappear from the Earth each day; 50,000 species every year
- Humans are to blame for the greatest mass extinction of species since the Dinosaurs disappeared 65 million years ago.
- Every habitat on every continent contains endangered species.
- Over the past 600 million years, extinction has only taken place at a rate of one species a year. Now, in the world's rainforests alone, we are losing 27,000 a year; 72 species a day; three every hour.
- In all of Earth Mother's four billion-year history, she has experienced five major extinctions. We are currently on the verge of another one.
- Animals are dying out an alarming rate: a thousand times faster than the natural rate of extinction.
- The population of the world's wild Tigers has declined by 95% in the past hundred years. Of the five known species of Tiger, three are now classified as extinct. There are only 5,000 Tigers left in the wild. One Tiger is killed every day.
- The population of the world's wild Black Rhinoceros has declined by 97% in the past 30 years.
- The population of the world's Orangutan has declined by 50% in the last decade. Sumatran Orangutans are currently listed as severely threatened and it is predicted that they will be extinct within the next five years.
- The population of the world's Sharks has declined by 80% in the past 15 years. 100 million Sharks are caught annually to feed consumer demand for Shark-fin soup.
- There are only 4,500 Snow Leopards left in the wild.
- Every species of Asian Bear is currently classified as endangered as they continue to be poached for their gall bladders and paws (which are amputated without anaesthetic). Currently, 7,000 Bears are imprisoned on bile farms.

- Sea Turtles have swum the world's oceans since the reign of the Dinosaurs and today face extinction.
- One thousand Dolphins are killed every day; one every two minutes.
- In the wild, Elephants live up to 70 years, but today very few enjoy a natural death.
- The population of the world's wild Asian Elephants has declined by 75%.
- At least 30,000 Blue Whales were once killed annually. Less than 6,000 Blue Whales exist in the world's oceans today. It will take more than a hundred years of serious, international protection to save them from extinction.
- One in eight bird species are in danger of extinction.
- One in three amphibian species are in danger of extinction.
- Half of the world's Freshwater Turtle species are in danger of extinction.
- Nearly half of the world's 235 species of primate are threatened by extinction.
- Less than 500 Mountain Gorillas exist in the wild today.
- Less than 300 Sumatran Rhinoceroses exist in the wild today.
- Less than 60 Javan Rhinoceroses exist in the wild today.
- Less than 50 Florida Cougars exist in the wild today.
- Less than 200 Siberian Tigers exist in the wild today.
- Less than 3,000 Komodo Dragons exist in the wild today.
- Less than 150 Golden Lion Tamarins exist in the wild today.
- Less than 1,600 Giant Pandas exist in the wild today.

Things that you can do to help
- Boycott travelling animal shows in which animals are often neglected or abused.
- Never purchase wild or exotic animals as pets. Many of these animals are taken directly from the wild and purchasing them only exacerbates the inhumane trade in exotic animals as 'pets'.
- Share your views by contacting your local newspaper, magazine or radio station regarding issues regarding animal welfare, or write to your local, state, and federal government officials about upcoming bills and/or animal rights.
- Arrange for an animal expert to visit your children's school and speak to your child's class in an attempt to raise awareness or dissuade the misconceptions surrounding some species of animal.
- Buy products and goods that do not have wrapping that will end up in landfill areas; areas that reduce natural habitat for wildlife.
- Reuse what you can, recycle what you can't, but no matter what, try to reduce the output of household garbage.
- Cut up six-pack rings that hold together soft drink and alcohol cans, thus reducing the chances of them becoming caught around the necks of birds and animals.
- Never take wild animals out of the wild and keep them as a pet.
- Encourage birds and small native mammals into your garden by planting 'feed' trees; it is during the colder periods that birds have the greatest difficulty finding plentiful food.
- Place a bird-bath in your garden or a bowl of fresh water under your garden tap.
- Initiate a community-based campaign to clean up a stream, wetland or park.
- Volunteer at your local animal shelter or apprentice yourself to a wildlife rescue officer.
- Avoid using chemical-based products in and around your home.
- Avoid products that rely on animal testing.
- Boycott companies that rely on vivisection and other such research techniques.
- Only buy products that are manufactured from materials that have been harvested in a sustainable way and boycott companies uncommitted to biodiversity, conservation and sustainable forest management.
- Only use humane animal traps. That way the target animal can be re-housed and you won't run the risk of accidentally killing other animals as well.

INTRODUCTION

My earliest conscious memory of seeing 'animal spirits' was an amazing and totally unexpected experience. I was about eight years of age, chatting with my younger sister in the kitchen of our home. Mid-conversation, we both stopped talking and looked toward the archaic Vulcan wall heater that hung on our kitchen wall. I finally whispered, 'Do you see that?' and she replied in a quaky voice, 'Yes'. We did not speak of it for a long time, but when we did we agreed that what we had seen looked suspiciously like little white Rabbits falling from the ceiling. Seriously! Although my sister is still very intuitive today, she has never admitted to seeing animals again. I, on the other hand, was followed everywhere I went by a large, black (domestic) Cat from that day on. I saw him on the bathroom vanity, on the coffee table and in the garden. He 'slept' on my bed and peered (and smiled) at me around corners and sat on my desk as I did my homework. Although I was never able to touch him, when I told my family, 'The Cat's here again', their flippant, 'Oh, is it?' response, led me to believe that they could see him too and that it was no big deal.

The Rabbit experience was a bit scary, as so many first-time mystical experiences are, but as I was a child who loved animals, the initial shock soon gave way to excitement. I literally began to seek them out. I looked for them everywhere, and that was when I first realised that the energy I had always felt with people held form. The form it began to take, when I really concentrated, was animalistic. I was able to determine whether people were trustworthy or not by simply 'feeling' their animals, or by asking myself, 'Do I feel comfortable with that animal?' I tried to tell my family but they sort of ignored me when I did. I guess our traditional church-oriented family history prevented them from asking questions. They simply did not understand, and so to avoid being asked tricky questions, they just ignored me in the hope it would go away. But it didn't, and so I grew up believing it was natural – like breathing, and because no one sat around discussing our amazing ability to breathe, I figured it was the same deal with seeing people's animals. So as a kid, I did not go around telling people 'I can see animal spirits'. What was the point? I thought everyone could do it.

Totemic blueprints

By writing *World Animal Dreaming*, I hope to foster a deeper appreciation of the animals that you share a spiritual bond with. I also hope to broaden the understanding of the animals that physically share this planet with us by endorsing them as more than just pets or playthings.

Animals, to me, are and always have been sacred messengers of Spirit and I am thrilled to have been given this opportunity to share the symbolisms that I have grown to celebrate as my personal relationship with Spirit. When I saw animals as a child, I instinctively knew 'stuff' about them and their lives. I discovered that not only did the animals offer insight into their past, present and future, they also held the keys that promised to help them unlock their pathways to success. I began to see animals as a projection of the soul, a blueprint; an externalised symbolic expression of personality and character: aspects for which people were grieving, or that needed healing or required attention. The readings I offer within the pages of this book, therefore, represent the interpretations of those blueprints... interpretations that helped *me* to better understand *myself* and the people I shared my world with. I discovered that we all call upon any number of these blueprints every day, to support us and enhance the quality and worthiness of our life.

As I grew and developed spiritually, I then began to see these blueprints as 'totems', or power allies that offered explanation into where a person was at and was then able to use this knowledge to 'read' them and to determine whether or not I trusted them or how I might help them or learn from them. I discovered that we might employ any number of these blueprints or 'totems' simultaneously or independently many times during the course of a day. They come and go, like spiritual helpers, 'angels' or guides. But it is my understanding that we are born with a pre-determined set of totemic blueprints that effectively afford us as individuals a sense of unity and purpose. They represent our strengths and our weaknesses. They represent our power, connection to Spirit and our soul essence. They also symbolise our shadow side, or those facets of ourselves we are unwilling or not yet ready to face. Each set of totemic blueprints are made up of several aspects that are represented in different ways, each one significant and sacred to the individual. These aspects embody our fundamental character and personality, our principles and ethics; our ability to express our beliefs, our wants, needs and desires; our sense of home and security, creativity, sexuality and potential; our vocation, calling, hobbies and health, relationships, legal issues, death, spirituality, religion, education, wisdom and travel; our purpose and Personal Power. Essentially, these aspects form the blueprints of individual expression, factors that dominate our life and how we live it. And these blueprints, to me, are physically embodied within the plethora of animals that share this planet with us.

I often refer to Spirit in my writing. To me, Spirit is the Creator; the One, the Source, the keeper of Great Mystery and the Void. It is both the god in his many forms and the goddess in hers. Spirit is all that is known to be unknowable, to be explored but never fully understood. Spirit is Magic.

It is Breath. Spirit represents balance: the fine line that exists between all that is 'light' and all that is 'dark'. Spirit demands that we trust, remember and know. It is both tangible and non-tangible and is found within all things feminine and all things masculine. It is both physical and non-physical. It is the tilling of the fields, the birthing of the children, the nurturing of the people and the changing of the seasons. It is the power found within one's dreams, intuition and the sacred darkness of the womb. It is war, lightning, sexual energy, passion and sunshine. It is rampant during the hunt and savoured in the kill.

Physical encounters

By sharing some of these animals with you, as well as the 'messages' I have grown to trust, I hope you may build on this foundation and develop *your own* relationship with the animals, the Earth Mother and Spirit. *World Animal Dreaming* was not written as an encyclopaedia of wisdom but was meant to serve more as an introductory guide; a base on which its readers may develop their own wisdom. Use the blank pages at the rear of the book to take notes, record observations and to journal your dreams. This is your link to the ways of animals (and yourself) through which you must feel comfortable to build on your inherent knowledge. Do not for one minute assume that *my* truth has to be *your* truth. The interpretations I have listed in this book represent a lifetime of personal discovery and interaction – *my* personal history with animals, and with this understanding, I invite you to use this book as a foundation on which to share *your* personal history.

World Animal Dreaming will not only help you identify 'What bird (or animal, etc) is that?' but also offer insight into what it might be trying to tell you. For example, the next time you have an unexpected physical encounter with an animal, instead of wondering, 'What was that all about?' refer to this book for *guidance*. Listen to your own feelings; the thoughts you were having just before the encounter or what was taking place in your life at the time, and use these insights to help ascertain the message the animal was trying to impart, its lesson or what it was trying to suggest you do. The messages are pure, untainted by judgment and free of guilt. They are offered directly to you from the Earth Mother.

Another option is to look upon this book as a source of daily affirmation. Before you rise from bed in the morning, take up the book and ask your higher self this question, 'How should I approach my day so that I might notice and embrace the opportunities that are presented to me, offering me the chance to grow, heal and prosper?' Then, simply open the book at random. You have asked a question imbued with intent so the answer you receive will be presented with equal respect. The first animal that you turn to is your messenger. If you make a pact with yourself to honour the wisdom offered by that animal, your day should reward you well or, at least be littered with opportunities to better handle familiar obstacles or limiting circumstances with a sense of empowered ownership and personal integrity.

Dreaming

Throughout this book the word 'Dreaming' denotes the wisdom and symbolic interpretation of the animals listed and has intentionally been used slightly out of context, the word referring more to the 'medicine' of the animal rather than its 'Dreaming'. To experience an animal by chance, and to have that animal share its wisdom on a spiritual level, is like absorbing aspects of its strength and power, or its medicine: energetic knowledge that can inspire change and healing within an individual. To experience a live Eagle, for example, could suggest the embracing of a spiritual life and the true, heartfelt honouring of Spirit's ways, with the discovery of a feather or a dead Eagle possibly implying the opposite or reverse: an understanding obtained in much the same way as the intended meanings of tarot cards are interpreted. When referring to the wisdom of the animals in this book, the word 'Dreaming' needs to be respectively viewed from the context of 'medicine', wisdom or teachings (as outlined above), because the word 'Dreaming' traditionally refers to the very deep, ancient relationship between a person or family group, the land and the Ancestor Spirits. The true 'Dreaming' of the animals can never truly be appreciated after just one brief encounter, unless you have a solid understanding of your family ancestral knowledge like the Indigenous People of Australia do. The word 'Dreaming', like the word 'totem', refers to ancient knowledge and ancestral lineage that outlines the family tree of a person, their family and their homeland while also helping to explain the creation of the Earth and everything on it.

Always in the oral tradition, legends from the Indigenous People of Australia's 'Dreamtime' explained daily phenomena and some were meant for initiated men's ears only. Much of the true essence of these stories, however, have been lost over time in translation, misinterpretation and the blending of one tribe's legend with the next by non-Aboriginal authors. Therefore I have deliberately excluded tribal or ancestral names, precise story outlines and spiritual associations shared with the animals by any particular people for fear of dishonouring their heritage and perhaps ignorantly recording false information. When writing this book it was not my intention to humiliate anger or distress any of Australia's Indigenous People (or any other culture or nation indigenous to any land mentioned in this book). Rather, it is my intention to value and record the primal connection that we, as a united people, hold with our animal brothers and sisters.

When next you feel lost or confused, simply raise your issue with the Earth Mother by audibly asking a relevant question. Once the question has been aired, all you need do is to listen and wait. The Earth Mother will send the animal best suited to offer explanation; the animal whose Dreaming best harnesses the issue and its productive outcome.

Ancient wisdom

Some say that in the beginning there was eternal darkness – a gentle void; a blanket of fertile nothingness that enveloped the Universal plains. The Great Mother was an ever-unfolding massive expanse of nurturing energy that lovingly wrapped around everything she encountered, drawing all into her protective womb. Then, a great physical power stirred and grew, expanding to many times its original size while waiting restlessly for the right time to stretch its masculine consciousness out into the Universe. The Great Mother, feeling the shifting forces at work, ventured forth to explore and a great eruption occurred. A cataclysmic explosion of such magnitude that torrents of red-hot liquid rock and gas went shooting out into the Universe, spewing molten rivers of fire and steam into the previously dormant, peaceful void. The Great Mother gathered together this rampant energy, pulling it deep within her womb where it continued to boil and where a calming, fertile atmospheric sheath formed around the new force, gradually taming the fiery passion. Within this sheath, the gaseous shards of liquid fire sent shooting into the void became the planets; the original 'stone people'. Our own Earth Mother was then birthed from the molten rock, and from her soil came the first 'standing people', the plants, shrubs, healing herbs and trees and. As the atmosphere reached equilibrium original bacterial life-forms wiggled into being followed by the insects and arachnids, the 'swimming beings' and those who dared to venture ashore to become the original 'winged ones', the hoofed and the clawed.

The phrase, 'we are all related' reminds us of the inherent relationship we forged with Nature at the beginning of time. A relationship that espouses the belief that man and animal are related: that all things are equal and that we are *all one*. One life-form depends upon the other. On a cellular level, we remember this ancient connection and integrate it on a subconscious level every day, but it is now time to make that relationship tangible again.

World Animal Dreaming represents the remembering of this sacred and ancient relationship.

The Dreamtime

According to the Indigenous People of Australia, the Dreamtime was the time before time, when the world was new and the Ancestor Spirits were wandering the Earth, often in human shape, helping to bring form to the land, the plants and the animals. Some Indigenous People refer to this time as 'The Dreaming' while others refer to their personal spiritual connection to the Ancients as The Dreaming. As the Ancestor Spirits wandered the Earth they set about forming links between groups and individuals and shaped the horizon by creating mountains and valleys, rivers and streams as they travelled. Places marked by the Ancestors held great spiritual significance for the people and stories and legends related to their Dreaming then emerged. This was a sacred time, alive with the magic of Creation; a time that is now gone but still imbued with great power for the people who continue to believe that the Spirits are present, disguised in the forms they adopted when the Earth was new.

The Indigenous People of Australia viewed Creation as based on a sacred 'power of seed' which was deposited deep within the Earth at the beginning of time. With the power of this seed, it is said, every worldly event or life progression that occurred left behind a residue of its energy within the Earth. Everything of the natural world was read as a symbolic diary, acted out in the beginning by the Ancestors. As with the tiny seed, the fertility of a place was weighed against the memory of its origin. This was called 'The Dreaming', which represented the sacred core of Earth Mother. The term 'Dreaming' could relate to one's personal spirituality or 'medicine', or the belief system held by the person's family or clan as a whole. Every clan member was allocated an animal totem at the moment of their birth: an animal spirit that not only offered the individual the strength of its wisdom, but that also protected the individual as they explored life by perhaps warding off illness or by removing obstacles and impending danger. During the Dreamtime, people could become animals and the animals could become people. The animals, on a cellular level, still remember this time, and now it is time for us remember to it, too.

Shape-shifting personified the memory for the ancient people. The donning of animal skins and body parts, the application of body paint (often mixed from blood, mud and clay), the mimicking and translation of animal movement and sound, ritualistic dance, hallucinogenic substances, smoke, fire and monotonous rhythm were typically combined to invoke and harness the spirit of certain animals for particular reasons. Shape-shifting fuses the spirit of an animal with that of an individual seeking its wisdom. By demonstrating their willingness to look at their physical form as a corporeal representation of an animal's spirit, shape-shifting helped drop inhibitions and ego so that they could walk as one with Spirit.

Sacred wisdom

Ancient Egypt also honoured the memory of animals and adorned towns and villages with animals sacred to their Ancestors. It was believed that the gods and goddesses, for example, could manifest in the form of particular species, and it was thought that honouring the animals would please their associated deity. Animals considered the incarnated forms of the gods and goddesses were treated well, living in or near sacred temples.

Cats, both domestic and wild, were considered benevolent and sacred to the people of Egypt, with many gods and goddesses taking Cat form (Bast, for example). The Cow (as Hathor) came to symbolise the mother of the pharaoh and feminine fertility, while the Bull was a symbol of masculinity and the pharaoh. The Cobra was a fertility goddess who was sometimes depicted nursing children. She was the protector of pharaoh and could punish criminals with her venom by bringing about blindness. The Crocodile was sacred to Ammut who was known as 'the devourer of the dead', punishing evil-doers by eating their hearts. The Crocodile was also sacred to Sobek, portrayed as a human with the head of a crocodile or as a Crocodile itself. The temples of Sobek usually had sacred lakes containing Crocodiles that were fed and cared for by specially trained priests. Falcons and Hawks were sacred to the god Horus. They were said to have protective powers associated with royalty and were often depicted hovering over the head of the pharaoh with outstretched wings. The Ibis was regarded as the reincarnation of Thoth, the god of knowledge, who took the form of an Ibis-headed man. The Jackal is associated with Anubis, the god of embalming and mummification, who was depicted as a black collared Jackal (or Dog) or a man with the head of a black Jackal or Dog. The Jackal was considered a guide to the newly dead because they were often seen haunting areas where tombs were built. Lions were believed associated with the rising and the setting of the sun and so were revered as guardians of the horizon. Sekhmet was shown either as a lioness, or a lioness-headed woman, who came into being as the Eye of Ra to destroy man and avenge the name of Ra. Sekhmet, however, was also known for her healing powers.

To many, the 'hunt' was symbolic of the search for the sacred self or the journey of the warrior as he quested for an explanation or deeper understanding of his very soul. The soul was, more often than not, depicted as an elusive white Stag (as in Arthurian legend, for example), while the hunt symbolically introduced the individual to his Inner Landscape (his inner self) by leading him deep into a 'dark, ominous forest'. I have journeyed with the White Stag many times. I stalked the Stag for years after reading about him as a kid in stories of King Arthur and Camelot. I wanted to corner the elusive Stag and to bring him down; to prove myself to the king and to the other knights. As a kid with low self-esteem, I felt slaying the Stag could only result in great things happening for me on all levels. Slaying the Stag represented power, freedom, acceptance and clarity. I often found him waiting for me in a grove of birch trees, standing by a stream, shaking its antlers. He would spy me for a bit, and then take flight.

We would run and run and run. Branches would whip my face. Tears would stream down my cheeks and mix with the sweat and dirt that built up from the chase and I never wanted the hunt to end. I thought for years that I was chasing the Stag. As it turns out, however, the Stag was always in control. He was leading me, taking me deeper and deeper into the darkness. It was fun. We loved each other. He took me on many adventures and, without my knowing, led me deep into the forests of my soul and gave me time to find peace with what I found there. He led me to a place of sacred healing and personal acceptance.

In Asia the innate belief that the spirit of man and the spirit of the animals are not dissimilar and that when a man passes into the next world, there is no reason he will not someday be reborn back into this world as an animal. It is for this reason that the animals are considered sacred with compassion toward them deeply integrated into the daily routine and ceremony of the people. In India, for example, one mouthful of food is left uneaten from every meal as an offering to Crow – a bird said to carry the memory of the dead in its heart. Greens, symbols of wealth and wisdom, are shared with Cow and other domesticated animals as thanks for their bountiful donation.

Animals are prominent in Chinese spirituality as well, particularly in the interpretations of the zodiac and the ancient practise of feng shui. According to the teachings of feng shui, for example, there are four primary beasts, known as celestial animals that must be honoured in order to harness the power and potential of the four elements – energies most welcomed into the home as they are thought to provide protection, strength and prosperity to those that live and work within. Black Turtle, which governs the North and the energies of winter, represents longevity, strength and endurance. Green Dragon (as the guardian of the East and ambassador of spring), offers protection, vigilance and goodness. Red Phoenix, ruler of the South and messenger of summer, wards off negativity while representing the five human traits – virtue, responsibility, conduct, compassion and dependability. White Tiger, as the consort of Green Dragon, embodies the West and the energies of autumn. White Tiger not only emits submissive, feminine power: she is also extremely protective and strong.

Ever since time began, man and beast have worked, lived and played alongside one another, offering companionship, food, shelter, protection and strength. Dog was the first to strike an agreement with man in Asia around 150,000 BC, offering his teeth for protection, body for warmth and his heart for companionship. Sheep and Goat first offered their domesticated meat and fleece to the people of the Middle East around 8,000 BC, roughly the same time Pig was first penned by the Chinese. Cow, again in the Middle East, became a beast of burden around 6,000 BC, while Horse was first saddled somewhere in the Ukraine around 4,000 BC. Donkey, too, was first employed as a pack animal in Egypt around 4,000 BC. Water Buffalo was yoked around 4,000 BC too, but by the people of China. Cat, a relatively 'recent' addition to the list, caught her first mouse in a human dwelling around 35,000 BC, while Camel became a friend of the Arabian nomad around 2,500 BC.

Man and beast have always shared an innate bond, a friendship, a reliance on one another other. Man, after all, is a mammal like any other: a warm-blooded, hair-covered creature that produces live young and suckles from the breast. We are no different, the animals and us. We are one. The animals are our brothers and sisters. They are the voice of the Earth Mother – her ambassadors, sent by her to inspire us (her children) in times of need. The wisdom of the animals represents the archetypes of human strength and weakness: the aspects of self we endeavour to integrate or banish from our lives.

This book represents the remembering of this sacred and ancient relationship.

Earth wisdom

Ancient wisdom clearly illustrates our relationship to all things. What may be initially seen as inert, the ancient teachings depict as living. It is said that all things of Nature, ultimately being created from the one source, deserve equal honour and respect. As a result, the traditions of many Indigenous people encompass Nature as a whole, with the understanding that Spirit lives within all things of Nature, forming the core of their belief system. The teachings imply that the Earth is our mother – that from her we came and to her we shall return. She supplies us with everything we need and loves unconditionally as mothers do. She instructs us well in all of life's lessons – about giving and taking, love and war, birth, death and rebirth. She teaches symbolically, her lessons clearly marking our rites of passage with the changing of the seasons, the transition of day into night, the waxing and waning of the moon and the ebb and flow of Grandmother Ocean's tides.

Earth Mother employs the animals as mentors, healers and guides; each symbolically gifted with a sacred message intended to guide us to a place of wholeness – individually and as a united people. The animals present themselves when we need them most and share their knowledge unconditionally. Her animals, our 'creature-teachers', can assist us in the manifestation of change; they can help bring about healing for ourselves and for others. There is an animal with the wisdom to help us with every aspect of our lives including those in the spiritual sense that can be invoked as vibrational teachers, totems and spiritual guides.

With the dawn of the New Age in Western culture, an enhanced interest in the mysteries of creation emerged. Everyone began to look again to the ways of Spirit and Nature for confirmation. Dolphin, as the apparent ambassador of the New Age movement was depicted on wind chimes, t-shirts, posters and gift cards to name a few. Such fascination saw Dolphin move from a mere creature of scientific wonder to a mystical beast of spiritual awakening and rebirth heralding a time of higher learning, healing and self-discovery and great change.

Dolphin brought with her not just permission to delve into the spiritual aspects of life, free of the restraints expected from traditional religion, but also the chance to finally Walk one's Talk. Dolphin witnessed the rebirth of ancient cultural beliefs into the New Age movement and was there to welcome a powerful emergence that brought with it a plethora of spiritual concepts that helped to initiate a shift in global consciousness. We are learning to love our neighbours and ourselves, to accept diversity and to feel empathy for our animal brothers and sisters. We now care more about the rainforests, oceans, rivers and streams than we do about the softness and whiteness of our toilet paper and we as a people can only get stronger, wiser and more accepting with Dolphin there to guide us. Dolphin is there when we are born and acts as a spiritual midwife. She 'pilots' us through the birth process in much the same way as her family will accompany a boat out of port to the open sea. Earth Mother is there too, as we navigate our way through life, offering support and protection when needed. She inspires our dreams, meditations and aspirations as she lovingly watches from the sidelines until called upon once again to help plot our course back to Spirit.

Sadly, many people remain ignorant to the fact that Earth Mother is in constant communication with them. As children of Earth Mother, the ancestral link we share with the land is equally as powerful as the bonds that link us to our biological family. Earth Mother is nurturing, receptive in nature and deeply imbued with compassion, love and the power to heal. She births everything at the beginning of its life, and devotedly reclaims it at its death. She draws within her womb all that is needed to create and recreate. She absorbs and integrates what she experiences into her sacred wisdom, tenderly recording every event like a mother who keeps a diary of her child's haircuts, lost teeth and first day at school.

Whale is the keeper of Earth Mother's sacred records. She witnesses the proceedings that collectively authenticate the spiritual makeup of the Earth, the memories of each and every event that has ever contributed to her shaping and stores them within her Dreaming. Whale uses this information to help us remember the spiritual history of those areas sacred to our personal journey. She offers ways to work with the land, to enhance our medicine, our lives and the planet as a whole. Whales communicate through low-frequency sound; sound waves that harbour memories of ancient knowledge. Earth Mother knows that the only way we can truly 'heal' the planet is to reconnect with our Earth Mother and walk as one.

All the meditation, conscious focusing of energy, prayer, sacred song and healing chants we can muster will only help settle the unrest and ease the pain until we are ready to consciously show liability for our past behaviour and to heal ourselves. We all yearn to take control of our lives and to make a difference to the world. We all yearn to believe in ourselves, to have faith in our ability to heal and to realise our true potential. The realisation that Earth Mother can nurture within us the wisdom to make our healing possible opens a pathway to power for those who seek her counsel.

It is time for us all to join hands, to walk as one and to venture into our united future as 'a people'. It is with this vision that I present *World Animal Dreaming* to you, a book that brings all the animals of the world together as a single voice. They come as a voice that sings from the heart of Earth Mother in the hope that we will all hear her call and return to the 'old ways' and remember that we are ALL children of the Earth Mother. We are all brothers and sisters, after all, and we are all equal.

THE SYMBOLIC LANGUAGE
OF THE ANIMALS

Since time began, people have wandered the Earth participating in religions that both encouraged magic and held knowledge and wisdom for their followers. Globally, practitioners were seen as Wise elders, Healers and Shamans and were the keepers of Sacred Knowledge. They knew that with this knowledge came great power. To honour this, much of the work was done in secret and passed on through oral tradition from one to the next. These individuals, because of their specialised spiritual training, could commune with Nature and spoke with the spirits and deity alike. They listened to what they had to say while learning to understand their Dreaming. They taught by example that everything was sacred and that Nature whispers to those who seek their counsel. They believed that everything on Earth, particularly the animals, had a lesson to teach. They made it their mission to learn each and every one and to use this accumulated power to manifest their qualities into their own lives.

When the people called upon the power of the animals, they were seeking complete harmonious union with the strength of that animal's being. They were asking for the animal to share its secrets; its Dreaming, its key to what makes it unique and therefore vulnerable to attack. Quietening the mind, easing the tension of the inner self and listening with an intuitive ear led to the miraculous being found in the silence. The sacred silence was, and still is, the secret link to the receiving of Spirit and its messages. The knowledge that the animals can impart creates a pathway to power – a pathway that must be trodden with awe and respect. The power gained lies in our deeper understanding of our role in life, the honouring of every living being as a teacher, and the maintaining of a reverent attitude that espouses equality.

'Mi taku oyasin', a well-known Native American phrase used in ceremony that means 'We are all related', acts as a reminder that we are part of the whole and all birthed from the one Source. We are not alone, but rather essential aspects of the cosmos, and it is with this belief that this compilation of Animal Dreaming is offered, supported by the sacred understanding that Spirit lives within all things of Nature, and that the animals speak to those who listen – a philosophy that forms the hub of many ancient cultures.

No matter what the origin, it is a universal understanding that each animal, as our brother or sister, has a lesson to communicate as part of their Dreaming: their acumen and their reason for being. As the wisdom and their interpretations will naturally differ from one nation to the next, common aspects of each Dreaming have been united or combined with common understanding and basic observation to help form 'a universal one'; a generic yet relevant list of life lessons for a people who yearn to walk as one with the understanding that 'we are all related', physically, emotionally and spiritually.

Reading the secret language of nature

The animals have always left signs for the observant, indicating not only their physical presence, but also symbolic messages intended for those who seek them out as teachers and counsellors. Wild animals are elusive, timid and shy. This is why Fox may leave footprints; Wombat may leave droppings on a log and Goanna may leave scratch marks on a tree. In doing so, they are saying, 'I have your answer, but you will need to decipher it by first determining who I am'. In order to recognise the signs and omens the animals are presenting, we must first learn how to interpret their 'signatures'. Searching for these signs and recording what we see in a journal or specimen box, even if we do not need answers or confirmation at the time, is an excellent way of remembering how to listen with our eyes in preparation for when we may need to seek assistance from Nature in the future.

A footprint is an obvious sign to look for when searching for signs left by the animals. Ideal places to look for clear impressions are in the damp soil and mud along riverbanks, around the edges of dams and lakes, or in the fresh moist sand on any beach first thing in the morning. Any damp soil, clay or sand will hold a solid footprint, but it must be damp if you wish to preserve it by casting it in plaster. To do so, mix the plaster powder with water until you get a thick, fluid paste and pour it carefully into the imprint. Once set, lift out the cast and label the back with a marker pen.

When deciding what animal to label the casting as, first consider these observations:

- Dogs and Foxes have four toe footprints, and their claws are easily seen.
- Cats, also having four toes evident, do not have claw marks (Cats are able to retract their claws).
- Goats and Deer have two triangular toe shapes and no heel mark, while Pigs do. Horses leave a crescent moon shape.
- Web-footed birds leave claw and heel marks and that's about it, while non-web-footed birds leave the whole print, toes and all.

Scratch marks on the ground or on the sides of trees are other physical ways of determining the presence of animals and the messages they are trying to impart. Rabbits, Koalas, Cats, Goannas and Lyrebirds are animals that leave distinctive marks or signs. Rabbits will scratch little holes in the ground in plain view, often-repeated five or six times in any given place and no deeper than 10 centimetres. These little scratches are called 'scrapes' and are not intended as possible entrances to burrows, as is sometimes assumed, but rather a way of marking territories. Rabbit droppings littering the entrance to a burrow are a way of determining whether a burrow is in use or not. Abandoned burrows will have no droppings scattered at the entrance, while a warren that is still in use will. Take a photo of the scrapes, and add them to your journal or specimen box.

Koalas and Goannas will often mark a tree as they climb up the trunk. These marks are not intentional, and are simply the result of the animal's claws digging deeply into the bark. Their mark is generally repeated, in even intervals, up the trunk, at least until a limb strong enough to support the weight of such an animal branches out from the tree. Lyrebirds, although highly elusive by nature, will give their presence away by scratching at the loose edges of a well-trodden bush-walking track in search of grubs and insects, just like Blackbirds do in our backyard gardens. The presence of Cats is easily detected by their habit of sharpening their claws on tree trunks. Cats will often revisit a favourite scratching tree, removing much of the bark over a period of time. A fresh scratch can be identified by the colour difference to the older scars. A fresh scratch will be darker or wetter-looking than any previous marks. Cat scratches are also usually only found approximately 1 metre up the side of the tree's trunk. Place a large piece of paper over the scratch marks found on the trunk of trees, and rub a grey-lead pencil over it. This will transfer the marks onto the paper. Looking at the position found, and the depth of the scratches, attempts to identify the animal that left the marks, along with your reasons and symbolic interpretations for why you have found them. Record your findings in your journal and add your rubbings to your specimen box.

Eye colour at night is another way of identifying an animal, even if they are unable to be seen. At night, we may catch in our torchlight what is typically called 'eye shine'. Red Foxes give off a bright-green eye shine, Owls give off a yellow, and Rabbits reflect red while some Frogs offer green.

Some animal's marking techniques are potent enough even for the human nose to detect. Foxes can easily be detected by the musky smell of their urine. Most obvious in the early morning, the scent will quickly fade during the heat of the day or with the slightest hint of rain. Try 'looking' for the smell of Fox around chook sheds, bird aviaries or Rabbit hutches. To identify the smell of the Fox scent is an excellent way of determining whether your animals are at risk. As a practice exercise to heighten your receptivity to following scent trails, have a friend mark a path for you using cheap, potent aftershave and then, using your nose only, try to follow the scent, marking it as you go with flour.

Droppings, or scats, are easy to find signs to look out for when seeking the wisdom of the animals in your area. Wombats display their droppings like trophies on top of logs or large stones as a way of clearly identifying their territorial boundaries. Foxes and Cats bury their droppings, so when looking for them, search carefully for signs of disturbed leaf litter and scratch marks in the soil immediately surrounding the site. Rabbit droppings look like currants and will be found sprinkled haphazardly near entrances to burrows and favourite 'scrape' sites. Owl scats are obvious and usually contain the remains of unfortunate creatures consumed during a previous meal. Owls must swallow their food whole, subsequently discarding the parts they cannot digest. It is interesting to collect the scats of Owls, and to keep the dissected scraps in paper bags. Visit the same spot again and again, and you can determine if the Owl whose scats you have collected targets a 'favourite' prey, or if it is an opportunist hunter.

Fresh leaf and fruit litter found on the ground beneath a tree day after day indicates the regular visitation of a bird or animal species that relies on that tree for its sustenance. Possums and most species of Parrot: Rosellas, Galahs, King Parrots, Gang Gangs, Black and White Cockatoos and Corellas are all culprits of this seemingly destructive habit.

Listening for and recording bush sounds is also an excellent way of identifying elusive creatures which may have messages for us, but are too shy to present themselves in the physical sense. Deep growling sounds may indicate the presence of Koala, Possum or Tawny Frogmouth watching from an overhanging branch. A high-pitched twittering sound may herald the arrival of a family of Bats. A whip-like sound may hint at Lyrebirds nesting close by, while the common sound of laughter will obviously suggest the presence of Kookaburra.

Recognising the presence of the animals is a great achievement and something to be proud of, particularly if you have identified the animal through observation and personal realisation instead of using a reference book. Once the animal track or sign has been observed, and the animal has been correctly identified, the next step is to look at the issues manifesting in your life at that time and relate it or them to the Dreaming of that animal by asking yourself these questions:

- What were you thinking about when you found the sign or mark, or identified the presence of the particular animal?
- What had you been focusing on during the hours leading up to the discovery of the sign or mark?
- What life issue are you currently working through?

The lessons these animals are trying to teach us may not be immediately apparent, and may take some personal investigation, research or soul searching to clarify.

Honouring the spirit of a road kill animal

Sometimes, when we are out driving in the car or walking through the park, we may come across an animal that has either been killed by passing traffic or that has died of natural causes. Often, we have no time or opportunity to stop and move their broken bodies off the road so that they don't suffer any more than they already have, but when we do have time and we get the urge to 'honour' the animal's spirit in some way, it's good to know that there are several beautiful ways this can be done:

- **Releasing the spirit:** When you're unable to stop to 'help' an animal that has been killed on the road because you're on a deadline or there's so much traffic on the road that pulling over is made impossible, visualise the animal's spirit 'stepping out' of the physical body, giving itself a shake and then either taking flight or running / hopping off the road (as it would if the animal had just stopped to have a rest). By visualising its spirit leaving the body, you're able to encourage it to return to Spirit intact and in full integrity. While the discarded body may continue to suffer physically, at least you can rest easy knowing the animal's spirit has been released.

- **Offering a humble burial:** When you're able to stop but you don't receive any messages to retain anything belonging to the animal (wings, etc), carry the animal's body to the side of the road and cover it with leaves, twigs or a light sprinkling of soil or gravel, the whole while asking the Spirits to fly the animal's soul back to the Creator. Visualise the animal's spirit stepping out of its physical body before making its way safely 'home'. No one can be sure if animals see 'the light' or even if there is any such thing in their world, so you'll have to trust that when you ask the Spirits to fly the soul home, welcome the inherent feeling of peace that comes with the knowing that they have found their way and that all is well.

- **Smudging the body of a dead animal:** If you have white sage in your car, you may like to smudge (see section on smudging further in this chapter) the animal's body before you release its spirit and then again after you have. With the first smudging, ask the animal's soul to remain calm and receptive to your love and support. With the first smudging, try calling in the Spirits with the intention of asking them to guide the animal's soul back to the Creator. With the second smudging, ask the spirit to leave the body and ride upon the sacred smoke as it rises and returns to the Creator. During the second smudging, ask the Earth Mother to welcome the physical body back to her belly, so that it may be reassimilated quickly and honourably and made available for rebirth when the animal's soul has recovered and returned from the Creator's embrace.

- **The most sacred of harvests:** It sometimes happens that when you move the body of a dead animal to the safety of the nature strip or the side of the road, you may feel the need to 'harvest' some feathers or remove a wing or a foot/paw. It's for this reason that you could keep (in the boot of your car) a 'shaman's kit': a smudge wand, matches, a sharp knife, a pair of strong scissors (the sort that are designed to cut up roasted chickens, for example), a packet of baby wipes, a towel or similar-sized cloth, some plastic lunch bags, some stiff cardboard and some clothes pegs. After smudging the dead animal and releasing its spirit (as described above), still your mind and 'ask' the animal if it would mind you taking some of its feathers or removing its foot or wing. You will feel a positive 'yes' or a definite 'no' in your solar plexus. A yes may be experienced as a sense of peace, tears suddenly welling up, butterflies in the stomach or an overall 'good' feeling. A no will be felt completely differently: a sick feeling in the gut, nausea, dizziness, a knot in the stomach, an obvious sense of foreboding or a sense of doubt.

Never assume that it's okay to just start plucking feathers at random... it's simply impolite and dishonours the spirit of the animal. If it's a 'no', then simply bury the animal (either on the roadside as described above, or at home later). If it's a 'yes', smudge the animal again, paying special attention to where you're going to cut. If it's just the feathers you want, ask the bird what feathers it would like to share (and don't take any others), before smudging the body while offering thanks and gratitude. Then simply pull the feathers out. Sometimes they come out easily, which suggests you're allowed to take as many as you like, but sometimes it's very hard to remove the feathers, which means that you're only allowed to take one or two. Never force the issue, and only take what you need as opposed to 'what you want'. When you've finished smudging, take up your scissors, or a pair of garden secateurs, and cut confidently through the flesh and bone and remove the wing or foot. Don't worry about the animal's blood as, after death, the blood stops flowing. Smudge the body again, and then smudge the removed body parts, offering thanks and gratitude. Wrap the removed parts in a towel with some sage, or put them in a plastic back to take home. If you have stiff cardboard and clothes pegs in your kit, stretch the wings or talons or feet out and peg them as open and wide as you can so that, if they start to dry out, they dry in a way that showcases their beauty. Crush some sage up in your hand, and sprinkle it over the wings or feet.

Remember that once the wing or feet begin to dry, they will become stiff and hard making it impossible to manipulate their joints. So, if you plan to wait until you get home to stretch them, leave straightaway. When you're home, peg them out immediately and sit them somewhere warm and dry and sprinkle them with dry sage, as a way of honouring them. As they will completely dehydrate naturally, there's no need to do anything special to preserve them. In a warm, dry place, they will keep for ages and never smell. Bury the rest of the animal's body as described above, asking the whole while for the soul to make its way back to the Creator. When the wing or foot has dried out completely, wrap it in cloth and put it in the freezer to kill any mites before they begin to eat the feathers and dried-out flesh.

Feral or introduced animals

Australia is richly stocked with many beautiful animals and birds, many of which are found nowhere else in the world. Our land is home to a diverse collection of introduced animals; animals originally brought to Australia by European settlers over 200 years ago and accidentally or intentionally released into the environment for one reason or another. I have said many times, although some of the animals here in Australia are 'feral', and as such, are harmful to our country's carefully balanced and delicate ecosystem (and as such, I would like it made clear that I do not endorse their presence), none of them are here by any fault of their own. They may not be indigenous to Australia, and their introduction may have negatively altered the bio-network of Australia forever, but we must remember that many of us are not native to this land either, with our very arrival all those years ago dramatically initiating the more obvious changes we see today. We need to transform the way we view these animals and look to the lessons hidden behind their presence while acknowledging them as the powerful teachers that they are, instead of persecuting them and labelling them as worthless vermin. After all, like us, all the animals, whether feral or not, are indigenous to the Earth Mother and when viewed in this light, are nothing less than sacred.

Obviously, the situation cannot be reversed overnight, especially not with rifles and poison. We cannot fix the mistakes of our Ancestors, but we can show responsibility to the Earth Mother by taking responsibility for our own lives. Animals that we shun reflect facets we choose to ignore about ourselves and they represent qualities we resent in others, too. They symbolise our jealousies and our secret desires, or the things we yearn to do but are afraid to acknowledge or embrace. The animals, as the voice of the Earth Mother, are simply trying to point out our inadequacies; those aspects we avoid, suppress or blame others for. It is a waste of time to 'band-aid' the situation by eliminating the 'feral animals' in an attempt to hide our shortcomings. It is like treating the symptoms without considering the cause. How we perceive the world is actually reflective of how we see ourselves. To see beauty in something is reflective of the beauty we see within ourselves. But, to see ugliness in something is a sure fire sign of healing we need to address within ourselves. If something disgusts or angers us, for example, we need to ask 'Why?'. We need to ask ourselves where this very same situation is being played out in our life, and whether or not it is something we are doing ourselves. It is not the animals themselves that are the problem, but rather the 'medicine' or lesson represented by animals that upset us or put us on edge. Once we identify the reasons for why the animals annoy us, we can integrate their lessons into our life, heal that aspect of ourselves and then release all judgment of the animal. The more people do this, the less the animals will feel compelled to remain. The more we take responsibility for our own healing, the more the animals and the Earth Mother will support us. If we fail to heed their requests, however, the more the Earth Mother will continue to send the messengers. They will just keep on coming, like the letters that were sent to Harry Potter inviting him to attend Hogwarts in the first Harry Potter film. The more he failed to reply, the more letters were sent until he had little choice but to submit. If we were to just surrender and take responsibility for our own lives, the 'ferals' would surrender, too. Sure, they will always be there (for as long as we are, at least), but chances are the need for them to be there in such undisciplined numbers would subside as the Earth Mother called them back to her.

Meeting your power animal totem – a meditative journey

Preparing for meditation

Smudging

A tradition made popular by the Native American people, smudging uses the smoke from burning white sage to cleanse and strengthen the energy field or aura. To smudge, place the sage in a heatproof dish. Take a match and light the sage until it starts to smoulder. Using a feather brush the smoke around your body while asking the spirit of the sage to remove any negative energy from your aura. Visualise the energy leaving your aura and returning to the Universe via the smoke.

Guided visualisation meditation

Finding your animal totem

By slipping into a meditatively induced altered state and requesting the wisdom of the animal spirit world, you will inevitably meet your totem or power ally. This beast will be of a species with which you already feel a bond. This creature will become your friend, your teacher and your life partner.

Still your conscious mind and silence the inner chatter. Wait for the moment when you intuitively feel the need to open your consciousness to the other realms. Ensure that your subconscious mind is receptive and alert by speaking to your conscious mind. Allow visions and symbolic images to waft through your mind. Keep your focus within yourself. Let any thoughts just go by. When you catch yourself engaged in an external conscious thought, just take a deep breath and bring yourself back to your centre.

Picture yourself on a great grassy plane, dotted with the most beautifully coloured wild flowers. From where you are standing you can see two very different sights. To your right is a path leading up to a steep mountain peak, and to your left is a path leading down into a deep valley. The point at which you are standing is in fact the intersection of time and reality; a mingling point of reality and 'the Other Worlds', of the physical and the mystical. It is where the miraculous can be found.

Visualise yourself taking the left path as it leads down into the deep valley. You walk until you are standing at the edge of a forest beside a huge standing stone that seems to be guarding the path that leads into the forest. On the side of the standing stone is a word, engraved into the surface. This is an affirmation word which describes and represents your potential at present. Take note of this word.

You start down the path, and to your left you notice an animal standing at the edge of the path. It says nothing, and will follow you as you pass. It means you no harm and for this meditation, will act as your guardian to ensure your safe passage.

You carry on down the path which seems to self-illuminate, despite the forest being pitch-dark, enabling you to see and not stumble. You see many things as you walk. Thick overhanging branches, incredible, brightly coloured butterflies and birds, sweet-smelling flowers and huge insects, like beetles and spiders; all too beautiful to be afraid of. All the while you feel eyes watching you, from amongst the trees. They are not threatening eyes; they are curious and caring eyes. You know you are safe, because your guardian is not far behind, keeping a close watch on you.

Continue to walk until you come to a great clearing. The area has been carefully cleared and here, and only here, is the forest floor covered in a lush green lawn, as if manicured. In the centre of the clearing, surrounded by huge stones, is a massive fire. This fire is so big you cannot see the top of the flames. The glow is so intense, you can see perfectly. You would think that with a fire this big that the trees would be scorched and the grass would be withered, but they are not. You would also think that with a fire this big that the heat being radiated out would be so ferocious it would be impossible to venture too close, but it is not. The flames of this magical fire are golden-orange in colour, like any standard fire, but the flames are cool to the touch. The fuel under the fire is burning, yet it is not diminishing. This is a sacred fire, protected by the forest. This is the Father Fire, sent to Earth Mother by Grandfather Sun when time was new. It was sent as the original spark destined to ignite the fire of life and all new beginnings. It is the Fire of Spirit, the one thing that links our inner fires to the Great Fire of Spirit. This fire means you no harm and even if you were to put your hand into the flames, you would never receive a burn. Put your hand in and see for yourself. Feel the flames licking your hand. Feel the sensation of the flames enveloping your fingers and your wrist, but without any heat.

You sit in front of the fire, cross-legged on the ground. You close your eyes and find your inner peace. Feel the glowing love of Spirit fill you to the core, sent to you by the raging flames of this gentle fire.

Open your eyes and stare into the flames, the whole time asking for your true and powerful totem animal to present itself to you, even for just a little while. Focus on this thought, and clear your mind of other things.Keep your intent pure and your eagerness at a minimum. As with all animals, you will not be approached if you are radiating urgent and unsettling energies.

As you stare, notice a pair of eyes staring back at you. They are not human eyes and you realise this, but you cannot, as yet, make out what sort of eyes they are. Gradually a face forms around the eyes, and you notice a neck, followed by a body and legs. The animal is now whole and gingerly steps out of the flames and sits in front of you, perhaps to have a scratch or a stretch. This animal is your totem animal, and this animal may be a bird, a beast, a reptile or an insect. It may even be a fish, in which case your environment may have changed without you noticing.

Watch how the animal relates to you. Does it circle around you, or rub up against you? Does it sit in your lap, or touch you with its nose? Does it make any sound? Does it make any 'threatening', or sudden moves? If it has ears, are they upright, or laid back? Does it have a tail? If so, is it upright, hanging down, or tucked under its body? Take note of these things, and any other obvious features.

After spending time with your animal/bird/reptile/insect, becoming accustomed with one another and possibly communicating about this and that, say goodbye and allow the animal to return to the flames. It must not follow you out of the forest, so insist on it returning to the Father Fire. Wait patiently if you have to.

Once the animal has returned to the realm of Spirit, look down to the ground beside you; in the grass you will notice a word. A word of wisdom that is meant as a message to guide you and link you to this animal once you part. This word will open up the communication link between the animal and yourself, and will act as a symbol of its Dreaming to you.

Begin walking back up the path. You will notice that your guardian animal is still following you. You will also notice that it made no gesture towards your totem animal, as they have already met. Spend some time returning up the path. Notice the things you saw on the way in, and notice that although the forest is as black as pitch, the path continues to illuminate the way. At the end of the path, where the edge of the forest meets the grassy plain, your guardian will step back to the side of the path, where it met you, and nod a farewell. Make your way to the standing stone, and take note of the engraved word. You will notice that the original word is still there, but underneath another word has been added. This word symbolises your possible potential now that you have the power of your totem animal walking beside you. Take note of this word, and add it to the other two words. You now have three words. Say them in your mind. Do they prompt any feelings, thoughts or emotions in you as you say them?

Take your time to walk across the grassy plain once more, again stopping to observe and enjoy the wild flowers.

Make a silent prayer to Spirit for a reason sacred to you and to offer thanks for the messages and visions experienced during the meditation. Ask Spirit to surround the Earth in a healing and protective green aura and focus it mainly on the animal kingdom. Wiggle your fingers and toes as you return to the physical room and open your eyes when you are ready.

THE ANIMALS

Aardvark
Opening

 Also known as Earth Pig or Ant Bear, Aardvark is an extremely gifted digger. He digs his way into a Termite mound and pokes about with his long tongue (which is coated with gluey saliva) to which the Termites stick fast. According to legend, if you place the dried root of a lotus plant under your tongue and confidently say the words *'Sign Arggis'*, any door that was previously locked to you will miraculously open. The same is said about the herb, moonwort. When placed in keyholes, locks holding their doors fast will surrender their hold, opening the way for intrusion.

Using his powerful claws, Aardvark can easily dig a hole faster than several men armed with shovels. When dried, ground and mixed with the root of a particular tree, Aardvark's claws (plus other body parts) are bound in skin and worn over the chest by those seeking its power and is believed that any barrier will prove ineffective to those who bear Aardvark's charm. The same may be said for those who are disciplined enough to master Aardvark's wisdom. An effective earth mover, Aardvark teaches us to plough through all apparent obstructions and to view them as lessons rich with opportunity for enhancement. Aardvark never takes no as a final answer and is always digging for truth, greater awareness and soul nourishment. Doors may appear locked to those who stand alongside an Aardvark person, but not for long. 'Never say never' is Aardvark's mantra. To recognise the presence of Aardvark is to sense a temporary opening, so dig when Aardvark makes a house call, as it will prove beneficial to your advancement.

Albatross

Encumbrance

The wingspan of the largest species of Albatross represents the largest of any bird (exceeding 3.5 metres) and she is famous for travelling great distances without needing to rest. She is able to sustain energy and soar for extended periods of time because of a tendon that locks the wing when fully extended and minimises muscle expenditure. A common notion warns that if an Albatross is killed, her death is sure to bring bad luck to a ship and its inhabitants. To figuratively carry an 'Albatross around one's neck' therefore, is to be plagued by constant bad luck.

Albatross offers clarity, deeper appreciation and peace regarding issues that hamper physical, spiritual and mental freedom. Albatross allows us to soar with greater ease through tumultuous periods in our life, forewarning us of obstacles that threaten to burden our load or impede our progress. She also rewards with emotional and spiritual resilience and sacred understanding capable of lifting us to ever greater heights. Issues that cause deep concern, personal difficulty or jeopardise our movements are dissuaded with the assistance of Albatross. She offers to carry for us the burdensome and troublesome loads that tie us down or lock us into a continual state of grief and apparent hardship. Albatross helps us appreciate and seek freedom; freedom from grief, pain and lack perceived as being caused by poor circumstance or 'bad luck'. She enables us to work constructively through all blockages and to deal with life's burdens by helping us take responsibility for them and find reason for their being. Denying oneself the chance to be free of encumbrance is like willingly going through life with an Albatross strung about one's neck.

Alligator

Preparation

Alligator walks with two different gaits: a clumsy shamble, dragging her tail, or a 'high walk' where she walks on her toes with tail held aloft and in this manner can reach speeds of up to 40 kilometres per hour. Alligator eats a wide range of prey animals, and are even known to eat carrion. Alligator has powerful jaws with razor-sharp teeth and grabs her prey dragging it into the water, where she rolls it over and over until it is drowned. It is then stashed under the water, or dragged around until the meat is rotten enough to tear apart and eat. Like all reptiles, Alligator cannot generate her own body warmth, and so must rely on the sun's rays to maintain her body temperature. Alligator can go several months before needing food.

Alligator people are masters of preparation. They never rush into things and never push for things to happen before their time. Alligator people know that to do so could mean losing everything they have worked hard to achieve, or worse still, missing an opportunity to enhance the quality of their life. When Alligator people initiate change or move toward any new phase of life, they do so with patience and meticulous concentration, spending quality time readying for the shift in perception. In doing so, they ensure that they are always fully equipped and prepared to take advantage of the event. Alligator calls for us to be patient during times of inactivity and reminds us that we are offered periods of dormancy in order to rest up and contemplate our next course of action. Alligator guides us to a place of trust, allowing us to ease unnoticed into position or sidle up to a problem issue, so that we might plan our attack with accuracy and precision. Alligator helps us find clarity and stillness to see above the emotions or circumstances that cloud our judgment and hinder our progress. She instils a sense of peace and faith and enables us to be still, patient and grateful for what we have achieved thus far. Only then will we have the stamina required to fully take advantage of that which is rightfully ours when the time is right.

Alpaca and Llama
Offerings

 Alpacas and Llamas are domesticated South American animals and are herded in large flocks; Alpaca for her fleece and Llama as a beast of burden. Alpaca and Llama foetuses are collected, dried and sold in markets. Purchased as potent offerings to the gods, they are buried under the foundations of new buildings to ensure their stability and longevity. Like all members of their family, Alpacas and Llamas spit when they are annoyed or feel threatened. It was thought that the souls of the dead could enter and reside within Alpaca or Llama. Their offerings to the people include abundance, foundation and validation.

The outwardly gentle and servile Alpaca has an inbuilt hatred and 'no fear' attitude towards Dogs and Foxes, making her a powerful guardian of other domestic animals such as Goats and Sheep, especially during birthing time. Alpaca is known to run down, trample and kill predatory animals. Through experience, Alpaca has come to realise that to offer something of personal worth, of an incomparable sacredness, the rewards are great and equally as inconceivable. Because of the sacrifices Alpaca readily makes with her fleece and young, she has been rewarded with the role of protector, guardian and guide to the young of others, the provider of nourishment to many and the bringer of warmth to even more. Alpaca is the totem of people who have experienced or witnessed the effects of personal loss, but make it their mission to enrich or improve the lives of others. Those who foster children, care for the sick and dying or who provide shelter and food for the homeless and abandoned carry the wisdom of Alpaca in their hearts and honour its essence by simply rising from bed each morning.

• Guanaco – *Intervention*

As a member of the Camel family, Guanaco can survive for extended periods without water and is hunted for her meat and fur. Although domesticated Llama and Alpaca are both descendants of Guanaco, Guanaco herself is both volatile and unpredictable and requires a dangerous exotic animal license to be kept in captivity and is considered not commercially 'viable'.

Guanaco is the totem of those who constantly find themselves overlooked in favour of others more qualified, talented or better known. Symbolic of the kid always chosen last for the team, Guanaco tempers disappointment, jealousy and resentment by reinstating integrity and authenticity. If something is 'meant to be', everything standing between us and it must comply to ensure its fulfilment. Things that are deemed 'meant to be' are usually things associated with our Purpose or greater Gift of Power. In order to realise either, it is understood that we must be prepared to take risks and physically and mentally do what we must to bring them to fruition. Sometimes, however, we unwittingly focus our attentions on goals that, although apparently beneficial and productive and in line with our Purpose, are not 'meant to be'. We are disappointed and confused when we are hampered by obstacles beyond our control. Guanaco invites us to surrender control and yield to unavoidability. If something is not 'meant to be', it will never be realised no matter how hard we fight for it. Guanaco offers divine intervention and takes us by the hand and leads us back to our rightful path, offering us the chance to regain truth and clarity. When Guanaco makes a house call, expect tears of relief, realisation and confirmation. Guanaco is a guide; an interventional signpost designed to offer those who have unknowingly taken a wrong turn a chance to fall back in line and, when the time is right, realise our true Purpose and the reason for us being prevented from settling for second best.

• Vicuna – *Neutrality*

Vicuna only yields small quantities of wool per year, which is highly prized and very difficult to produce commercially. Vicuna resists domestication and runs blindly at fences leaping over them whenever possible. She can also be unpredictable and volatile. Crossbreeding with Alpacas for wool production unfortunately renders offspring sterile after two generations.

Vicuna is an animal that offers allegiance to no one and finds ways to avoid having to share with others. She figures that because she takes very little for herself, she should be able to keep what she does have. Vicuna teaches us to never take anything for granted and to show appreciation for what we have. Vicuna does not support those who abuse or take advantage of others, and will ensure that plans and actions to do so will be foiled.

Vicuna people do not like being taken advantage of. They hate being lied to, backed into a corner or made to feel responsible for the wellbeing of others. They can be cold, indifferent and outwardly uncaring, preferring to focus their attentions on their own wants and needs. Vicuna offers endurance to people who have spent a life surviving as opposed to living and watches over those who have known poverty, hardship or lack, and are afraid of having what little they have taken away. Vicuna provides warmth, protection and nourishment to those who mistrust or are fearful of authority or those in more dominant positions than themselves, while ever so gently, over a period of time, nurturing trust and faith in human kindness.

Ant
Strength

 Ant is capable of carrying many times his own body weight in his jaws, thereby making his industrious life that much easier. Ant also depends on strength of mind to anticipate and outsmart his opponent's every move. An engineer and schemer, Ant is forceful and charged with might and endurance. A communal creature, he appreciates and harnesses the strength found in numbers and reminds us that to work cooperatively toward a collective goal will ensure more efficient results.

Ant knows only too well the danger of the 'too many chiefs and not enough Indians' scenario and nurtures within us the understanding that in order to succeed as a family or group, everyone must be prepared to knuckle down and play an equal part. In doing so, everyone comes away believing they have a voice and that they contributed jointly to a job well done. Ant also teaches patience, which in its own way is a form of strength demonstrating that even the highest mountain can be moved, one grain at a time. Most people can recall a time when they have had their kitchen invaded by Ants. When this happens, thank the Ants for their sacred lesson, because this mass visitation will, in some way, coincide with you pushing for something to happen before its time or complaining that something is taking too long to eventuate or materialise despite being overdue. By simply surrendering to inevitability and accepting that all will be revealed in its own time will see the Ants disappear as quickly as they arrived. Ant gives us strength of mind, body and spirit, a sense of community and dogged patience. To understand and harness this power will see us become the sole engineers of our lives, able to lay solid life foundations upon which opportunities can be realised and honest success assured.

Antelope
Radiance

There are several species of Antelope in Africa, including the Topi, Sable Antelope, Impala, Kob, Roan Antelope, Addax, Bongo, Eland and Waterbuck. After a gestation period of eight to nine months, most Antelopes produce a single calf, which is kept hidden from predators for the first week of its life. Antelopes travel in herds of up to 24 animals and are largely nomadic by nature.

According to legend, Antelope holds great significance for the African Bushmen, as she is the only animal who knows where to find the hiding place of the god capable of taking on her form. It is a common attribute of ancient spirituality to see the animals as representing aspects of deity, embodying their most favourable characteristics or of lending their bodies as vehicles through which deity might speak directly to the people. A lunar-influenced creature, Antelope was sacred to Astarte, the Great goddess of the Middle East who was a goddess of balance, holding death and destruction in one hand and birth and regeneration in the other. She presided over the souls of the departed and was often depicted wearing crescent-shaped horns on her head. Also sporting curved horns, Antelope reminds us that no matter what happens in our life, Spirit will always provide a guiding light, a symbol of hope and a way of guiding us out of the shadows. Antelope equates these periods of hardship and pain to the darkness of night-time when issues appear more overwhelming. She reminds us to look to the morning star for affirmation and see it as heralding the dawn of a new day. In order for anything to be born (for any project to be allowed to start, or new relationship, for example, to be realised) some aspect of your life must be allowed to die. Calling in the energies of Antelope to guide the process, however, ensures that the most potent time to initiate the necessary endings are harnessed, making way for fertile new beginnings. To follow the radiance of Antelope is a guarantee that everything will work out for the best.

• Blackbuck – *Kindness*

Blackbuck browses the desert regions of India, Pakistan and Nepal and is classified as vulnerable meaning she is at risk of extinction (in the wild). According to the fundamental teachings of most Earth-based cultures, the ancients viewed all things as birthed from the One Source, and as such, deserving of equality and respect. To hold this stance is to honour the wisdom of Blackbuck; and that promises reward and abundance to those who consciously 'walk gently upon the Earth'.

Those who look to the wisdom of Blackbuck are guaranteed abundance and favour when they embrace the core essence of its acumen: kindness.

Kindness is something Blackbuck espouses we shower upon all things of Nature: the trees, stones, animals and plants with the understanding that all things of Nature are inherently our brothers and sisters, as well as a respect for humanity and the sacred place we hold within the Wheel of Life. When we are able to look upon everyone and everything as our equal, through eyes free of greed, intolerance and control, we begin to realise who we truly are. As we acknowledge the beauty in all things, we rekindle an ancient bond between them and us. Everyone is born with the wisdom of Blackbuck within their hearts: it represents our collective potential and destiny. Unfortunately, the majority of people are oblivious to its presence. Only love, both for ourselves and for everything of Creation, can dissolve the barriers that prevent us from realising unity. What we exude we also attract, so if we truly believe that we are never alone, we won't be, and if we view ourselves as living a life of unconditional love, surrounded by beauty, so we shall be.

• Dik Dik – *Promise*

A dwarf Antelope, Dik Dik mates for life and many pairs unite to form large herds when food is plentiful. An animal of diminutive size, Dik Dik (named after the noise she makes when startled) does not let her stature get in the way of her sense of honour.

Dik Dik demonstrates the level of unconditional love available to those confident enough to first seek it within themselves; a sacred awareness realised by those who Walk their Talk and feel proud in relation to who and what they are. Dik Dik people give their heart completely to their mate, with the mutual promise of unreserved love, protection and service. They have discovered that the only way to find true love is to first find it within one's self and truly feel it for one's self. Dik Dik instils a sense of understanding, appreciation and partnership into all of our relationships and reminds us that no matter what foundation our relationships are based on, they must be honoured with equality and tolerance, with communication and a shared vision binding all things together. To promise to always be there for another is the most powerful way of affirming one's commitment to oneself.

• Duiker – *Discernment*

Duiker ranges from golden-tan to Zebra-striped in colour and the males are equipped with very sharp horns to defend their territory. A creature not afraid to experiment with her diet or to explore different arenas of life, Duiker is known to 'duik': dive into undergrowth and shrubbery when threatened. Those drawn to the wisdom of this animal are encouraged to let their guard down, to experiment with their senses, to trust their own judgment and to know that life is there for the living. For those who are afraid to try new things or to embrace the unknown, sit in silent contemplation and invoke the wisdom of Duiker all the while asking it to share her sense of audacity and adventure. Alternatively, Duiker is also a powerful guide for those who constantly shun prudence in favour of pleasure. Instead of always 'duiking' when caught raiding gardens or orchards, for example, Duiker will provide the courage needed to seek permission or to wait for an invitation to share. An ambassador of the clarity that comes with knowing when to act and when to show discretion, Duiker's message is that of discernment.

• Gazelle – *Nimbleness*

Gazelle is favourite prey for many of Africa's predators and both sexes usually have horns. As if always embarking on giant 'leaps of faith', Gazelle provides quick thinking, lightning-fast reflexes and the ability to identify fertile ground well before it is physically in sight.

Gazelle offers the chance and ability to leap from one opportunity to the next by encouraging us to take carefully calculated risks and educated guesses The nimble-footed Gazelle is a graceful animal of extreme beauty that charms others by taking them on great adventures; chases that lead them into new lands and higher realms of thinking. Daring others to follow its fresh lines of thinking and her innovative ways of doing things, quick-talking Gazelle is always aware of those who will follow to a point and then take over when success is guaranteed. To walk a path influenced by Gazelle is to know a fast-moving lifestyle fraught with danger and possible failure, but if piloted carefully under the influence and watchful eye of Gazelle, it will prove to be a path of triumph and incentive. To nurture success always keep one step ahead of your opponent, while radiating a constant (be it illusory) aura of composure and enthusiasm that suggests greater, stronger aptitude.

• Gemsbok – *Dignity*

Also known as South African Oryx or Oryx Gazelle, Gemsbok feeds primarily on grasses, leaves and shoots and inhabits dry grasslands and desert areas of South-East Africa. An animal of intense physical beauty and strength, Gemsbok walks proudly with a commanding confidence that may be mistaken for boorishness.

Displaying a deeply integrated sense of worth, Gemsbok encourages those who look to her for affirmation to continually radiate composure, to never jeopardise one's reputation with common behaviour and to maintain dignity as one's priority. To find oneself exploring the wisdom of Gemsbok is to consider one's motives and legitimacy. Gemsbok prompts us to examine our authenticity; to evaluate how we truly feel about ourselves and the value we place on our values and beliefs. To come from a place of ego is not the path endorsed by Gemsbok ... one may just find oneself the victim of a hungry Lion. Believing oneself worthy of a dignified life is to have faith in one's character. Radiating self-love is not an offence, but expecting others to worship you without merit is.

• Gerenuk – *Good Spirit*

 Meaning 'Giraffe-necked' in Somali, Gerenuk is commonly seen standing on her hind legs feeding on branches out of reach of other herbivores and is known as a Stilt Walker. A Legend has it that African tribesmen strapped stilts to their legs so that they could continue to live normal lives in spite of invading waters. The most widely accepted reason for stilt walking, however, was birthed from stories of tribal wise men that walked on stilts in order to identify and exorcise evil spirits.

Call in Gerenuk when you need to look at life from a different, fresh perspective and when you feel restricted, insignificant or blinkered by your sentiment. Look to the graceful 'stilt walker' when you require a 'leg up' or when you need support navigating your way through life. When the emotional pool of life turns rough, invoke Gerenuk and ask her to share her strength and acumen. She will help you identify the negative influences in your life by revealing interference and deception. Confrontation is minimised, too, and kept amiable with the wisdom of Gerenuk, who knows the importance of Walking one's Talk and honouring one's innate truth.

• Nilgai – *Wellbeing*

 Nilgai is Asia's largest Antelope and resembles a horse. Nilgai has excellent hearing and eyesight, but a poor sense of smell. Both sexes move swiftly, demonstrate powerful stamina and emit quiet but earnest vocalisations when startled.

Nilgai embodies the importance of wellbeing and offers the traditional symbology of the colour blue (due to the 'colour' of the animal's coat): clarity, good health, peace, balance and clear communication. Holding vibrational correspondence to the sixth (or throat) chakra, the colour blue is often invoked to induce a sense of calm and benefit. Nilgai supports the path of those seeking connectedness, wellbeing and good health by awakening choice and Personal Power. Imbued with great endurance and speed, Nilgai provides those who seek out her wisdom with dogged determination and the self-worth needed to view themselves as worthy of peace and clarity. Often speaking in hushed tones, those working with the wisdom of Nilgai make powerful and effective healers, counsellors and social workers; their inherently empathetic nature enhanced by an unwavering trust in their intuitive abilities.

• Oryx – *The Unicorn*

Oryx inhabits the steppe regions and deserts of the Arabian Peninsula and is currently classified as an endangered species. The Unicorn's ancient origins as a heraldic creature announcing the changing of the seasons has seen it evolve many times, from Bull to Goat to Rhinoceros. One reason offered by historians for the Unicorn's transition from Goat to Horse is apparently linked to several Horse skulls found in an ancient Siberian burial mound, each adorned with an elaborate single leather horn attached by straps to the centre of the forehead. It is believed that these horns were revered as potent symbols of masculine sexuality.

Unicorn remains a symbol of purity, true intent and spiritual insight, and with this as her gift to us, is powerfully protective as she elevates one's ability to distinguish the noble from the dire in everything we do. The horn of the Unicorn was said to be able to heal and neutralise poisons. Oryx Dreaming, therefore, represents hope and inspiration; one's 'exposed' soul – no longer feeling the need to remain hidden behind a well-established disguise. She offers a beacon that draws to itself encouragement and faith; the ability to transform confusion into hope. Oryx promises that when you follow her lead there will always be light ahead. She heralds a time of rebirth and hope during those moments when you know you are doing the right thing even though it may not feel like it at the time. Oryx ensures that things will work out for the best.

• Springbok – *Contribution*

Springbok leaps to heights of 3.5 metres, with legs held vertical to the body (an act known as *pronking*), when fleeing from predators. Thanks to poaching and habitat destruction, herd numbers seldom reach more than 1,500. Considered a symbol of abundance and fortuity due to the huge number of animals that once made up the herds, Springbok was honoured as a main contributor to the wellbeing and nourishment of the people.

To invoke the wisdom of Springbok is to acknowledge the contributions we make and the support we offer friends, family or the community as a whole. It is to recognise our worth as a resource to the people as well as accepting the praise that we deserve from those who have benefited. To look to Springbok as a guide or totem is to acknowledge our role as a primary provider, main caregiver or sole 'breadwinner' for the family or clan. Springbok people usually do more than their fair share of chores and generally with minimal expectation of others to contribute. Springbok encourages us to slow down, to savour the rewards of our hard work and maybe approach others for assistance when we try to take on too much; to lessen our expectation of ourselves or relinquish some control over how things are to be done. Springbok endorses the 'fair share' philosophy by reminding us that although it is honourable to contribute to any family or community-based project it is unbalanced to be the sole provider of goods or services when there are others who are capable of helping out.

Armadillo
Shield

Armadillo is a timid, 'reinforced' creature that inhabits the warm grasslands and forests of southern and Central America. He is protected by plates of skin-covered bony armour that enable some species to curl into a ball when threatened. Armadillo's armoury is said to act as a shield, protecting humanity from all that is deemed unfavourable.

Armadillo rolls himself into a ball, defending us from attack and deflecting negative interference. Armadillo only unrolls when it is clear that we are willing to experience what is being offered to us. If we choose not to comply, Armadillo stays closed to possibility. Saying 'No' is one of the hardest things in life to do, particularly when we are made to feel guilty or weak. Armadillo recognises this and so offers endurance, stamina and a sense of authenticity as we retreat. Although it might feel as though we are offered little or no choice at the time, everything 'big' we experience in this life has been agreed to by us, at one time or another, consciously or not. Armadillo's shield, therefore, does not protect us from the significant inevitabilities of life, but rather the level of confusion and fear we are subjected to as a result. Armadillo protects us from the ravages of guilt, shock and pain that wrack our body after any major event. He helps us recover to the point where we can regain a sense of clarity and understanding and cradles us as we ask questions and seek out the answers. He shields us from interference that may hinder our quest for reason. Although we are bombarded by many things deemed unfavourable, Armadillo opens our hearts to the understanding that everything happens for a reason, and that there is no such thing as coincidence, mistakes or accidents. Everything is pre-planned and agreed to by all parties – including us.

Auk
Concession

Auk loosely resembles Penguin but they are not related. The Auk family includes Guillemot, Murre and Puffin which has the genus *Fratercula*; Latin for 'little brother' or 'friar'. Many of the friars that emerged in Medieval Europe were committed to a life of poverty, relying on the charity of others to support them. Their role was to go out and preach to the people. Living a minimalist life, friars sacrificed a life of material possession in favour of spiritual attainment.

In similar fashion, Auk has sacrificed flight and mobility on land in exchange for greater aptitude in the water. Auk strikes a concession between what our society deems essential and what we view as sacred, especially when the two contradict one another, or when our views demand greater attention, time or effort to personally maintain. Although his wings adapted to underwater 'flight' beautifully, an ability that afforded him greater food and abundance, Auk had to consider the broader wellbeing of his clan and so retained the fundamental ability to fly, albeit in a cumbersome manner. Auk nurtures those interests, beliefs, wants or needs that conflict with the traditional ways of the family, community or workplace. He allows us to be ourselves, to cooperatively adapt the way we do things in order to honour our personal views, while retaining a balanced sense of responsibility and commitment to those who love or support us. Auk helps to integrate what we hold dear into our life in a way that does not impinge on or compromise the familiar ways or the conventional comings and goings of others. He affords time and opportunity to meaningfully celebrate what makes our heart sing in a way that does not demand others fall in line or follow suit, and that does not restrict or demand explanation for what, why or how we do it.

Axolotl
Fate

Axolotl, or 'Mexican Walking Fish', is a type of Salamander that remains in the larval phase even as a sexually-mature adult. He never undergoes metamorphosis to become a land-dwelling creature. Despite being enjoyed the world over as a popular aquarium pet, wild Axolotl is today classified as an endangered species.

Xolotl was the Aztec/Toltec god of lightning and death who is often depicted as a skeleton or as a dog-headed man and led the souls of the dead to the Underworld. Xolotl was said to push the sun at sunset towards the ocean and guard it during the night as it journeyed the Underworld. The name Axolotl is derived from the Aztec *atl* meaning water, and *xolotl* meaning dog. According to Greek legend, Themis, the goddess of Necessity was said to have given birth to three daughters who became known as the Three Fates who spun the thread of life; determining how long each thread would be and cutting the thread when it was time for death. The Three Fates are said to laugh at our pathetic attempts to cheat them, because we always fail. Axolotl reminds us that we cannot hide from Fate and that nothing we do or say can thwart the inevitably of her master plan. Axolotl comforts us in our quest for understanding by explaining that all good things must come to an end and that with every ending, a new beginning is guaranteed; with every death we are rewarded with a birth and with every relationship, job, project or home that is lost to us, a new, better, more fruitful proposition is presented to us for consideration. It is only when we resist change that we find ourselves paralysed by fear, grief and confusion. When we surrender to change, we soon discover sacred reason for the things that seemingly happen against our will, with Fate offering rewards to those who embrace her higher wisdom.

Baboon
Petition

 Baboon travels in family troops of many females and several unrelated mature males. Baboon is considered a wise man: an elder and teacher of high esteem. On the word of legend, Baboon's acumen was often sought out by the other animals who viewed him as a spiritual messenger or sacred oracle. In support of his Egyptian mythical association, the classification name for the Baboon is *Papio Anubis.* Anubis, the Jackal-headed god of the Underworld, was responsible for the manipulation of the balances that weighed all hearts against the Feather of Maat; the Mother of Truth. Only those whose hearts weighed even were permitted to venture into the Other World.

Baboon encourages us to listen to all sides of a story before forming judgments one way or another. Baboon instils the importance of weighing up the facts before making suggestions, decisions or final rulings. He endorses the adage that 'it (always) takes two to tango' and the advice 'never judge a book by its cover'. To work with Baboon's wisdom is to understand that although things may seem cut and dried on the surface, there is always more to a story than initially meets the eye. And to always determine what is right and what is wrong by examining all the facts, petitions put forward and perspectives before saying, doing or deciding anything.

• Mandrill – *Enigma*

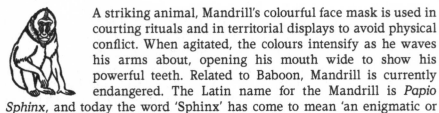 A striking animal, Mandrill's colourful face mask is used in courting rituals and in territorial displays to avoid physical conflict. When agitated, the colours intensify as he waves his arms about, opening his mouth wide to show his powerful teeth. Related to Baboon, Mandrill is currently endangered. The Latin name for the Mandrill is *Papio Sphinx*, and today the word 'Sphinx' has come to mean 'an enigmatic or mysterious person'.

To walk in the light of Mandrill is to be called an enigmatic person. It is to be labelled 'unknowable', suggesting that although you may know a lot about other people, their lives and their loves, most people actually know very little about you. Although acceptable to a certain point, Mandrill warns that such a lifestyle may someday lead to loneliness and resentment on our part. Mandrill encourages us to lay our cards on the table and to be open and upfront about who and what we are before embarking on any new venture or relationship. He supports us as we grow from child to elder. He nurtures us from birth, helping us to be our true and impeccable selves, while supporting us as we rebirth after we topple from ego-imposed pedestals. Unlike his namesake, Mandrill warns us to avoid speaking in riddles or using deceit as protection. The gentle Mandrill, who only ever bares his teeth when discouraging prospective aggressors, teaches us to Walk our Talk, to show integrity and to champion wisdom, strength and nobility as our cause instead of imposing dishonesty or belligerence.

Badger
Compliance

 Badger is nocturnal by nature and thousands of European Badgers are killed annually as a result of Badger baiting and other illegal means. Along with the Australian Wombat, Badger is one of Earth Mother's keepers of sacred herbal lore; the medicinal properties of the plants, flowers and herbs.

If Badger is currently nagging at you to take heed, consider the fact that you may need to visit a natural therapist that specialises in herbal remedies. Thank Badger for his wisdom and be sure to follow whatever you unearth through with resolve and tenacity – energy befitting the wisdom of Badger. As a solitary creature, it could be said that Badger is grumpy and impatient because his friends so rarely come to visit him, with the obvious reason being his lack of visitors. Badger is all about regaining control, being organised and maintaining one's personal direction in life. Badger is not for the faint-hearted – he expects that we all fall quickly and willingly into line in an attempt to realise the bigger picture, to conform to Universal flow, let down our guard and shun frailty, vulnerability and defencelessness of any sort. When hurried before their time or backed into a corner, Badger people can be unassailable and punitive in nature and often come across as being avariciousness, materialistic and parsimonious. They hate change and are often guilty of refusing to acknowledge or even consider perspectives or points of view different to their own. As a result, Badger people often find themselves cut off from those around them; emotionally and spiritually stagnating in a vain attempt to maintain the status quo. Badger demands that we take responsibility for our life and our own healing. He asks us to be gentler on ourselves and others and encourages us to consider the thoughts and beliefs of others and to honour them accordingly. He reminds us that we all need to be free to determine the direction of our own lives.

• Honey Badger – *Self-absorption*

Honey Badger, or *Ratel*, is a determined carnivore with a reputation for being Africa's most audacious animal. Reclusive by nature, he will tackle highly venomous Cobra and Black Mamba when pressed. Honey Badger begins life as a joyful and merry being, and then over time, slowly becomes more and more cynical and introverted due to limited life experience and painful worldly observation.

Honey Badger people believe that if they don't do what rewards them themselves, no one else will. Those around them are usually left a little shell-shocked by the change, and because it emerges so gradually, they very rarely notice the transformation until it is too late. Those who embrace Honey Badger tend to display belligerent, determined and self-inspired behaviour. Their main lesson in life, as a result, is to soften and control their aggressive tendencies and to reduce it to a level more assertive in nature, thus allowing for input from all sides. They must learn to listen to all concerned and consider more than their own perspective by respecting the beliefs of others and (once again) valuing those currently sharing their life path. Honey Badger is driven by what makes him feel good at the time, and generally with little consideration of how his actions affect those around him. He will readily take advantage of the efforts employed by another, the generosities offered by friends and family or the hospitality of strangers who know no better. If you are being presented with Honey Badger, ask yourself these questions: Are you (or someone close to you) looking at life from a more self-absorbed angle than normal? Are you taking advantage of the goodwill of others in a way that only supports your personal gain? Are your actions hurting, limiting or draining the potential of another? Do you take more than you give back? Are you more often than not, aggressive, short-tempered, negative, or limited in your perceptions? If the answers to these questions profit your best interests only, and this resonates well with you, then you are working with the shadow side of Honey Badger and it is time to start appreciating the support being offered by relaxing your control, addressing your fears and offering something back.

Bandicoot
Industry

Solitary and nocturnal by nature, Bandicoot is a small, omnivorous marsupial. Urban development has severely fragmented Australia's Bandicoot populations and he falls prey to several animals. Bandicoot was believed to have birthed himself from the side of an Ancestor Spirit, leaving behind a gaping cavity, which he filled with honeysuckle nectar. He was regarded as a thief in early Australian history because he stole flowers and vegetables from orchards, fruit stands and market gardens.

Because he was prepared to take risks and do what was needed to ensure his survival, Bandicoot was awarded the wisdom of ambition and industry. His inquisitive nose, constantly probing the ground while exploring every window of opportunity, gave him the reputation of fruitfulness. Bandicoot people, though reserved, shy and humble, are hard workers; always on the go, always searching for ways to make their life richer and more abundant. They are driven by self-worth and carry the 'I deserve it' badge proudly on their sleeve. They are the quiet achievers, the true essence of Australian industry; the embodiment of achievement. Bandicoot promises a time of reward and acknowledgement for hard work, resourceful thinking and fruitful attitude. He foretells the birth of 'something sweet'; the realisation of a goal or some ambition erroneously assumed to be a long way off. Bandicoot warns against taking advantage of or 'borrowing' resources not intended for your use.

Bat
Rebirth

 Bat is the only mammal capable of true flight. According to superstition, Bat roosting under one's eaves is a warning of possible gossip and jealousy aimed at the head of the house, while Bat appearing in the home is an inauspicious warning of negative witchcraft or ill-wishing aimed at the entire household.

Bat reminds us, therefore, that just as a baby rests inverted in the womb waiting for its moment of birth, the Bat hangs upturned in the cave waiting for night to fall. The cave is an ancient analogy made in reference to the womb of Earth Mother. As Bat exits her cave each night she essentially re-creates the act of birth as well as demonstrating our desire to step out of the darkness of uncertainty and to symbolically rebirth ourselves. The image of Bat flying out of her cave denotes desire for new beginnings or the chance to start from scratch in one or more areas of our life. She alludes to the idea of completely rebirthing who and what we are, as if re-emerging from our mother's womb as a new being. Rebirth signifies shedding all the outworn aspects of our life. It represents a complete reshuffle of how we view the world and how we see ourselves within it. Bat heralds a symbolic death, a sudden ending or closure, followed by a new beginning and primes us for an ending of something that no longer serves us and offers us the chance for expansion and growth. Bat prepares us for rebirth, symbolised by the stepping into a new phase or facet of life. It is our destiny to grow and essentially become our future. It is Spirit's will but we can initiate rebirth, the aspect of the familiar self that is dying must be acknowledged and dealt with to allow the process to flow smoothly. We cannot expect new doors to open if we are not prepared close old ones. Just as trash and waste will eventually clog and kill any natural body of water, emotional and spiritual obstacles will eventually strangle our sense of choice, limiting our potential and hindering our renewed perception of self. Bat asks that we consciously face our emotional issues and remove the obstacles.

• Vampire Bat – *Energy*

 Although Vampire Bat does require fresh blood (from livestock) for her sustenance, she never attacks humans. In essence, vampirism is an attempt to reclaim something believed lost. It is inherently the nature of the Vampire to require the life force of an outside host in order to survive because they do not have sufficient energy of their own. Therefore, a Spiritual Vampire is someone who uses someone else's Spirit in order to survive. These misguided beings believe that they are unable to create what they want in life using their own energy. For the first time in their life, they mistakenly believe that they have power, when in truth they are powerless. An Emotional Vampire plays on the emotions in order to gain power over another by employing fear, guilt, bullying, and victimisation. A Spiritual Vampire will initially prompt you to feel energetic, happy and excited, after which your energy levels will dwindle, possibly below your normal range. The key is to be aware of your energy levels and emotions after each encounter. Emotional Vampires are more common and easier to identify. If you've ever felt tired for no apparent reason after spending time with someone, you've probably encountered an Emotional Vampire. They are the emotional blackmailers. They create an aura of innocence; a façade of good-intention and authenticity.

Vampire Bat affords us the power to simply walk away from these people. She offers us the skills to vanquish their control; to let them go. Vampire Bat reminds us that our energy is for our use only. Energy cannot be taken or stolen against your will, but it can be misappropriated if you allow it to be. The trick is to prevent this from happening by saying 'No'. Spiritual and Emotional Vampires are natural-born manipulators, so the easiest way to deal with them is to totally cut off their supply. When their source of energy dries up, they will either learn to survive on their own or seek out an alternative 'food' source.

Bear
Going within

Hunted since prehistoric times for her meat and fur, the eight existing species of Bear are spread throughout the Northern Hemisphere and Southern Hemisphere, including North America, South America, Europe and Asia. Six of the eight species of Bear are omnivorous, while Polar Bear is mostly carnivorous and Giant Panda mainly eats bamboo. Typically solitary and diurnal, all Bears have an excellent sense of smell, can run very fast and are skilful climbers and swimmers, and most retire to their dens where they 'sleep' away the winter.

• Asiatic Black Bear – *The prostitute*

 Asiatic Black Bear, also known as Himalayan, Tibetan or Moon Bear, and little is known about her ways. Despite a clear and obvious lack of proven medicinal worth, Moon Bear's bile is harvested and sold as a traditional remedy for ailments and is hunted and served as delicacies in restaurants. Moon Bear hibernates during the winter months and loses a great deal of weight which must be recouped when she 'wakes up' in the spring. In central Asia, the moon is described as a mirror that reflects all things of the world. To sit and ponder the reflection of the moon in a pool of water is believed to be the best remedy for a person suffering from depression, concern or anxiety.

A creature that symbolically sits in the West on the great Wheel of Life, Bear generically invites us to ponder life, to seek sacred silence and to meditatively journey deep within so that we might productively explore our inner perceptions as we watch the moon grow in size and power. She prompts us to seek and trust answers found deep within our inner knowing before considering the acumen of others. Bear invites us to stand introspectively, facing the sun as it sets. Such a stance creates opportunity for reflection, calm and self-assessment. Moon Bear reflects the inherent prostitute that exists within all of us: that part of us that is willing to compromise our mind, body and spirit in order to feel whole, better or worthy. She represents the shadow-side tendency to sell ourselves short, sell ourselves out, to reject personal values and morals and to ignore sanctified beliefs in order to gain or maintain security, support, affiliation or endorsement. She allows us to make excuses for our actions, no matter how lame, and to tell ourselves that we believe them to be true. Moon Bear demonstrates the pointlessness of believing the self-initiated façades, illusions and lies we hide behind in order to avoid taking responsibility for our actions and reactions. Moon Bear demands that we take down the figurative 'for sale sign' that has presented our most sacred and prized features to the highest bidder for generations, and that we begin to put things right (on a personal and global scale) by saying 'No more'. Some things are priceless and cannot be replaced.

• Black Bear – *Introspection*

 Largely solitary by nature, (except when accompanied by a dependant cub), Black Bears is an opportunist feeder, eating whatever is available. Black Bear traditionally sits in the West on the Great Wheel of Life and encourages us to silence the inner chatter, to sit in silent contemplation and to find the answers we seek within the solitude of our subconscious mind. The silence is the key to higher understanding; the key that unlocks the line of communication between our higher self and Spirit.

Black Bear's cave represents the womb of Earth Mother and the wisdom stored deep within the subconscious mind. As such, the cave is a symbol of growth, with the act of entering being a return to the centre of the sacred self, a 'death' of sorts', and our emergence signifying the act of rebirth.

Black Bear instils a sense of self-sufficiency while endorsing trust in our intuition and personal belief, rather than relying on those of family and friends. Black Bear guides us deep within that part of our subconscious mind and teaches us to release that which no longer serves us, thus making way for new beginnings. Because of this quality, Black Bear people are often described as 'dreamers' and, when fully misunderstood, 'time-wasters', when in reality, due to an enhanced sensitivity to their physical surroundings, they are otherwise engaged; filtering and integrating what their conscious mind tells them in contradiction of what their subconscious mind inherently knows. They enjoy their own company, are very creative and are profoundly visual. The totem of healers, teachers and dream interpreters, Black Bear is the keeper of one's inner knowing and it is only when we embrace her wisdom that we fully break through the illusion of personal limitation and false belief and find clarity and awareness within ourselves embracing the wisdom of the Void. Black Bear offers insight that will see us ponder life, contemplate our spiritual path and make productive, self-empowering, goal-achieving choices later in life.

• Brown Bear – *Primordia*

 Brown Bear is now extinct in Europe due to excessive hunting and survives today in North America as Grizzly Bear, an animal of little or no genetic difference. At first glance, Brown Bear's awkward gape made her appear dopey and slow but this was not the case. Brown Bear could reach speeds of up to 56 kilometres per hour (at short bursts), was an adept climber and readily took to water. Brown Bear was a flat-footed, largely nocturnal mammal that slept in dens and hibernated lightly during the winter months. To all appearances as a fierce predator, Brown Bear preferred to feed on roots, berries, fungi, fish, insects and small mammals.

Bear, emerging from her womb-like cave after a period of winter dormancy followed closely by new-born young, has long carried the symbology of rebirth and renewal. She Bears were revered as the embodiment of the Celtic goddess, Artio, whose name contains residue of the traditional name for Bear; *Art*. Brown Bear remains the totem of the Artist; the one who bears witness to the world around her and preserves it forever in sculpture, on canvas or some similar, figurative way, She represents the celebration and awakening of dormant ability, personal rebirth and self-healing. A hibernating animal, Brown Bear is the guardian of the Inner Landscape or the Underworld; the place we journey to in times of contemplative and introspective need. Brown Bear nurtures us as we meditatively comprehend the reason for things, as we nut them out for ourselves, as we wait patiently for the right moment to initiate new ideas, for opportunities to be presented or for potentials to be verified. As she sleeps deep within her cave, she stimulates a deeper understanding of our dreams, plans and visions of the future, while awakening our latent potential, thus symbolically 'licking us into shape'.

• Giant Panda – *Sorrow*

 Scientists still cannot agree as to whether Giant Panda belongs to the Bear family or not. Despite the fact that Giant Panda has a similar build, powerful jaw and strong Bear-like claws (as well as having similar blood proteins), she does not hibernate and her diet is completely different to Bear's. Giant Panda is typically observed in people who 'cry for the people'; people who find themselves driven to make the lives of others more tolerable.

Giant Panda people are very compassionate, empathetic and sensitive to the suffering of others. In extreme cases, they look at the state of the world and literally cry overwhelmed with sadness and grief stricken by the insignificance of their lone voice. They feel as if they should be doing more to support the people, with no idea of how to go about offering it. If unable to channel their passion productively, Giant Panda people often burn out or break down emotionally beneath the burden of guilt and sadness they bear on behalf of the world. Giant Panda affords those who embrace its wisdom a deeper understanding and introspective advantage when it comes to helping others reclaim clarity. They are generally able to distance themselves from the emotional circumstance of others in order to see and appreciate why things happen and what needs to be done to bring about positive change. Giant Panda people are encouraged to look to the esoteric properties of bamboo for stamina and protection when opening their hearts to others. Bamboo is used as a divinatory tool in Chinese temples and can designate negative or positive omens according to how it is handled. Giant Panda warns of becoming too involved in another's process of change when unprotected against getting too involved and personally affected by its conclusion. Giant Panda endorses 'crying for the people' as a viable and sacred medicine, but not when it is offered at the emotional expense of the one carrying it. Thus, Giant Panda offers her support to those who hold personal wellbeing on par with those they support.

• Grizzly Bear – *Fatherliness*

 A threatened species, Grizzly Bear was once found throughout Asia, Africa and Europe and his fur turns grey with age, affording him a salt and pepper or 'grizzled' appearance. The word 'grizzled' means distinguished, eminent, greying, aged and mature. Everything about Grizzly Bear supports these evocative words as he is indeed a distinguished creature carrying an air of weathered maturity. The stance he adopts when standing on two legs is both intimidating and protective. The arms outstretched is reminiscent of the 'bear hug', while the slow plodding stroll of Grizzly Bear invites an unrushed, casual approach to life.

Grizzly Bear silently and carefully mulls over the arguments, petitions and requirements of all involved parties before sharing his view. His decisions are sound, based solely on years of experience, aged wisdom and profound consideration. A thinker and a philosopher, he gains his wisdom from mystical sources and appears to remember everything. Grizzly Bear people are usually reserved, reticent types who rarely offer their opinion without invitation. Grizzly Bear people watch from afar but seldom interject or draw attention to their curiosity. When a Grizzly Bear person does offer their point of view via stories or recollections based on his (or her) own life experiences, however, everyone stops and listens. They are hardly ever overpowering or unreasonable but when they do demonstrate these negative qualities, they are generally damaged in some way. They are always aware of their weaknesses and (although reluctant to discuss or explain) are willing to heal them, but simply cannot find the tools or hone the skills without support. Grizzly Bear teaches the art of deliberation and the weighing of all possibilities and endorses the avoidance of making rash decisions or pushing for things before their time. To embrace Grizzly Bear is like being welcomed home; a protective place of understanding, appreciation and wholeness.

• Kodiak Bear – *Retrospection*

 Kodiak Bear is extremely sensitive to his environment, and as such, offers a measure to the health and vitality of the ecosystem sustaining him and there are currently several factors affecting the creature's future. Although Kodiak Bear will venture into backyards and gardens in search of food, raiding dustbins and compost heaps, he is best known for his ability to catch Salmon.

Kodiak Bear prompts us to look retrospectively over our life and to reflect upon the lessons, experiences and opportunities we have been afforded since childhood. In doing so, we may ask 'What would I do differently?' or 'How would I handle that situation if I had the chance to do it all over?' Had Zeus, for example, handled his affair more covertly, or if he had honoured his wife by not enjoying his infidelity in the first place, Callisto's fate (and that of her son) would have panned out differently. By placing her in the heavens as the constellation Ursa Major, Zeus was forever reminded of his betrayal, Callisto of her artlessness, and Arcas of his bravery. Kodiak Bear nurtures a sense of reason and fortitude that can never be hindered by the opinions, desires or motivations of another. Kodiak Bear celebrates every experience as a chance to learn more and to enhance one's wisdom. He explains that even when life seems to push you back or force you forward, you can regain equilibrium by reflecting on the reasons that landed you there in the first place. By remaining steadfast in your convictions and by questioning the motivations behind the things that you do, you will avoid the pressure created by those who would otherwise manipulate you for their personal gain. Confirmation can be sought, too, by considering the medicine ways of Kodiak Bear's favourite prey: the Salmon. The silvery, reflective skin of the Salmon also invites retrospection. Salmon inspires deeper consideration of the experiences life presents us with, and the lessons hidden within each. In hindsight, Salmon reminds us that we can usually see the reason for why 'things' happen and that nothing happens by chance.

• Polar Bear – *Brotherhood*

Polar Bear is the world's largest land-dwelling carnivore. The people of the North revere Polar Bear as a source of great spiritual power, physical endurance and wisdom. To them, Polar Bear is not just another animal – he is family with many believing they are his direct descendants.

Considered the 'Spirit of the North', he is an animal of ancient power, a keeper of wisdom and a guardian of the Spirit World and offers deep and meaningful insight into the world of Spirit. He takes us on a tour, a 'hands-on' exploration of the other realms and the joys that are to be found there. Polar Bear opens a portal between the worlds and a bridge that links the elemental forces of nature and our inherent relationship with all things. He allows us to travel back to the Dreamtime; the sacred point in time that witnessed the Creation of the world and brings us back, too, to our own personal point of Creation, when we first realised that the power to dream, decide and formulate our future was ours alone. Polar Bear affords the chance to reassess our beliefs, our values and our personal commitment to walk gently upon the Earth. He helps us feel good about being in our own skin again and to see ourselves as being a part of the whole and not apart from the whole. Polar Bear asks that we make a pact to help our brother raise awareness to the plight of the North, and as recompense, trust in the knowledge that he will help us heal by teaching us to trust our emotions and express our feelings, instead of biting our tongue. He asks that we remember our place in the greater scheme of things and contemplate the very real fact that if mighty Polar Bear (a creature perched on the top of its food chain) is not strong enough to defend himself against the effects of global warming and pollution, then who are we to assume that we will be any better off? Polar Bear ignites the desire to partake in a spiritual quest that will see our life regain its integrity, wholesomeness and clarity; a journey that will see our gifts of power emerge, purpose realised and our connection to Spirit become richer, deeper and inherently fertile.

• Sloth Bear – *Familiarity*

Sloth Bear feeds primarily on Termites (made easy by the evolution of his mouth) and is abundant throughout India, Sri Lanka, Bangladesh, Bhutan and Nepal. According to Asian tradition, the protruding tongue was a sign of fecundity, power and positive chi-energy, and was likened to the emergence and growth of the erect male penis. The lips were said to symbolically resemble the vulva and the tongue protruding from the lips was seen as an imitation of sexual penetration. To this day, the vulva is properly referred to as *labiae* (meaning 'lips') while the Latin *lingus* ('tongue') is a derivative of the term *lingam*, which refers to the male penis.

Sloth Bear invites us to ponder the relationships we enjoy with the people in our life and to assess the level of familiarity we share with each of them. Sloth Bear encourages us to consider whether or not we have honoured these relationships properly by showing them the respect they are worthy of. He invokes a sense of accountability and respect for all relationships, by explaining that what might be appropriate in one situation may not be appropriate in another, that all are worthy of equal esteem and that the best way to earn respect is to first show it toward others in a way fitting of what you feel you deserve.

• Sun Bear – *Recognition*

Malayan Sun Bear is the smallest member of the Bear family and is often kept as a pet because of his playfulness and appeal. Most are abandoned at maturity, however, as he becomes increasingly difficult to handle and control.

Traditionally Bear invites us to stand introspectively, facing the sun as it sets creating opportunity for contemplation and inner assessment. However, Sun Bear encourages us to stand with clarity and watch the sun as it *rises*. Such a stance forces us to consider our ponderings in a tangible way; to look within ourselves for the clues that will initiate substantial new beginnings and produce the keys needed to unlock doors that promise hope, abundance and good health in the physical sense. According to the ways of the tarot, 'the Sun' card reveals the true essence of whom and what we are. It represents the promise of a new day. In this context, Sun Bear infuses greater endurance and support. He guarantees recognition of opportunity and how to ensure its success. His warming, solar energy offers reassurance and healing. He refreshes and confirms and prepares us for the next leg of our journey. Sun Bear creates a sense of enthusiasm, warmth and illumination capable of rebirthing one's spirit. To want to explore the energy of Sun Bear comes as a very positive sign. If you have called upon his wisdom to help clarify a situation, or to help you make a decision, the answer to your question will most likely be a resounding, 'Yes'. Sun Bear is an indicator of happiness, good health, rewarding relationships, financial security and a happy home and ensures healing in any situation or circumstance.

Beaver

Industriousness

 Beaver is affectionately known as the 'sacred centre of the land' because he creates rich habitats and safe havens for other, sometimes endangered, creatures by building dams in streams and creating clean-water wetlands. According to European folklore, Beaver is said to embody resourcefulness, peacefulness and vigilance.

Beaver speaks of accomplishment, strong connection to home and family and community spirit. Beaver energy invokes and harnesses the elemental energies of Wood, Earth and Water and is blessed with the medicine name of 'achiever'. He encourages us to harness our resources, to work hard and to strive for a goal. Beaver encourages us to deal with any emotional stagnation that may threaten to block creative flow, to surrender fears and weaknesses, settle differences and to seek alternative solutions to obstacles that hinder growth. Beaver works hard to build his lodge and so do Beaver people. They work particularly well as a member of a team and focus best on communal goals that promise to benefit everyone equally. Beaver people find security in always having alternative plans up their sleeve in case everything they have worked hard for gets 'washed away'. Beaver endorses the fact that when we limit our beliefs or ignore our options, we stem the flow of opportunity that promises to enter our life. Beaver, simply put, demonstrates the fact that fear, denial and a lack of planning will inevitably block your efficiency and flow of abundance if you allow them to. Beaver reminds us that if we work as a team, knuckle down and remain vigilant, we will never 'go under'. We will remain strong, in control with our head safely 'above water'.

Bee

Potential

Bee is a flying insect that plays an important role in the pollination of flowers and flowering shrubs. Bee may travel thousands of kilometres and visit millions of flowers to gather enough nectar to make just one jar of honey. Bee was once revered as a bridge between the natural world and the Underworld. Images of Bee were used to adorn the walls of tombs and it was once believed that Bee was the embodiment of the souls of priestesses who once dedicated their lives to Aphrodite.

Bee promotes the celebration of life, the realisation of potential and the ability to make good from every opportunity and affords the 'Midas Touch' to those who embrace her wisdom. Bee endorses the value of organised community, dedicated team work and the harnessing of a group vision. In order to reach a desired level of achievement or to build the strongest of foundations in life, we often must enlist the support and knowledge of others and trust that they will work for the common good, just as Drone Bees demonstrate loyalty and commitment to their Queen. Bee nurtures us as we celebrate the magic of life and discover the wonder and fertility in every experience. Bee can be invoked to aid fertility on all levels, particularly when one is attempting to conceive a child or establish a new business or project. Bee provides a fertile base on which any 'seed' or concept may take root, grow and prove viable. If you are birthing a new business, for example, view yourself as the Queen Bee. Invoke Bee to ensure the sustainable increase in the size and productivity of your 'hive', building it up to the point where 'drones' are required to eventually run the business on your behalf leaving you to either sit back and reap the rewards or create yet another hive.

Bilby

Harnessing fear

Bilby digs tunnels and has been affectionately labelled as Australia's answer to the Rabbit. Vulnerability is a keynote of Bilby, who now sits on the edge of extinction. Fear surrounds this unassuming marsupial, demonstrated by both the animal's nervy disposition and the concerns the authorities hold for her survival in the wild. The problem with fear is that it spreads like wildfire. We journey through life working largely from two basic manuals, each respectively labelled *Love* and *Fear*. Most people favour one over the other, checking the pages for answers and seeking confirmation modelled largely on previous experience.

Bilby invites us to consider which book we favour and that we be honest to ourselves. Curiously, most of us don't bother to check the book of *Fear* anymore. We may have enjoyed one or two of the lessons from the book of

Love, but we have all experienced most (if not all) of the lessons offered by the book of *Fear*. Bilby offers the challenge to abandon the book of *Fear* and to study the book of *Love* wholeheartedly. She calls to us to bring what we have read to fruition by consciously acting on the advice offered. Fear, once welcomed into your life, takes root like an invasive, noxious weed and is very hard to expel. Start small. With every thought that passes through your mind, consider whether or not it comes from a place of fear or a place of love, trust and acceptance. Try trusting yourself instead. You have everything you need within you to move you ahead in the world. Our perception of the place we hold in the world often affects how others act and react toward us. What we radiate is what we attract. If we radiate fear, we will attract it, but if we radiate trust and unconditional love we will be showered with the consequent rewards. Bilby listens for, harnesses and carries the burdens created by our fears. Know though, that this will only be a temporary arrangement. It is vitally important that you realise where your fears lie, and for you to develop your own strategies of how to reverse their influence within your life. Bilby teaches us to control our fears so that they do not envelop our soul and block us from realising our potential.

Binturong
Propagation

 Binturong is an essential propagator of forest plant life. Once the fruit she eats has been digested, the discarded seed and stones are scattered via her droppings throughout the forested regions, where they quickly take root in the fertile soil and grow. There is a system of propagation based on ancient observation of the phases and influences of the moon that is just as relevant today. It requires that we observe the ebbs and flows of Nature and the rhythms of the land and coordinate our activities in the garden around the most fertile periods of the lunar month based on these influences. Each week is based on the observed phases of the moon and are said to fruitfully harness the force and power afforded the Earth at these times.

Binturong invites us to learn and integrate the subtle fluctuations of Nature into our lives, to harness their power and to allow them to productively influence our lives. Binturong encourages us to aid in the future sustenance of the planet by remembering that after we have gone, our children will be left to deal with our inadequacies. Binturong asks that we set a good example by returning to the ancient observations and teachings of Nature when working our gardens, by planting by the moon, choosing ancient, hardy pest-resistant fruit trees and vegetable crops and shunning the tendency to rely on chemical based fertilisers and growth hormones that eventually lead to the further pollution of our soil and waterways – not to mention our minds and bodies. Binturong espouses the belief that if we nurture the Earth Mother, she will nurture us.

Bird of Paradise

Temptation

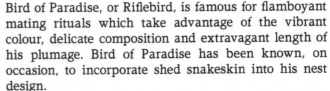

Bird of Paradise, or Riflebird, is famous for flamboyant mating rituals which take advantage of the vibrant colour, delicate composition and extravagant length of his plumage. Bird of Paradise has been known, on occasion, to incorporate shed snakeskin into his nest design.

Bird of Paradise endorses the lesson made apparent by the legend of Adam and Eve; supposedly the first man and woman to be created by the hands of God. The biblical story tells of Adam and Eve being offered a life of beauty and plenty within the Garden of Eden, except for the fruit from the Tree of the Knowledge of Good and Evil. The devil disguised as a Snake hid in the tree and tricked Eve into eating a piece of the Tree's fruit by telling her that if she ate from the tree, she would become like God, able to decide for herself what was right and what was wrong. God was angered by their betrayal and banished them forever. Although truth can be found in the wily words of the Snake, Bird of Paradise warns against making 'shot-gun' decisions, especially those triggered by temptation-fuelled spontaneity. He explains that decisions not properly thought through usually end in disaster, landing us in a quandary of what to do to reverse our actions, cover our trail or talk ourselves back into the 'good books' of those we love and hold sacred. Temptation is only positive when offered in a productive way, and when the offer can be harnessed and channelled as an opportunity to grow, heal and better our life of that of those dear to us. Willingness to take educated risks, for example, is to demonstrate trust and to follow a path inspired and directed by sound judgment. When you are onto a good thing, stick to it, and don't dance with the devil by tempting fate, unless you are fully prepared to live by the consequences.

Bison

Sacred unity

Bison or Buffalo is the largest Earth-bound mammal native to North America and one of the most ancient animals. Buffalo is a symbol of life. It is the embodiment of sacredness and was once seen as a channel for divine communication and a means of gaining insight, guidance and encouragement from Spirit.

Buffalo unites the mundane with the miraculous. She builds on what is regarded as a practical and fruitful life by integrating a meaningful, unified spiritual foundation offering choice, balance and wholeness. Buffalo reminds us that integrating prayer and appreciation into everyday life is a sacred way of re-establishing a sense of worthiness and abundance within ourselves. By honouring the sacred, we enhance the mundane. When we acknowledge the divine and welcome it into our life, we allow it to manifest in everything we do. We literally begin to notice Spirit and the miracles of Creation in everyday things. To acknowledge Spirit and to welcome it into your life is to know you are not alone. When you call to Spirit, you call to those *in Spirit*. You call to the Spirit *within all things* and *within yourself*. And in doing so, you also call to the Creator Spirit and the protective, nurturing energies of the Earth Mother. Sacred Unity can only be achieved when we are fully committed to consciously doing what needs to be done to support its ideal. Enjoying a practical and fruitful life means living, breathing and celebrating our very existence in a similar way in *everything* we do. To be supported, for example, we must be prepared to support. To be loved unconditionally, we must be prepared to love unconditionally. To be trusted, we must learn to trust. Most of all, we must learn to empower ourselves with these qualities as gifts of self-love. How we live our life on a tangible level must reflect our beliefs and our sense of self worth. When it does, we are truly working with Buffalo Dreaming.

• White Buffalo – *Miracle*

 The Plains Indians consider White Buffalo as a gift from Father Sun. White Buffalo was, and is, sacred. Carefully prepared White Buffalo skins (referred to as 'robes') were traditionally displayed in full sunlight outside the lodge of the tribe's medicine elder as a sign of respect and thanks to the sun. White Buffalo robes were also worn into battle as sacred talismans of protection. When a White Buffalo was slaughtered, great care was taken with respectful prayer offered throughout the process. It was believed that the white robes enhanced healing ceremonies and offered the people greater chance of recovering from illness. Medicine bundles were also wrapped in white robes as a sign of sacredness for the contents and as a way of offering them protection.

The Lakota, Dakota and Nakota Nations are collectively referred to as the Sioux and its people are warriors. The White Buffalo Calf Woman sits at the heart of the Sioux Nation and offers beauty and conviction to their legends. Before she came, it is said, the people wandered aimlessly across the land. She rekindled the flame of Spirit within their hearts and minds and she has been honoured ever since for her gift of wisdom through ritual and ceremony. Many believe that the White Buffalo Calf named 'Miracle' (born August 20, 1994), and every other White Buffalo Calf born since, collectively herald the re-uniting of humanity and the reawakening of Oneness: the state of mind, body and spirit that rejects solitude, fear and abandonment and re-establishes sacred connection to Spirit, the Earth Mother and 'the people'. White Buffalo symbolises hope and renewal, harmony among all people and a joining of all races of man so that we may walk together, united as 'a people'.

Blackbird

Song

Blackbird has been introduced to lands far from their native home, including Australia and New Zealand, and is considered a pest by many. He is a songbird and member of the Thrush family. The male Blackbird is often heard singing in the early morning, late afternoon or early evening. He sings during nesting time, serenading his mate as she sits on her eggs. Blackbird only sings at specific times of the year, and only during certain hours of the day.

Blackbird is considered the gatekeeper to the Other Worlds. His song beckons us to enter, explore and follow a spiritual path that will inevitably broaden our self-awareness and intuitive knowing. Blackbird's song praises us for the level of commitment we show while living our physical life, while urging us to open our consciousness to a spiritual path that will lead us to a more fulfilled place of wholeness and knowing. It is potent enough to heal mental, physical and spiritual dis-ease and offers a unique way to reconnect with others, the Universe and ourselves. Sometimes those who are directed to embrace Blackbird and to sing a healing song are guided to put their mouth directly on or over the affected area of the body and to 'sing' into the site of dis-ease, while using the rattle or drum to ground and reassure their client. It is said that both the vibration and the melody carry strong healing powers, especially when delivered with pure intent and a lack of ego. Healing song has been reported to powerfully affect the emotional body, too. When people receive the unconditional love as it flows exclusively around them, they are often deeply moved. Blackbird reminds us that healing songs do not require any type of musical aptitude; it is about tapping into our own soul song and releasing it without concern for 'how it sounds.'

Asian Buffalo

Effort

Found throughout most of Southern Asia, docile Asian Buffalo is easily domesticated (unlike his African cousin, Cape Buffalo) and is employed in the cultivation of rice paddies. Also called Water Buffalo, this large breed of cattle has insufficient sweat glands, making it necessary for him to wallow in pools of water or mud in order to keep cool. Asian Buffalo (along with Horse and Camel) has long been used as a beast of burden by the indigenous people who share the land with him. As a result of this ancient association, Asian Buffalo has grown to understand this sacred role and honours servitude as his Dreaming.

Asian Buffalo's efforts have not gone unnoticed and people from many cultures realise that without Asian Buffalo they would not be able to sustain the lifestyle required to productively support their communities. In many traditions, Asian Buffalo has been rewarded with the gifts of sacredness and protection as a way of acknowledging his efforts. Asian Buffalo reminds us that to embrace demanding employ will eventually lead to reward – for the self and others – and that without personal effort, one cannot expect to progress on any level. This is Asian Buffalo's gift.

• Cape Buffalo – *Defiance*

Cape Buffalo is respectfully labelled the most dangerous animal in Africa. It is a fact that more people have been killed by Cape Buffalo than by any other animal in Africa, with all attempts to domesticate the species through crossbreeding with cultivated breeds proving impossible.

Cape Buffalo is a relative of Water Buffalo and endorses effort, the willingness to contribute and absorb another's burden and to selflessly work hard. Water Buffalo offers strength and resolve while espousing the belief that effort and dedication usually lead to reward. Cape Buffalo, however, does not support this philosophy at all, proposing instead that we *don't* offer contribution on any level. An animal that defiantly refuses to be yoked, Cape Buffalo affords strength and resolve to those breaking free from oppression and abuse. To explore the wisdom of Cape Buffalo is to fight back and take a personal stand against persecution. It is to say 'No more' to control, fear and manipulation and to shun *the system*. Showing little respect for Lions, Cape Buffalo rejects languor, demanding that people show accountability for their own lives and behaviour instead of dumping responsibility and expecting others to bow and scrape. Cape Buffalo people are slaves to no one – they are free-spirited, wild individuals who live each day as they come. Usually unemployed and burdened by few material possessions and displaying an inherent rebellious streak, Cape Buffalo people (who are naturally gifted dreamers, artists and craftsmen), do not take kindly to offers of charity or government assistance, preferring to improvise and make do instead of 'selling their soul to the devil'.

Butterfly
Transformation

Butterfly is only capable of flight when her body reaches a certain temperature and basks in the sun to harness the sun's energy. It is said that Butterfly offers new life and the chance to transform ourselves on all levels; to become stronger, prouder and more willing to trust.

As Butterfly moves from Caterpillar to Chrysalis to Butterfly, she demonstrates trust in her ability to grow and adapt. While in the form of a

Caterpillar, Butterfly represents us as we take our first steps toward conscious growth and personal development. Caterpillar is slow and cumbersome; the embodiment of how we view ourselves as we struggle to absorb new information and develop new skills. As Caterpillar builds her protective Chrysalis and begins to metamorphose, we begin to internalise our newfound wisdom. We begin to examine and question; file and discard. By the time Caterpillar decides to emerge as the beautiful Butterfly, we announce that we are ready to test our newfound wings and take our wisdom out into the world, to share it around and hopefully enhance the lives of others. The sight of Butterfly breaking free of her Chrysalis was seen as a re-enactment of rebirth. As such, Butterfly is a powerful symbol for anyone contemplating change or who is in the midst of major transformation. Butterfly promises that when contemplating change, we will be offered three tangible windows of opportunity to harness our goal. Each window will only last for the duration of one week but should the window be missed for one reason or another, rest assured you will be presented with two other opportunities. As Butterfly is deaf, she encourages us to listen to our other senses when we are in doubt as to when to call in change. Listen with your heart instead of your ears and go within for guidance instead of listening to the advice of others because true and effective change can only be fully appreciated when you are ready to integrate it on all levels.

Camel
Reserves

Camels are even-toed ungulates that bear distinctive 'humps' on their back. Both the Dromedary, or one-humped camel, and the Bactrian, or two-humped camel, have been domesticated. They provide milk, meat and fleece and are used as beasts of burden.

• Bactrian Camel – *Stockpile*

 Bactrian Camel stores fat in his two humps, which offers nourishment when food is scarce. He can survive several days without having to drink water and stores water in special 'stomach pouches'. When water is available, Bactrian Camel drinks only to replace what he has absorbed. He was first domesticated over 3,500 years ago and remains vital to the desert communities of Asia.

Bactrian Camel endorses readiness and encourages those who embrace his wisdom to be organised for any eventuality. He prepares us for the future by ensuring we have all that we need and more. He endorses never being caught short or being unrehearsed for any emergency and helps us progress from one day to the next in a fruitful way, supported by foresight and direction. Bactrian Camel ensures that we are nourished and nurtured adequately so that we may remain strong and of service to others. Those working with Bactrian Camel are usually effective savers, but are sometimes accused of hoarding or stockpiling items in excess of what is immediately required. Those interested in honouring the medicine ways of Bactrian Camel would do well therefore, to pose questions to themselves in an attempt to prepare and develop the endurance inherently afforded to Bactrian Camel people. Bactrian Camel poses questions so that we may know who we are, what support we have around us and who and what we can be sure of or rely upon in times of emergency. Bactrian Camel espouses the fact that if we can confidently answer these questions, we will be prepared for anything because we will have all we need to survive stored within us, stockpiled 'just in case'. When we know who and what we are, we no longer need to look externally for confirmation. We no longer need to seek out teachers, healers or leaders. We become the only leaders we need and, armed with this knowledge, we can never go unprepared again.

• Dromedary Camel – *Replenishment*

 Dromedary Camel stores fat in his single hump and also can survive several days without having to drink water. According to tradition, Dromedary Camel is said to represent compliance and submissiveness, royalty, solemnity, endurance and self-control. Dromedary Camel only endorses compliance and submissiveness, however, when such qualities offer reciprocal benefit. When they support another party's best interest above your own, however, he offers solemnity and endurance to take the reins and steer life in a more fruitful direction.

With his long eyelashes and pad-like feet, Dromedary Camel is perfectly equipped for arid conditions, sand storms and strong desert winds: symbolic of the emotional barrenness that inspires many to step out on their own and quest for purpose, self-worth and unconditional love. He offers fortitude to those pondering a journey that offers little emotional or financial encouragement and no premeditated destination. He offers sound navigation and guaranteed 'survival' to those prepared to take a risk, trust absolutely and do it hard for a while in order to be open to opportunity and the chance of betterment. Dromedary Camel helps us survive difficult times, particularly when we feel emotionally, spiritually and physically parched. His appearance can be seen as a warning that the path ahead may be difficult – dry, arid and possibly devoid of emotional support, love and incentive. If we are to traverse it with ease or with any degree of success, we must trust that we have all that we need within us and know that, by journey's end, we will be replenished. When we invoke the support of Camel Dreaming, we emerge emotionally stronger and more self-reliant.

Capybara

Now

Resembling giant Guinea Pig in appearance, Capybara is the world's largest living rodent and spends a lot of time in the water, swimming and feeding on the waterweed. Of solid, grounded disposition, Capybara lives a contented live, neither pushing for the future nor grieving for the past.

Capybara instils a sense of peace by explaining that when we panic about the future or waste time fretting over our past, we miss out on the possibilities being offered to us in the now. Capybara helps us heal the past by guiding us back to the first experience that ever contributed to us being 'damaged', to review it for flaws and to find the reason for why Spirit would put us through such a thing. Capybara helps us ask, 'Why would Spirit expect us to, or rather *need* us to experience such things?' All experiences, whether deemed by us as 'good' or 'bad' form the foundation of spiritual training and offer apprenticeship; learning from which powerful knowledge can be gleaned. Each experience includes a lesson that, if approached with a willingness to understand, will offer clarity and insight into who we are and what we can become. Capybara helps us know our future, too, by asking that we picture in our mind an approaching event that is creating concern or trepidation. Capybara helps us appreciate the life we are living today and rejects putting things off until tomorrow. He slams excuses and compromise for things that happened yesterday. Capybara reminds us that our children are only children once, for example, and that it is not until we lose something dear to our heart that we begin to appreciate its sacredness. Capybara states that love should never be taken for granted and that we end and begin each day with an 'I love you', and that we never part company with those we love without making peace, saying sorry or acknowledging their opinion with a hug.

Cassowary

Respect

Solitary and secretive by nature Cassowary has razor-sharp claws which he uses to defend himself and his chicks. Like Emu, the male raises the young. Sacred Space has been a fundamental aspect of most ancient philosophies since the Earth was new. All creatures have their own roles to play in the Web of Life, with each creature occupying space vital to its very existence. To respect the territory of others will ensure that they respect yours; a simple mind-set embraced by all of Earth Mother's creatures. Humans also build and maintain their own physical environments that, if respected, have the potential to become Sacred Space for themselves and others. We only have one Earth and it is up to us to honour the space we inhabit while we are here.

Cassowary is awe-inspiring and carries a reputation that commands respect. He has been known to run down and kill humans that step uninvited into his territory. Cassowary speaks of respect and warns us that what we put out is what we get back. Cassowary instils an innate respect for the belongings, beliefs, sacred space and loved ones of others, while also inspiring equal respect within the self. Cassowary is proud of what he is and what he represents. He is proud of his black feathers and his blue face, his flabby neck and the horn on his head. He knows he stands apart visually from other birds, but he does not let that hinder his growth. Despite the fact that he will never fly amongst the clouds, Cassowary struts through life radiating self-love. It is not important what others think of you. How you view yourself is what counts. Cassowary explains that in order to attract respect it is vital to emanate self-respect and show pride in your achievements, radiate self-worth and adopt and mirror the favourable qualities of the people that are drawn to you rather than focusing on their negative traits.

Cat
Sexuality and protection

 Cat is a small ancestor of the African Wild Cat, an animal first domesticated over 3,500 years ago by the ancient Egyptians, and is today one of the world's most popular choice of family pet. Cat is a skilled predator, indiscriminately stalking a very wide range of prey and is very intelligent, learning simple tasks with ease and dexterity. I have found that most people can generally be split into two categories – Dog people and Cat people. Dog people are usually needier than Cat people, seeking out constant company or steady partners. Cat people are more aloof and usually only seek company when they need stimulation or confirmation. Dog people are 'earthier' than Cat people who prefer fine food eaten in restaurants and friends who are 'someone'.

Cat encourages us to honour our sense of sensuality, self-worth and inherent self-love, and to see ourselves worthy of new beginnings, creation and rebirth. Powerfully sensual, too, self-confident and aloof, Cat can be invoked as a powerful form of sexual healing and protection (she is the designated guardian of the female sexual region and the root or base chakra). Cat is often referred to as the 'pussy' Cat, a slang term, often considered vulgar, that figuratively links the animal to the archaic 'yoni' symbol, the vulva, the place of origins and the ultimate representation of primed fertility. Black Cat affords the strength and self-empowerment to confront sexually related issues face on and to do what needs to be done to reclaim a sense of peace and self-worth. Cat provides a voice that is guaranteed to be heard; a voice that will both attract the attention of qualified support and ward off and expose the unwanted advances of 'stray Toms' who harass, taunt and abuse their sexual power. As long as Cat walks with you, protection, maturity and rebirth is assured. The path ahead remains full of fertile promise and potent opportunity as Cat offers support enough to fulfil any goal, to heal any issue and to bring any dream to fruition.

• African Wild Cat – *Protection*

Very little is known about the behaviour of African Wild Cat, apart from her solitary lifestyle and that she is probably territorial by nature. She is barely distinguishable from today's domestic Cat. In Egyptian lore, African Wild Cat symbolised the womb and pregnancy because it was believed that the energies of the moon fertilised the male seed and allowed it to grow in the womb. 'Puss' (a slang term often considered vulgar derived from the Egyptian, *Pasht*), refers to African Wild Cat's ability to shield the female sexual region of all women against intrusion, to defend the womb and to protect the unborn child.

The powerfully caring energies of Cat, however, can be harnessed and integrated into all areas of our life (whether we be male or female) as a physical, emotional and spiritual guardian of the family, the child, those displaying the wayward or 'home angel, street devil' blueprint, lovers, partners, siblings and friends. The protective qualities of African Wild Cat may also be invoked to ensure the development of new projects, investments or anything representing personal growth and advancement. African Wild Cat is capable of nurturing the fruitfulness of that which represents new life, but when invoked for the opposite reason, as the guardian of the womb, she is equally capable of thwarting any viable but unwanted 'seed' from germinating.

• Asiatic Golden Cat – *Alliance*

Like Puma, Asian Golden Cat is largely solitary in nature, but unlike any other species of Cat, the male Asian Golden Cat will support his mate and help raise the kittens. Everyone yearns to live life to the fullest, emancipated from all expectation and dependability and showing accountability for one's action is the only way to ensure that life remains free of impediments and obligation. However, Asiatic Golden Cat warns that if you find yourself in a situation that impairs your hopes and plans for the future, then follow its advice and form an alliance with someone of similar character, station or circumstance: someone who understands or shares your situation, someone who will benefit equally from your support as you will from theirs.

Like a light at the end of an otherwise dark tunnel, Asian Golden Cat eases the burden of fear, isolation and liability by offering vitality, prudence and reliability to any relationship. Under the guidance of Asiatic Golden Cat, young, frivolous, naive girls become motivated, protective, nurturing women while childish, bombastic, callow boys become hardworking, loyal, sympathetic men. Incandescent Asian Golden Cat will also make alliance-forming house calls to bring awareness to possible cries for help that have gone unheard or warning signs that have gone unheeded (intentionally or not) in relation to drug or alcohol abuse, sexual molestation, mental illness, violence, misdiagnosis or oppression.

• Fishing Cat – *Reconnaissance*

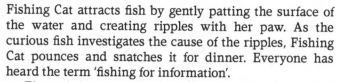

Fishing Cat attracts fish by gently patting the surface of the water and creating ripples with her paw. As the curious fish investigates the cause of the ripples, Fishing Cat pounces and snatches it for dinner. Everyone has heard the term 'fishing for information'.

The wisdom of Fishing Cat embraces a similar understanding, while offering the skills needed to ensure success and integrity in our search for truth. We have all had a gut feeling that nags at our conscious mind at one time or another and attempt to write it off as judgment, mistrust or jealousy; traits we were raised to view as negative and limiting. But sometimes we need to get to the core of the issues to regain peace of mind. Water, the element most closely associated with Fishing Cat, has long been considered a symbol of the emotions, cleansing and feminine energy. Animals depend on it by residing in, on or near it therefore, can be seen as ambassadors of this energy, imbued with specialised designed to guide and shape our intuition, innate creativity and imagination. Fishing Cat instils a trust in our intuition and our ability to 'just know' when something is not right. It nurtures a solid belief in our self-worth while prompting dedication to the maintenance of that worth and the strength needed to test our resolve. It helps us to separate ourselves from emotional ties, personal wants and desires and preconceived confidence long enough to distinguish cold truth from naïve certainty. It affords stability to face our worse fears and to productively handle and deal with the consequences, no matter how unsettling they may be. Fishing Cat coaches the delicate art of asking subtle yet probing questions; to 'test the water' and lay the bait that will help uncover truth without raising suspicion or demanding deeper enquiry.

• Ocelot – *Secrecy*

Poaching for her beautiful pelt and the illegal international pet trade has contributed to a marked decline in wild populations of Ocelot, along with deforestation. Once found throughout North, Central and South America, Ocelot has all but disappeared. A creature of the night and its shadows, Ocelot was said to carry the markings of the night sky upon her back. Like the typical 'golden' Jaguars ('Sun Jaguars'), Ocelot represents a balanced view of both the light and the dark aspects of life, indicated by the contrasting patterns on her coat.

Long revered for her elusiveness, silent deportment and love of dark, lonely places Ocelot was said to carry the medicine of the Secret Keeper, with all things related to it demanding an element of discretion and diplomacy. She does not lay blame or place judgment, and expects the same level of respect from those who carry her Dreaming and sees everything and everyone as being deserving of choice. The appearance of Ocelot usually indicates secrets and denotes things hidden from plain view, obscured by complicated stories, vague excuses and forced smiles. Out of respect for the individual, however, Ocelot never reveals the person in question, but instead makes a brief appearance and leaves because it believes it is not her place to offer judgment. Ocelot can confirm deception in other personal relationships, too. *How* they are deceiving you, and why, will never be exposed, however, as Ocelot never reveals a secret, but rest assured that when she does shed light, she is never wrong.

• Serval – *Covertness*

Serval is one of Africa's seven species of indigenous Wild Cat, or *Makanu*. Serval, like all Cats, is an animal of both lunar and solar influence, indicated by the changing dilation and contraction of her eyes. As a nocturnal animal, Serval represents mystery and stealth, while, as a diurnal animal, she symbolises elusiveness and solitude. Serval is timid, reserved and furtive by nature.

Those drawn to explore the wisdom of Serval, therefore, are being reminded to look within themselves for their innate strengths and distinctive character traits as a way of fortifying their confidence. Serval people are unique and stand alone, often feeling isolated from their kin because of unusual physical appearance, outlandish beliefs, passionate emotions or extraordinary natural ability. Serval people are forced to walk their path alone because of the higher purpose Spirit has in store for them. Serval offers the gift of stealth, the veil of covertness that both protects and provides. Serval people 'march to the beat of their own drum' and, as such, are born to *serve all*, to selflessly birth a better world for the rest of us from the creativeness of their own minds. Serval people are richly rewarded by Spirit, however, when the time is right for them to step out of the shadows into the spotlight of recognition.

Cattle
Nourishment

The term 'cattle' describes any domesticated herbivorous even-toed, hoofed mammal of the family *Bovidae*. Cattle were first captive bred for their meat, milk and other products, as well as beasts of burden, around 6,000 BC. Most of the contemporary breeds of dairy and beef cattle originated in Europe, while those more 'ancient' breeds, typically characterised by a shoulder hump and/or low-hanging dewlap, originated largely in India, with many now distributed throughout Africa, Asia,

Australia and North, Central and South America. Cattle have four chambered stomachs, a decreased number of teeth (compared with other herbivorous mammal), with no upper incisors. Most breeds also have horns that are not shed after the breeding season. Cattle are widely distributed throughout the world.

• Cow – *Motherhood*

Cow has long been regarded as a lunar-influenced creature; a celestial beast that exemplifies the nurturing qualities of the Earth Mother. Cow also carries deep association with the Mother Goddess in her many guises, with Cow itself literally acting as 'wet-nurse' to humanity for thousands of years. Ancient legends from all over the world refer to Cow as the personification of the Great Goddess who birthed the Earth or whose milk flowed as the four primordial rivers that nourished the ancient race of man, while the Milky Way constellation was said to have been born from the udder of Isis-Hathor.

Cow offers the horn of plenty to those who embrace her wisdom, as well as fertility and sustenance. Cow embodies what it means to be a mother and her role as giver of life, caregiver and protector of children. She prompts us to ask how we might rate the relationship we currently share with our mother and initiates healing that must take place between you if you are to continue to grow as a person. She offers permission to review the effectiveness of our mother's role and, in turn, our own role as a mother. Cow Dreaming releases us (and them) from the cyclical roller-coaster of past and future 'mother-issues' and the associated emotional burdens, unproductive parenting patterns and fruitless maternal programs. Cow demonstrates that when we set about healing our 'mother issues', we effectively remove them from our personal history, thus removing them on a genetic level from our children's personal history, too.

• Bull – *Potency*

In Celtic history, the number of Cattle an individual possessed indicated the degree of wealth his family held. Bull, in particular, was revered as a symbol of potency, abundance, power, prosperity and fecundity. To this day, the phrase 'a Bull Market' is still used to describe a potent and rapidly escalating stock market. Celtic warriors were considered brave and strong, possessing the strength and endurance of Bull and White Bulls were ritually sacrificed to make the point. White Bull represented the sun and was held sacred as a symbol of new life. Cow, meanwhile, was said to embody the nurturing qualities of the goddess and the Earth Mother herself. Bull calls for hard work, dedication and endurance. This is the only way we can expect to achieve any goal, do well and live a fruitful life.

Bull people are steadfast and determined when striving to achieve a goal. They are often perceived as being stubborn and inflexible. They live life to the full, with a tendency to be self-destructive when not kept in check.

They have strong personalities and, when their positive qualities are nurtured, grow to become mature, stable and awe-inspiring leaders. Bull espouses taking our time and not rushing at things like a 'Bull at a gate', or bustling through life like a 'Bull in a china shop', because the results would be ill-managed and quite disastrous. Instead the Bull favours the quieter, more exacting approach to cement true advantage.

• Banteng – *Obstinacy*

Naturally active during both night and day, the shy nature of Banteng has forced him to become primarily nocturnal in areas of concentrated human population and has been widely domesticated throughout Asia, but most notably in Bali. According to Asian folklore, the Banteng is a yin-influenced creature that sits traditionally in the North as a representative of the winter solstice. Although a symbol of obstinacy and potent energy, he exudes feminine vibration. A sign of longevity, it is thought that Banteng can live for thousands of years.

Banteng literally oozes from the earth; his immutable and peaceful power driving those who embrace him, fuelled by an abundant, steadfast power. Banteng is deliberate and retiring. Banteng loosens and ploughs the ground, gradually working the earth to make it fertile. He represents calm, obstinate and tenacious power and offers support, grace and capitulation. It seems that once motivated in a certain direction, it is almost impossible to dissuade Banteng people who love things to be done well, with perfection and efficiency their only expectation. Although occasionally stubborn, intolerant, secretive and reserved, Banteng people are honest, responsible and persevering. Banteng reminds us to appreciate the little things. He encourages us to set a goal and to strive to achieve it promising those who show determination, faith and commitment to their responsibilities will be rewarded with abundance, stability and freedom.

• Texas Longhorn – *Resistance*

Texas Longhorn once formed the foundation stock of America's cattle industry and was ideally suited to the harsh environment. Texas Longhorn embraces the wisdom of Cow, Bull and Buffalo, combining them and presenting them as a united package guaranteed to offer stability, endurance and prosperity.

Texas Longhorn provides the chance to establish and build a future of abundance, security and contentment, a lifestyle that provides all that you and your family could ever want or need but not without hard work and sacrifice. Texas Longhorn willingly shares his wisdom with those prepared to knuckle down and give life a go. He supports those who yearn to take stock of their lives and who dream to build a future based on honesty and self-pride for themselves and their family. He offers those who have previously lost everything or who have known grief or hardship a second chance and opportunity to rebuild and fruitfully start again with minimal foundation. Texas Longhorn people find themselves learning new skills with ease and dexterity. Texas Longhorn people realise that in order to make something of yourself, you must be prepared to work hard and build on the basics, relying on what you have and saving for what you don't. Texas Longhorn people espouse the 'from humble beginnings, great empires can grow' mentality with everything they do.

• Watussi – *Renewal*

Watussi is a breed of cattle considered sacred to the people of Africa where it is not uncommon for cattle to be bred solely for ritualistic purposes and kept only for its milk and blood. Almost every significant rite of passage is marked by the gift of blood, and blood drained from a Watussi is seen as a sacred source of life-giving abundance.

Watussi represents a primordial connection to the gods for the people; a symbol of manifestation, rebirth and power. Through blood-letting, Watussi creates a path that leads the people on a journey, delivering them into the supernatural world of the gods and Ancestor Spirits creating a porthole into the Underworld; a place that inspires powerful change, total release and complete and final endings. Watussi forces us to acknowledge our shadow side, to face our demons and to undergo a ritualistic death or self-sacrifice or sorts so that our old self might die an honourable death so that our true self might emerge. In doing so, Watussi promises renewal. Watussi reminds us that our Ancestor Spirits are never that far away, that we are never alone, that the veil between our world and that of Spirit is only as thick as our faith allows and that blood is thicker than water, no matter where in the world you live.

Chamois
Kismet

Chamois is a large, goat-like mammal and inhabits rugged, rocky environments. A favourite talisman carried by gamblers to enhance their level of kismet, it is traditionally crafted from a scrap of Chamois leather, a square of red flannel, a shark's tooth, some pine tree sap and a drop of Dove's blood. In today's world, Chamois leather is favoured for its softness and suppleness and is considered an ideal cloth for cleaning and polishing. It is a contemporary allegory that suggests the car we drive and the condition in which we keep it says a lot about our character, priorities and potential. The word *kismet* is Turkish for 'portion'

or 'lot' and has come to mean 'fate' or 'destiny' or to describe one's 'lot in life'. The word kismet helps to clarify the fixed natural order of the Universe and the unavoidable, unalterable progression of life.

Chamois is concerned with kismet. Chamois embraces the fact that fate and destiny cannot be duped or manipulated. A gambler can attempt to harness all the luck in the world, for example, but if he is not meant to win, he won't – there is little we can do to change the Universal master plan. We agreed to experience our life just the way it is long before incarnating into this physical existence. We have a choice though: to live a whole, impeccable and productive life, or to not. If we live our life with an air of abundance and if we work hard to fulfil that destiny, we can only do well. When we live our life, and all the while strive to improve 'our lot' and that of others, then kismet may shine on us and support us on our way.

Cheetah
Vigour

 Cheetah is built for speed and practically every part of Cheetah is adapted to maximise her potential. The alliances formed between males last for life. They hunt and live together, maintaining regions that often overlap several female territories. Males and females only ever come together to mate and the female raises her cubs alone.

Cheetah is the totem of those who fret over body image, health, fitness and what others might think. Striving to always better their perceived position in life, those who carry Cheetah learn at an early age the importance of personal pacing and self-reliance. Progressing in bursts, Cheetah people tire easily and know, from experience, the limits to which they can extend themselves physically and emotionally before burning out. Cheetah people agonise over being labelled unsupportive, self-centred or sexist and often suffer from nervous skin allergies, high blood pressure and stress. They are more often than not overly emotional people and are not ashamed to show it publicly. Sometimes scarred by unresolved past hurts or deep-set grief, those who look to the wisdom of Cheetah would do well to open themselves up to members of their own sex to reclaim and rebuild stamina, morale and personal authentication. Cheetah implies a need to slow down, to pace ourselves and to set personal boundaries. She encourages us to take responsibility for our health and wellbeing, relationships and our own integrity. Cheetah offers stamina and vigour to get out into the world and to make a difference, by supporting those prepared to improve their place within it.

Chevrotain
Tenderness

Chevrotain, or Mouse Deer, is not a true Deer at all. With species indigenous to both Asia and Africa, she represents the smallest member of the hoofed mammal family and her diminutive size makes her ideal prey for Snakes, Eagles and native Cats.

Chevrotain is both warm and inviting and surrounds those who embrace her with an aura of compassion and empathy. Not afraid to defend what they hold sacred, Chevrotain people dislike pointless confrontation and would rather agree to disagree when given the option. Emotion-driven and highly perceptive, those who carry Chevrotain are kind and affectionate, despite appearing standoffish or aloof on first meeting. Chevrotain protects those who seek her acumen by instilling within them a sense of self-preservation that, at first glance, can make them appear cold and superior. Chevrotain people take time to get to know. They offer little insight into their character or private lives, but once their protective façade is penetrated, they demand unwavering loyalty and commitment. Easily distracted by kindness, a generous (but genuine) offer or suggestion will be all it takes to dissolve any tension and unrest. Chevrotain offers insight into the subtler, more symbolic ways of the world. In times of confusion and misunderstanding, Chevrotain brings about a sense of clarity, sympathy and understanding by helping us to read between the lines or follow our intuition. She offers wisdom gently, often 'downloading' deeper understanding and broader points of view while we sleep, or when we find our conscious mind wandering during daydreams.

Chimpanzee
Ascension

Believed to be the closest relative of man, Chimpanzee enjoys a lifespan of over 50 years and is famous for his use of tools, such as adapting sticks to extract Termites from their mounds. Threatened by loss of habitat and poaching, Chimpanzee leads a very structured life with signals, verbal demonstrations and 'language' ascertaining the community standing of an individual. The Swahili word for Chimpanzee is *ki-mpanzi*, which means 'little climber'. Indigenous inhabitants of Africa's rainforest regions hold the Chimpanzee in high regard. Some honour them as protectors of the people and as forms of deity.

Those who carry the wisdom of the Chimpanzee are thought to be particularly blessed by Spirit and protected by the gods. Chimpanzee endorses the belief that those who see themselves as worthy of great things will be afforded opportunity, advancements of sort and the chance to transcend the mundane. Chimpanzee is not an animal to sit contently on the bottom rung of the ladder of life and strives to always ascend and better himself. Chimpanzee people find themselves continually climbing to ever greater heights, relentlessly scanning the horizon for ways to improve themselves even more. Seemingly born with silver spoons in their mouths, Chimpanzee people work hard and rely on their intuition to see clearly into the future because they trust and celebrate their relationship with Spirit, and as a result, are always seen to do well.

Chinchilla
Self

 Due to his rareness as a seriously endangered wild species, Chinchilla is not often sighted. He is about half the size of a Rabbit, and is often kept as a family pet. It is said that the stronger a person's jaw line, the greater their degree of vitality and fortitude. Those with defined jaw lines are often pigheaded, for example, while a proportionately large chin suggests an individual driven by passion and faith. Chinchilla, affectionately referred to as the *Chin*, is an animal of great strength and endurance. Despite being hunted to the edge of extinction by greed and manipulation, Chinchilla refuses to succumb and climbs proudly on top of a rock and surveys his territory as if silently contemplating the current state of the world. Even those kept as pets are said to show poise and determination, squeezing behind cabinets so that they may scale them from behind.

An animal of privileged reputation, Chinchilla remains proud of himself and his achievements despite being exploited and profited from by everyone he has ever met. Chinchilla reminds us of our inherent self-worth by explaining that no matter what we have done, what we have agreed to or what has been impinged upon us against our will, we are still beautiful and loved by Spirit. No matter how small or insignificant your experiences may have made you feel, you are still a powerful, capable, talented person deserving of respect and love. Chinchilla helps us tap into our strengths and talents, our unique gifts and attributes so that we may reclaim our sense of self and be, once again, proud of who and what we are. Chinchilla reinstates inner strength, courage and self-pride and encourages us to hold our head high with our chin confidently projected.

Chipmunk
Chit

 Although Chipmunk is largely solitary by nature, he will unite with others in song. The name 'Chipmunk' was a misinterpretation of the Algonquin word *chit-monk*, which originated from the 'chit, chit, chit' noise uttered by the little mammal. Chipmunk is very curious and

bold. Politeness, generosity and thoughtfulness are traits firmly imbedded in Chipmunk's heart and deeply imbued within his wisdom.

Chipmunk espouses doing things for the sake of doing them, or because it is the right thing to do, with little or no thought of immediate recompense. Those who embrace the wisdom of Chipmunk are usually those motivated by the joy a simple act of kindness affords; their only repayment often being the look of surprise and happiness on the recipient's face. Chipmunk people have an inherent understanding and sense of empathy for those genuinely less fortunate than themselves. To be able to venture out into the world with sought-after skills (that would typically earn a respectable wage), and to offer and employ them in service to others, while trusting (with no guarantee) that you will be reimbursed at some time in the future is to fully appreciate the sacredness of Chipmunk. Chipmunk people, when provoked, enjoy a wide vocabulary that is both sharp and succinct and will do what it takes to reclaim lost personal power (and money). Chipmunk endorses bartering, where goods are exchanged for services rendered or services are offered and held on promise. Remember, though, to negotiate a set value for your exchange and work from there. If this feels awkward or you are excited by the potential of such a system, initiate a full-blown bartering system within your community – a network that encourages the exchange of goods and services instead of money with an in-depth directory that lists the goods and services, the offering party's credentials, testimonials, contact details and a fair and negotiable 'point value' for each of the goods and services offered.

Civet

Magnetism

 Although referred to as Civet Cat, Civet is not a Cat at all and is more closely related to the Mongoose. Civet is endangered in some districts due to over-hunting for his pelt and sweet-tasting meat or as a favoured source of musk. The word 'musk' is derived from the Sanskrit word *mucks*, meaning 'testicle'. Musk was once celebrated as the 'perfect scent' and Civet musk is believed to offer incentives similar to those exuded by human pheromones; primary compounds that trigger sexual activity in most creatures.

Those who carry the energy of Civet are usually magnetic of character, captivating and exciting, loved by members of the opposite sex as well as their own, but, strangely, equally despised. The totem of the bad boy and super model (hence the term 'cat-walk'), Civet is witnessed in those considered 'cool', beautiful and 'the most likely to succeed'. Civet, however, has a downside in that he dissuades as easily as he attracts. Civet people tend to appear 'out of reach', or 'too cool' for normal folk to be associated with. It takes a very self-assured individual to approach a Civet person with the intention of initiating a relationship. Civet people, therefore, must decide what they seek in a perfect mate and take it upon themselves to approach and initiate all relationships, friendships and associations, hence ensuring their success and personal productivity on all levels.

Coatimundi
Survival

Coatimundi, or Coati, looks very much like a Raccoon – in fact, the two are related. Coatimundi is carnivorous and has an insatiable appetite. The term *coatimundi* apparently suggests a 'lone Coati' in the Tupi language, referring to the animal's solitary lifestyle.

Coatimundi is the totem of those traumatised by a significant other. Coatimundi people have, at some point in their life, been displaced emotionally; their yin and yang forcefully unbalanced by confusion, pain or self-repugnance. According to shamanic lore, when an experience is traumatic we can become disassociated from our soul essence in order to survive the ordeal and essentially numb the pain. We then tend to behave in a way that contradicts the 'normal' or expected response. The fear of being ridiculed, shunned, ignored or disbelieved is a common result ; so they keep silent 'just in case'. Coatimundi offers a voice. He offers strength and resolve to reclaim one's power and reunite the individual with their soul essence. Coatimundi people are survivors. They are gentle, humble and kind. They can, at times, appear needy, self-condemning and morose, traits indicative of low self-esteem, momentary flash-backs and unresolved pockets of healing. The stripy tail of Coatimundi promises to help reclaim a sense of balance, sound navigation and self-pride, while the elongated muzzle offers direction, self-recognition and ability to Walk their Talk confidently into a safe new future where they will feel free to be themselves. Coatimundi people need to remember, though, that an experience so powerful and potentially overwhelming as physical, mental or sexual abuse needs to be turned into something positive and good. 'What doesn't kill you makes you stronger' is an affirmation that must be remembered as a personal mantra. Coatimundi people have much to offer their community, particularly in the form of sound counsel strengthened by a foundation of experience and effective strategy. With a wealth of knowledge to shore them up, Coatimundi people are well equipped to facilitate profound healing in others of similar background, while the whole time beautifying their own view of the world.

Colugo

Safety net

Colugo, or Flying Lemur, is not a Lemur at all. Lemurs are only found on the island of Madagascar, while Colugo is native to tropical forests and woodlands of South-East Asia. Despite what their folk name suggests, Colugo cannot 'fly' and glide from tree to tree on folds of skin that extend from their neck to their wrists, from the wrists to their ankles and from the ankles to the tip of their tail. Female Colugos will hang upside down from a branch, cradling their young on their bellies 'hammock-style', their folds of skin creating a safety net. It is thought that the hammock was conceived by people of the Mayan culture, where being elevated meant that there was nothing to hinder the cool evening breeze and they were out of reach from venomous wildlife. It was also was adopted by sailors because it afforded them a balanced night's sleep with the hammocks swaying in harmony with the ship's undulations. The hammock-like stance adopted by Colugo suggests a nurturing, protective quality found also in those who carry Colugo energy.

Colugo people are able to move freely from one situation to the next, with little effort and minimal stress. They are an inspiration to others because they trust completely that things will work out no matter how unforgiving the shortcomings may threaten to be. Because of their positive attitude, their efforts rarely go unrewarded. Colugo people consider themselves supported at all times by Spirit and those who share their lives. Colugo people are very supportive of others. They are optimistic, positive and cheerful. They believe that everyone deserves a chance and that everyone should have a go. Colugo lifts us to new heights. He offers promise and support and a balancing quality that invites us to take a leap of faith and to shun fear by providing a safety net guaranteed to catch us should we fall and cradle us until we feel confident to step out and try again. Colugo welcomes us home after a hard day. Womblike in energy, Colugo offers the chance to find comfort in the reassuring arms of a friend or family member and the encouragement to try again tomorrow.

Condor

Reunion

Californian Condor remains the 'most famous' of the Condors with ancestry dating back to the Pleistocene Age. Despite his ancient origins, he is now teetering on the edge of extinction. Californian Condor is the largest and rarest bird found in North America, with only three individuals known to exist in the wild and about 85 in captivity and it is unlikely that numbers will ever reach a level to classify the species as 'stable'. Incan prophesies once warned of a division that would take place between the indigenous people of America. The colonisation of the Americas created a rift between the North and the South, fulfilling the prophesy. The people believed that the split not only caused the continents to energetically divide, but that it also triggered an imbalance between the masculine and feminine found within all things of Nature and the colours represented by humanity. A ceremony was then forged that would see the 'Eagle of the North' reunite with the 'Condor of the South' heralding a time of peace, abundance and reunion for the people. According to ancient teachings, both the Eagle and the Condor sit in the East on the Wheel of Life: the place of vision, energy, clarity, illumination, realisation and new beginnings. In the East, we learn to unite energy with vision so that we may bring about effective change.

Condor calls upon the people to assist with the reunification of the planet and to share sacred knowledge the world so desperately needs. Condor motivates us to collectively reach out and share the knowledge we have inherently stored within our conscious selves and to help spread awareness and understanding that will effectively rebirth humanity and the world as a whole. Condor people are inspired to restore balance and encourage us to forgive, to heal and to surrender all pain, anger and grief to Spirit. They are driven to assist others make the transition from the old world to the new by embracing and remembering the 'ancient ways'. The collective knowledge of the ancient cultures is an essential ingredient if reunification here on Earth is to take place.

Cormorant
Support

 Although Cormorant spends much time in the water, her plumage lacks the essential waterproofing components belonging to other seabirds and so she spends time on shore with wings outstretched, drying her feathers in the sun. *Ukai*, or Cormorant fishing, is a Japanese fishing technique that involves employing a tame Cormorant by means of a leash attached to a small metal ring fastened around the base of her neck that allows the bird to catch fish, but prevents her from swallowing them. Cormorant offers relief to those who constantly surrender their power or who feel their strength and feelings of joy seeping away or being drained unmercifully by others (much like the ring around Cormorant's neck preventing her from enjoying the fruits of her labour). 'Takers' drain energy on a conscious level and prey on emotional weakness in order to strengthen themselves; and to rope others in.

Cormorant espouses the fact that help is only supportive when it is appreciated and willingly reciprocated. It need only be acknowledged in an honourable and honest way. Cormorant offers a sympathetic hand to those willing to embrace the lesson found in needing to ask for help. She supports those who celebrate the humility required to seek help and the sacred wisdom found in being offered it. Such wisdom offers endurance and opportunity to build a foundation of self-reliance, so that the need for external help becomes increasingly less frequent. Cormorant reminds us to guard against emotional draining and encourages us to develop the strength to say 'No'. The figurative ring may then be removed from our neck enabling us to dive deep back into life without fear of interference or manipulation.

Coyote
The Joker

 The Coyote (a name derived from the Aztec word, *coyotl*), or Little Wolf, is an animal typically associated with the open plains of the 'Wild West'. Coyote has a powerful sense of smell; hearing and vision with a reputation for being incredibly adaptable, resourceful and sly. Coyote will usually only take livestock when wild food is scarce or when environmental conditions or poor health force his hand.

Coyote endorses the learning of lessons through laughter and jokes and forces us to laugh at ourselves, to see the folly of our ways and to learn from our mistakes. By questioning our beliefs and testing our commitment to them, Coyote either shows them up as being superficial and unfounded or proves their merit, thus concreting them as viable aspects of our personal wisdom. Coyote helps us realise our greater potential by making fun of the earnestness and blind dedication we waste on habits and beliefs that are no longer valid or purposeful. Coyote reminds us that enlightenment is best found in experience, with every experience offering a chance to better ourselves. Coyote does not see it as dishonourable to be the recipient of a valuable practical joke, but jokes that belittle our self-worth are not respectable and are not endorsed by Coyote. Coyote nurtures sacred understanding between what is morally sound and what is not. Coyote combines all things prudent with the imprudent; the revered with the disrespected. He calls for us to laugh and be laughed at. He unites all things opposite and encourages us to throw caution to the wind and experience trial and error. Coyote returns us to a state of child-like innocence and teaches us to laugh for the sake of laughing, to experience pleasure, to shun fear and apprehension and to celebrate life.

Crane
Goodwill

Crane, generically, is classified as the tallest bird capable of flight. Most indigenous traditions and religious beliefs that embrace the wisdom of Crane do so out of reverence and devotion for the bird. Despite this, Cranes of Asia (in particular) continue to suffer an alarming decline in numbers. Crane is both majestic and elegant, with the most recognised 'Asian' species being Japanese Crane; a pure white bird with a glorious red crest romanticised to live for a thousand years. According to Japanese, Chinese and Korean belief, Crane symbolises goodwill and long life. Origami Cranes are often used to decorate war memorials as symbols of peace, for example, and are often given to the sick and dying to wish them quick recovery or safe passage after death. Origami Cranes are also folded (in lots of 1,000) to invite good luck and to inspire wishes to come true. The Japanese favour Crane imagery, particularly when designing wedding kimonos, because Cranes mate for life and show eternal devotion to their partners. In Christian belief, Crane is viewed loosely as a symbol of renewal and resurrection.

Crane guides the released souls of the recently departed back to Spirit, a sacred (and ancient) association that marks the Crane as an ambassador of endings and 'death': a word that often refers to a dramatic change that initiates a significant new beginning. To see Crane flying into the sun, however, is said to indicate a longing to bring about a rise in one's social standing. A creature that traditionally refers to cycles, progression and eternal growth, the appearance of Crane readies us for peace and harmony after a time of upheaval. Crane invokes good luck and good health. Those who carry Crane make loyal friends, committed partners and are usually people who need little excuse to celebrate even the smallest blessings offered in life. Crane rewards those who consciously integrate its wisdom into their life with long, fruitful lives and gratifying relationships.

Crocodile
Creative force

Common throughout the world as both a saltwater and freshwater species, Crocodile is said to have remained relatively unchanged since the reign of the Dinosaurs. Despite her ungainly appearance, Crocodile is capable of reaching great speeds, even when on land. Mud has for centuries held esoteric symbology as the blood of the Earth Mother's womb, and is therefore associated with the feminine principles of life, death and, as a result, birth. As an emissary of the Earth Mother's blood, therefore, Crocodile is also a symbol of the creative forces of the world. Common in Egyptian, African and Australian Aboriginal mythology, Crocodile is described as a force capable of delivering both tenderness and annihilation.

According to Crocodile, death and birth are both vital stages of initiation. As such, Crocodile primes us to close one door so that another may open. Crocodile people are both gentle and loving, but, due to circumstance, often appear hard-nosed and strong. They honour both qualities, but rarely combine the two. They take immediate and steadfast responsibility for all aspects of their life and never feel squeamish about doing what it takes to honour the process. Crocodile people are frequently forced to fend for themselves and seek emotional nourishment from whoever is willing to offer it. A bi-product of being forced to think outside the box in order to survive, Crocodile people can turn any negative experience into a positive one and are able to see opportunity in the direst of situations. Crocodile people show deep appreciation for the things they have achieved, obtained or experienced, and when they open their hearts to possibility, make devoted partners and parents. As a land-dwelling animal and an aquatic one, Crocodile acts as a doorkeeper to both the tangible world and the Underworld; the embodiment of both life and death in their purest forms. Crocodile, with eyes positioned on the top of her head, encourages us to see above and beyond physical limitation and emotional burden so that we may trust our intuition and inherent ability to manifest our heart's desire.

Crow
Law

 Crow is a gregarious and extremely intelligent bird: social and joyfully interactive with others. She is very protective of her mate and offspring, but will also defend other unrelated individuals when they are threatened. She is among a handful of creatures known to use tools in their pursuit to achieve set goals quicker. Bestowed with the mysteries and knowledge of Creation (it is said that the Records of all Creation are bound in a book made entirely of Crow feathers), Crow is the keeper of sacred law and the keeper of ancient records. As such, Crow sometimes changes the rules by shape-shifting (appearing as a Wolf in Sheep's clothing, for example) or duplicates by consciously creating a double of herself to test our commitment and personal resolve. Travelling in collectives known infamously as 'Murders', the feathers of the Crow are said to be powerful amulets that symbolise mortality. As a creature of the Void (the Universal Womb, the source of all understanding, inspiration and knowing), Crow exists in the past, present and future simultaneously; perceiving the darkness within light and the light within darkness while seeing all worlds and dimensions from every conceivable vantage point.

Therefore, Crow's power is great and her teachings strong and she is concerned with justice, truth and ethical principles. Governed by an unprecedented understanding of Universal law, she speaks of truth and wisdom unheard of in any human law system. When we call to Spirit for help, for example, we simultaneously invite change. Crow paves the way for change by ensuring that we are well equipped to face the consequences.

An animal that endorses the fact that in order to open new doors you must first be prepared to properly shut old ones, Crow is an animal that inspires the cycle of birth, death and rebirth. When it comes to initiating the change that Crow has modelled us for, we must be prepared to take it by the horns and battle it until it is defeated and complete. If we shy away at the last moment, Crow becomes annoyed that we have not honoured our end of the bargain. When one honours the ways of Crow and strives to live by the laws determined by Creation, however, we are permitted to leave this world and move to the next with clear memory of our life experiences. Ruled by the element Air, Crow is the keeper of the intellect. She is responsible, therefore, for thought and reason – and, when invoked, is said to be capable of promoting clarity of mind for the individual. By breathing life into our future, by turning messages from Spirit into 'flesh', we are honouring the laws of Crow and positively shape-shifting our consciousness. On a more personal level, Crow portents love, emotions, intuition and intimacy – ideals that suggest positive forces at work within our lives.

Deer
Softness

Deer are ruminant mammal that belong to a family that includes: White-Tailed Deer, Mule Deer, Elk, Moose, Red Deer, Reindeer (or Caribou), Fallow Deer, Roe Deer, Sika Deer, Samba Deer, Chital Deer and Muntjac. Male Deer (except Chinese Water Deer) and female Reindeer grow and shed antlers each year, with an extra tine or point appearing annually until the animal has reached full maturity.

• Caribou or Reindeer – *Vertigo*

 Caribou, (or Elk or Reindeer) was first domesticated over 2,000 years ago and is still kept by the Arctic people of Europe and Asia. Caribou is famous for his extensive migratory habits. Caribou is traditionally associated with stamina and endurance, balance and control equipped to withstand severe cold and harsh conditions.

His wisdom offers insight into how we might regain stability or a solid foot-hold, especially when life becomes overwhelming or unsteady. He provides reassurance during times of emotional indifference or when we are trying to reclaim feeling after emotional pain and suffering. Caribou supports us as we combat stress-related dizziness, nausea and light-headedness caused by taking risks or 'walking on thin ice'. The antlers (branching from the third eye or brow chakra), suggest an intuitive knowing and higher degree of understanding that inspires peace and surrender, and the acceptance that things will work out okay. Caribou picks us up after a time of turmoil and puts us back on track. He promises to provide warmth and comfort as well as the physical strength and determination to reach new heights free of fear or trepidation.

• Chital Deer – *Heart of the world*

 Chital Deer, also known as the Spotted Deer or Axis Deer, normally lives on the grasslands of India and Sri Lanka but will venture into neighbouring forests to browse on fallen fruit and leaves. All early civilisations assumed their realm to be the most beautiful, the most powerful and, of course, the most blessed by the gods, with their capital (typically built directly at the hub of their territory) representing the Axis of the World; the navel or *umbilicus* of the Earth. The ancient Romans believed their empire to sit at the centre of the Earth, so much so that they named the sea that formed the heart of their dominion *mare nostrum*, or our sea, and affectionately referred to it as the Mediterranean, which blatantly translates to 'Middle of the Earth'. 'A Man's Home is his Castle' is affectionately used by many people who see their home and family as the focal point of their lives.

Chital Deer endorses our home and family as the centre of the world; the hub of our existence, while reinforcing our self-worth and belief that the Universe rotates around us. In order to make an effectual difference to the world, or to ensure your voice is heard, Chital Deer encourages you to view yourself as the centre of the world, the *axis mundi* from which all inspiration transpires. Chital Deer is never arrogant, narcissistic, loud or boorish, however. Rather, she approaches the world with gentleness, peace and acceptance combined with a potent display of expectation. To invoke the Heart of the World attitude of Chital, you must display undying faith in the validity of your Personal Power. You must find your purpose and present it to the world as the missing link in the worldly scheme of things. You must believe in what you are doing unconditionally and honourably strive to help people understand its importance on all levels. Chital is not for procrastinators, self-doubters or self-saboteurs. She is the driving force and symbolic soap-box for those who yearn to get their message 'out there', who believe they have a mission and who know deep down that they hold within them a sacred key to the positive transformation of the planet.

• Elk – *Camaraderie*

 In Europe, Moose are referred to as Elk, while Red Deer and North American Elk are considered the same species. Elk is very strong and represents vigour, power and endurance. The strength of Elk can be found in his ability to just 'keep going'. There isn't anything that cannot be achieved when Elk offers his dynamic support and his motto is 'Never give up'.

Elk is potent and is imbued with fertility and abundance. Never shy of advertising his influence either, he bellows loudly during mating season. Elk is proud of who he is and enjoys living in his skin. Elk's potency lies in his ability to honour the balance between knowing what he must do for others and what he needs to do for himself, and he proves his worth when he impeccably identifies the correct time to respect both. Elk offers strength through his high opinion of comradeship and his ability to balance spending quality time his family and friends and colleagues. Elk encourages us to maintain our physical, mental and spiritual energies and helps us walk the subtle line of responsibility: responsibility for our own wants and needs and for those around us. Elk only seeks out a mate during the rut and says that no matter how dedicated you are to your partner, spouse or family, everyone needs a break. Elk helps us regain our inner strength by forcing us to be true to ourselves. Elk helps us recharge our endurance batteries by encouraging us to step away (temporarily) and 'forget' about the day-to-day responsibilities that, although sacred to us, weigh us down emotionally or spiritually. Elk people also find comfort in the security, peace and love found at home. They also find comfort in the knowing that with their sense of security comes trust and respect. Time away from commitment allows for introspection and silent contemplation. It provides for the chance to revaluate and to find the stamina to take things back home to the next level, to shift focus and to improve on what you have.

• Fallow Deer – *Confirmation*

Fallow Deer are farmed commercially for their meat, a practice that dates back thousands of years.

Fallow Deer reminds us to always approach life with a sense of trust, peace and gentleness; spiritual love that promises reward to those of us who demonstrate resolve and personal integrity. Fallow Deer is an animal that radiates unconditional acceptance and love. She is an animal that, symbolically, we are all born with; offering herself as a guide, mentor and source of spiritual power to each and every one of us. She represents our potential while reminding us that we are all related and that no one is any more or any less important than anybody else. She reminds us that if we radiate the essence of what her spirit represents – unconditional acceptance and love, we will never be faced with obstacles, never know lack and will never be judged or viewed from a perspective hampered by jealousy or fear. To shower fear with love will see fear being banished forever; like shining a torch into a darkened room, the light will dominate and the darkness will be vanquished. To look the forces, that would otherwise see you bow and scrape, dead in the eye with an outlook that simply says 'I love you and honour your path, but I choose to walk a path that loves me back', will see all obstacles drop to the wayside. Fallow Deer offers confirmation that the Other World is close. She inspires love, commitment, soul connection and spiritual purpose.

• Hog Deer – *Self-preservation*

Hog Deer gets his name from his habit of rushing through undergrowth with head held low, diving under obstacles like a wild Pig instead of leaping over them like most other species of Deer. Although the male Hog Deer is committed to a single mate (instead of sharing himself freely among a harem of breeding females), his sense of loyalty is aimed first and foremost toward himself and his own sense of self-preservation.

When invoked, Hog Deer promises a staunch partner and committed team; his faithful, protective nature envelopes all who call upon him, supported by an outwardly unsympathetic 'tough-love' philosophy. The true essence of Hog Deer, however, is found in his ability to lead by example and the powerful way in which he teaches independence and self-empowerment. When the going gets tough, Hog Deer offers suggestion and then leaves, deserting those who look to him to their own devices. He does not abandon or reject responsibility for his charge but, rather, steps aside and takes up the role of observer and mentor. When he leaves you alone to face your fears, Hog Deer supports the healing process by creating a protective diversion. Such chaos offers a chance to retreat, recharge and focus your mind so that you may productively revaluate your original intentions. It is not until we experience chaos do we begin to see with genuine clarity. Hog Deer forces you to develop self-preservation skills, stand your ground, speak your mind and be your true self. He is a powerful teacher, friend and healer who will blatantly approach life in a matter-of-fact, 'head down/bum up' manner. Despite Hog Deer's independent, determined Dreaming, those who carry his medicine are warned to avoid becoming obstinate, stubborn and intolerant of others. Hog Deer shuns those who willingly embrace the victim mentality, the role of martyr and those who purposefully avoid or vehemently deny the need for self-healing.

• Muntjac – *Fortitude*

Muntjac first appeared during the middle of the Miocene period, some 22 to 42 million years ago and reaches a height of 43-46 centimetres at maturity and usually weighs between 11 and 16 kilograms. Also called the Barking Deer, Muntjac will yap for over an hour when startled or when she senses danger.

Muntjac is reticent in demeanour, diminutive in stature and unassuming in carriage. She is an animal of honourable, humble character that has managed to slip under the radar and survive for tens of millions of years. The fortifying wisdom of Muntjac offers not only a solid foundation to sink one's teeth into in order to establish a grounded, balanced spiritual path, career or personal life, but she also imbues that foundation with endurance that promises to support and nourish for a lifetime. Muntjac people go into all relationships and partnerships with a sense of permanence. They abhor the 'fly-by-night' attitude because once they make a promise or commitment it is quickly set in stone. When invoking the wisdom of the Muntjac as a means of support, be prepared for all projects to progress slowly. Muntjac endorses the belief that if you want something to last, it must be allowed to grow at its own pace. Things that are hurried or rushed are usually weak in foundation, thus losing stamina and collapsing long before their time. Muntjac encourages a reserved, gentle, inconspicuous approach to all things. In life, Muntjac people rely on their quiet personas to 'camouflage' themselves, especially when in loud, threatening or unfamiliar settings. By no means timid or shy, the Muntjac person simply knows that if you want to progress and remain long term, you must first appear friendly, compliant and compromising, even if only to benefit your own means.

• Red Deer – *The Holy Grail*

 Red Deer, or Barbary Stag, is nervy and highly strung, making them unpredictable options for commercial farming. The male Red Deer is called a 'Stag', while the female is referred to as a 'Hind'. The male Red Deer produce antlers, which are shed after the rut. Red Deer antlers grow up and inward and look like rough tree bark. On reaching maturity, the antlers will typically display a total of 10 points, with some known to grow more. To walk in harmony with the Earth, to celebrate the path of Spirit and to ponder the meaning of life is to participate in a personal quest for White Stag; our Innate Self. White Stag, in Celtic mythology, often appeared as an omen indicating the nearness of the Other World.

When we pursue White Stag, the chase may lead us out into the world, daring us to take risks and to try new things. It may lead us to other realms and dimensions encouraging us to explore Spirit, past lives or our higher selves, but generally it leads us into the Underworld, or to a private and secret place known as the Inner Landscape. When we symbolically follow White Stag, we are being invited to journey deep within our consciousness where we are ultimately left to contemplate life and seek the wisdom of our inner silence. The fate of White Stag is symbolic of the evolutionary passage of the soul; the developmental journey of growth experienced when one readily embraces vital change on all planes of awareness. White Stag, as my own soul essence and power aspect, has helped me to find a place of trust within myself, to know my Inner Landscape and to systematically banish myself forever of 'evil'. I loved my Stag and still do. Red Deer (as the embodiment of the White Stag) protects us as we embark on a quest that will see us stalk and secure our sacred self. He leads us on an adventure that will offer many tests, obstacles and challenges that will see us champion our own sacred cause and face our personal demons, emerging on the other side a stronger, braver, and wiser individual.

• Rusa Deer – *Adornment*

Rusa Deer is largely nocturnal, but it is not uncommon to see her browsing during the day. When startled, Rusa Deer tucks her tail down (instead of carrying them erect like other Deer) and barks to announce restlessness.

Rusa Deer people are essentially gentle people with compassionate hearts who feel compelled to detach or separate themselves from the world around them. Separation is never planned. It just happens. Rusa Deer people are naturally wary. They are hard to get to know and have difficulty getting close to people. They take everything personally and assume that if there is tension in the air, then it is probably due to their presence, words or actions. Rusa people are not martyrs and do not blame themselves or hold themselves responsible for the misfortune of others, but they are insecure. As a result, they spend much of their time apologising, biting their tongue and covering their tracks. Consequently, Rusa Deer is the totem of those who go through life hiding behind façades intentionally designed to keep others at bay. People often mistake such 'camouflage' as a sign of suppressed rage, defiance or emotional incapability, when in fact most Rusa Deer people see their apparel as a form of 'power dressing' and their bodily adornment as a way of advertising their potency and ability to manifest soul-yearnings. Essentially, people drawn to the wisdom of Rusa Deer do so because they long to heal, shun fear and stand in their power. Rusa Deer people waste much of their energy suppressing true feelings and behaving detachedly and emotionally barren, but creating a façade is a fundamental survival strategy for those who walk with Rusa Deer; a shield that allows them to explore deeper, strive further and achieve higher than they would normally be able to.

• Samba Deer – *Alarm*

Samba (or Sambar) is not only one of the larger species of Deer, he is also the most widely spread. Instead of offering warning to the herd before fleeing, Samba Deer stands alert, emitting regular warning barks until the threat passes; a trait that sees many individuals fall prey to hunters and predators. Samba's repetitive alarm call is a definite sign of an imminent threat, with everyone in the know trusting its validity and seeking cover immediately.

Samba people honour their ancient relationship to all things. They inherently view themselves (along with all things of Nature) as being born of the One Source, with their life supporting the existence of everything else. Samba people live their lives in service to others, living each day in an interrelated way in harmony with the world around them. Samba Deer encourages us to walk gently upon the Earth and reawakens us to this ancient truth, while helping us to remember how to read the signs and hear the silent whispers of the Earth Mother. Those drawn to the wisdom of Samba are usually very sensitive to the environment and the energies of other people, despite being described as having physically powerful and intense personalities. Samba people are naturally watchful, wary and highly intuitive individuals who are often labelled as being paranoid, cynical and suspicious of others. Samba offers clarity by revealing untruths, deception and things otherwise hidden or veiled by darkness. The unexpected appearance of Samba is usually followed closely by a revelation or disclosure and it should be remembered that if a Samba person offers warning, make sure you heed it (if only to keep them quiet). Samba people NEVER cry Wolf, and in heeding their cautionary words, you will be spared great disruption, emotionally, physically or financially.

• Sika Deer – *Free will*

 Sika (meaning 'small Deer') is sacred to the Japanese culture. Some species of Sika are enhanced by white spots, which 'fade' as the coat grows thicker with the onset of winter. Males grow a lush mane and narrow, erect antlers that measure almost one metre in length at maturity. Along with the hoofs, the antlers are used to defend the harem, which can consist of up to 12 breeding females. Sika Deer feeds mainly at night, although she is occasionally seen browsing during the day. Sika is a very vocal animal, using a wide range of calls including quiet chirrups, piercing screeches and urgent barks.

There is a Japanese legend that speaks of a Shinto Prophet who once visited the city of Nara in the year 768 AD riding a majestic White Stag. As a result, ever since that day, Sika Deer have been allowed to roam the city at will. To honour the Priest's visit, a team of observers was established soon after. This team remains active today and is known as the Nara Park Sika Deer Research Group. According to this group's historical records, Japanese Army Officers gifted a White Sika Stag to the Emperor of Japan, who in turn gifted the animal to Nara Park. Since then, sightings of the sacred White Deer have been reported. Deer promotes compassion, a quality said to aid in the hearing of human thought and the ability to speak in any language. The soft, gentle eyes of the Deer are thought to *gaze with compassion over all realms of being,* according to Buddhist belief. For those who feel obligated, silenced or oppressed, Sika Deer offers a voice and the chance to have it heard on many levels. Those at the mercy of the law, for example, would do well to invoke the Sika. Her energy will surely attract sympathetic aide and a compassionate ear. Sika, as an enlightened creature, reveals secret agendas and covert motives of those who may, outwardly, appear true and wholesome. She allows those who walk with her to know, inherently, the hearts of others and to communicate readily with any one from any culture through the language of love, compassion and integrity. She offers freedom to explore and to exercise free will when it comes to decision making, personal growth and independence. Sika Deer teaches compassion and spiritual devotion. She offers relief from the mundane while delivering you into a state of tranquillity, harmony and bliss. Sika dissolves the boundaries that confine, the burdens that weigh heavy on the heart and the responsibilities that imprison. Sika is a gift from Spirit, a sacred offering that, if realised and embraced, will instil inner contentment, acceptance and peace.

• Swamp Deer – *Inundation*

Swamp Deer remains close to water at all times and navigates her way through swamps and marshes without sinking into the soft ground.

Swamp Deer offers stability and a guiding hand to those who find themselves inundated or overwhelmed by the responsibilities of work, personal relationships, family, parenthood or life in general. The appearance of Swamp Deer suggests an avenue that, if explored with integrity, will lead both the individual and the group to a place of higher or deeper understanding. While in their brown coat phase, Swamp Deer people may appear somewhat obsessive in character, while demonstrating excessive or compulsive behaviour. They yield to pressure gladly, subconsciously deciding that it is easier to resign than to endure and to seek firmer ground. When they give up, Swamp Deer people do not waste time, slipping quickly into a state of deep depression that often requires supportive (usually medical) intervention. However, while in the brown coat phase, Swamp Deer people are also very receptive and 'open' to suggestion and are usually very sensitive to the subtler forces of creation, making communication with spirit beings. However, when the Swamp Deer person eventually passes into his or her red coat phase (as they usually do when they acknowledge and integrate the animal into their life on a meaningful, interrelated level), they experience a shift of consciousness, a boost in physical energy and a sense of clarity never witnessed before. Swamp Deer people who have followed the guidance of their totem's acumen know an inner vitality and generally enjoy good health and wholesome social interaction. However, they need to watch their tempers.

• Tufted Deer – *Simulation*

Tufted Deer is so named because of the dark brown crest that grows on her head, which can reach 17 centimetres in length often covering her simple, spike-like antlers. Tufted Deer is a secretive creature that does much to disguise her true appearance. Not only does she mask her retreat by hiding the white underside of her tail when startled, she also conceals her antlers among the long hair that grows from her forehead. It is the fang-like teeth that reveal the true potency of

Tufted Deer's Dreaming and offer warning that 'things may not be what they seem'.

Tufted Deer explains one should never make assumptions based on appearances alone. Tufted Deer reminds us that just as there are angelic forces that yearn to inspire us and see us prosper and heal, there are opposing forces (of equal strength and power) that would happily starve us of purpose and see us shrivel up and die. To assume that everything of Spirit is good and beautiful is just as ignorant as assuming that all aspects of the dark are inherently evil. Although it remains a universal truth that the light side will never intentionally betray you, the dark side will readily permeate the light, negatively affecting all that it encounters like a cancerous tumour. But, while this is the case, the dark side offers valid lessons and experiences that, although usually devastating in nature, offer opportunities to grow and broaden one's view of life. Therefore, while walking a path of impeccability, it is a wise man that acknowledges the good and bad in all things, but only draws to him those things that promise to benefit him in a balanced way while questioning their authenticity all the while. To see a Deer with fangs is puzzling. It may *look* like a Deer, but although it radiates the gentle energy of its kind, the presence of fangs is contradictory. And so to experience Tufted Deer is to be encouraged to ask: 'Is what I am witnessing really happening? Is this for the best? Can I trust what is being offered to me? Is this person/place or thing on the level? And to ask them in about all areas of life, particularly those that are spiritually oriented.

• White-tailed Deer – *Gentleness*

White-tailed Deer is an opportunist. She readily adapts to any number of environments and food types and has been known to eat insects and carrion can swim far out to sea to avoid predators.

An ancient species of Deer, White-tailed Deer teaches unconditional love and the knowledge that to walk gently upon the Earth means to walk in balance, in beauty and in honour of everything and everyone who shares this planet with us. White-tailed Deer asks that we respect the right of all things of Nature to enjoy abundant, interrelated lives and to realise that the impact we have on our environment now will determine the quality of our lives in the future. White-tailed Deer expects that we treat everyone and everything as an equal; to treat others the way we would like to be treated. She does not insist on those who embrace her wisdom to live a life of piety, but does ask that we remain mindful of our actions and the affect they have on others. Everyone is inherently imbued with the qualities of White-tailed Deer. She represents our collective potential and unity as a people. Sadly, many are unaware of its spirit and remain disconnected from the world around them, lost in a quagmire of bitterness. Indiscriminate but sincere displays of compassion and empathy are the strengths found in those who carry White-tailed Deer Dreaming. White-tailed Deer nurtures the understanding that so long as you live your life in an interrelated way, you will never feel inadequate, unattractive or unimportant again – and you will most certainly never feel alone. White-tailed Deer embodies the future vision of humanity walking as one, hand-in-hand and united as a people.

Dingo
Trickster

The golden-furred Dingo is celebrated as Australia's first 'feral' species. He is believed to be the descendant of the Asian 'Wild' Dog, brought to Australia around 40,000 years ago by our Indigenous People as a companion. Children are the embodiment of innocence and epitomise virtue and purity. They look out on Creation through the eyes of an Angel, seeing beauty in all things and trusting that the world will protect them. A child will instinctively see the innate decency in the psyche of another. To be reminded of the true meaning of innocence is to be reminded of the Spirit of Life and what it means to be nourished to the very core of our being.

Dingo represents each of us as we naively step out into the world for the first time; the child who acts on every impulse with little consideration of outcome. Dingo symbolises our eagerness to venture out into the world, to explore new horizons and to try new things. Dingo people live on a day-to-day basis, never planning ahead and are always ready to tackle whatever comes their way, ever eager to open up to new realms of possibility. Dingo does not endorse stagnation, fear, worry or doubt. He doesn't represent ignorance but rather impulsiveness and a child's spontaneity. Dingo people often fail to notice the obstacles evident in day-to-day life. They are naturally friendly but socially naïve and have difficulty grasping social etiquette or the subtle, unspoken rules expected in relationships. Dingo people often bite off more than they can chew, then sit back licking their wounds, trying to figure out what just happened. Dingo nurtures the gentle souls who remain oblivious to the hardships they will encounter as they begin their lives. Dingo teaches by example, illustrating the need to learn from our mistakes and to not to take life too seriously. He helps us ground our sense of responsibility so that we do not make the same mistakes again and again. Innocence is a beautiful gift, but ignorance is dangerous. Dingo embraces the adage, 'Knowledge is Power', while explaining that any quest for knowledge may simultaneously lead to further lessons. Embrace them, lick your wounds and keep going. Every step forward is a step closer to better understanding the ways of the world and your place within it.

Dog
Loyalty

Dog has been domesticated for over 14,000 years, with some studies suggesting as long as 150,000 years. Today we have hundreds of different breeds with equally as many variations in size, temperament and appearance. Dog is a highly social, pack-oriented creature and has lived with and worked in close proximity with humans in so many ways that his loyalty has earned him the title of 'man's best friend'. Dog is, by human standards, colour blind, because of the flatness of his lenses, which limits the degree of detail he can detect, despite most breeds having a much greater field of vision than humans. Along with excellent field vision, Dog is also able to detect very low-frequency sounds and can quickly and accurately pinpoint the exact source of any noise. Not only that, but Dog also excels in detecting scents.

Unconditional love is a gift from Great Mystery. It personifies the true essence of Spirit. Some say that it represents the elusive fifth element, that when united with the traditional four – Earth, Air, Fire and Water, the result is Creation itself. Dog encourages us to celebrate life and those that we hold dear. He offers the belief that the best way to demonstrate our feelings are through our actions. When doubt is plaguing a relationship, words from the heart can help band-aid the problem, but they rarely cure it. Dog encourages us to celebrate life and, if we belief it is worth the effort, to celebrate our loves, no matter what needs to be done to prove the point. Due to Dog's inherent sense of loyalty, Dog embodies the most pure example of unconditional love, faith and tolerance possible. To treat Dog with respect and commitment will see the animal return that love and devotion tenfold; if not more. Clearly a remissive creature, Dog instils the ability to forgive when appropriate, to accept imperfection in others, to realise that no one is perfect and to maintain loyalty and truth, to others and to ourselves. As a creature coached in pack mentality, Dog teaches us to understand legitimately ordered hierarchies within our community, while maintaining faith in our own values and belief systems. Dog nurtures the understanding that for things to flow smoothly there often has to be a pack leader and that to achieve something for the self the rest of the pack must be considered. It also strongly promotes allegiance to the self, particularly when there are 'pups' involved. Dog will only take abuse for so long before it turns on its aggressor in order to retain its own power, to protect what it holds dear and to maintain its sense of integrity. Dog is a powerful teacher that inspires trust, love and acceptance: qualities that can only be realised in others when first fully established within the self.

• Hunting Dog – *Equality*

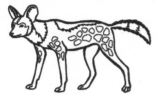

African Hunting or Wild Dog's coat is decorated with irregular patches and no two Dogs ever look the same, hence his folk name: the 'Painted Dog'. Falling prey to habitat loss and canine diseases transmitted by feral and domestic Dogs, the species is classified as endangered. Powerfully adaptive, though, African Hunting Dog has been found foraging in the snows of Mount Kilimanjaro (an altitude of over 18,000 feet).

Hunting Dog affirms the belief held by the ancient cultures that we, as children of the Earth Mother, each hold sacred position in the scheme of things; that we all represent a vital strand in the Web of Life and that we are all equal. He demonstrates that although we are all unique and separate on one level, we are reliant and unified on another. A casual but effective hunter, Hunting Dog knows that if we each stand in our Power and move forward with confidence in ourselves and trust in our people, we are honouring our sacred place within the Web of Life, particularly if we strive to discover and embrace our purpose. To slack off, deny responsibility or play the part of the victim ultimately weakens the Web of Life and disrespects the agreement we forged with Spirit before embarking on our Earth Walk. It also robs our brothers and sisters of the chance to better their lives. Everything happens for a reason and all things have their place. Hunting Dog encourages us to acknowledge our uniqueness, to discover our purpose and to adapt on all levels with the expectations and lessons that are presented to us so that we may live abundant, whole, interrelated lives.

• Raccoon Dog – *Labelling*

Although the initial resemblance is uncanny, Raccoon Dog bears absolutely no relation to Raccoon. He is definitely a member of the Dog family, hibernates during the winter months and enjoys an omnivorous diet. In the wilds of Asia, Raccoon Dog has been hunted almost to extinction and is now protected by law.

As is generic for all Dogs, Raccoon Dog fundamentally reminds us to demonstrate loyalty to ourselves before falling victim to the demands of others. Before you can expel energy on others, for example, you must first have enough in reserve to sustain your own needs. Raccoon Dog observes the sacredness of honouring your own needs by encouraging the celebration of what makes you unique. Raccoon Dog supports those who are assumed to be something they are not; those who are labelled, pigeon-holed or categorised according to superficial appearance, dress code or body language. Put simply, people who are mistaken for something they are not are people who feel the presence of Raccoon Dog. Innocently mistaking someone for something they are not is blameless and acceptable, especially when apologies are offered or when the error is put right in a jovial way. Maintaining the ruse by maliciously labelling the recipient of the mix-up, however, is totally unacceptable and dishonourable to Raccoon Dog. He nurtures the understanding that we are all blessed with qualities that will serve us best and that will someday see us reach our intended potential, even if these qualities, at first glance, seem to hinder our growth or hamper our self-esteem. Raccoon Dog reminds us, too, to have compassion and understanding of these qualities when we witness them in others, even if they conflict with assumed normalities and traditional perspectives.

• Red Dog – *Relationships*

 Also referred to as Wild Dog or Dhole, the 'Red Dog' of Asia is the essentially slighter, red-haired 'cousins' of Grey Wolf. Red Dog travels in family-oriented packs of 20 or more, in which hierarchy is savagely established and respected and where all adults care for the pups, related or not. It seems that no matter how badly a Dog is treated, its sense of loyalty and trust remains true.

Dog teaches us to accept faults in others (when appropriate) and ourselves while appreciating that no one is perfect. He affirms loyalty and the need to remain true to our commitments and obligations. But, when there are 'pups' involved, Dog promotes, above all, loyalty to the self. To lose sight of our own sense of worth will inevitably result in us losing sight of our purpose and consequently we are no good to anyone, especially our children. The sheer joy and security found in a solid relationship is awe-inspiring, especially when the wants and needs of both parties are productively acknowledged and celebrated. Companionship and unconditional love are two key phrases used to describe the generic of 'Dog'. Red Dog, however, focuses on the motivations that inspire us to remain in relationships that may no longer be fruitful or personally beneficial. The wisdom of Red Dog speaks of basic survival, security and grounding, polarity, movement, sexuality, pleasure and emotional security. So long as you are able to weave these qualities into your relationships while maintaining personal integrity, then the wisdom of Red Dog is being honoured and held sacred. But the moment you believe, for one reason or another, one or more are not being reciprocated, you may want to consult the wisdom of Red Dog and ask him to help you hunt your perceptions and reclaim your sense of personal loyalty. In doing so, commitments and obligations will be afforded rightful prominence, as will your sense of purpose, character and self-pride.

Dolphin
Breath

Anyone who has witnessed the joyful behaviour of Dolphin at play would agree that they are both beautiful and awe-inspiring. Dolphin leaps not only to entertain human spectators, however, she also do it to impress a mate, to shepherd fish and for the personal thrill it affords her. Such displays strengthen the social bonds held between members of the pod, while developing trust and teamwork required for survival as a herd. The most abundant is the common Dolphin who comes together to form herds of several thousand. Marine Dolphin is there when we are born. She guides us from the watery world of the womb and delivers us into the physical world.

Dolphin inherently resides within each and every one of us. As we journey though life, Dolphin journeys with us, checking constantly to ensure that every breath we take is one of self-respect and purpose. Dolphin welcomes Spirit into our life by breathing life into the spark that resides in each of us – the spark, that if fed and nurtured, has potential to become a flame; a flame that links us directly to the unconditional life-giving, life-affirming fire of Spirit. Our sense of security, our confidence, our relationships, and even the type of employment we seek, are all issues that are determined by the quality of the time spent in our mother's womb and how we drew our first breath. Apparently we sign sacred contracts that outline every aspect of our Earth Walk from the moment we are born, to the time we are destined to leave again. Essentially, this means that the life we were born into, the people we meet, the friends and foe that cross our path and even the marks we make on the world while we are here, are all pre-destined. Dolphin reminds us to revisit our sacred breath in order to fuel the fire of passion each time we conceive and 'birth' new ideas, create new things or embark on new relationships. She offers the life-giving ingredient that must be acknowledged before any new project can be brought to fruition: breath. Dolphin asks us to review our life and to ask questions that may trigger heartfelt reactions in relation to the time spent in the womb. See this as an opportunity to reclaim your power, to rebirth and to finally honour the first breath you took as you entered the world. Dolphin remains with us, like a guiding light, navigating our progress from the birth canal out into the wide world. She offers support and protection. She inspires our dreams, desires and aspirations as she lovingly watches from the sideline, and she will remain there until called upon one last time to plot our course back to Spirit. To honour Dolphin and her gift is to ensure that the first breath we take in life is healthy and strong, and that the last one we take is more of a sigh; one that confirms contentment with our efforts and achievements during life.

• River Dolphin – *Conduit*

All species of River Dolphin are endangered due to damming, pollution and hunting. River Dolphin prefers the muddy, torpid water trapped at junction points of streams and waterways, where the undercurrent flows slower allowing her to preserve energy when hunting and she is nocturnal.

River Dolphin is the conduit that channels the affects of sacred breath throughout our conscious and subconscious bodies, so that we may witness the rewards of simply acknowledging the validity of good health and clarity in our everyday lives. River Dolphin endeavours to enrich our lives and bring us, as a people, closer to ourselves and the Earth Mother so that we may realise our potential and hers. River Dolphin augments a greater resistance to anxiety and trauma. When invoked, she fortifies, rejuvenates and refreshes both the physical and etheric bodies, while enhancing confidence, determination and courage on a discernible level by acting as a symbolic sluice. Patrolling the 'veins' of the Earth Mother in rivers and waterways, she ensures they flow smoothly while keeping a close eye out for blockages and stagnation; threats that may otherwise prevent the healthy flow of energy through the body. River Dolphin Dreaming, however, is also very practical. Her wisdom espouses a simple observation: that by Walking our Talk, we can ensure a vigorous flow of life-giving blood throughout our body by simply keeping our rivers and waterways clean and healthy. By demonstrating our intent for all to see, what we present on an external level mirrors what we are experiencing on an internal point of view and vice versa.

Donkey
Modesty

Donkey is well known for his stubbornness but he is not so much stubborn as intelligent, with a strong sense of self-preservation. If Donkey feels that something is not in his favour, all the coercion in the world will not make him do it. They are not easily forced or frightened into doing something they do not want to do. Donkey has been used as a 'beast of burden' for centuries due to his great stamina and is more economical to keep. He is also demonstrative and gentle and is perfect for teaching children to ride.

Donkey inherently understands his role as a 'servant' to others and accepts his purpose, but holds inherent yearning for personal achievement and respect. He plods discreetly through life, holding sacred a deep sense of resolution; a knowing that his loyalty and servitude will be compensated some day, if not by its owner, then by Spirit. Donkey nurtures the understanding that when we seek out what we need, we are more often than not rewarded with more when the time is right. Donkey encourages us to keep our head down and to work from a place of humility. To do anything else right now, could attract 'negative' attention and see the result of our hard work and diligence evaporate. Donkey people are quiet achievers. They are modest, reticent and hate attention. They are happy to work under a boss, attracting favourable attention and recognition for their efforts. Donkey offers solid foundation and helps build reputation and experience, until the day comes that offers a chance to strike out on one's own. Donkey people are marked from day one with an aura of greatness. Their modest, humble personas target them for higher recognition, because although they innately believe themselves worthy, they assume nothing. Donkey assists in the construction of a solid, fruitful life. He encourages us to listen to our own judgment, to work hard, but to never be manipulated by personal greed or another's lust for power. When approached with modesty, Donkey promises to take us from the ordinary to the extraordinary.

• Onager – *Target*

 Onager, Asiatic Ass or Syrian Ass, is native to the steppe and desert regions of Mongolia, Iran, Tibet, India and Pakistan and has been known to go for long periods without water. Onager was once found throughout Israel until he was completely exterminated during the early twentieth century. Fourteen pairs of subspecies were successfully reintroduced in the 1980s and although not a true Syrian Onager, the released Persian Onager has returned to the landscape a much-loved creature. Onager is said to kick stones back as it runs from predators and apparently the power discharged by a fleeing Onager led to the creation of a catapult, which was called the *onager catapult* and considered heavy artillery in its day.

Intent is what fuels Onager Dreaming. Knowing what your intentions are before you commence any journey or relationship while being aware of how the consequences of your actions will affect others is to honour the wisdom of Onager. An animal not afraid of hard work and discipline, Onager warns against stubbornness, arrogance and thoughtlessness. Onager supports those who strive to make their lives bigger and better, especially when they remain humble in their approach and demeanour. Onager people survive and thrive because they are born with an inherent target or goal at which they aim all their energy and intent. They realise that in order to attain any goal, they need to work hard and remain focused and disciplined while making do with what they have. They subconsciously know that to slip into resentment and anger would distract them from their goal and hinder their progress. Onager encourages us to remain mindful of our target, focused in our intentions and to strive for accuracy, impeccability and truth in all that we do. To lose sight of our target will see us lose direction, self-control and dignity. It will see us waste energy and be seen as undisciplined and sloppy, thus inadvertently damaging or destroying the good relationships forged with those who would normally support and encourage us in our quest for a prosperous life.

Dormouse
Rest

Dormouse hibernates for up to six months of the year (depending on the weather), waking only to feed on cached stores of seed and grain. Her name derives from the Anglo-Norman *dormeus* meaning 'sleepy', and closely resembles the word dormant, which means inactive or asleep.

Dormouse is all about taking time out for you and encourages us to step away from the routine aspects of life and to return to our centre of being and remember what is important to us. She encourages us to look after ourselves on all levels and forces us to shut ourselves off to become 'dormant' and restful; to find sanctuary in stillness and comfort in our own company. Dormouse also endorses the reduction of stress through meaningful and productive activity coupled with a healthy diet Dormouse not only endorses physical rest and rehabilitation, she also supports the need for mental relaxation and to still the mind and allow it to focus and partake in the activity with you, in a meaningful, loving way. Make every activity a sacred one and life itself will become a celebration. Create gaps in your daily schedule to include rest and relaxation. If you are tired, take a nap. Meditation, guided visualisation, focused breathing and massage are also powerful tools that could be built into any 'healthy body, healthy mind' program, because they help to alleviate stress and apprehension. To cap off your new course of personal therapy, spoil yourself every now and then by doing things you love to do. Whatever you do, though, Dormouse asks that you make a pact to do it for you and you alone.

Dove
Peace

There are approximately 300 species of Dove in the world and her call is said to inspire feelings of peace, reassurance and homecoming within those lucky enough to hear it. Dove has long been a universal symbol of peace and devotion, with Noah supposedly releasing a Dove after the great flood of biblical times. Dove was said to have returned with an olive branch in her beak, indicating the presence of dry land and the end of the flood. Dove was also said to have watched over the baptism of the infant Jesus. In politics, the term 'dove' is used to describe those who favour peaceful resolution, as opposed to 'hawks', which do not.

Dove inspires peace and harmony by offering balance and stability, particularly after a time of emotional upheaval or pain. She provides the tools needed to effectively welcome ourselves home so that we might get our life back on track. Dove settles the heart, re-establishes clarity and surrenders fear and trepidation. A messenger of God and a beacon of hope, she reveals light at the end of the tunnel, illuminating the way to fertile ground where we may rest, recuperate and start over. Dove symbolises self-love, replenishment, inner peace, unconditional love and trust. Dove people are trustworthy, faithful, gentle and sincere. They never raise their voice (or a suspicious eyebrow), are unconditionally forgiving and only ever see the good in people. Dove people are often deceived, however, by people who prey on human kindness and who repeatedly fail to know when they are being taken advantage of.

Dragon
Treasure

 Although most cultures make reference to Dragon in the spiritual history of their land and people, when we picture Dragon in our mind, we automatically see the scary beast of faerie tales. Although this fabulous imagery is familiar to most people, Dragon's power actually lays in his ability to shed his skin and emerge as a new, magically altered being. Dragon demonstrates for us the 'will to dare' by teaching courage, strength and self-knowledge. He encourages us to face our fears, to combat them and transform them into personal gifts of inner strength and power. Many traditions regard Dragon as protectors of the elements; Earth, Water, Air and Fire. Earth Dragon guards the treasures of the Earth as her 'legacy' to those of us who honour and respect the Earth as our Mother and speaks of abundance and the wisdom obtained as we reach the maturity of old age. Water Dragon guides us as we meditate and contemplate and teaches us the art of introspection by encouraging us to calm the inner chatter so that we may find the silence within.

The winged Dragon of the Air brings clarity of mind while sharing the gifts of intuition and heightened intellect, while the flame-breathing Dragon reminds us to honour the fire in our belly, the passion that drives our creative force, while teaching lessons of enthusiasm and innocence. Fire Dragon is the most potent at puberty when we seem to know everything, but in fact know nothing. Dragon harnesses the elements as ingredients of power and strength and unites them in the sacred act of Creation. Dragon carries the supreme quality of manifestation and instils an unquenchable thirst for higher understanding, spiritual knowing and occult lore. To slay Dragon is to engage in a battle between the light and the dark aspects of self; the vanquishing of one's inherent darkness to make way for the emergence of self-mastery, clarity and impeccability. To figuratively rescue the princess from the clutches of Dragon is to free oneself from bondage and tyranny, while stealing Dragon's cached wealth is to win the treasure found in the attainment of spiritual knowledge and wisdom. Dragon people are determined, self-governing, perceptive and scholarly. They are sound judges of character, inspiring leaders and empowering, knowledgeable individuals. They enjoy a solitary, luxurious lifestyle and the accumulation of wealth.

• Rainbow Serpent – *Shaping the land through legend*

When time was new, Earth Mother was flat and grey, with no mountains or valleys. The Indigenous People of Australia believe that the landscape was formed by the massive bulk of a Great Rainbow Serpent as it made its way across the land.

Rainbow Serpent's gift is that of 'shaping the land' and teaches us how to reshape the inner landscape that has become our personal reality, by encouraging us to face, combat and transform our fears into gifts of strength and power. Rainbow Serpent was a teacher spirit that showed the people how to dig for food and how to breathe. It was believed that Rainbow Serpent shaped babies inside the wombs of women, and so was revered as a source of great fertile power and creative potency. Rainbow Serpent teaches us to banish the 'What ifs?' from our lives; the fears and limitations that hinder our growth as people. She encourages us to breathe, relax and create and instils a sense of calm and faith in our ability to manifest all that we need to support the lifestyles we yearn for. Rainbow Serpent was the mightiest and most revered of the Dreamtime beings, so feared by the other creatures that they stayed well away from her and when she became tired of shaping the Earth, she found a waterhole and sank into its depths. Each time the other animals visited the waterhole they were very careful not to disturb her. The Rainbow Serpent is not a creature to tempt fate with. Although it is safe to acknowledge the superficial lessons of the Rainbow Serpent, you are advised to never attempt to invoke this powerful spirit without permission, traditional understanding or ancestral guidance. Be warned: even Australia's Indigenous People remain fearful of disturbing Rainbow Serpent as she spreads across the sky, for fear of the unknown consequences.

Dragonfly

Illusion

The oldest flying insect found in fossil form strongly resembles the contemporary Dragonfly and Dragonfly larvae form the dietary foundation of many larger species of fish. Dragonfly, like Butterfly, embodies the regenerative powers that lend themselves to the concept of rebirth. After mating, Dragonfly deposits her eggs in water, where they hatch and develop into ferocious aquatic larvae before transmuting into adult Dragonflies. Born into the world as an aquatic organism, Dragonfly experiences a symbolic death at the midpoint of its life and re-emerges as an apparent new creature, with deceptively iridescent wings that seem to glisten, reflecting the changing light.

Dragonfly lends himself to the principles of agility and activity, replacing the illusion of separation with the truth of unity. Dragonfly helps us to break free of self-created illusion and those created on our behalf by others of good intention; illusions that essentially restrict our natural development and ability to choose for ourselves. Dragonfly previously held great magical power, once inhabiting another body and knowing another life. Due to an overwhelming sense of self-importance and a puffed up ego, Dragonfly's appearance and skill were forever altered through the wily ways of a Trickster Spirit. A character that was always willing to boast of his paranormal prowess, Dragonfly was eventually caught in her own illusion. Allowing himself to be taunted by the Trickster Spirit, Dragonfly took the form of a delicate, wraithlike insect, but with the mystical change came the death of her magical knowledge. Trapped forever in the body we see today, Dragonfly constantly darts from one bulrush to another, regularly checking his reflection in the pond water while looking for the Trickster Spirit that duped him into giving up her supernatural powers. Thus, Dragonfly offers us the chance to rebirth our sentient selves and dissolve feelings of misconception and illusion and helps us see that many limitations initiated by our physical reality are undesirable boundaries, designed to prevent us from shifting our consciousness and growing spiritually and emotionally.

Duck
Emotional stability

Duck is graceful in the air, is a powerful swimmer and is skilled at diving to great depths in search of food. Sometimes it is necessary to hide how we truly feel in order to maintain a look of confidence and detachment as we navigate our way through even the most difficult periods.

Like Swan, Duck helps us retain an air of grace, peace and tranquillity. She helps us create a façade of indifference, elegance and complete and utter calm, even when we are barely resisting the temptation to cry, run or clam up. Duck helps us balance our emotions so that we do not vent our emotions publicly. In the wrong setting, such a display would see us lose credibility or surrender our power. In those rare instances, what we feel inside may not be something we need to advertise. Duck people are masters of emotional disguise. They are able to appear strong and centred, even when experiencing the most emotionally unsettling situations life can muster. They remain focused and dedicated to their responsibilities, seemingly able to separate themselves from life's burdens in order to operate effectively and efficiently at work or with friends. They tend to keep personal things personal, to the point when even the closest of family members may not notice a change in disposition. Duck people must avoid systematically shutting people out however, by allowing themselves to trust a select few who are willing to offer a supportive shoulder to cry on or an empathetic ear. Duck suggests that when the emotional pool gets too rough, simply swim ashore and ground yourself. Duck offers the tools to successfully and gracefully navigate our way through even the most tumultuous periods and to explore and honour our emotions at all times.

• Eider Duck – *Quilting*

Eider Duck is famous for her thick and heavy down. Eider down is the favoured filling for most good-quality duvets and quilts and has the best thermal insulating properties of any natural material. Quilting was introduced into Europe from the Middle East during the late eleventh century and afforded women an opportunity to gather together socially. The women would each create a reflective 'block'; a square that recorded sacred memory.

Eider Duck endorses the preservation of this ancient art and inspires us to pass on the wisdom gained from these important times and to see the quilt as an opportunity to honour our personal history and our inherent wisdom. Eider Duck people are often considered the keepers of ancient or ancestral knowledge. They are the ones family members look to for confirmation and support in times of crisis. Eider Duck people are very warm, welcoming and homely. Eider Duck people have often known hardship and emotional insecurity as young people and so feel it important to nurture those around them, providing a sense of belonging and stability in everything they do. To look to Eider Duck for guidance is to present aspects of your personal history in a way that offers someone else a valid reason for their past, better understanding of their present and clarity and direction for their future. It is to feel the need to acknowledge the wisdom found in personal experience and to record and share it in a tangible, permanent, practical way. The quilt offers one such opportunity, as well as providing a sacred sharing time in which to contemplate, reminisce and dream with those you trust.

• Mandarin Duck – *Bliss*

Mandarin Duck holds great mystical association in Asia and, according to the ancient art of feng shui, is considered sacred for his contribution to healthy and long-lasting relationships. There is a Japanese folktale that explains how Mandarin Duck became a symbol of love and fidelity. The story tells of a feudal lord who becomes so taken by the beauty of Mandarin Duck's plumage that he decides to trap him and take him home to add to his garden. The little Duck, separated from his beloved mate, becomes so distressed he begins to die of a broken heart despite the many other birds that already inhabit the garden. One day the lord's servant girl was stealing a kiss with her samurai lover, when they happened to spy the miserable little Duck sitting under a bush. Relating to the true love and loyalty expressed by the little Duck and feeling for his sadness, they decide to secret him away and reunite him with his mate. Of course, such a decision was totally against the lord's wishes, and on learning of their refusal to return the Duck, he became so infuriated that he condemned them both to death.

According to this legend, Mandarin Duck is said to mate for life. When he finds find a suitable mate, it is told, he remains with that partner until death. But, should they ever be separated against their will before that fated day, they quickly languish and waste away. And so, the traditional teachings of feng shui welcome Mandarin Duck as a symbol of reciprocal respect, consideration and faithfulness. His presence is said to ensure strong and long-lasting relationships, while simply displaying Mandarin Duck figurines beside the bed is believed to enhance the passion and mutual pleasure of one's love life by inspiring those who employ his charm to communicate openly, candidly share all needs, wants and desires and to basically appreciate one another's company for what it is. Mandarin Duck Dreaming, therefore, affirms an unwavering state of love and fidelity between spouses and lovers alike, while offering sound advice and proven solutions to those currently experiencing relationship difficulties.

• Wood Duck – *Altruism*

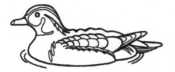

Also called Woody, Summer Duck, Acorn Duck, Swamp Duck or Squealer, Wood Duck has the most striking plumage of any Duck in North America. Wood Duck is very protective of his young (and each other) and will post a sentry to 'keep watch' for possible threats.

Wood Duck endorses altruism: unselfish behaviour that borders on self-sacrifice. He nurtures strength of character, dependability and commitment. He affords an emotionally stable, balanced view of the world and helps us integrate this into our lives as a true and productive perspective. Wood Duck is powerfully protective and establishes an air of confidence, bravery and chivalry that is sensed and admired by all who witness it. Wood Duck people are usually very attractive, charming and witty, but generally take it in their stride as they are not driven by ego. In Australia however, the term 'Wood Duck' is not so poignant and is generally reserved for individuals who display the shadow side of the little Duck's Dreaming: irrational, immature, reckless behaviour. They show little consideration for others, seeking self-gratification at any cost – until the following day when their decadent conduct comes back to haunt them and they rally their family and friends to offer support as they battle headaches and nausea.

Dugong
Healing the womb

Also known as the 'Madonna of the Sea' and Sea Cow, Dugong is a large marine mammal that inhabits Australia's tropical waters and due to hunting her for her meat and 'oil' and a decrease in availability of sea-grass, she is now listed as an endangered species. Sacred in African culture as the *Manatee*, Dugong is thought to have once been human in form, transformed by either curse or blessing. Mistaken for mermaids by early sea-goers, Dugong is thought to have fuelled belief in the legendary Siren, and is now classified as belonging to the order Sirenia. Dugong serenades its young, soothing it with sacred song. She is a slow-moving, gentle creature that grazes on aquatic plants. Suckling her calf from her pectoral breast, Sea Cow is archetypal of the mother and therefore, the womb. Harmless to other sea-creatures, Dugong (a lunar-influenced creature) symbolises all energies that nourish, procreate and are maternal.

Dugong reminds us to nurture ourselves if we are mothers and to honour our mother for the part she has played in our life. She reminds women that they must heal themselves on levels deeper than the mere physical. She speaks of the power that only comes from women collectives: the power of a sister's cry and the learning of discernment, through loss, abuse or matriarchal neglect. Dugong reminds women that their power comes from their womb and that their healing represents their connection to Spirit. All women share sacred genetic memory of all that has gone before them and what is yet to come: the wrongs exacted upon them by men, the wrongs they have imposed upon their sisters and the wrongs their sisters have inflicted upon them. These are the things that women must heal and this is the wisdom of Dugong. She speaks of the journey into the memories of the Grandmother Spirit and the need for all women to heal collectively from the womb.

Eagle
The all-seeing eye

'Eagle' is the common name used to describe several members of the family, *Accipitridae*. Most of the 60-plus species of Eagle inhabit Eurasia and Africa, with two species found in the United States and Canada, nine in Central America and South America, and only three in Australia.

• Bald Eagle – *Oneness*

 Once common throughout the United States, populations of wild Bald Eagle have declined gradually since the early 1700s due to pesticides used in agriculture, habitat loss and pollution. Bald Eagle was officially declared the National Insignia of the United States in 1782 and has since become the living symbol of *freedom, unity, spirit and the pursuit of excellence* for the people of America and more recently, the people of the collective world. Bald Eagle reminds us that God doesn't just live 'out there' and that being close to God doesn't need to be difficult.

Bald Eagle, as an emissary of the Creator Spirit, suggests that perhaps you have been using the 'wrong' words and looking to God from the 'wrong'

perspective and suggests you try using instead the word 'Spirit'. You may feel a stronger connection to that word and with Spirit as your ally, you will feel confident to march out into the world and find yourself. You will feel that you are one of the people, not apart from them. Spirit is our link to Creation. Spirit inspired Creation. Spirit is Creation. It refers to those in Spirit and it is the life force found within all things. It is God but it is also the goddess. It's the Angels, your spirit guides, your totems and the Faeries. It is the life force found in water, fire, wind and Earth. It is the power of thought, the emotion of love, the power of silence and the process known as death. It is you. And it is the people. Spirit binds us together and makes us 'One'. And the Bald Eagle card is reminding you that you are 'One'; 'One *with* The One'. When I refer to Spirit, I refer to those *in Spirit*. I refer to the life force found in our brothers and sisters: the plants, the trees, the stones, animals and birds. I refer to the life found in Water, Fire, Wind and Earth. I refer to the power of thought, the emotion of love, the power of silence and the process known as death. And I refer to the people. Spirit is what binds us together. It is what makes us '*One*'.

• Harpy Eagle – *Torment*

 Despite their immense power, Harpy Eagle populations have been decimated due to deforestation as a result of logging and agricultural encroachment. Harpy Eagle is so named after the 'Harpies', or Snatchers, of Greek mythology. Harpies were half-woman, half-bird, who snatched the souls of the dead as they journeyed to the Underworld. According to early interpretations, Harpies were originally described as beautiful winged women, but in later translations they became winged hags with sharp talons; a version that carries to the present day. The Harpies were considered to be emissaries of retribution who abducted souls and tortured them as punishment for the erroneous ways of the people who once housed them. Malicious and cruel, they embodied the devastating potential of the wind. We are all promised a gift of power and the chance to realise our purpose before incarnating into this plane of existence, but unless our faith is tried, we fail to develop the drive or ambition to realise either.

Harpy Eagle delivers a spiritual trial designed to test our resolve and commitment to life so that we might discover our reason for being. Those who show willingness to heal by exploring the lessons hidden within every life experience and who seek to achieve the highest of their potential are allowed to pass and 'survive' the quest, to be rewarded with spiritual nourishment and growth. Harpy Eagle indicates a form of grief that has not yet been fully integrated, but which can be with divine counselling and grounded, spiritual instruction. It can also denote mental torment created by unresolved guilt. Harpy Eagle conveys the potential for self-imposed punishment and emotional bondage that must be surrendered to Spirit in order for one to live a full and productive life. A bird of impeccable carriage and high spiritual standing, Harpy Eagle offers swift and sound release from crippling emotional burden and overwhelming despair. A bird that embodies the very fundamental nature of Spirit, Harpy Eagle reintroduces clarity and peace by dispelling personal darkness and restoring soul essence.

• Wedge-tailed Eagle – *Spirit*

Wedge-tailed Eagle is Australia's largest bird of prey and has keen eyesight, capable of visually identifying prey from over 1.5 kilometres away. According to Aboriginal lore, Eagle is an emissary of birth, death and rebirth and is revered as the one whose role it is to shepherd the souls of the recently departed back to The Dreamtime. Likewise, in many other Earth-based cultures Eagle is representational of the Creator Spirit because of his ability to reach breathtaking altitudes. With eyes that are capable of detecting the slightest hint of earth-bound movement he witnesses the fears we keep locked deep within our consciousness and those weaknesses that represent our vulnerabilities, discomforts and inabilities.

Wedge-tailed Eagle is said to have a sacred capacity to know our heart of hearts, our sincere and purest intent, and thus our true essence. Wedge-tailed Eagle offers faith in the knowledge that Spirit is watching and guiding us as we go about our everyday lives, particularly when we are faced with perplexing resolutions or complicated life choices. Wedge-tailed Eagle helps us view all life circumstances from widely varying perspectives and to appreciate the whole picture while simultaneously seizing all potentials tight in the talons of our personal future vision. To step forward supports advancement and growth, while to step back offers a chance stay put or further contemplate the situation. Equally as legitimate though, is the cold hard fact that the act of moving forward poses the very real threat of failure, while to step back offers retreat and a chance to reassess. To walk to the edge of any of life's symbolic precipices and to step off is to take a leap of faith, to trust in Spirit 100% and to know what it means to 'Walk one's Talk'. While facing the very real possibility that you might figuratively plummet to your demise, the very act of stepping forward will result in Spirit noticing your determination to grow and progress, and Wedge-tailed-tail Eagle symbolically swooping to catch you on his back before the rocks break your fall, leading you to a very real place of accomplishment and success. Wedge-tailed Eagle offers the strength, bravery and discipline we need to reach ever greater heights as we live our physical lives, while reminding us to always retain a healthy sense of humbleness, to reject blind recklessness, and to never lose spiritual sight of our original intent.

Echidna
Personal protection

 Echidna is an egg-laying mammal closely related to Platypus and is protected by spines that cover the majority of his body. Echidna bustles through life and when disturbed quickly digs himself into the ground. He effectively shuts himself off from the world and prevents anyone from interfering or getting too close to him.

In much the same way as Echidna we are often guilty of approaching life with a similar degree of dogged determination and stubbornness. We suppress the wider perspective that often comes from the experience and wisdom of others and reject different ways of viewing a problem in favour of a stance we have always taken. Echidna helps us understand the fundamental distinction between denial and determination or, more to the point, the difference between not wanting assistance and not needing support. Despite his steadfast, purposeful mindset toward the physical aspects of life, Echidna unconsciously integrates aspects of Ant Wisdom into his in an attempt to enhance his understanding of life. Echidna is obstinate and easily irritated, while Ant is patient. Echidna knows that Ant holds an elusive ingredient that will help make his life that much richer and his connection to Spirit that much deeper. Echidna actually instils the necessity for a balance. Although he promotes ambition powered by intuition, passion and determination, he reminds us to constantly remain vigilant to the wisdom and wider perspective of the experience of others. With his incredibly sharp quills, Echidna offers protection when we wish to be alone or when we want to have our views recognised and our beliefs respected. It permits only those we trust and want near to venture within our sacred space during these times, energetically protecting our vulnerable side and our most private feelings from everyone else. Echidna opens our heart so that we may nurture others and receive the nurturing they can offer us. Echidna teaches us to drop our guard, relax our personal protection, develop tolerance and learn to trust. Echidna reminds us that we do not have to tackle life alone, that life presents choices that often hinge on whether or not we are open to acknowledging the love that surrounds us. Outwardly impatient toward those who offer assistance and seemingly unyielding in his life mission, Echidna reminds us that to intentionally keep others at a distance is okay, but only when it is practiced with integrity to the self. Demonstrated by the lack of quills on his vulnerable belly, Echidna patiently endorses the taking of calculated risks by allowing others to get close to us, prompting us to gently trust in the knowledge that their energy will serve us well in whatever form it takes.

Elephant
Self-awareness

There are two species of Elephant in existence today: African Elephant and Asian Elephant who are surviving descendants of the now extinct Mammoth and Mastodon. She is the largest living land-dwelling mammal, and can live up to 70 years in the wild. Elephant communicates by touch, sight, and sound, relying on infrasound and seismic communication to converse over long distances. Her intelligence is comparable to that of primates and cetaceans, as is her apparent self-awareness and ability to show obvious emotion for the dead and dying.

• African Elephant – *Commitment*

 Weighing in at over 6,000 kilograms as an adult, African Elephant has longer tusks and larger ears than her Asian cousin and only comes into oestrus (season) once every three to nine years. Female calves stay with their mother's group, while males leave once they reach sexual maturity and eventually establish their own territory. Elephants have been known to live 65 years in the wild, with the dead being mourned for years after. It is not uncommon for remains of a deceased loved one to be visited year after year, with time taken by those still living to 'cry' and silently reminisce before moving on. Elephants embrace a matriarchal system, with the mothers and their offspring forming the hub of the community. Relationships between group members are tight, with each member honoured for their individual strengths. For this reason, it is the oldest non-reproducing females that lead the herd because of their extensive knowledge and wisdom. Due to rustlers African Elephant is classified as endangered.

An animal revered for her wisdom and as an elder and teacher of high esteem, on the word of legend, African Elephant's acumen was regularly sought out by the animals who saw her as a spiritual messenger and sacred oracle; a wise chief who, without bias, settled disputes among the other animals. African Elephant is considered an animal too kind and trusting for her own good who is said to feel pity for even immoral individuals, and so often finds herself badly deceived. Due to her enduring memory, loyalty and sense of obligation, African Elephant reawakens our duty to the promises we make and the commitments we forge as we go through life. African Elephant endorses a greater sense of responsibility, while encouraging us to address and honour the promises we have made and those we have broken. She helps remove the illusions created by unspoken assurances we assume have been made, as well as the trauma caused when these 'promises' are not honoured and offers strength and endurance to those who feel betrayed or forsaken. When invoked, African Elephant establishes a powerful sense of commitment to the self and a belief in our own self-worth.

• Asian Elephant – *Gratitude*

Asian Elephant is significantly smaller than her African 'cousins' and often doesn't produce tusks. Although Elephant has sat at the heart of the Asian culture for the past 4,000 years (at least), the survival of the species is now at threat due to the ever-growing human population and resultant fragmentation of Elephant's forest habitat as well as illegal poaching and shootings. According to Hindu belief, Elephant is revered for her memory, loyalty, gratitude, generosity and gentleness. She has become a symbol of sovereignty, spiritual strength and intelligence. Ganesha, the Hindu god of wisdom (among other things), has the head of a single-tusked Elephant and is often depicted riding on the back of a Mouse. The appearance of White Elephant was said to have proclaimed the birth of Gautama Buddha, and as a result, White Elephant has become a sacred symbol of appreciation.

White Elephant and Ganesha are both said to offer deliverance from the obstacles created by the mundane aspects of life, aspects such as embarrassment and limiting circumstance. Elephant's power, gentleness and humility also make her a sacred symbol of victory of life over death, or the ability to welcome change. A personal record-keeper of sorts, Asian Elephant harnesses sacred memory and loyalty to one's ancestry. She helps us to understand and embrace the reasons for why we are faced with difficulty and encumbrance as we grow and what it is that we are supposed to do with these experiences. When we take the time to explore these reasons, and we learn to honour the lessons hidden deep within each, we begin to understand our sacred purpose and deepen our relationship with Spirit. In deepening our relationship with Spirit, we break through the veils that separate us from those *in Spirit*. By welcoming those *in Spirit* into our conscious lives, we enhance the integrity of the wisdom we have gained from honouring our lessons. When we speak, generations past speak with us and through us. And when our Ancestors speak through us, the unconditional love experienced is both humbling and awe-inspiring, invoking a sense of gratitude that cannot be put into words. The strength that comes with truly knowing that you are no longer alone removes any worry or concern of being tricked, hindered or embarrassed by limitation again because if your heart is illuminated by the guiding hand of Spirit, so your life path will be, too. And that is something to be extremely thankful for.

• Pygmy Elephant – *Evolution*

Borneo Pygmy Elephant, a recently discovered subspecies of Asian Elephant, is reportedly much smaller and more peaceable than regular Asian Elephants. Elephants are big: mammoth means huge. But here we have a species of tiny Elephant.

Pygmy Elephant is an animal that defiantly flouts our perceptions and the comfort that lies in assumptions by stepping out and breaking away from familiarity by simply being different. African Elephant espouses commitment to family and community, while Asian Elephant harnesses sacred memory and loyalty to one's ancestry. Pygmy Elephant however, encourages us to internalise this wisdom and to channel it back into ourselves. Today's children, for example, are doing just that. They are saying, 'Enough is enough. What about me?' Evolution is a word that means development or advancement and used to describe an event that enhances awareness and deepens understanding while forcing us to revaluate all that we once held close and revered as sacred truth. Today's children are acting up because we haven't got the courage to do it ourselves. Instead, we have created a forum for them to speak and now that they are, we don't know what to do about it. We are beginning to look for truth and harmony in all that we do. We are moving away from power and control and into a place of balance. And we are demanding that our leaders and those in command follow suit – just as our kids are expecting of us. Pygmy Elephant is encouraging us to celebrate this powerful time of change. With her sudden and unexpected appearance, she announced to the world, 'The time is now'. Pygmy Elephant encourages each and every one of us to channel resentment and feelings of isolation into something good, powerful and meaningful, instead of using them as excuses to feel sorry for ourselves, to act up or to rebel against authority. Pygmy Elephant demonstrates that when you take time out for yourself you enhance yourself, you evolve. She reminds us that just because we may have unique ideas, unconventional ways of doing things or controversial views, we must never apologise or hide who we are. These traits are what make us unique. We must never let the limiting beliefs of others put us down or confine us to a box.

Emu

Masculinity

 Emu is the world's second largest flightless bird and is a fast runner and adept swimmer. Naturally curious, even wild Emus cannot resist investigating any activity that is out of the ordinary. Sacred Aboriginal rites were performed around Emu and his eggs, some associations linking the bird with the nurturing energies of the sun and the protector of the children. Traditionally, women were seen as the emissaries of the metaphysical realms, fulfilling the role of the romantic, the prophet, the healer, the educator and philosopher. Men have always been the active ones: the developers, the hunters and collectors, the foot soldiers and the defenders. Men once sat in counsel opposite their women as counterparts and equals, collectively at peace within their role as the ones expected to physically manifest the dreams and visions of their women. Emu honours the energy of the opposite sex while strengthening and

improving a public image of his own. Masculine energy is witnessed or experienced rather than being physically contained. Feminine energy however is generally tangible and real to the touch.

Emu successfully embraces both the active aspect of the traditional role of men while energetically honouring what it means to be male on a vibrational level. Male Emu adopts the sole responsibility of raising his chicks, incubating them under his body until they hatch and then keeping them close until they are old enough to fend for themselves; a rare event indeed, even in the animal kingdom. The Emu, being a grounded, flightless bird, offers real and grounded relief to the single father. As a 'yang' totem, Emu demonstrates the practical skills needed to guide and raise a child when the nurturing and protective energies of the mother are absent. Alternatively, Emu can also assist the single mother by offering the masculine support lacking in the absent father, so that her energies may be preserved and rejuvenated. Assuming that the Emu energy is being radiated through the heart of the mother or the residual energy of their absent father, the children will acknowledge the harmony created within the relationship they have with their mother. Emu advocates the belief that if one is to maintain and enhance one's degree of endurance one must learn to only ever work at one's own pace and to honour one's known limitations. It demonstrates how to integrate the positive and supportive aspects of both our 'yin' and 'yang' sides by drawing their wisdom into everything we do, thus enriching our view of the world. By living for today, instead of wasting energy worrying about tomorrow, or resentfully revisiting yesterday, we will maintain our endurance and realise the potential to both do and dream simultaneously. Our life will begin to offer fertile foundations, realistic dreams and chances to move productively into the future.

Flamingo

Sifting

There are two species of Flamingo in Africa: the Greater and Lesser. Made famous by her powder-puff pink plumage (tinted by the crustaceans that form the basis of her diet), Flamingo is often found in mixed groups. Demonstrated by the deepening hue of the Flamingo's plumage with every invertebrate it eats, Flamingo offers permission to pamper and love ourselves. She says that if you can't love and respect yourself unconditionally, she won't radiate a sense of self-worth. If you don't see yourself as being worthy of true love, Flamingo explains that you can't expect others to know that you are yearning to be. What you radiate is what you attract. Like attracts like; a simple adage endorsed by Flamingo.

Flamingo is inspiring, cleansing and motivating. Equally, she is soothing, caring and approving. Flamingo helps one sort through the forgotten mess and garbage stuffed to the back of the 'wardrobe of life'. A symbolic sieve, Flamingo helps to determine what is useful in one's life and what will create baggage. Imbued with acceptance and unconditional love, Flamingo awakens one's inherent romantic and creative nature, especially within those who have endeavoured to heal issues of the heart or those who genuinely feel at peace with themselves. Flamingo's strong sense of justice creates a hurdle for anyone not working from the heart. While assisting in the discrimination of truth from dishonesty, energy emitted from a pure heart-space confuses those who work solely from power and control. Impeccably speaking from the heart, Flamingo helps us uncover, implement and share our genuine purpose. Resembling a fishing hook, Flamingo's bill trawls for and lands emotional support and, in doing so, helps us trust our own judgments. She helps us to navigate our life path by heightening our other senses to the truth in a sometimes dark and desolate world.

Fly and Maggot
Awareness

Blowfly lays Maggots in the carcasses of road kill, waste and garbage. He assists Nature by removing the decaying bodies of the dead thereby helping to control disease. Apart from this, scientists know little about the true 'purpose' of the common Fly. Australia is famous for its Black Houseflies, Horseflies and Blowflies, which are prevalent in warm summer months. Associated with demons and plague in early writings, Fly was seen as a vehicle of decay and destruction by the Hebrews and an envoy of evil, sin and pestilence by the Christians. Some African tribes celebrate a Fly god, while others see Fly as a symbol of the soul that should be honoured and never killed. In Australia, where Flies swarm in their millions, Fly is seen as an uninvited guest at barbeques and outdoor gatherings and a bother to babies, animals and those who work outside. Flies have become such a part of Australian life that they have crept into colloquial conversation, with sayings like 'I'd like to be a Fly on the wall when she finds out about that' and 'There are no Flies on you, are there mate?' Such clichés highlight Fly as creatures of awareness.

Shape shifters and bi-locators, Fly is a spy who watches, listens and absorbs knowledge not intended for him. Another aspect of this pinpoints negative energy, particularly in areas where Flies swarm. Such areas may be infested with vibrations or dark-side entities that need to be removed or cleansed. Fly also warns of people who carry dark-side entities or welcome them into their spiritual life. Fly encourages us to develop our awareness so that we may become learned in the darker aspects of Creation, more aware of the less obvious and develop our shape-shifting abilities so that we can 'be' in two places at once.

Fox
The magician

Fox is the common name give to any omnivorous mammal belonging to the *Canidae* family. Fox is best known for his erect, triangular ears, pointed and slightly upturned snout, and his long bushy tail, which is also known as a 'brush'.

• Arctic Fox – *Fox fire*

The Arctic Fox, or White Fox, has a heavy white coat during winter, but as soon as the snow begins to melt, it is shed in favour of a brown one. Some Arctic Foxes sport a heavy, pale bluish-grey coat in winter, which sheds to reveal thinner but darker bluish-grey coat in the summer. These animals are known as Blue Foxes. Arctic Fox enjoys a wide distribution because of his ability to adapt to the cold and accept a wide variety of prey, sometimes forced to abandon customary hunting grounds and travel nomadically for food. The Northern Lights, or the *Aurora Borealis*, Latin for 'Red Dawn of the North', is the name given to the eerie light-show phenomenon that traverses the northern skies. The Northern Lights are created when flares erupt from the surface of the sun, spewing vast numbers of solar particles into space, which form plasma clouds. Northern Lights are formed when these clouds collide with the Earth's atmosphere. The more solar particles that collide with the gas molecules in the atmosphere, the more lights we will see moving across the sky. The Finnish people called the Northern Lights *Revontulet*, which meant 'Fox Fire'. They believed that Arctic Fox started fires that reflected the lights by showering the Earth with snow, which she brushed up with her tail.

Arctic Fox births the realisation that, as the master of our own destiny, we are fully qualified to create. Arctic Fox delivers all the necessary tools to shape a bright and abundant future. A true alchemist, Arctic Fox inspires the belief that our yearning alone can breathe life into our dreams and ambitions. She reminds us, though, that in order to do so we must first step out of doubt and into conviction. In her productive phase, Arctic Fox represents the active, masculine power of creative desire and allows us to influence the world and shape our future through willpower alone. Arctic Fox stimulates us to harness the creative energies of the Universe and to marry them with the physical skills we have developed during our life. She points out that if we are to manifest any positive change within our life, we must first take control of our life and demand respect by instilling a sense of it within ourselves, for ourselves. Some people view the negative aspects of Arctic Fox as being representational of our dark side but without shadows created by the dark, we are unable to see the light and, without hope or promise, we cannot create. Arctic Fox is, therefore, simply a necessary harbinger of balance.

• Fennec Fox – *Riddles*

Fennec Fox inhabit has prominent, oversized ears that enable him to hear prey hiding under the sand. Just as Horned Owl lends her eyes so that we may see in the darkness, helping us determine lies and dishonesty hidden behind a veil of false integrity, camouflaged and undetectable to trusting eyes, Fennec Fox helps clarify the ambiguous intention secreted within words and phrases that could otherwise be misinterpreted as barefaced truth.

Fennec Fox helps us translate the riddle-like fashion in which some people speak in the hope of misrepresenting their true intentions. Fennec Fox translates cryptic expression and double meaning, and so should be invoked when seeking the advice or assistance from people whose best interests are likely to be considered first and possibly in favour of our own. The Fennec Fox knows only too well the danger of trusting the superficial sounds we might hear; sounds that we assume are saying one thing (like the presence of a plump, juicy Lizard hiding under the sand), but are actually telling us something completely different (that the Lizard is in fact an angry Scorpion) or, worse, the complete opposite or nothing at all. Fennec Fox protects us from the sting we feel when we realise we have been duped or blatantly lied to and offers support. Fennec Fox encourages us to speak little and to listen more; to make notes to be used in our defence when the truth behind the spoken word is revealed and to take a witness who can confirm what was said.

• Kit Fox – *Shadows*

Kit Fox, also known as the Swift Fox, grows only to the size of a domestic Cat and is quite unafraid of man, but will retreat quickly to her den when startled. She is easily trapped and shot, a tendency that has witnessed a dramatic decline in Kit Fox numbers. Kit Fox lives in the shadows and is an animal of the night: a creature of mystery and elusiveness. Twilight is Kit Fox's power time, that time between late afternoon and evening when it is too late to be called day but too early to be classified as night.

Kit Fox is a fringe-dweller who lives between the worlds. Known to share territory with humans while keeping her distance, she represents those who live on the outskirts of society, but who yearn to be included, involved and welcomed. Kit Fox often builds her den along fence rows, indicating a desire to stay within her comfort zone while safely contemplating the wider world from a familiar point of view. Kit Fox nurtures those among us who are too shy to show their true selves. Afraid to draw attention, Kit Fox people long to be like everyone else, but lack the confidence to integrate.

A creature known to lurk in the shadows as a way of ensuring her survival, Kit Fox is demonstrated by those who desire to come 'out of hiding' and introduce, perhaps for the first time, their true selves and share their potentials and gifts of knowledge and experience. Kit Fox covers her tracks and hides her presence behind a veil of cunning and distrust. Kit Fox inspires us to leave the shadows, to break through our insecurities and say to the world, 'Here I am. Now deal with it', and affords the self-confidence and inner strength to put ourselves 'out there', no matter how insignificant the initial steps may seem. Kit Fox allows us to stand in our power by instilling believe that we can master any situation and overcome any limitation by reminding us that we are just as important, worthy and sacred as the next person.

• Red Fox – *Kenning*

Red Fox is a handsome creature and is known to establish his den in close proximity to human dwellings, raiding compost heaps, orchards and poultry sheds for Chickens and eggs. Legend says that a Fox that finds himself plagued by Fleas will take some fleece caught on the barbed wire surrounding a sheep paddock and carry it into a flowing river. As the Fox moves deeper and deeper into the water, his Fleas move higher and higher to avoid the water, until they have nowhere to go but into the fleece held firmly between the Fox's jaws. The Fox then sends the fleece down the river. Stories like this, coupled with his uncanny ability to blend into his surroundings, being both obvious in his movements while inconspicuously keeping to the shadows, lead to his reputation for cunning, 'kenning' and craftiness. Kenning and cunning both derive from the meaning 'to know' or to show foresight, discernment and strength from experience.

As a trickster and sly-one, Red Fox is also an animal gifted with both wisdom and profound clarity; qualities that enhance his chances of survival and family fertility. He is an animal that takes productive advantage of any situation, no matter how vague. Red Fox affords the wisdom to look at the world from varying perspectives, to consider the options at our disposal and to execute any plan with precision and dexterity. Red Fox offers an inherent ability to fruitfully and respectfully profit from the world and promotes a sense of adaptability, good humour and responsibility; qualities that ensure our journey out into the world will prove both abundant and rewarding. He advises us to not take ourselves too seriously and to learn and grow in maturity with every mistake we make. Red Fox dares us to review our beliefs and values and life in general in a similar fashion to how we might ponder our likeness in a mirror; to consider our mistakes, weaknesses and insecurities and to knowingly and pensively integrate the acumen afforded by each into our lives.

Frog
Cleansing

Australia is blessed with over 200 species of native Frogs and the slightest change in environment conditions seriously affects their wellbeing. Frog has thin, porous skin, which means she not only lose body moisture quickly on warm days (hence being more active at night) she also absorbs chemicals from the air and water. Despite the impressive range of Frog species, populations are declining at a rapid pace due to pollution, introduced species of fish and Cane Toads. Earth Mother Australia's Outback bakes under an unrelenting sun, with the ancient rocks buried beneath the red sands capturing and holding the energy of the sun's rays. The heat is maintained until well into the night, when it is then replaced by a deathly chill that competes for supremacy with the heat of the day, permeating the bones while whispering promises of death into the ears of those reckless enough to spend an unprepared night alone in the wilderness. And then the rain comes bringing new life to the land, initiating a chain of events that completely transforms the horizon. The physical regeneration is awe-inspiring, with an absolute desert becoming a tapestry of colour and sound almost overnight. Just as thunder and lightning may herald the coming of an invigorating storm, Frog choruses approaching rain.

On a symbolic level, Frog signifies a need to settle the emotional dust that blocks our vision and she helps us cleanse our Spirit by stimulating the release of sacred tears, intended to rid our souls of unexpressed emotion. Instinctively we are preparing our bodies for fruitful new beginnings. We are readying ourselves for the end of an emotional drought and the conclusion of a period of barrenness. When we journey through life devoid of emotional cleansing, we grow numb to the possibility of change and simply forget what life was like before the drought. When embraced in a productive way however, our tears welcome fertility and growth. Intentionally ignoring issues that deserve our attention is to live half a life. It takes a great degree of courage, resolve and trust but once the darker side of our soul is confronted without fear, the energy once used to keep it in check is freed up and life suddenly becomes less burdensome. New life cannot be expected to establish itself in a desert devoid of sustenance. One action helps shape the next and we cannot expect new doors to open if we remain afraid to shut old ones. Where there is no love, encouragement or support there is little chance of emotional growth. Without rain, there is no life. Without tears there can be no healing. Frog reminds us to take time out for ourselves, to remove negativity and fear from our life and to release emotional baggage. Frog teaches us to welcome and honour our tears and to see them as a healthy way to cleanse the soul of pain, grief, fear and longing. She offers us the chance to recharge our batteries and to reclaim a sense of balance and healing within our lives.

• Poison Arrow Frog – *Inflection*

Poison Arrow Frog, or Poison Dart Frog, is brilliantly coloured to warn predators of his extreme toxicity which he obtains by eating certain insects that have fed upon poisonous plants. Captive Poison Arrow Frog is therefore often harmless, although some species are toxic enough to poison an adult human. Poison Arrow Frog is threatened by habitat loss and atmospheric impurities carried by the rain that feeds his habitats.

Poison Arrow Frog people do not mince words but when they do elect to bite their tongue their opinion is betrayed by their facial expression or the glint in their eye. Poison Arrow Frog people are observant and listen well. They are worldly, street-wise and usually well educated and consider themselves qualified to offer judgment or argue a point. They can be impatient, intolerant and blunt in their attitude and due to of their resolute natures, frank use of language and penchant for accuracy and truth, and are hard to get to know. Poison Frog people may not intentionally look down their nose or purposefully use venomous inflection, but they are always considered judgmental, threatening and condescending. Poison Arrow Frog asks that we not only watch our words, but also how we deliver them. He encourages us to be mindful of our facial expression, too, particularly the way in which our eyes can convey how we truly feel about something or someone. Just as an arrow hits its target in accordance with the integrity in which it is drawn and released, our eyes can focus and send our true intentions and perceptions with equal velocity and accuracy. Poison Arrow Frog reminds us that our emotions: happiness, pleasure, humour, frustration, anger and resentment, are all portrayed with equal potency via our eyes. He nurtures the fact so that we may communicate how we truly feel in times of discussion, with little fear of being misconstrued or misinterpreted by those listening to the subtle 'words' uttered by our body instead of those spoken via our mouth.

Galapagos Tortoise
Longevity

Of the 14 described subspecies of Galapagos Tortoise, 11 still exist. Like all reptiles, Galapagos Tortoise is diurnal and depends on the sun to warm her body supplying her with the energy to spend the day grazing. She sleeps almost 16 hours a day, half-submerged in mud or water, which conserves body heat. Galapagos Tortoise lives for approximately a hundred years and has formed a close relationship with Galapagos Finch whom she allows to feed on the ticks and parasites found in her creases. Apart from the Galapagos Hawk, Galapagos Tortoise has only one predator: man.

Galapagos Tortoise instils a sense of peace, stamina, focused vision and longevity. It is ancient association that labels Tortoise as the 'totem of the Earth Mother'. Both Tortoise and the traditional teachings of the Earth Mother espouse living in harmony with the environment and that all things of Nature are essentially born of the one source. Galapagos Tortoise says that if we take each day as it comes, living our life with integrity and peace in our hearts, in support of our brothers and sisters, we can achieve wondrous things. As long as we dedicate an equal degree of respect and dedication to everything we do and everyone we meet, our journey will be supported and guaranteed success. Galapagos Tortoise endorses taking our time and maintaining focus on each task at hand. Galapagos Tortoise people are usually reserved, patient and introspective. They like to consider all options before committing to any one in particular, after which they spend significant time pondering their course of action. Despite their apparent procrastination, though, once a Galapagos Tortoise person has their sights set on a goal, nothing can dissuade their forward march. It may take a while for their ambitions to be realised, but Galapagos Tortoise people always hit their target. With peace, stamina and focused vision, Galapagos Tortoise offers staying power and a long, healthy, productive life, so long as it is one lived in harmony with all things and with respect for all people.

Genet
Chastity

 Cat-like and nocturnal in behaviour, the Ancient Egyptians and Greeks once trained pet Genet to act as a Rat catcher, just as the Berbers of Northern Africa still do today. Genet has anal glands that secrete a scent advertising her sexual, social or territorial status. When startled or threatened, she expels a powerful, off-putting odour designed to repel aggressors. Genet is also called Genet Cat, due to her retractable claws, Cat-like features and feline traits. Female Cats are called Queens, while the rather vulgar expression 'Pussy Cat' archaically links them to the unsullied womb of the virgin.

It is said that while the Virgin Mary was giving birth in the stable of Bethlehem, a Queen Cat was at the same moment giving birth to kittens. Similarly, Bast, the Egyptian Cat-headed goddess of fecundity, was responsible for love, fidelity and the birth chamber, but was forever revered as a virgin. Genet reinstates women (and men) to a place of purity, a chaste state of innocence and perfection when the sacred act of coupling becomes a violent act of rape. She strips us of guilt, shame and tainted reputation, reinstating an air of virginal wholesomeness. Genet sees beyond the physical content of meaningless encounters, maintaining a sense of chaste perfection for sex workers for example, who see little alternative to their legitimate way in which they support their family or lifestyle. Genet separates the act of sex from the joy of love-making, returning even the most seasoned prostitute to a sensual, first-time lover when embraced by the man (or woman) of their dreams. She nurtures victims of rape and sexual domination too, by maintaining the knowledge that virginity taken against one's will is no fault of the victim. Genet helps us see clearly and better understand the role we play in our sexual growth and speaks of truth as she demystifies sex by turning something previously espoused as demeaning, dirty or painful into an act of joy, love and nurturing. She turns an act used for centuries to control, manipulate and conquer into an act of promise, creation and union and reinstates hope and sexual healing. Genet reinstates the belief that even those experienced in the art of sex can be chaste in character; that even those of 'many partners' can champion what it means to be a virgin at heart.

Giant Anteater

Patience

Giant Anteater belongs to the order Xenarthra or Edentata, which means 'without teeth'. He has very poor eyesight but well-honed hearing, a good sense of smell and is adept at opening Termite mounds and Ant nests – the hub of their favourite source of nourishment.

Anteater can be, at times, unpredictable. Anteater betrays the key to his wisdom by mention of his own name. He is an animal that feeds primarily on Ants and Termites, suggesting a desire to integrate patience and to shun the self-sabotage archetype that so many of us carry. Anteater people are typically hard on their themselves, and can be quite impatient. They want to achieve and they want to achieve now, in as little time and with as little effort as possible. While striving to fulfil their ambitions, however, they tend to sabotage their chances in the process. Very capable while working at their optimum level, they bully themselves to reach higher, by setting unobtainable goals bound by unrealistic deadlines. Anteater invites us to be gentler on ourselves and to strive for goals we know we can reach. He encourages us to aim higher, but to focus for now on what we can comfortably achieve with the skills and resources currently at our disposal. Anteater explains that to undertake more before we are ready may result in us achieving less, or coming out with nothing.

Gibbon
Phobia

 Gibbon belongs to the Ape family and shares kinship with Chimpanzee, Gorilla and Orangutan. He is highly intelligent, forms intricate communal troupes and parents each of his young until they are several years old. Although Gibbon is able to perform astonishing acrobatic feats while showing little concern for the heights he scales or the distance he might fall should he lose his grip, he (along with several other species of primate) is terrified of water.

Those moved to explore the wisdom of Gibbon, despite their natural ability to consciously swing from one task to another with little effort, quickly and easily grasp new responsibilities, hook into new concepts before they are integrated on a common level and comprehend new theories, technologies and assessments with minimal instruction, they are often haunted by phobias, unconscious blockages and limiting beliefs. Gibbon can be called upon to identify the cause of one's phobias, exposing the true fears disguised within them. Gibbon encourages us to examine our phobias and to see through them, exposing them as nothing more than superficial cloaks hiding tangible yet healable fears. Because our phobias are symbolic of the deeper fears hidden deep within our shadow aspect, they hold within their very nature the key to their own banishment. All we need to do is find the symbolic key that will inevitably release the chains that bind us.

An index of phobias and their implications:
- *Hydrophobia*: a fear of water and drowning – suggests a fear or history of being emotionally shackled, overwhelmed or controlled by another's power, charisma or dishonesty.
- *Arachnophobia*: a fear of Spiders – suggests an inability to harness change, make independent choices or to start over. Often those suffering from a fear of Spiders have endured a life governed by indoctrination, apprehension and manipulation.
- *Zoophobia*: a fear of wild animals – suggests a fear of opportunity, change and potential. To 'fear' all animals is to shun the guiding voice of our Higher Self, the Earth Mother, our Ancestors and Spirit.
- *Melissophobia*: a fear of Bees – suggests a fear of success, abundance and advancement. To 'fear' Bees is to turn away from one's responsibility to develop and personally and financially accomplish.
- *Ornithophobia*: a fear of Birds – suggests a lack of trust in one's higher self and one's own judgment. It also suggests a fear of being cradled, nurtured and being 'mothered'. It may also suggest a fear of becoming a mother or, rather, of proving to be an effectual mother.
- *Gatophobia*: a fear of Cats – suggests a fear of being alone, of standing in one's power and of making decisions based on one's independent wants and desires. A fear of Cats may also suggest a fear of intimacy, affection or an unresolved history of sexual abuse or a lowly attitude toward sexual activity and its associated connotations.

- *Cynophobia*: a fear of Dogs – suggests a fear of commitment, making promises or of having promises broken. Dogs are synonymous with loyalty, friendship and unconditional love, and a fear of Dogs suggests a lack of faith in these qualities.
- *Ichthyophobia*: a fear of handling or touching Fish – suggests a lack of trust in one's ability to bring one's dreams to fruition. Fish are symbolic of our inherent intuitive nature, with a fear of Fish representing a resistance to trust our innate or 'gut' feelings, intuitive notions and contemplative abilities.
- *Doraphobia*: a fear of fur or skins of animals – represents a fear of change, endings or symbolic 'death'. It also indicates a fear of shedding, releasing or stepping out of one's established comfort zone.
- *Hippophobia*: a fear of Horses – suggests a fear of initiating one's life journey, of making decisions and of harnessing one's Personal Power. Horse has the potential to birth a realisation of one's purpose, with a fear of Horse implying procrastination, stagnation or a fear of discovering what that purpose may be.
- *Entomophobia*: a fear of insects – suggests an inability to see the value in silence, stillness and introspection. People who are afraid of insects are generally anxious about spending too much time in their own company for fear of being enveloped by personal demons, personal darkness, dire memories, guilt, shame or regret.
- *Musophobia*: a fear of Mice – suggests a mistrust of anyone or anything requiring contractual agreements, endorsements or promises. Those who have been negatively influenced by broken leases, business partnerships, marriages or other legally bound affiliations often share a fear or mistrust of Mice.
- *Mottephobia*: a fear of Moths – suggests a fear or mistrust of God, Spirit, Creation, Great Mystery, the Source, Religion or Spirituality. Moth is attracted to naked flame or any illuminated light globe, suggesting a desire to be close to 'the Light' or the life-giving 'Source'. A fear of Moths, therefore, clearly suggests the opposite.
- *Ophidiophobia*: fear of Snakes – suggests an inability or unwillingness to address the past and to shed the outworn or outmoded aspects that no longer serve us. A potent symbol of good health (as recognised by the medical profession), Snake promises new beginnings to those who are willing to acknowledge, embrace and release their shadow qualities.

Giraffe

Intersection

Enjoying a lifespan of 25 years or more, Giraffe inhabits grassland and loosely wooded areas, feeding on leaves and branches of shrubs and its preferred species of tree, the acacia. After a gestation period of approximately 460 days, female Giraffe gives birth in a standing position, with the newborn calf falling unceremoniously to the ground. Giraffe is considered a sacred vehicle of supernatural power and African Bushmen performed ritualistic dance and ceremony to harness her wisdom.

Giraffe effectively demonstrates the interconnecting relationship that inherently links the physical plane, the Underworld and the Spiritual Realms. Like a tree, Giraffe stands in all three worlds simultaneously, offering acumen ingrained with sacred experience. An emblematic intersection or 'cross over' point between the worlds, Giraffe offers choice and understanding to those who seek her wisdom. Offering insight into death, grief, fear, pain, and healing, Giraffe's feet suggest the need to explore the past, to make well all wounds and to productively explore one's Inner Landscape, while helping to maintain a strong footing in (and an illuminated pathway back to) reality. Giraffe's torso reminds us to remain practical, to strive for realistic goals and to productively process the mundane aspects of everyday life as they present themselves, and in doing so, offers buoyancy, grounding and stability. The head of Giraffe, as it probes the heavens, browsing the branches of the tallest trees, offers permission to explore the world's religions and spiritual paths, and to develop our sacred gifts. Each branch of the tree suggests a unique opportunity to grow personally and spiritually, be it through the recognised face of organised religion, pagan tradition, or the 'New Age' movement. No matter what the source, Giraffe seeks to introduce us to an aspect of Spirit/God that delivers us back to a place of inner peace, totality and good health. As a whole, Giraffe illustrates the great cycle of life; the symbolic journey we take as we repeatedly visit each world during the course of our life.

Goat

Determination

Goat reverts back to his wild state with very little effort. Feral Goats are found in many countries and are harmful to the environment, affecting the native animals and vegetation. Goat can survive in areas unsuitable for other stock animals and are often kept by landowners to help combat encroachment of bush land and weeds.

Since the beginning of time, people have confused the emotion of 'love' with 'lust'. The energy of Goat, when allowed to dictate our actions, often sees longings superseded by prudence and discrimination. When channelled positively, however, he characterises healthy sexual yearning balanced with both hormones and healthy discretion. As such, Goat affords opportunity for all sexual relationships to evolve in a wholesome way. When negatively directing their potential, Goat people inconsequentially indulge themselves in shameless activity. When demonstrating their positive traits, however, Goat people are gentle and loving. They have an inherent love of animals, plants, the waterways, mountains and Nature. They are demonstrative, funny and sensitive. Goat people are often described as being the 'salt of the Earth', grounded and sound. As well as its creative potential, however, Goat represents survival instinct, determination and the quest for higher knowledge. Goat represents drive and the determination to push to greater heights and encourages us to break free of restriction and to set ourselves free of unreasonable expectation and bondage of any sort. This is why Goat constantly strives to obtain levels seemingly out of reach. It should be remembered however that never being satisfied with the things we have can lead to greed and discontent, qualities representative of the more negative aspect of Goat. To demonstrate a balanced sense of ambition and aspiration so that we can productively further ourselves on all levels, however, is a positive trait symbolic of the correct use of Goat Dreaming.

• Ibex – *Cushion*

 Ibex, probably the Wild Goat of the Old Testament, is surefooted and nimble and able to move at great speeds through rocky terrain. A traditional symbol of beauty, Ibex was believed to traverse this terrain by throwing herself from one ledge to the next, cushioning her fall by landing on her horns. Legend has it that the horns were made of some elastic material that enabled Ibex to bounce.

When invoked, Ibex can help ease the pain after unexpected shock, surprise or trauma and supplies a cushion that shields us from the full impact of emotional pain and suffering, while offering the chance to realise and integrate possible reasons for the event. She supports us through the initial numbness, shoring us up as we seek answers. Offering counselling of sorts, Ibex provides a solid foothold on life so that we may soldier on. She helps us deal with the feeling of being 'stuck between a rock and a hard place' by lifting us to a higher realm of understanding where we will feel encouraged to pray, talk or scream at the heavens. Ibex provides the space to vent our emotions and ask 'Why?' When appealed to, Ibex lessens the blow after we are hit hard by events that knock us around spiritually and that threaten to shatter our perceptions, beliefs and familiar view of the world. Ibex does not offer reasons for why things happen. She would never dare to be so forward. She does, however, create the meditative forum to ask the questions of Spirit that will allow us to find the answers we seek. She helps us gain an authentic sense of peace, a deeper appreciation of Great Mystery and endurance in the quest for higher appreciation.

• Mountain Goat – *The mother*

 Mountain Goat is also well suited to living on rocky terrain but it is not unknown for her to accidentally slip and fall to her death. The sexes travel separately until the breeding season, with females remaining close to the kidding grounds and males roaming in search of receptive females. The young can stand and climb shortly after birth, but remain close to their mother until the following year's young are born. Mountain Goat relies heavily on the sustenance of the Earth Mother's mountains to protect and provide for her. Mountains (along with the humble letter 'm') have long held sacred association as the 'breasts of Earth Mother', the Twin Peaks that give birth to the sun each morning.

Mountain Goat reminds us that we are never alone; that just when we begin to believe we have been forsaken by all who love us, we remember that we are constantly being cradled in the protective arms of our Earth Mother. Mountain Goat reunites us with our roots, with our ancient origins. She helps us reclaim our inherent heart-felt connection to the 'old ways' and the ways of the goddess. On a less tangible level, Mountain Goat also encourages you take a quest that will see you journey within yourself, reconnecting to the 'mother archetype' that resides within each of us. Mountain Goat offers her support to those who find themselves in turmoil because of this illusion, by encouraging them to journey within to welcome their 'inner mother' home. When we are able to embrace our 'mother archetype', we learn to mother ourselves. We no longer feel the need to seek nourishment and love on an external level because we are empowered by self-love and self-nurturing. When we embrace our 'mother archetype', we journey to the sacred mountain located within our Inner Landscape where we awaken our inner goddess so that we may live fertile, abundant lives, full of sustenance and bountiful harvest.

Goose
Mother Goose

Geese are large waterfowl that can be broken into three genera: Anser, or Grey Geese, which includes all domestic Geese and Swan (Chinese) Geese; Chen, White Geese, and Branta or Black Geese, which includes the Canada Goose. The term goose applies to the female, the male is known as a gander, while young birds are known as goslings.

• Canada Goose – *Adventure*

Canada Goose migrates south each year. At the onset of autumn, they congregate and prepare for the long and gruelling journey as a flock flying in the familiar 'V' formation and follow established routes learned from their parents. Fairytales were originally shared as a means of stimulating community spirit. Originally told in the oral tradition, their function was to entertain and educate adults and to help them better understand the world and the customs of the village in which they lived. Often narratives, they contain elements of fantasy and wonder that were rarely restricted to any one place or timeframe and typically included royalty, common folk and animals that spoke and acted like people. *Mother Goose* has become the archetypal teller of fairytales and nursery rhymes but no specific writer has ever been truthfully identified as its author. These tales lift us out of the physical realm of expectation and deliver us into a world of non-ordinary reality; a world of wonder and possibility that stimulates the imagination while cutting portals into the 'Other Worlds'. They offer a solid, grounded foundation on which to explore the world in which we live from a position of fantasy and 'make believe'. In the world of fairytale, nothing is out of reach, everything is possible and thoughts and secret yearnings are easily obtained and teaches us how to face fears and embrace our shadow side, while helping to explain and bring into perspective the darker aspects of existence. As adults, we can revisit this sacred time and, similarly, these magical places by invoking the wisdom of Goose.

Because of her instinct to travel to far off lands at certain times of the year, Canada Goose (and that of all migratory Geese) re-establishes the childhood fantasy of fabulous adventures to legendary places. Canada Goose opens the window of opportunity, exploration and wonder. She stimulates spontaneity; to live life as an adventure, and to share the thrill of discovery with our children. She reminds us that not only do children have sacred requirements, the inner child does too, and that if we forget to honour the existence of our inner child, the realm of Faerie will be lost to us forever. Canada Goose Dreaming, therefore, reawakens the Peter Pan archetype, the inner child who yearns to remember its dreams, to once again believe in Faeries and Dragons and to revisit magical lands long ago lost to our imagination.

• Greylag Goose – *Monogamy*

Greylag Goose is the ancestor of most contemporary breeds of domestic farmyard Goose. The name 'Greylag' is said to have derived from the fact that they have grey legs or that they 'lagged behind' while other breeds migrated. 'The Goose that laid the Golden Egg' was originally the Egyptian goddess, Hathor; said to be the one who gave birth to the sun. It was once sacrilege to kill a Goose in midwinter, because the sun was said to return to the womb of its mother during this time, gaining in strength to be reborn in the new season. Being the oldest breed of domestic Goose, Graylag feathers were traditionally used to stuff quilts and duvets and quilts and have long held ancient symbolism surrounding fertility and marital fidelity. Sleeping on bedding made of Goose down, for example, was thought to ensure fertility and fidelity due to the bird's faithfulness to her mate and devotion to her young.

Greylag Goose espouses loyalty and sexual commitment and promises a fruitful relationship and the inevitable realisation of children. Greylag Goose Dreaming, when invoked, is potent medicine for those who yearn to conceive and carry a child full term. Greylag Goose foretells the safe arrival of a healthy baby and a nursery filled with laughter, joy and coos of delight. Greylag Goose people are true, honest and proud. They strut their stuff with confidence and are said to march through life with the air of a soldier patrolling his grounds. Greylag Goose people enjoy a productive, abundant married life, producing many children and even more grandchildren, celebrating life with hearty meals and warm fires surrounded by family and friends. Greylag Goose people rarely go without, lacking nothing in life for the simple reason that they know true wealth. They never need worry about money, for example, because they know where their wealth lies; their family. Greylag Goose reminds us that when we revere our children and partner as the most important aspects of our life, we live safe in the knowledge that we are truly blessed and abundant in the most sacred of ways. Armed with this understanding, money and material possessions readily flow into our life when we need them to, with little or no effort or need for concern.

• Nile Goose – *Duality*

 Egyptian Goose bonds for life and makes an excellent parent. She is an opportunist when it comes to nesting preferences; nesting on the ground, in burrows, on cliff ledges or in abandoned nests of other birds. Egyptian Goose was domesticated and considered sacred by the ancient Egyptians. The power found within the feminine is neither different nor the same as the power found within the masculine for, although they are opposites, they are equal at every degree.

Nile Goose endorses the fact that now is the time for humanity to understand our role as masculine and feminine energy forms, to come together as one and to live in harmony and balance with each other instead of arguing over who is the stronger sex and why. As men, it is time for us to remember the sacredness and power of the opposite sex while taking responsibility for improving public image of our own, and women need to do the same. Today's men are *tired* of being 'blokes' who play footy, watch porn and drink beer. They *want* to do more, but their women need to show them how by encouraging them and providing space to explore, ask 'silly' questions without fear of ridicule and to make mistakes. Women must drop expectation and realise that their men are largely innocent (not ignorant) to the ways of Spirit and that they need time and patience if they are to catch up. Nile Goose celebrates the fact that we have come full circle. She rejoices in the fact that we are once again looking to one other as brothers and sisters, equals and as vital strands in the Web of Live. Incidentally, it is worth noting that 'Amen' is a magical Hebrew word meaning 'let it be'; a word used to invoke divine response to a prayer. Maybe, just maybe, the truth revealed by summoning Nile Goose is the answer we have been calling for.

• Snow Goose – *Winter solstice*

 The Indigenous People of North America have long celebrated the seasonal migration of Snow Goose and they became known as *Chen Hyperboreus*, which means 'from beyond the north'. It is a baffling mystery how, despite the barren arctic tundra, Snow Goose is able to find the exact same nesting grounds year after year; the same grounds where she was hatched. Snow Goose finds a mate during the winter feeding season and forges a bond bound to last a lifetime. Goslings follow the first moving object they see when they hatch, which is called imprinting. Snow Goose has long been associated with the North Wind and is said to vibrationally embody the energy of the winter solstice. It was once assumed that the days growing shorter in December meant that the sun was dying. The people grew afraid that the sun would not return if it were allowed to dwindle to nothing, so rituals were performed before December 21 (the winter solstice) with the intention of placating the sun. During the festivities, no one was permitted to work and slaves and masters exchanged roles, or at least were treated as equals. St. Augustine, the first Archbishop of Canterbury, was believed to have downplayed the sacredness of the winter solstice by declaring that Goose heralded the 'The Great Freezing'. He assumed that when a harsh winter beset the land its intention was to worry or thin the Snow Goose population; a battle that symbolised the constant tug-of-war between all that was feared and perceived as evil and all that was good and wholesome.

Snow Goose people are generally born around the time of the winter solstice. They are sensible and determined, responsible and cautious but can appear to lack emotion or sympathy at times. They are chatterers and love to gossip. They are loyal in their relationships, but rarely fall in love at first sight. Although undemonstrative in public, in private Snow Goose people are passionate lovers and committed parents. They are dependable providers and are generally very house-proud. Snow Goose calls for us to be persistent in our search for security, with all our ambitions set to be hard-earned and elusive. It often feels as though we are restricted and limited in our options when working with Snow Goose Dreaming, but despite her rather pessimistic flavour, Snow Goose is a celebration of promise, hope and strength. She suggests a plentiful harvest, new beginnings and light, while heralding refreshment, rebirth and renewal on all levels.

Gopher
Sacred geometry

 Solitary, territorial and aggressive, Gopher is a burrowing rodent and is polygamous. The word 'gopher' comes from the French *gaufre*, meaning 'honeycomb', in relation to the complex subterranean network of tunnels the Gopher builds as his den. Gopher obtains enough moisture from the plant life he eats, so rarely needs to go in search of water. It is a popular notion that sees all things of Nature following a Universal pattern or geometric blueprint. The Pythagoreans, for example, sought to decipher the mysteries of Nature by meditating on the endless triangular web created when the sides of a hexagon are extended, its lines meeting in the centre of an adjacent hexagon. When the pattern is repeated over and over, a honeycomb pattern becomes evident with each corner forming a perfect 60-degree angle. Sacred geometry represents the inseparable relationship that exists between us *(the part)* and the Universe *(the whole)*. The collective principle of *oneness*, a belief that we are all related; that we are all fundamental parts of the bigger picture rather than independent entities living apart from it. The principles espoused by the concept of sacred geometry are demonstrated by the sacred 'Web of Life'. We each represent individual threads in the Web of Life. Each of us depends upon the authenticity of those who stand closest to us and, as sacred strands ourselves we, in turn must lend support and stability to those leading from us. The honeycomb network of tunnels built by the Gopher similarly embodies sacred geometry.

Gopher offers interconnectedness to those who seek his wisdom. Gopher provides a sense of authenticity to the individual, while offering opportunity to expand one's consciousness to include their environment and those who share it. Gopher offers safe haven to those who wish to work alone, while affording communal alternative to those who don't. Gopher knows that no matter how effective his network of tunnels, without the land that supports it, he would never survive. He understands, too, however, that as a single entity, his mere presence nurtures a grander network that branches out from his own and provides support (no matter how insignificant) to the very environment that surrounds it. Thus, the honeycomb pattern (and the wisdom of Gopher) ostensibly explains the fundamental balancing force of the cosmos, while explaining the fragile place that we, as humble two-leggeds, hold within it.

Gorilla
Essence

Despite his powerful appearance, Gorilla is a gentle vegetarian who prefers to discourage confrontation by beating his chest and hooting aggressively. After a gestation period of 270 days, a single baby is born. Gorilla is currently at risk of extermination and extinction because of the increasing demand for his meat. Gorilla represents our potential to overcome the greatest obstacles with gentleness, unconditional love, faith and commitment. The Silverback maintains his position, not with muscle or brawn, but with a gentle heart and compassion. We as a race could learn a great deal from this animal, but instead we choose to murder and eat them. Gorilla eats plants and vegetation and rarely takes the life of another for food. He cries, dreams and holds hopes for his children. Gorilla shares 97% of the same DNA as we do, making him one of our closest living relatives represented in the animal kingdom. If we lose him, we lose our very foothold on reality; we lose faith in everything along with the potential of our race.

Those finding themselves investigating the acumen of Gorilla are being primed for a time of personal reflection. Gorilla invites us to look closely at our lives and to consider where we could be gentler on ourselves. Being that Gorilla will do everything in his power to avoid confrontation, those working with Gorilla often do not address important issues in their lives in favour of keeping peace with those around them. Gorilla people take their responsibilities seriously, often living as if the world itself may collapse in a heap if they let their guard down. They live to make others happy, only feeling safe and secure when those around them are at peace. Gorilla people rarely leave places of employ or relationships (although they may secretly entertain the idea) even when they are grieving for change or yearning to follow their hearts. To avoid falling victim to the wants and needs of others, Gorilla encourages us to contemplate the things that may offer freedom and joy. To embrace Gorilla is to return to one's essence and consider those things that make our hearts sing. Gorilla asks us to be honest and to show gentleness and loyalty to ourselves instead of beating our chest in an act of defiance and evasion, burning ourselves out emotionally and physically as a puppet to expectation and tradition.

Grouse
Doorway

Once considered a game species, Grouse was regularly hunted for sport and food. He is famous for his elaborate courtship displays; a sacred dance that concludes with the male and female coming together to mate. Many native people recognise the sacredness espoused by the ritualistic dance of Grouse. The dance follows the path of the spiral: a path that leads you deep within your centre and reunites you with all of creation. The spiral is an ancient symbol of inner journey, spiritual vision and self-illumination. Grouse guides us through the time-honoured dance of life that promises to reunite us with the ebbs and flows of Nature and the cyclic ritual that is our own body.

Grouse raises our awareness to the magic of the menstrual cycle, for example, a sacred facet of life that powerfully re-enacts the process of life, death and rebirth, the progressive phases of moon and the ever-rotating seasons. The dance of the Sufi is an act of surrender. As they twirl, the dancers raise their left hand to receive divine blessings and lower their right hand as a sign of offering. They twirl to acknowledge that everything in life moves in a circular way and to seek harmony with that Universal motion. They twirl to surrender to and unite with the Divine and to attain a higher level of consciousness. Their intention is not to lose themselves in the frenzy of the dance however, but rather to find their sacred place in the greater scheme of things leading them to their inner world where they may reunite with their innate self. The word *dervish* literally means 'door' and portrays one who stands pondering the path to spiritual enlightenment. Grouse also represents this path that leads you deep within your Inner Landscape where you will be offered the chance to surrender and re-emerge as a whole, healed individual who knows their purpose and believes themselves equal and worthy of all things.

Guinea Fowl

Forewarning

Travelling in flocks of several hundred monogamous pairs, Guinea Fowl is an incredibly noisy bird, emitting a rapid, ear-piercing 'clack clack' call at the slightest hint of danger. Although female Guinea Fowl will often contribute to a single communal nest, both the male and the female care for the brood once hatched. Terrestrial during daylight hours, Guinea Fowl typically roosts in trees at night to avoid predators. Guinea Fowl is also considered as an effective watchdog. Naturally wary of strangers, he warns landowners of predatory animals and human trespassers.

According to Greek legend, African Guinea Fowl was said to correspond energetically with the protective properties of amber, the fossilised resin of pine trees. Sophocles, the Greek playwright, poetically noted that Guinea Fowl wept tears of amber which was prescribed by healers as a means of deterring chronic depression and suicidal tendencies. Honouring his vibrational connection to the powerful healing stone, Guinea Fowl benefits those who are feeling weighed down with responsibilities. His loud clacking call warns of approaching darkness. Guinea Fowl feathers can be carried to reverse and send back pessimistic thoughts and the influence of negative 'witchcraft'. Invoke Guinea Fowl or carry his feathers the moment you feel powerless or out of control. With his aggressive, no-nonsense attitude to life, the appearance of Guinea Fowl will enhance mental clarity while validating, grounding and stabilising one's life path.

Guinea Pig
Motivation

Now 'famous' as a laboratory animal, Guinea Pig, or Cavy, was domesticated over 6,000 years ago by the people of Peru and has become a much loved pet in many households the world over due to his unassuming nature, minimal needs and his wide variety of colours and hair lengths. Guinea Pig is easily housed, rarely jumps, bites or scratches and is not known for his burrowing abilities: these traits having bred out over generations of domestication.

The term 'guinea pig' has come to refer to someone used to trial new ideas, skills or products. For example, one might say, 'I used my good friend as a Guinea Pig for a new recipe'. As such, Guinea Pig offers his wisdom as a guiding light; a beacon that illuminates the way to new discovery. Guinea Pig is the test pilot that leads the way to the innovation of new forms of healing, medicine and scientific exploration. Guinea Pig people are driven by discovery. They are passionate about helping people and find great joy in helping people find better ways to help people. Guinea Pig people often find themselves taking one step forward and two steps back as they endeavour to find answers to questions that may unlock the secrets to new opportunity. Despite countless setbacks however, they usually remain steadfast in their resolve, willing to trial and error in their quest for explanations. Few truly understand the motives that drive the Guinea Pig person, but all are amazed and grateful for the fruits of his labour. A guide that illuminates the way, Guinea Pig physically channels new information, giving of himself to benefit the people. Guinea Pig primes us for new discovery, a surprise suggestion or new idea, the investigation of an alternative form of healing, medicine or health treatment or an offer to participate in some innovative undertaking that promises to enhance the planet.

Gull
Correct behaviour

Gull has lived in close proximity to humans for thousands of years and belongs to a large family represented by many species, most of which nest inland. Gull takes advantage of updrafts of air and soars over large distances with very physical little effort. Gull eats almost anything and is a valuable scavenger. She is territorial and ruthless in her defence. During territorial defence, mating ritual or parent/chick interaction, Gull exhibits a complex series of communicative behaviour displaying intricate body language and emitting calls that are multifaceted in both form and function. A Gull trying to woo a mate will perform a 'threat' pose, but in a modified sequence that alters the initial meaning of the display.

Gull offers insight into the acceptable and expected protocol of any new group, community or association we may have joined or are considering joining. Everyone has attended a dinner party and has felt unsure as to what knife or fork to use first, for example. There is nothing worse than the first day at a new school or job and not recognising anyone. Worse still, making a social mistake that makes you look and feel silly. Often these experiences are made worse by stress and uncertainty. Gull gives us the presence of mind to calmly observe others before taking action ourselves (just as Gull casually glides over the rough waves, assessing the torrid sea below before descending to its surface to fish). Gull makes us aware of group dynamics and hierarchy so that we do not tread on toes. She encourages us to wait for and recognise appropriate cues and signals so that we appear knowing. Gull teaches us the 'correct behaviour' in any situation.

Hamster

Keepsake

 When foraging for food, Hamster packs as much as she can into her expandable cheek pouches and carries it back to her burrow to consume later. She is commonly kept as a pet and as a laboratory animal because of her high rate of fertility with the most popular pet being Syrian or Golden Hamster. All Golden Hamsters originated from a single 'golden' female found in Syria in 1930 along with a nest of 12 young. The word 'Hamster' is a derivative of the German verb *hamstern*, which means 'to hoard', while the word 'hoard' has come to mean 'accumulate or collect'.

Hamster people love to keep reminders of times past; souvenirs of holidays, celebrations, photographs and rites of passage. Hamster is all about research and the quiet accumulation of knowledge; a compendium that celebrates humanity and our role in it. She supports us as we accrue a library of recollections that will support and educate future generations of their past. She encourages us to dig up our past, to probe our ancestral lineage and to explore the history of the land we call home in search of truth, and to record all that we find for the benefit of ourselves and our children. Hamster demonstrates that when we take the time to discover our past, carefully examine our 'family tree' and employ experts to access 'family heirlooms', we sometimes unearth golden surprises that not only enrich the perceptions of our Ancestors, but promise to enhance the quality of our life and that of future generations. Hamster speaks of unexpected inheritance usually discovered in the form of valuables discarded or overlooked as 'junk'. She also helps us find answers to questions that have plagued the family for years and reclaim the power or wealth wrongfully meted out by perfidious relatives. She respectfully exhumes family 'skeletons', secrets and deceptions that have shaped our lineage up til now and reveals what could have been if they had been truthfully and honourably exposed earlier.

Hare
Lunar energy

Brown Hare is larger than Rabbits and adapts quickly to new environments, surviving in habitats known to offer little or no protection against the elements and predators. Hare is solitary by nature and sleeps in shallow indentations (called a 'form') dug into the ground, protected by a shrub, hedge, brambles or tall grass. When disturbed, Hare will bolt, her tail tucked low and her body carried high on long, powerful legs.

Easter is a Christian sacrosanct religious holiday and the term 'Easter' originated with the Scandinavian goddess Oestra; a moon goddess whose responsibilities included spring and fecundity and who was sometimes depicted bearing the head of a Hare. The 'Easter Bunny' was birthed as a concept from the legend of Oestra's Hare; a symbol of fertility, renewal, and return of spring. So potent was Oestra's ability to inspire fertility, the word *oestrus* was established to announce when an animal went into 'season', heat or rut and describes the period of heightened sexual interaction between the sexes in preparation for spring. The menstrual cycle in women was once referred to as the 'Moon Flow', and it was observed that this fertile time often fell around the time of the full moon. Sanskrit describes the moon as being *cacin*, which translates to 'marked with the Hare'. Hindus believe that the spots on the moon can be clearly seen forming the shape of a Hare. Superstition once ruled that woman should not pray to God because God was the 'God of Men'. Instead, it was considered more appropriate for women to pray to their own heavenly body: the moon. Hare suggests 'drawing down the moon', a ritual used to empower and unite the feminine essence with the goddess. The three 'main' phases are celebrated: the waxing or 'new' moon is said to embody the qualities of the 'maiden' and inspire inspiration, bravery, change, improving health, career and job prospects, patience, love and romance. The full moon is said to represent the 'mother' with a full, round belly, our children's potential, decision making, self-empowerment, healing and dreams, while the waning moon describes the 'crone', or when a soul is preparing to pass to the Underworld. Hare governs the feminine side of intuition, esoteric knowledge, wisdom, higher learning and the power that the understanding can bring if harnessed and channelled productively. She represents the greater balancing force that cradles and nurtures the perceived world, and personifies the mysterious or unconscious energy that provides the fertile basis on which creative events occur. She also represents the dormant potential just waiting for the active (physical or masculine) principle to bring things to fruition.

Arctic Hare
Avoidance

 Arctic Hare has grey/brown fur during the summer months and bright white fur in the winter. In the northern-most regions however, she may retain her white coat all year round and raises her multiple young in fur-lined nests built in depressions in the ground, protected behind rocks or under a coarse bush.

Arctic Hare encourages us to live our dreams, be carefree and true to ourselves. She calls for us to listen to our intuition, to remain loyal to our imaginings and to avoid allowing logic or reason to persuade our decisions. Although this is a beautiful way of approaching life, Arctic Hare people can be impractical and irresponsible as a result. They are romantics who go with the flow and flit from one thing to the next. They can appear 'moonstruck' or suffering from inspired madness. Creative, spontaneous and 'fun', Arctic Hare people make ineffective decision makers; their actions often adversely affected by the people they meet and the peripheral circumstances at the time. They are adaptable, independent, selfish and, at times, dismissive. They appear to honour what others demand of them, but instead, only create the illusion of dependability to avoid the pressure of expectation. They are loyal first and foremost to their own yearnings, wants and desires. Arctic Hare people have a definite need for comfort, security and elegance. They *love* decadence and finery. But, on the other hand, they hate being confined or depended upon. Their feelings are changeable. They are unpredictable and shrewd. They avoid commitment and confrontation and when we expect them to be brave and willing to face adversity, they will duck for cover and flee, but when we think they might run, they are courageous and enduring. Arctic Hare people, although fickle, are honest, cautious and diplomatic. They never hurry, but are always on time. Arctic Hare people treasure marriage, closeness and good friends, but make for undisciplined parents and role-models. Arctic Hare suggests that our obsession for freedom and beauty be moderated with accountability and invites us to consider how our carefree existence may affect us later. Balance and temperance are the keys to harnessing Arctic Hare Dreaming. We don't want to reach old age and realise that we are alone, sad, bitter and broke; a common side effect of a life spent dancing naked in the moonlight without a care in the world or a second thought for those around us.

• Jackrabbit – *Aphrodisia*

A member of the Hare family, Jackrabbit is a solitary creature, except during the mating season when she may congregate in very small groups and produce between one and four litters a year. It is said that a pinch of dried Jackrabbit holds powerful aphrodisiacal qualities, potent enough to invite the physical affections of another. Whether fact or fiction, traditional local folklore offers much insight into the wisdom of all animals. All members of the Rabbit and Hare family enjoy abundant fertility (as compensation for being targeted as a favourite source of food by so many carnivorous animals).

Jackrabbit is imbued with powerful sexual energy, both personally and when invoked on a symbolic level as an aid or support by those who admire her for her wisdom and medicine. Jackrabbit Dreaming, when invoked with pure intent, affords fertility-boosting qualities even when all hopes have been lost. She helps clear fear and worry, which are powerful enough to block creativity on any level, while inviting submissiveness, tenderness and trust; ingredients that jointly offer possibility. Jackrabbit shuns solitude by dispelling fear. Jackrabbit people yearn to be loved, needed and missed. When they do meet potential partners, they often sabotage their chances of a relationship by rushing in too quickly, being overly protective or jealous, or backing off almost immediately blaming themselves for the perceived incompatibility. Jackrabbit people, too, often have trouble conceiving or carrying full term. Jackrabbit people are vulnerable to negative suggestion and tend to believe the fears or inadequacies of others, integrating them into their own lives as personal truth. Jackrabbit Dreaming therefore, reverses such fear, packages it neatly and sends it back to its source. Jackrabbit inspires excitement, happiness and sensuality, and is useful in the combating of all fear and insecurity so that any new venture or phase (represented by a baby or not) may be considered as a possibility and eventually birthed as reality.

• Snowshoe Hare – *Quick wit*

Snowshoe Hare, or Varying Hare, takes his name from his broad, heavily furred feet that allow him to safely traverse deep snow (in much the same way a pair of snowshoes afford human travellers safe navigation). His coat changes colour with the seasons: tawny brown in the summer and snow-white in the winter (for obvious reasons).

Snowshoe Hare carries the wisdom of trickster and hero for the people who share his land because of his quick-thinking mind, which is nimble enough to outsmart even the most physically gifted. As if blessed by the elements themselves, Snowshoe Hare is said to embody the qualities of both wind and water, with some saying he 'stole the sun' and others referring to him as 'brother to the snow'. Snowshoe Hare is the totem of those gifted with a sharp mind. Expert problem solvers, Snowshoe Hare people are adept at avoiding confrontation, negotiating deals and 'skating on thin ice' with no fear of negative repercussion. They are skilled at bluffing and hiding their true emotions behind a veneer of indifference. Snowshoe Hare people are adaptable, charming and talented. They acclimatise easily to new settings or situations and blend well into a crowd, instantly (and with incredible ease) becoming everyone's friend and ally – as if they had always been there. Snowshoe Hare endorses shrewd flexibility and preparedness. Snowshoe Hare people are often described as being born with silver spoons in their mouth, with 'the gods' smiling favourably on them at all times. Those who embrace his wisdom must be able to chop and change, travel light, take educated risks and be prepared to snap into action with little or no warning. If they remain committed in their efforts and alert to the pitfalls, good fortune, abundance and nimbleness will be theirs for the taking.

Hawk

Messages

 Hawk is a diurnal carnivore, meaning he hunts live prey during the day. Some members of the Hawk family can reach great speeds while in flight and are capable of taking prey while flying. Venerated as an Ancestor by some of the Indigenous People of Australia, Hawk was regarded as the protector of the Warrior Spirit. He is revered as a primary messenger deity of Creation in ancient Greek, Egyptian, Native American, Ainu and Madagascan folklore, and is seen therefore, as an omen of good tidings and is viewed as a positive warning, a harbinger of healthy change and a portent of success in battle. Hawk is said to be one of the great solar birds supposedly able to stare directly at the sun without squinting. To be able to look directly into the sun and not have to look away is symbolic of being able to look directly at an issue and to see what needs to be acknowledged and addressed. To witness a Hawk in flight, to hear his cry, or to find one of his feathers suggests that Creation is on the march and that we should prepare to receive a message or sign from Spirit.

Hawk prefers that we look at life from the viewpoint of the bigger picture, as he does with far-seeing eyes. Hawk primes us to ask for and receive the signs of Spirit; signs that will guide us to the next phase of our life. Hawk warns that we may be viewing the world from a limited vantage point and that other issues may be hampering our vision. He helps initiate forward movement by forcing us to challenge our personal demons and welcome long overdue, but necessary, confrontations. One cannot expect new life to spring from desolation unless a promise is made to honour the process. Like Bilby who tends to view the world with fear and trepidation, we can expect life to remain static when we choose to not to broaden our perspective, embrace the bigger picture and initiate forward movement.

• Pale Chanting Goshawk – *Candidness*

 Pale Chanting Goshawk is often found perched on open branches in plain view of his prey; a tendency rarely practiced by other raptors. Pale Chanting Goshawk has a cousin, Dark Chanting Goshawk, who has darker banding on his feathers but similar to look at in every other way.

A member of the Hawk family, Goshawk is generically seen as a messenger of Spirit: an omen of change, prosperity, new beginnings, change or conception. Each species of Hawk identifies a specific genre of message that independently offers a greater level of awareness and wider perspective of life. The message delivered by Pale Chanting Goshawk is that of honesty. To have him make an appearance is to be warned that you must be frank, open and up front about something at this time. 'Truth at all costs' must be your mantra. Do not hesitate, avoid or deny the truth from being revealed. You may be asked a question or be pushed to offer an opinion, and the only advice at hand is that you speak from a place of honour – no matter what trepidation you may feel regarding the possible outcome. Dark Chanting Goshawk however, suggests that you dampen the level of candidness you would normally surrender and encourages honesty at all costs. He suggests you answer questions with questions, so that you can buy time or stall the inevitable unveiling of truth. Answering in riddles is different from hiding or deceiving. Choosing to only reveal a truth when the question is specifically worded is a way of protecting another, for example, while maintaining personal integrity.

• Gyrfalcon – *Orientation*

 Gyrfalcon is a raptorial bird of prey indigenous to the Arctic tundra and is the largest and most powerful of the Falcons. During medieval times, Gyrfalcon was the most valued of all Falcons, possessed only by royalty who sought the bird as a symbol of eminence and power. There was nothing they liked better than being seen in public accompanied by hoards of falconers carrying Gyrfalcons on their wrists. The Gyrfalcon was named after its habit of flying in circles; the word 'gyrate' suggests revolving around a fixed point or axis, to move in spiral or spiral-like course or to move in a cyclical fashion.

Gyrfalcon encourages us to maintain focus on all desired goals; to circle, watch and wait for the perfect moment to initiate their realisation and to nurture a confident, forward momentum when offered a tangible window of opportunity to grasp their potential and bring them to fruition. Gyrfalcon people are those whose sights are set on majestic heights and whose ambitions are set apart from those of the average man. They are keenly aware of their abilities and show impeccable resolve in their desire to see their targets reached. Gyrfalcon illustrates that the most successful ideas are those allowed to unfold in their own time and which we never lose faith in, or indiscriminately chop and change as we see fit. Gyrfalcon people are supreme hunters, stalking their prey with integrity and grace. They stealthily circle their objective and never deviate from their master plan. Their motto is 'onwards and upwards', striving for ever-higher vantage points, never losing focus of their original plan. Gyrfalcon endorses a steady forward march, with the only back-pedalling being that which ensures new direction or the refinement of the bigger picture.

Hedgehog
Anointing

Hedgehog is a small spiny mammal said to be immune to many toxins and poisons. Hedgehog spines are actually hollow hairs strengthened by keratin and are only shed when Hedgehog is stressed or ill. When threatened, Hedgehog will roll into a tight ball, defensively pointing her spines outward. Hedgehog is nocturnal and hibernates during the winter months. 'Groundhog Day' is an American practice derived from European tradition introduced during the eighteenth century. The emergence of animals such as Hedgehog symbolised the imminent arrival of spring. Hedgehog is said to perform a ritual called anointing. When she comes across a foreign scent, for example, she secretes an aromatic froth from her mouth which she mixes with the new smell or taste and applies it to her spines in an attempt to disguise her own odour with the new one. She is also said to chew the skin of Toads, mangling the venom from the dead animal's parotoid glands, mixing it with her own saliva and then coating her spines with the concoction. The 'anointed' spines then apparently prove more painful and irritating when hapless predators try to eat them.

Hedgehog should be invoked when it is apparent that the winds of change have stopped blowing in an advantageous direction, or when our luck seems to have dried up or frozen over. Hedgehog helps to improve our chances of success by offering a window of opportunity to initiate new beginnings, but only when approached with a pure heart and true intent. One of the easiest and most familiar ways to inspire positive change is to burn a candle with an objective or desired outcome in mind. To enhance the potency of the ritual though, one should consider the colour of the candle to be used (with each colour said to carry specific symbolism and vibrational 'medicine'), and then anoint the candle with an oil imbued with qualities that support the outcome. As you light the candle, state your 'wish' out loud and allow the candle to burn down and go out naturally.

Hippopotamus

Volatility

Hippopotamus is a Greek word meaning 'River Horse'. Forced to spend much of her daylight hours submerged due to the fact that her skin loses moisture at an alarming rate when exposed to the air, Hippopotamus will nibble on aquatic plants while 'floating' with only her eyes and nostrils evident above the water. Loafing on the river banks in a deceptively mild-mannered way, Hippopotamus is responsible for the bulk of animal-related human deaths in Africa and regularly play-fights to establish and maintain hierarchy, but when provoked, the males will fight to the death.

People who find the strength to eventually say 'no more' after years of abuse or oppression generally discover what it means to carry the energy of Hippopotamus by accident. Those of us who live a life of pretence, forced silence or persecution are like submerged Hippopotamus: calmly drifting through the cool waters of an otherwise unsympathetic and perilous environment, interacting productively with our friends and family on a day-to-day basis while going through the motions of a 'normal' life, but unbeknownst to anyone, internally steaming like a volcano on the verge of emotional eruption. Hippopotamus offers a voice to those who find themselves silenced by external forces. Preferring that we seek help and put trust in others; that we speak up and let others know how we are faring and that we do everything we can to regain our Personal Power instead of constantly and willingly giving it away, Hippopotamus rejects the implementation of the victim mentality and the overindulgence of the 'prostitute' trait found innately within each of us. Hippopotamus endorses the fact that we all have a voice, that we are all equal and that without our input, the world would be less than perfect.

• Pygmy Hippopotamus – *Divinity*

Fossilised remnants reveal that numerous species of Hippopotamus once inhabited Africa. Only two remain today, however, with Pygmy Hippopotamus being the smallest. According to archaic lore, the Hippopotamus was a divine embodiment of the goddess Taueret or Ta-urt, wife of Set, who was also portrayed, at times, as a red Hippopotamus. Due to a lack of sebaceous or temperature-regulating glands, both breeds of Hippopotamus secrete a pink-red liquid that dries to form a protective lacquer on the surface of the skin: a discharge that works as protection against both sun-burn and parasitic insect bites, but which was first erroneously believed to be blood 'sweated' out by the animal (a phenomenon interpreted as a promise of new life, longevity and potent fertility from the goddess herself). The appearance of a pregnant Pygmy Hippopotamus was received as an auspicious symbol of both abundance and fecundity.

The realisation that life is rich and rewarding is an understanding birthed from a deep appreciation of Pygmy Hippopotamus Dreaming. Life is what you make of it. Spirituality is a way of life, to be integrated into every step you take. It is to celebrate your abilities and to use them as a way of enhancing the lives of those around you. As you begin to explore the feminine force that inherently stirs within all people, you open a doorway that welcomes powerful new beginnings. You invite a tidal wave of insight, emotion and spiritual belonging to flood in, reawakening an ancient yet dormant relationship with the goddess archetype. If you have recently noticed Pygmy Hippo, a spiritual approach toward life is needed at this time, as well as the understanding that Spirit is watching everything you do. To allow your actions to be guided by Spirit and to call to the Ancestors for inspiration is to comprehend the essence of Pygmy Hippopotamus Dreaming. You are a wholesome personification of the Creator Spirit. The god and the goddess reside deep within your soul. You walk in balance. The blood of the Earth Mother flows through your veins, to be 'expressed' when needed, and with this knowing, you are divine. You hold the power within you to manifest, to heal and to communicate on all levels.

Hoopoe
Ambivalence

 A reticent bird, Hoopoe prefers the single life or to travel in pairs, although relaxed flocks will often band together during the migration season. Hoopoe is a cavity-nester, seeking out hollows and cracks in rocky outcrops or in the walls of buildings. A 'soul bird' and a messenger of the spirit world, Hoopoe is said to be gifted with the ability to detect underground springs and hidden wells and is therefore considered sacred, in part for her water-divining skills, but also for her role as 'the doctor bird'. As with many sacred animals however, Hoopoe has two faces. On one hand, the bird was held in high esteem because she was believed to bring food to her ailing parents (an honourable trait) and because she presented a viable source of mystical knowledge to the people, but on the other she was feared as a harbinger of deception and loathing.

To carry the ambivalent wisdom of Hoopoe is to walk in two worlds: one in which you enjoy being self-assured, sociable and admired by others, and another in which you find yourself feeling reserved, hesitant and discounted. These two worlds may be how you are received in life or it may be how you perceive your place within it. This is not only confusing for you, but very off-putting for those who are trying to share your world. It is hard to read people who chop and change emotionally. People who are dissatisfied or disillusioned with life tend to have difficulty initiating new friendships or sustaining established ones. If you find yourself being drawn to investigate Hoopoe, the wisdom essentially boils down to you needing to make decisions. To be true to yourself instils within your soul a sense of peace, harmony and unconditional love. When one is in this space, others feel the shift and are instinctively drawn to the energy. They begin to see you as you now see yourself. So, if you want people to treat you with disdain and fear, continue radiating disturbing, unsettled energy. But if you would prefer people to admire you for becoming who you were meant to be and for believing in your intuition, dreams and self-purpose, then learn to love yourself. Ease up on the self-punishment and reclaim your Personal Power.

Hornbill

Providence

 Hornbill becomes quite tame when exposed to human contact and although he will kill and eat Snakes and Lizards, he can often be found scavenging around restaurants at dinnertime, feeding on morsels thrown to him by fascinated tourists. 'Horned One' was an archaic title of Mother Hera as the divine Moon Cow, because her horns were said to be imbued with the fertile energies of the moon. She was acknowledged in many belief systems, in both feminine and masculine form, but typically depicted as a 'horned' deity of fertility, abundance, sexual energy and protection. Today, the death of the old year and the 'birth' of the new are still celebrated with the victorious trumpeting of horns. Hornbill kills Snakes and are deemed providential because he creates a place free of both venomous Snakes and evil spirits. A spiritual filter of sorts, Hornbill is seen as the eliminators of those that would bring 'negative' visions, thoughts and illness, dark-side entities and malevolent souls. Hornbill, it is thought, only kills Snakes that threaten the wellbeing of the people.

If you have had Hornbill make himself known to you, then be warned that you have some filtering to do, and if done properly your life will begin to flow gainfully. Hornbill suggests that the Ancestors are watching and guiding your actions at present, and that no matter how unlikely it may seem, your luck and fortune are about to change. Before the providential wisdom of Hornbill can be integrated fully, however, understand that you are being primed to address some interference from the past that may be haunting you and blocking your potential, or some meddling occurring (on any level) right now. Be aware, too, that Hornbill's relationship with Snake (an ancient phallic representation of sexual potency) suggests the chance to confront perpetrators of sexual interference or control by helping to create a safe environment in which you will be heard and protected. Hornbill reminds us that before we can live a productive, abundant life (you are a naturally lucky and blessed person), blockages, interference and fear must be exorcised before the energy previously used to support them can be fruitfully employed to bring new projects, relationships or cycles to fruition.

Horse
Personal power

Since the beginning of time, no single animal has afforded mankind the gift of physical freedom as Horse has. However, he has gradually been abandoned for the convenience of the motor vehicle but still kept for leisure, sports and entertainment. Wild Horses run free in many parts of the world, either as a native species or as a feral (introduced and set free) breed. Australia, for example, is famous for the Brumby, a resilient, 'wild' horse which is a derivation of the domestic Horse brought to Australia during European settlement. A universal symbol of strength and endurance, Horse is represented in myth and legend as a revered cohort of the Gods and as a potent spiritual creature in his own right. When Horse was first introduced to the people, he strengthened their view of the world, affording them greater understanding of the land because he allowed them to explore the horizon on a scale never experienced before. Although his introduction brought disruption to tradition, Horse quickly became a sacred animal to many ancient cultures and was a symbol of strength and power.

Due to his ancient association with transport and travel, Horse reveals the true essence of Personal Power: our inherent gift or sacred philosophy that drives us onward and upward. Horse brings to light what it means to be unique and sacred, by highlighting our Personal Power. Personal Power is first realised the moment we are conceived, with the hope that we will embrace it and share it with others and teach them how to awaken their own during the course of our life. Personal Power is knowledge; acumen accumulated over lifetimes of experience that lifts us from the mundane and delivers us into the realisation of unlimited potential. When knowledge is gathered and is used for the betterment of the self (and others), it gathers in energy. This energy becomes passion, the motivation to move forward, grow and expand on all levels. Personal Power is awareness that comes from being connected to Spirit and all things of Nature. Personal Power is the embodiment of personal wisdom of the remembering of who we truly are. It is a gift to the people from Creation and represents our purpose and the reason for which we were born. It offers us the chance to make a difference in the world and to make life richer for others. Traditionally, Horse stands at each of the four cardinal points on the great Wheel of Life, with yellow Palomino protecting the East, Red Chestnut standing in the South, Black Horse guarding the West and Grey Horse representing the energies of the North (according to Northern Hemisphere tradition). Each of the four directions offer a sacred gift of knowledge that can only be attained when we symbolically journey to each point and integrate the wisdom into our conscious lives. With the East comes the gift of illumination and clarity, and with the North, innocence and passion. In the West we learn to understand the concepts of introspection and contemplation, and in the South we are offered maturity and discernment. With this symbology to uphold, Horse encourages us to put our ears back and gallop in the first direction that takes our fancy. Horse channels knowledge from every corner of the spiritual globe so that we may develop a unified belief system that will contribute to the enrichment of our Personal Power, while priming us for a journey to a place of great personal Power: our inner self. Horse stimulates the passion to shun idleness and stagnation, qualities that threaten to dampen the creative aspects of our soul. He encourages us to move forward, for it doesn't matter which direction we initially take in our quest for Personal Power. As long as we take the first step to finding it, we will.

• Mongolian Wild Horse – *Renaissance*

 Mongolian Wild Horse, or Przewalski's Horse, is one of the few surviving species of true 'Wild Horse' left in the world. Because of his habit of constantly raiding crops and breaking through fences, Mongolian Wild Horse was killed in the thousands, delivering him into extinction as a wild species. Of the 800 or so that survived in public zoos and private collections throughout the world, many were united in a captive breeding program that saw 55 animals in the late 1990s successfully reintroduced into the wilds of Mongolia. According to legend, there is a Horse stationed at each of the four cardinal points on the great Wheel of Life, with Yellow Horse (Palomino) in the East (according to Northern Hemisphere tradition), White Horse (Grey) in the North, Black in the West and Red Horse (Chestnut) in the South. Each of the four points represents a rite of passage that must be explored when we journey forward symbolically (and physically) around the Wheel of Life. Each rite of passage is imbued with a sacred lesson intended to enhance the potency of the journey and, in turn, our life as a whole, with each Horse respectively charged with their delivery.

The powerful animal directs us to put our ears back, to gallop in the first direction that takes our fancy, collect the knowledge that speaks the loudest and the truest from every corner of the spiritual globe, and from that develop our own personal belief system. Typically, Horse refers to travel, conscious movement forward and decisions and action that see us venture out into the world in order to find our fortune and discover our purpose. Horse rejects stillness and stagnation by encouraging us to experiment with new ideas, explore new territories and reach ever greater heights. A Horse in its purest, wildest, most ancient form, however, the Mongolian Wild Horse encourages us to travel *back* and *within* to explore our personal or family history for clues as to our purpose and Personal Power. Mongolian Wild Horse reminds us of the wealth of experience, library of knowledge and sacred understanding stored on a genetic level within each and every cell of our subconscious body, our past life associations and the inherent gifts and abilities passed down from one generation to the next. Acumen held sacred by 'the people' is what motivates Mongolian Wild Horse Dreaming. He offers permission to work with what we have, to take the knowledge that has supported our family for possibly generations and to remodel it so that it offers traditional understanding in a contemporary way. If you carry Mongolian Wild Horse Dreaming, consider the possibility that your purpose may include rebirthing the ancient or traditional ways of *your* people. You may very well be a messenger or storyteller. Changing personal history is a powerful tool that, once mastered, allows us to remove blockages and limiting programs by travelling back to where they first emerged. By dealing with them there, they are effectively eliminated, roots and all, from our consciousness, thus, allowing us to 'forget' they were ever there at all.

• Pony – *Challenge*

 The term 'Pony' usually refers to certain breeds of small Horse, and is often described as unpredictable, intolerant and unsuitable as a child's mount. Ponies were commonly used as 'Pit Ponies' in mainland Britain to haul coal out of the mines when, in the mid-nineteenth century, it became illegal to employ children to do such work. During this time, thousands of Shetland Ponies worked and lived their entire lives working the dark underground tunnels. There are several legends, especially in Celtic folklore, that link Pony with the sea, and equally as many that associate him with rivers or lakes. Those unlucky enough to mount these Ponies would usually see themselves carried into the water and drowned; a ride that embodies the classic journey to the Underworld depicted in traditional tales the world over. Like the 'Pit Ponies' themselves, many who visited the Underworld did so knowing they may never see the light of day again. Perhaps the most famous, though, is Kelpie: a water spirit said to take the form of a White Pony with a mane reminiscent of the foam created by the waves of the sea. It is said that if a human rider is quick enough to replace Kelpie's bridle with a regular one, Kelpie will make a wonderful and compliant Pony. The secret, however, in keeping a Kelpie is to not imprison him for too long or he may curse the lives of the rider and his family.

Pony asks that you be sure of what you want before embarking on any quest or adventure. Although you may seem to get what you want by invoking Pony Dreaming, if your intentions are not clear or pure, the warning is that you might get more than what you bargained for, with your original objective being discarded or destroyed along the way. In most cases, those who dare to explore the wisdom of Pony start off okay, but after a while (be it because they become nonchalant or because their ego gets in the way), they seem to lose control and come off second best. If you are prepared to work hard, stay focused, be accountable at all times for your behaviour and attitude and remain on task even when things seem to go askew, then chances are Pony will support your venture and see you eventually come out on top. Pony does not offer an easy ride or a quick trip to success and challenges us at every turn, often inspiring fear, doubt and momentary periods of blind panic. Pony people yearn to venture out into the world to explore and to seek their fortune and often demand that others help them or support them on their way. Pony people regularly set themselves up for a fall, getting kicked back into submission over and over. Not until they are willing to bite back, however, and take responsibility for their attitude and obligation to their own wellbeing, will they overcome their weaknesses and find the strength and endurance to take up the reigns and reclaim control of their life. Pony only offers the high road to those fully prepared to make it on their own two feet and his wisdom is one that is both superficially empowering but emotionally devastating when handled with indifference.

Hummingbird
Wonder

 Hummingbird is famous for her ability to hover like a miniature helicopter and her name comes from the characteristic humming sound made by her wings. Hummingbird is the only species of bird capable of deliberate reverse flight and plays an important role in the pollination process, especially among trumpet-shaped flowers. Hummingbirds is among the world's smallest birds, with Bee Hummingbird recognised as the smallest bird in the world. It is said that if you capture Hummingbird and put her in a cage, she will surely die. Hummingbird's love of freedom is so passionate and her appreciation for beauty so rich, that anything that hinders the celebration of either weighs heavily on her heart.

Vibrating pure joy and excitement, Hummingbird resonates from the heart, nurturing integrity, impeccability and peace within those who embrace her. She reawakens our dormant sense of wonder for life and helps us recognise the beauty that surrounds us every day. Hummingbird alerts us to the threat of being negatively restricted, bound or confined (figuratively or not) by physical or mental responsibility. Hummingbird is lost on those who allow themselves to fall victim to domestic slavery or who put their wants, needs and desires aside in favour of those around them. She turns a spotlight on depression, resentment and frustration by helping us realise when we have fallen prey to their dark influence, energies and blinkered indications. Hummingbird people celebrate life to the fullest and refuse to suffer restriction of any kind. They bathe in the nectar of life, laugh from the heart and cry at the slightest hint of beauty. Although willing to take responsibility for their past and show accountability for their actions, they abhor being bound by expectation, gagged by guilt or regret or yoked by responsibility (except when appropriately remunerated or emotionally compensated). Hummingbird people often flit from one job to the next, have many friends and prefer to eat organically. Hummingbird encourages us to live life to the fullest, to hold freedom high on the agenda and to view the world with a wonder and innocence usually reserved for wide-eyed children.

Hyena

Eminence

Related to Mongoose, Hyena was once thought to be androgynous. Equipped with a mock penis, it is the most aggressive female who leads the pack with the most dominant defending her administration with little or no mercy until her eventual death, with her oldest daughter, or 'princess', naturally succeeding unless challenged, killed or deposed. Hyena is the only mammal known to practise genetic selection, where the oldest or strongest cub will kill or 'weed out' weaker or opposing siblings to ensure its own longevity. Hyena is the natural enemy of Lion; a relationship which should be considered by those who carry Hyena energy.

Hyena is a powerful totem for the able woman who relies on her own resources or who chooses to walk her path 'devoid' of men and their influences. Hyena can also be seen as the protector of men who have a history of giving their power over to the central women in their lives. Men who resonate with Hyena are usually in the midst of healing after years of abuse while remembering the strength of their yang aspect. They are discovering what it means to be a true male and, possibly for the first time in their lives, trusting their ability to dream and create. Those who resonate with Hyena deplore laziness, forceful control and people who dump responsibility on others, although they themselves tend to hide behind a façade of imposed confidence and frankness. Happy to nourish their soles on whatever titbit of praise or attention is offered to them, they forcefully instruct those around them to stand in their power. Scarred from being abandoned or feeling isolated, and forced to trust only their judgment in all situations, those who carry Hyena grow up viewing themselves as being the only ones capable of effectively bringing about change, maintaining control or keeping equilibrium within the home or workplace. Those who work with Hyena energy find themselves intentionally cleaning up after those around them, willingly tending to the wants and needs of their community and allowing their defensive egos to dominate. 'Skulking in the shadows' their worry is that someone may notice their countless fears and weaknesses, and so in order to avoid such interference, they keep others at bay by radiating an overwhelming sense of order and control. Their rigid view of the world may last a lifetime, or at least until they have cleared the programming that initially birthed the belief that they are unsupported or considered lesser by the key people in their lives. Then and only then is their laughter heard and felt to be true. Hyena people tend to laugh falsely, with a desire to hide how they truly feel about their lot in life. Hyena people are usually so busy proving their worth to themselves that they essentially forget who they are, what their childhood dreams were and what they were put here to do. The truth is all people, including those who work with Hyena, are divine beings, capable of achieving wondrous things. Hyena people, unfortunately, are usually the last to productively grasp the magnitude of their eminence, that's all.

Hyrax
Veracity

Hyrax is about the size of a Rabbit, but has squat, rounded ears, flattened claws that resemble hooves and a short tail and his feet sweat profusely as he runs, enhancing his traction. Despite his rodent-like appearance, Hyrax is actually a distant cousin of Elephant and Aardvark. Hyrax populations fluctuate depending on living conditions, with numbers peaking in rainy periods and social groups varying in size according to the availability of physical room. When feeding, Hyrax crops the grass with his side teeth instead of snipping it with his front teeth. The Bible makes occasional mention of the 'Coney', a reference assumed to be directed at Rabbit, but was in fact describing the Rabbit-like Hyrax. In Christian tradition the Coney was a symbol of over-abundant fertility and lust and was depicted settled at the feet of the Virgin Mary as a symbol of humanity's triumph over temptation. With this ancient connection to truth and integrity, the impeccable Hyrax stands by his obligation to ensure that we live veracious lives.

Although mistaken for an animal of a different species, Hyrax believes that everything happens for a reason and that there is no such thing as a mistake or a coincidence. Bound with ancestral devotion to the teachings of his cousin, African Elephant, Hyrax is heavily imbued with the pledge to honour his commitments and to set an impeccable example for others. To live impeccably is to live 'free of sin': a promise to always do what is right and good and to always speak the truth. Sure, as sentient beings we are born with an inquisitive mind but Hyrax, with his enhanced foothold and tendency to eat using its molars, urges us to watch how we navigate our physical path and to 'chew' on things a while before making rash or shallow decisions.

Jackal
Death

Jackal mates for life, is very family-oriented and will occasionally congregate in small packs. Both sexes patrol and defend territorial boundaries and unlike other Dogs that will howl in response to rival animals, Jackal will only answer the call of members of his own family. With a reputation for being a sly and cunning scavenger, Jackal is a profoundly successful hunter that adapts with ease to new environments. Anubis was a canine-headed, pointy-eared funerary deity of ancient Egypt charged with the duty of embalming and preparing the dead. Priests wearing masks of Anubis washed the entrails and watched over the physical body and the place in which they rested. Anubis was probably a Jackal because these animals were commonly seen lingering around the tombs and cemeteries of the dead. He was responsible for guiding the dead to those who judged their souls and became the one who steadied the scales used to weigh the hearts of the recently departed against the Feather of Ma'at. Should the scales balance, the soul would be led by Anubis to the Underworld. Should the scales not balance, the heart was fed to Ammut the 'devourer of the dead', the annihilator of criminal souls in the Underworld, and the soul destroyed forever.

Jackal initiates and endorses dramatic change and watches over those experiencing it as they weigh things up and decide their next course of action. Jackal celebrates every process of change as being symbolic of death; a ritual that sees the familiar aspects of the self surrendered in favour of a new phase. Jackal supports all necessary endings; those aspects of life that we know must be permitted to die a natural death, to be relinquished and let go. Jackal sustains us as we bring closure to all outworn aspects of life, but reminds us to hold truth and integrity as our highest priority in a way that supports all parties involved. Our intent must weigh pure when we call upon Jackal to assist us bring about change. If we fail to demonstrate impeccability in all our dealings, Jackal will deny all knowledge and abandon us in our efforts to see old doors productively close in our favour. Jackal can also be appealed to in times of physical passing or actual death. Call upon Jackal's Spirit to guide the dearly departed to the Otherworld, offering them safe passage and protection and to offer comfort and peace to those left behind. Jackal people make powerful mediators, assisting in the peaceful, mutually beneficial resolution of divorce, business collapse and finalisation of partnerships of any kind. Natural-born purifiers and cleaners, Jackal people are honourable, hardworking, trustworthy and humble, often taking responsibility for tasks assigned to other people or willingly doing jobs on behalf of others that could be deemed lowly or demeaning.

Jackdaw
Narcissism

Jackdaw is related to Crow and Raven and is a social bird that travels noisily in large flocks, with mated pairs maintaining tight bonds within the flock. He is an opportunist feeder, taking insects, small mammal, eggs, seeds and grain, carrion and food scraps from rubbish bins. He nests in hollow trees, rock cavities, in ruined or abandoned buildings and in dense vegetation and his presence is said to presage the coming of rain. Folklore has it that Jackdaw can be easily caught with a shallow pan of oil; the vain bird becoming so entranced by his reflection that he sacrifices his own safety in favour of staring longingly into the pan. Sigmund Freud first penned the term *narcissism* in relation to human psychology after Greek mythology's Narcissus' irrational obsession with his own reflection. Narcissism, as a diagnosed condition, is usually associated with those who think and act in ways that border on an obsession and fixation with themselves, usually to the exclusion of family and friends.

Jackdaw people are usually self-indulgent, attention-seeking, dominant, ambitious and insensitive braggarts and rely heavily on others to help with their day-to-day responsibilities and decision making. They tend to view themselves as superior or worthy of life's benefits, but at no cost or effort on their part. Jackdaw people are sociable, so long as all dialogue centres round them and their interests. The moment someone else steals the spotlight, they become irritable and bored. They are famous for being prattlers, boasters, gossips and imitators. Jackdaw people often fall victim to the vain assumption that others find them engaging or attractive. To the further detriment of their reputation, too, Jackdaw people are prone to looking at themselves as they pass by any reflective surface. Legend states that Jackdaw will visit the laurel tree (bay) and consume its leaves as a medicine. Laurel leaves are said to induce prophetic dreams and enhance psychic ability and are revered for their protective and purifying qualities. Most pertinent, though, is the belief that laurel leaves can be used to ward off evil, mental disease and physical illness and when burned with sandalwood, are said to lift 'curses'. If narcissism can be classified as a 'curse', then the esoteric properties of the bay laurel should be investigated for its supportive and healing resources. Jackdaw, when invoked as a curative, inspires a sense of inner peace, harmony and self-forgiveness. He stills the mind so that we may regain clarity and silence. Instead of escaping into a beautiful, imaginary world where we fantasise about having total physical and emotional control over our life, Jackdaw helps make it a reality by creating a forum in which our voice will be heard, self-imposed illusions shattered and self-healing facilitated. Jackdaw nurtures us as we realise that we are capable of being loved and that we are capable of loving others. He differentiates what it means to love one's self as opposed to being *in love* with one's self as form of defence. He gently returns us to a loving heart, instilling personal fertility and long-awaited good fortune.

Jaguar
Impeccability

Often confused with Leopard, Jaguar has a stockier build with rosettes on her coat complete with internal spots. Black Jaguars are often called 'Black Panthers' – a species that just doesn't exist. Black Jaguar is simply a regular Jaguar displaying the melanistic gene; a trait that produces an almost black pigmentation in the skin and fur.

Black Jaguar is considered a 'yin' animal. She is a lunar-influenced creature: both feminine in nature and imbued with the element of water. She is feared and revered by the Indigenous People of South America for her sophistication and power. Regulated by the energy of the dark moon and the feminine forces of Nature, Black Jaguar has long been shrouded in mystery and powerful medicine, with ties to the complexities of change, death, the evolution of the soul and the embracing of the unknown. Jaguar nurtures us as we struggle to appreciate death as a process that promises to see us emerge whole and reborn. 'Regular' Jaguar (as a solar-influenced creature; an emissary of fire and the sun), sheds light on death, so that we may fear it less and honour it as a sacred gift of power. According to the wisdom of Jaguar, death is best seen as a process that inspires deeper understanding of change and transformation. Death represents all that is known to be unknowable in relation to Spirit, our inherent selves and the Universe. Death forces us to step out and appreciate life and to live ours closer to Spirit. In doing so, we make a vow to avenge the death; to make it mean something. If Jaguar has stepped solemnly into your cards today, you're being offered the chance to embrace the unknown and explore the Void. She encourages us to only ask questions that we are prepared to receive answers for, and to take heed and honour how we respond to them. Jaguar teaches us to walk the warrior's path to freedom and to embrace 'death' in its many guises with faith and integrity. She asks that we demonstrate impeccable self-respect by walking in truth, the whole time honouring the life we live and how we live it in relation to our personal reality, and that we do so in a way that demonstrates unwavering commitment to the vows we made before entering the Earth plane.

Jungle Fowl
Obligation

Jungle Fowl is the ancestor of all contemporary farmyard Chickens. Some of the 'older' domestic strains (the game breeds and Brown Leghorns, for example) still hold the residual, telling coloration and feather patterning of their wild ancestors. There are populations of feral Fowl in the northern quarters of Australia that demonstrate how quickly domestic birds revert to the original Jungle Fowl colouring and appearance when left to their own devices. Habitat loss, poaching and the illegal harvesting of eggs for private collections have contributed to the decline in Asia's wild population of Jungle Fowl. The survival of the species therefore, is not only of environmental and genetic importance, but also as an assurance of the strength and endurance of the village poultry relied upon by the people of Asia. The male Jungle Fowl (the Cock or Rooster) welcomes the sun's golden rays with a concord of morning chorus and, as such, is held in high regard as a bird of solar influence. In India the Rooster is considered to be the personification of the sun's warming energy. In Japan the Rooster is the quintessence of the day's first rays of light. In China he embodies the five most favourable qualities of humanity. It is a bird of prophecy; positive in character and behaviour – his proud stance and erect comb affording him a sense of power and wisdom.

Jungle Fowl's ankle barbs denote an air of military calibre and the courage needed to honourably triumph in battle. He is revered for his 'goodness' for it is observed that he distributes his food evenly among his family and he represents poise and promise, because of the confidence radiated each time he greets the sun – quite contrary to the antagonistic, conceited animal many describe the Rooster as being. Jungle Fowl symbolises the hero, the guardian and protector of the people and his crow is said to drive away ghosts and phantoms, sending them back to their world. In welcoming the light of day, Jungle Fowl is said to dissolve illusion, darkness, deception and confusion. Those who carry the wisdom of the Jungle Fowl are easily described as being truthful, candid, considerate and brave. Jungle Fowl people give of themselves readily and wholeheartedly. They regard it as an honour and privilege to be of service to others. When invoked with pure intent, Jungle Fowl holds the potential to bring any dream to fruition (legend says that Rooster could find an Earthworm in a desert). The downside, though, is that those who carry the wisdom of Jungle Fowl are usually very extravagant with their money (they would say they were generous), they have difficulty resisting temptation and are usually plagued by bad luck (as observed in the way Rooster scuffs the ground for his food). Jungle Fowl people, when working with their more 'negative' qualities, often deny their flaws by 'crowing', or bragging about exaggerated or fantasised achievements. Jungle Fowl people are romantic, seductive and alluring and love to be admired and are encouraged to shun narcissism, tactlessness and forcefulness.

Kangaroo

Family

 Members of the macropod family (Kangaroos and Wallabies) travel on powerful hind legs, using their long, thick tails to balance their body while hopping. Some species can travel at up to 60 kilometres per hour and are capable of leaping over obstacles up to 3 metres high. Anything that looks like a Kangaroo and weighs less than 20 kilograms is classified as a Wallaby. Wallaby prefers to lead a semi-solitary life, unlike Kangaroo that travels and lives in 'mobs'. Red Kangaroo stands taller than a man and weighs up to 85 kilograms and is classified as the largest marsupial in the world. Kangaroo rests in the shade during the heat of the day and feeds from late afternoon until well into the night when it is much cooler. She feeds mainly on grass and needs very little water and can actually survive without drinking for many months. So plentiful was Kangaroo that she was the staple diet of early Indigenous Australians.

• Grey Kangaroo – *Abundance*

Frankly, to pin all our hopes on the belief that money equals abundance will quickly see us realise the complete opposite. It is difficult to understand initially, but to constantly worry about money, or to obsess about hoarding wealth, is a sure-fire way of losing everything (especially our money). The more we hunt for something, the further away it gets. To know true love is to know the greatest of wealth. When we finally understand that true wealth is usually never represented by money or gold, and we release our monetary mindset, fear of lack can be transmuted into trust and the block that prevents us from realising 'wealth' can be removed forever. To let go of lack will essentially result in gain. Grey Kangaroo, a symbol of abundance, offered the people his rich meat and warm pelt. Thus, prosperity came to mean healthy children, a full stomach and a warm, dry sleeping place. They believed that the land would provide all that they needed and, that if they lived in harmony with the Earth Mother, their life would be safe and abundant forever.

Grey Kangaroo ensures that abundance will flourish for the self, the family and indeed for the people as a whole, particularly when we remain grateful for what we have and we live in harmony with all other things. He warns us however, that although to want more than we have is healthy (the trait of someone destined for bigger things), to want more than is necessary is avaricious and limiting. To focus our attention on material acquisition is to follow a path of delusion that will eventually lead to false promise and greed. Such a path can never nurture the soul, no matter how well it might sustain the pocket. A person may have all the monetary wealth in the world, but unless their soul is nourished with love and happiness, they will never know true abundance. Grey Kangaroo demonstrates that it is our right to have all our prayers answered and all our necessities satisfied. Grey Kangaroo reminds us that we should only ever ask for what we need rather than risk everything and push for what we want, followed by a sincere prayer of thanks to Spirit.

• Red Kangaroo – *Responsibility*

According to Aboriginal legend, Red Kangaroo was the first creature to take the responsibility of Dream Journeying its way across the land, retrieving sacred truths crucial to the future growth of the people. The knowledge discovered by Red Kangaroo was eventually brought back to the people, affording them a deeper understanding of their ancestral past and a stronger, more abundant sense of responsibility for their collective future. To take responsibility for our actions and to understand what is appropriate behaviour is to fully appreciate the wisdom of Red Kangaroo; an animal that speaks of family fertility, commitment and the promises we make when we assume the responsibilities of leadership and parenthood.

Red Kangaroo motivates us to re-evaluate the rationale on which we have developed our present life values and beliefs and encourages us to take responsibility for our own life and to seriously consider the fact that perhaps the time has come to push our grown Joey out of the pouch, to make way for another. Alternatively, Red Kangaroo affords us the time to reclaim aspects of the past we consciously put on hold long ago, or to realise dreams and aspirations for the future that once felt a lifetime away. Red Kangaroo helps us to maintain equilibrium and to always tackle life in a forward motion and that the primary responsibility of parenthood is to live a life of integrity and in doing so our wholesome example will trickle down to even the smallest Joey in the mob. Red Kangaroo is unique in her ability to have three young at once: one at foot, one in the pouch, and another forming in the womb. When Australia's environmental conditions are fertile with plentiful rain, lush and abundant feed and benevolent weather, Red Kangaroo lives a productive existence with the mob steadily increasing its numbers on an almost weekly basis. If the ideal conditions deteriorate however, bringing drought, fire or flood, female Red Kangaroo will do something quite extraordinary to ensure the wellbeing of her people. She will surrender the infant in the pouch and put the foetus in the womb into a state of suspended animation. The infant remains nourished and is continually fed by the mother, but it does not develop physically, waiting for the conditions of the land to improve. Red Kangaroo asks whether or not you are taking adequate responsibility for your role as parent or leader. Everything you do and the way in which you do it inherently instils itself in the consciousness of your children as acceptable behaviour. Therefore, ask yourself if you are taking your responsibility as parent or leader seriously. Are you honouring the pledge of responsibility you made to yourself before you started walking this life path, or would you say that you were in an emotional drought at the moment? If so, it may be time to re-animate some element of yourself, so that you can begin taking responsibility for your life and that of your children.

• Wallaby – *Progression*

 Wallaby, as a generic term, is a member of the Kangaroo family. Equipped with powerful hind legs, the many subspecies that make up the Wallaby family are capable of achieving great speeds, often covering great distances with seemingly very little effort. Because of the unusual shape of his hind legs and bulky tails, Wallaby cannot physically walk backwards.

The desire to move on from traumatic or oppressive events in our past is what instigates the foundation of most spiritual exploration and healing. Despite the motivation, however, few have the skills, the support or the experience to fully undertake such a venture on their own. We usually lack the skills or understanding to find the inherent sacredness that is destined to become our Purpose. People may say that we are dwelling in the past, or that we just don't want to move on when they witness us repeatedly revisiting our shadow space. In reality, the sacredness lying dormant within this space simply has not been realised. We have not allowed ourselves to visit the space with the intention of learning from it and using the process as a chance to rebirth ourselves. This is why Wallaby does not sponsor stagnation or reluctant movement of any sort, but instead promotes progression and personal growth. To demonstrate a desire to progress, even if it means temporarily revisiting the past, honours the wisdom of Wallaby. It can be said, despite the heartache that accompanies the theory, that some individuals have chosen to experience their particular life path, and to interfere would mean interrupting their karmic evolution. For these people, Wallaby offers the chance to progress from one day to the next, in a manner that nurtures their requirements and supports their soul. Spirit forgets no one. No one is left behind. Everyone's choices are honoured and supported by Great Mystery, including those aspects of Creation that can never be understood or are meant to remain a Mystery. Wallaby heralds a time of awakening: a 'wakeup call' of sorts. Wallaby encourages us to always move in a forward motion and to explore new horizons. He pushes us to take risks, to avoid the temptation to look back with regret and to never return to our old, familiar comfort zones once we have developed the confidence to leave. Remember that 'onwards and upwards' remains both the adage of Wallaby and the advice offered to those who seek his counsel.

• Bridled Nail-tail Wallaby – *Choice*

Bridled Nail-tail Wallaby, or Flashjack Wallaby, is a rare Wallaby that is so named because of the bridle-like markings that run down his neck and around his shoulders, and due to the strange 'nail' that extends from the tip of his tail.

Nail-tail Wallaby speaks of the desire to no longer be controlled, restrained, held back, bridled, yoked or 'nailed down' to anything and anyone for any reason, and of the lengths we will go to fight for our right to be free, be heard and be unconditionally loved for what and who we know we are.

Kiwi
Surrender

Kiwi's plumage enables him to camouflage himself easily by blending in with the plants and leaf litter found on the forest floor. Kiwi feeds on worms, insects and berries, which he finds with his strong legs and probing beak in the undergrowth and under rotting logs. According to Maori legend, Kiwi once had brightly coloured plumage and powerful wings. One day the Creator noticed that bugs were eating all the forest's plants and someone had to become 'Official Bug-Catcher'. All the birds were asked, one at a time, if they would leave the forest canopy forever and live on the forest floor to guard the forest's plants and destroy all the plant-eating bugs. One after the other they refused and Kiwi eventually volunteered knowing that the role meant great sacrifice and the loss of his colourful feathers and powerful wings. The Kiwi knew that if he did not offer, the forest would be lost forever and all the birds and animals would surely die. Kiwi surrendered his wings for the betterment of all and was rewarded by the Creator with a long, powerful beak and the sacred title of 'bravest and most famous bird'.

Kiwi's message is to 'surrender'; the knowledge that at times we must give something up in order to further our lives and those of others. Personal lifestyle is largely surrendered when a child is born for example, as parents often surrender aspects of their own selves so that their children's lives may be richer, more prosperous and healthier. It is not uncommon for parents to go without so that their children are warmly dressed and properly fed. Fear is also an aspect that, when surrendered, transforms our view of life because to always worry about the 'What ifs?' is to limit our potential. A doubt is simply a limiting decision. Kiwi encourages us to surrender all limiting beliefs and 'What ifs?' so that we may welcome abundance and success into our lives. Kiwi instils this understanding and can assist during tough transition periods. Kiwi may ask us to examine our lives and to decide what needs to be surrendered for the betterment of ourselves and others.

Koala

Journeys

 The closest relative to Wombat, Koala spends much of his time high in the canopy of eucalyptus forests, only coming down to move from one tree to another. The Koala will wedge his rump into a forked branch and sleep up to 18 hours a day. Koala is a marsupial mammal, meaning the female suckles her single young while carrying it in a pouch. Koala obtains most of the moisture he needs from eucalyptus leaves, which are said to have a soporific, hypnotic, sleep-inducing affect on the animal, and as a result, Koala rarely needs to drink fresh water. Koala is often called a Koala Bear; a name afforded him by his outwardly cute, cuddly appearance. Not only is Koala totally unrelated to Bears, a wild Koala will cause serious bodily harm to anyone silly enough to cuddle one. Revered and honoured by the Indigenous People of Australia because of an ancestral promise made during The Dreamtime, Koala is seen as the bringer of plentiful water, the protector of lakes and the caretaker of flowing streams and rivers. As a way of acknowledging its familial associations with water, Koala is recognised as a traditional custodian of the West on the Wheel of Life. By tradition, the teachings of the West prompt us to seek and trust answers found deep within our own inner knowing before considering the advice given by others. He embodies the ancient symbolic links made between water and the human spectrum of emotions,

Koala endorses the wisdom found in speaking less, while encouraging us to listen more. Koala fosters the notion that as spiritual beings we inherently know the answers to all of our questions, with the knowledge we seek stored deep within our consciousness. Koala demonstrates the sacredness of the healing journey we must take in our personal quest for answers and embraces the inner journey to the core of the deepest self. To journey with Koala is to quest for the ancient knowledge and spiritual awakening stored inherently within our consciousness. According to the ancient philosophies of many Earth-based healing traditions, the most effective path we can take in our quest for emotional, physical or spiritual stability involves first delivering ourselves into an altered state of consciousness. This is usually obtained via the ingestion of selective organic hallucinogens or by denying the body of nourishment for prolonged periods of time. To witness Koala in the wild will find you observing him in one of two states – awake, feeding and tending to his young, or dozing in a foetal position. It is believed that, via the altered state of awareness the animal slips into after ingesting the eucalyptus leaves, Koala is able to enter other realms of reality. Once there, it is thought that Koala gathers knowledge and is able to perform healing in ways not considered physically possible in the tangible world. Koala equips us to move beyond the physical restraints of our physical body and to travel to the inner realms. Koala embraces the sensation we experience when we start to shift into a healing state of consciousness, and begin to feel energy moving through our body from a source higher than any found in the mundane world. When we slip into this healing space, our conscious mind relaxes and becomes gradually less active. Our mind moves from a dynamic mental state into a relaxed space that allows us to respond intuitively. Our breathing becomes deeper and we shift into a new profound state of being. Koala assures us that we already know the answers to the questions we seek assistance with. He tells us that now is the time to start taking notice of our inner self, our innate connection to all the information of the Universe. Koala asks us to stop looking to others for corroboration, advice and wisdom; to take responsibility for our own life, our own path and our own destiny. Koala says that we must start our own journey; a quest that will unlock the answers we seek from a place hidden deep within our essence. And the journey must begin today. It must begin NOW. When we journey with the Koala, our potential for growth and transformation strengthens and our sense of self escalates. You just have to first take responsibility for your own healing and trust that all will evolve as it is meant to.

Kookaburra
Healing

Kookaburra is the largest member of the Kingfisher family and relies on the wait-and-pounce hunting technique. He finds a vantage point, and when prey appears, he drops from his perch and grabs it in his beak, oftentimes bashing it against a tree or rock to make sure it is dead. Kookaburra is a cavity nester, taking advantage of tree hollows and hollowed-out termite mounds. According to Aboriginal legend, Kookaburra was created to awaken the people, to herald the new day and to welcome the rising sun. To awaken can mean many different things however, as can the symbology of a new day. Kookaburra preys on Snake; an animal whose wisdom inspires us to surrender outworn values and belief systems so that we may heal, prosper and grow. While Snake can be seen as preparation for the next phase of your life, you are being told that before this new exciting change can take place, you must first acknowledge and deal with some facet of your old life that needs to be released. Snake sheds her old skin, making way for new growth. Kookaburra takes this process one step further, however, by first acknowledging the need for self-healing and then following up closely with swift execution. Taking responsibility for one's own healing is probably one of the most confronting things a person can do. It is often ignorance rather than defiance that sees most people denied the chance to heal.

Kookaburras have a distinctive call that strongly resembles human laughter and for this reason, some refer to the bird as the 'Laughing Kookaburra'. Many assume therefore, that the message of the Kookaburra is that of lightening up and learning to laugh at ourselves. It may be true that his laughter inspires others to laugh along and this rather obvious assessment of Kookaburra's is sometimes relevant but the truth is that if Kookaburra does make an appearance, his true message delves far deeper than his superficial laughter. Kookaburra's laugh is in fact a deceitful giggle, a scoff that suggests we may be covering up our true feelings; a tease intended to distract attention away from the real issue. Kookaburra's laughter denotes an inability to face one's fears, a failure to acknowledge an outworn value or belief system that no longer serves us, and a preference to keep things as they are. In this context, Kookaburra's laugh suggests denial at all costs, no matter how detrimental it may prove to be. However, when Kookaburra is observed sitting pensively silently watching the world go by, the message is quite different. From this perspective, Kookaburra is reassuring us that the healing that must be addressed within our life has been acknowledged, and that positive steps have been taken to bring about its commencement. A silent Kookaburra is a far more uplifting sign than the raucous laughter emanated by a chorus of mockery and taunt.

Lady Beetle
Good luck

Lady Beetle, also known as Ladybird and Ladybug, is best-known for her yellow, orange or red wing casings which are covered in little black spots, and her delicate black legs, head and antennae. Loved by gardeners the world over because a lot of the species prey on agricultural pests such as aphids, Lady Beetle can be found in almost all the major crop-growing regions of temperate and tropical countries.

In Germany, Lady Beetle arrives as a sign of fertility, or a warning that someone (a close friend or family member) is about to announce a pregnancy. Alternatively, Lady Beetle can also herald other forms of fertility such as an opportunity that promises to lead to bigger and better things – a job offer, a promotion, a financial windfall or a long-awaited contract. Associated with fairytales, magic and all things whimsical, Lady Beetle was commemorated in the well-known nursery rhyme, 'Ladybird, Ladybird', which is dated to circa 1744:

Ladybird, ladybird fly away home,
Your house is on fire and your children are gone,
All except one,
And her name is Ann,
And she hid under the baking pan.

Like many different species of insect including butterflies, dragonflies and bees, and due mainly to her metamorphic phases of development, Lady Beetle also shares long-standing connections to various deity and the heavenly realms. When associated with the Virgin Mary and the Norse fertility goddess Freyja, for example, Lady Beetle is referred to as 'Our Lady's bird'. But, when linked directly to God, Lady Beetle is sometimes referred to as the 'Little Animal of our Good Lord'. But the one thing she is most celebrated for is her apparent ability to attract good luck. Affectionately known as 'the Good Luck Bug' in countries that include Italy, Russia and Turkey, the appearance of Lady Beetle will see people either making wishes or preparing for a wish already made to come to fruition.

Lemming
Chinese whispers

Lemming's incisor teeth grow continuously and must be worn down by constant gnawing. He remains active all winter, finding food by burrowing through the snow and will cache grass and seeds. He is a solitary animal, meeting only to mate but will breed rapidly when conditions favour his requirements. 'Lemming' is common slang for someone who believes whatever they are told and blindly follows others, while ignoring better judgment and their inherent sense of self-preservation.

The expression was birthed from the erroneous belief that Lemmings committed suicide by marching off cliffs when food became scarce. When environmental conditions are at their optimum peak, Lemming populations undergo a dramatic increase that often reaches tens of thousands. With resources poorly equipped to sustain such an overwhelming population swell, the animals are forced to trek out into the wilderness in search of food. Although hunger inspires them to act irrationally, forcing them to migrate to more fertile, abundant lands, they do not suicide but rather run blindly, frantically searching of food. They fan out randomly from their home base, with little thought of direction or destination. They venture into foreign territories, cross fast-flowing rivers and, individually will occasionally swim out into the ocean (with the intention of swimming 'to the other side'), only to drown. A hunger-driven migration inevitably leads to many of the animals dying at the hands of predators, unfamiliar territory or starvation. Disney Studios produced *White Wilderness*: a documentary that supposedly caught 'rare' proof of Lemmings throwing themselves to their death but film crews had apparently herded the Lemmings toward the edge of a cliff and literally pushed them over, leaving them no choice but to plummet into the sea below. People believed what they had seen to be true thereby confirming the myth that Lemmings commit suicide.

Lemming calls for us to be sure of the details before espousing information gleaned from doubtful sources as fact. He asks that we avoid being a gossip, rumour-monger or tittle-tattle, as that sort of talk only leads to Chinese whispers, in which the original message is passed on from one person to another, while being contextually altered in the process. Lemming warns us that doing so only makes us look like liars and try-hards; people who boast and pretend to make themselves look and feel more popular, stronger and wiser. The appearance of Lemming confirms suspicions regarding the telling of an untruth or a story that has been stretched out of proportion to hide a hidden agenda or a misdemeanour that the teller would prefer to keep secret.

Lemur

Apparition

 Representing the most ancient branch of the order of primates, early Ancestors of Lemur evolved into Apes and Monkeys. Lemurs themselves, however, developed separately into their current forms. Found primarily on Madagascar, the ecological isolation afforded by the island and its wealth of natural habitat, has enabled Lemur to exist with relatively little interference from the outside world. The most universally recognised of the 43 individual species is Ringtailed Lemur, a true Lemur.

Lemur people appear apathetic on first meeting. They often separate themselves from emotional issues to disguise their fear, apprehension and lack of self-worth and are introverted and nonchalant. They are poor listeners but crave attention and often display egocentric qualities. They can appear unmotivated or disinterested, and may only offer their support begrudgingly or if it doesn't interfere with their own plans. Lemur people are onlookers and they hate change. When working in the negative, Lemur people tend to be cynical, judgmental, discouraging and teasing in their observations. They have difficulty maintaining relationships but keep many friends and even more associates. When displaying their positive traits, however, Lemur people are easygoing and peaceful. They are effective networkers, matchmakers and dot-joiners. They are composed, tolerant and objective in their approach to life. They make reliable friends and are gentle in their ways. Lemur people are funny, compassionate and nurturing. Reticent in nature, Lemur people can be submissive, attentive and universal yet spiritual in their belief. Laidback and accepting, Lemur people are profoundly clairvoyant, intuitive and knowledgeable. They are composed and stable and make fine leaders who negotiate affectively, are stable in foundation and are pacifists at heart. They make dependable, sociable partners, pleasant, cooperative workmates, attentive friends and inoffensive neighbours. The word Lemur actually means 'ghost'. Lemur, as the ambassador of the Ghost World may be preparing you for a 'ghostly visitation', or helping you to come to terms with supernatural activity that may be affecting you at present. Lemur stills our mind and supports us as we slip into a receptive state of being, making the event less stressful while easing the transition so that a line of communication may be successfully opened between us and those in Spirit. Visits from Ancestral Spirits are common, but they generally go unnoticed or are written off as 'something weird'. If Lemur makes his presence felt, take the time to listen to those 'weird' sensations, visions or occurrences as they may very well be indicating the presence of a deceased loved one bringing messages, confirmation and healing. A pull to explore Lemur, therefore, is to acknowledge a possible calling to study the specialised art of mediumship, spirit communication and clairvoyance.

Leopard
Augmentation

 Leopards range from pale cream to golden brown in colour. Blackish-brown rosettes cover the back and upper limbs, but become solid spots on the face and lower limbs. Female Leopard raises her offspring alone after giving birth to up to six cubs in a cave or thick undergrowth. Solitary by nature, male and female Leopards usually only come together to mate with territories often overlapping. Leopard is nocturnal generally and does his hunting at night dragging his kill into a tree so that it is out of reach of Lions and Hyenas. Classified as endangered due to habitat loss and poaching, Leopard has been completely eradicated from some areas of Africa.

It may be impossible to 'change' a Leopard's spots but we, as sentient beings, can make a conscious decision to grow and transform by learning new skills, broadening our horizons and deepening our relationships. We can no more rework Leopard's spots than enforce unwanted change on someone else, no matter how valuable we believe it to be. The only way one can change another's spots is to offer them choice, and hope that they see possibility rather than looking for the familiar 'What ifs?' People hear the word 'change' and panic. They see it as representing disturbance or confrontation or something requiring effort and a level of accountability and instantly resist. With every step away from our known comfort zones, we enhance our relationship with the world. With every question we ask, unusual flavour we try or untried door we test, we deepen and widen the perception we hold of our sacred self and our position in the Universe. We begin to see life as an adventure; a trial of the skills and knowledge we once regarded as familiar, while looking for the chance to improve them. We begin to strive for higher places, while endeavouring to grow inwardly and outwardly. In doing so, we accept the invitation issued by Leopard to augment our lives, thus making it richer, deeper and more meaningful for ourselves and others.

• Black Leopard – *Invisibility*

Leopard is easily recognised by her flaxen coat, distinctive patterning and long tail. Often confused with Jaguar, Leopard has a slighter build with rosettes devoid of internal spots. Black Leopards are often called 'Black Panthers' – a species that just doesn't exist. Black Leopards are simply regular Leopards displaying the melanistic gene, a trait that produces an almost black pigmentation in the skin and fur. Leopards displaying the melanistic gene are typically born into litters comprising both black and standard coloured offspring. It is believed that the darker coloration aids Leopard in her ability to stalk prey undetected.

Being alone is a regular occurrence for Black Leopard people, but *feeling* alone is even more common. They often feel insignificant, invisible and unimportant and tend to believe their presence in this world goes unobserved and that their leaving would go unnoticed. As opposed to those who *walk with* Black Leopard, those inspired to investigate the wisdom of the Black Leopard are asked to think about their role as isolators, condemners or abandoners of others and to consider the lasting affects their behaviour may have had on their 'victims', and to consider the possibility that their actions may reflect some time in their past when they were persecuted in some way; a time that may now require revisiting and releasing. Leopard calls for personal augmentation. It supports us as we go about changing personal programs, dumping indoctrination, family patterning and limiting beliefs and behaviour. Essentially, Leopard affords powerful and effective strategies to change our personal history so that we may prosper on all levels. Black Leopard Dreaming, however, while espousing the 'regular' medicine of its kind, builds confidence to stand in our own power, to step out of the shadows of doubt, self-loathing and grief, to find our voice and to express ourselves in whatever way serves us best. 'Regular' Leopard helps us to 'change our spots' by teaching compassion for others, how to see things from different perspectives and to consider what our treatment of others really says about how we perceive ourselves. Black Leopard Dreaming, however, asks that we focus our compassion on ourselves and what serves us right now. In essence, 'regular' Leopard asks that we contemplate our personal patterning and how we might consciously improve ourselves on an external level, while Black Leopard enhances self-image by allowing us to experience humility and to clearly see the beauty in the 'little things'. She augments our 'inner' perspectives, while instilling a deep sense of self-love, self-worth and self-appreciation, while helping us to forgive our past and, ultimately, ourselves.

• Clouded Leopard – *Clarity*

Clouded Leopard waits safely in ambush among the branches of the forest canopy for unsuspecting Deer or Pigs to happen by and when she tires of waiting, she might grab a Monkey or bird that ventures too close. Solitary, softly spoken Clouded Leopard is the smallest member of the Big Cat family. Due to overindulgence in the now illegal exotic pelt trade, Clouded Leopard is considered vulnerable as a species. An animal that seldom descends from the trees, Clouded Leopard relies on a high vantage point to assess her surroundings and to establish the things she requires for survival.

Clarity and truth achieved from a prime viewpoint are essential if Clouded Leopard is to continue her arboreal lifestyle. To have her outlook impaired or her integrity questioned would mean the animal going hungry or being forced to adapt or change her habits. Clouded Leopard affords us the power to maintain immaculate clear vision in all that we do and to remain true in accordance with the choices we make, be they good or bad. She reminds us to be constantly aware of our approach, prejudices and accountability in all areas of life and requires us to review our perceptions. Clouded Leopard's chosen lifestyle affords her equally as many advantages as disadvantages, but she does not expect any of the other animals to make her life easier. She does not force others to comply with her way of life or expect others to make excuses or feel guilty for her inadequacies. Clouded Leopard shares her wisdom from two opposing angles – from the stance of the animal itself and from the viewpoint of her intended victim. From the stance of Clouded Leopard, her wisdom comes as more of a warning: Do not participate in any activity for which you are not prepared to be held fully accountable for at a later date. Clarity and truth are the keynotes of Clouded

Leopard and she does not offer second chances to those who shun her advice. When Clouded Leopard makes a medicine call, be aware that cries of alarm, tears of shock or claims of naivety, virtue and denial will do nothing to ease the case made against you when you fall from grace or unstable self-fashioned pedestals. From the viewpoint of the Big Cat's victim, Clouded Leopard is both supportive and reassuring, and promises to return clarity to an otherwise foggy or clouded mind. It clears all feelings of hesitation, mental burden and anxiety. An honourable creature, Clouded Leopard takes full responsibility for luring her prey into her clutches. She does not hide the fact that she uses and sometimes abuses her position of power to get what she wants. With this knowing she offers her prey a sense of transparency. She knows she has not deceived her victim, or led it to believe anything but the inevitable. In doing so, the prey animal is prepared for its fate, armed with a sense of new beginning, hope, knowledge, power and above all, clarity. Clouded Leopard pardons her victims of all blame. She takes full responsibility for the role she plays in luring her prey into her clutches. According to Clouded Leopard, no one can be held responsible but the individual who uses and then abuses his or her position of power. With this realisation comes a sense of new beginning for the prey that eludes her influence, along with hope, knowledge, wisdom and above all, clarity.

• Snow Leopard – *Cynicism*

 A short, stocky feline, Snow Leopard is built for strength and endurance with a thick coat, long tail and large, powerful paws. Preying on Musk Oxen, Ibex and Wild Boar, Snow Leopard is a solitary animal now listed as endangered due to poaching and persecution by habitat-encroaching farmers, who fear her as a threat to livestock.

As a member of the Cat family, Snow Leopard shares the non-specific wisdom of her cousins when called upon in a sacred way. Cats generically act as the protector of the procreative region of all people and the inherent power we have to manifest and bring about productive and necessary change on all levels. However, due to generations of blind discrimination and ignorance on the part of the people who target her, Snow Leopard is an animal that no longer suffers fools lightly and shows little concern for the spiritual needs and yearnings of humans. As she has lost the patience of her cousins and their forgiving ways, Snow Leopard has become increasingly cynical over the years. Charged with awareness enough to afford those who seek her counsel great wisdom, Snow Leopard often replies to questions with grim sarcasm and cares not for dizzy, superficial, indulgent seekers, preferring to save her acumen for serious students of Earth Mother's ancient knowledge. Those inspired to explore the wisdom of Snow Leopard may find that the description given of the Snow Leopard also describes their current view of the world and the irrational, agitated feelings experienced of late. In order to regain your ability to trust yourself and others, manifest your heart's desire and realise your Personal Power, you will first need to address and heal these aspects of self. Snow Leopard may be tired and cynical, but she is not a lost cause. She wants to heal, feel joy and know inner peace, like everyone else, but is afraid to 'open up' for fear of being abused and oppressed. She has been forced into her pessimistic ways by years of ill-treatment and disregard, sentiments shared by those who embrace the wisdom of Snow Leopard. Snow Leopard warns those who look to her for guidance to initially expect little sympathy, but if they are dedicated and prepared to show commitment while promising to honour her input, they *may* be rewarded with meagre encouragement and vague direction. Snow Leopard empowers us to combat feelings of inadequacy by charging us with the power to speak up, experiment with change, trust people rather than automatically shutting them out, rely upon our intuition and take the occasional yet calculated leap of faith.

Lion

Languor

 Targeting animals such as Antelopes, Zebras, Giraffes and even baby Rhinoceroses, Lioness is generally entrusted with the responsibility of doing the hunting while Lion waits in the shade of a good tree. A powerful, striking and confident animal, Lion will feed first on the Lioness' return, growling and snapping at any animal that gets in his way. Lion lives in family groups known as 'prides' characteristically ruled by a single male (although alpha females do exist). It is not unusual for the females of a pride to be related and for all the cubs to be sired by the same male.

Lion, although a powerful and majestic creature, expects his mate to do all the domestic 'work': a trait symptomatic of the attitude born by many modern-day men. Lion asks us to look at our relationships in a way that highlights this possible and incredibly limiting mind-set. An animal that knows great pride, Lion is an animal that holds his head up and shakes his mane symbolically heralding the dawn of a new day or the realisation of a new beginning. According to legend Lion's golden mane symbolises the rays of the rising sun. Some Lions however, sport black manes suggesting a heavy heart, depression, sadness or disappointment. Those who resonate with black-maned Lion are often haunted by confusion and doubt. Time and introspection are the only cures for when black-maned Lion makes a house call. Those who carry the wisdom of Lion however, are usually powerfully confident, hardworking, inspirational and creative and whatever they touch usually turns to gold; they have the 'Midas Touch'. Lion is highly intelligent and is capable of bringing his visions to fruition. He promises warmth, protection and potent possibility. However, as with all things, there is also a downside. He can be incredibly lazy and outwardly unmotivated. Those working with Lion often require constant encouragement, ego boosting and confirmation of their influence to reach their fullest potential. Lion promises great things, but constantly seeks affirmation and verification of his power and his vital importance to the world. Suggesting the attainment of abundance and the reclaiming of Personal Power after a time of confusion, darkness and dormancy, Lion is indicative of the inevitable new dawn that must follow every night: an understanding that ignites realisation, clarity and inner strength. Lion says, 'Stop procrastinating and get on with it'. Languor is a limiting behaviour rooted in fear. Motivation is a decision. Self-confidence is a birth-rite. Remember this and you can (and will) achieve great things.

• White Lion – *Rectitude*

White Lion is a genetic rarity, but is not an albino variation of his kin. He has pigmentation, seen readily in his eyes, paw pads and lips. African legends about White Lions have been passed down from one generation to the next for centuries and unsubstantiated sightings were first documented in 1928. But the existence of White Lion was not confirmed until the mid-1970s with the discovery of two healthy white cubs.

According to African mythology White Lion is said to be messenger of the gods. He symbolises the golden light and the good that can be found in all creatures. Championing righteousness and promise, White Lion recognises the potential found in those that may be unjustly labelled by poor reputation or hearsay. White Lion prompts us to never judge a book by its cover, but rather to rely on the intuitional feelings we receive on meeting someone for the first time. White Lion teaches us to look for, identify and celebrate the golden glow of potential in others. Everyone has an inherent *golden glow*, but due to life circumstance or negative external influence experienced through life, the vibrancy of the glow can sometimes wane to the point of invisibility, and if our golden glow is allowed to remain dormant for too long, we run the risk of forgetting about its existence altogether. The golden glow is similar to life force, spirit essence or our innate power aspect, all of which offer vitality and purpose. If we become detached from our power aspect, we lose energy, passion and reason. Feelings of failure, despair and unattractiveness begin to creep into our consciousness, fogging our perception and hindering our progress. To have our golden glow recognised and endorsed by another is often all it takes to banish the impinging darkness forever so that we may re-ignite our power aspect. Thus, White Lion advocates that to see the good in people, or to breathe life back into our own golden glow instead of focusing on the less than positive aspects, is an alternative worth considering.

Lizard
Daydreaming

Lizards are reptiles found the world over, ranging dramatically in size from the 3-metre Komodo Dragon of Indonesia, to the 2.5-centimetres-long Grey's Skink of inland Australia. Some species lay eggs, while others such as the Blue-Tongue Lizard, give birth to live young. Like all reptiles, Lizards are ectothermic in nature ('cold-blooded' – creatures that rely on their environment to regulate body temperature) and must absorb the warmth of the sun to stimulate activity and generate energy. As Lizard basks in the sun, absorbing its life-giving rays, we incorrectly assume he is fast asleep. Nothing could be further from the truth. Lizard is, in fact, wide-awake, pensively journeying the realms of possibility.

Lizard is a master daydreamer and the ultimate tutor in the art of manifestation. His wisdom lies in the understanding that when we acknowledge our daydreams, we allow our higher selves to consider alternative life paths that we may have never consciously deemed plausible. Through our daydreams Lizard teaches us the importance of respecting and remembering the messages of Spirit while offering the skills in bringing these messages to fruition. All our daydreams should be recorded in a specially prepared journal for future reference, particularly if we experiences déjà vu on a recurring basis. Déjà vu occurs when we catch up physically with our daydreams. When we daydream we are energetically checking out our potential future selves. Daydreams are Spirit's way of allowing us to consciously explore our future while remaining corporally alert. Daydreaming can be compared to taking a walkabout or medicine walk, but instead of strolling through the woods, for example, daydreaming encourages us to stroll through the realms of Spirit. To receive a daydream that suggests healing or progress is to know that Spirit is guiding you to a place of greatness. Spirit is offering you a map, and you need to follow it with inherent clarity. Spirit never makes a mistake. The Spirits around you can inspire you, but only the Spirit within you can physically help you. When we listen to the inspiration offered by Spirit, and we do what needs to be done to physically affirm its potency, we, too, will never make mistakes again.

• Chameleon – *Ambience*

Found almost exclusively on the island of Madagascar, Chameleon is a unique species of Lizard capable of changing colour and communicates hunger, comfort, fear and even the readiness to mate through the tone of his skin, (rather than as a form of camouflage: a misconception adopted by most people). Exposure to daylight and the warmth of the sun, when pooled with the effects of certain internal chemical reactions, trigger Chameleon's pigment cells to either expand or contract, thus encouraging the tone of skin to favourably change. Chameleon has powerful pincer-like feet that grasp branches like a vice, enabling him to climb trees with very little effort and has eyes that are able to move autonomously, making it possible to study his surrounds with close to 360-degrees sight. Chameleon also has a very long, sticky tongue often twice as long as his body, that unrolls with lightning speed, snaring insects some distance away.

Chameleon is a slow-moving, reserved creature that encourages us to take our time to ponder the world from all angles and steadily seize possibilities as they present. What may initially seem like bad luck or unwanted change may, in time, turn out to be a blessing in disguise. Chameleon teaches us to grab all opportunities that are offered (the good and not so good) and to hold onto them until they have revealed their potential. Chameleon helps us adapt to new sensations, feelings, energy shifts, levels of awareness and emotional ups and downs. He demonstrates how to welcome change and to harness its potential. If Chameleon has made his presence felt, you may also need to consider your sensitivity to the atmosphere of your home and workplace. Chameleon's reliance on the health and wellbeing of his environment suggests a need to set the tone for positive change in ours. To change the energy of the environment in which you spend the majority of your time will not only improve its productivity as an abode or place of employ, it will inspire your mood as well. Your communication skills, health and general attitude will improve, as will your energy levels, relationships and potential to do more on all levels. It is like dropping a pebble into a pond ... the ripples that fan out from you will touch everyone and everything, motivating them to follow suit. Incidentally, Chameleon people live by the expression that 'beauty is only skin deep'. 'Things that sparkle are not always gold' is an axiom adopted by those who endorse Chameleon Dreaming; an observation based on personal experience. External beauty does not necessarily lend itself to the manifestation of inner beauty. Chameleon says that truly dazzling people are those who radiate unconditional beauty from their hearts, no matter how alluring or plain their physical appearance may be.

• Gecko – *The inner child*

Gecko inhabits the warm, tropical regions of the world. Most geckos cannot blink and most lack eyelids and have fixed lenses that enlarge in darkness. Instead, she has a transparent membrane that she licks to keep clean. Some Geckos are nocturnal and have excellent night vision, being 350 times more sensitive to light than humans. Gecko makes chirping sounds when communicating with other geckos and is and are known for her suction pad-like toe pads that allows her to scale smooth and vertical surfaces (and ceilings) with ease. Many can lose their tail as a form of defence.

Gecko is a symbol of luck, rebirth and life. A common tribal tattoo, the early Polynesians saw Gecko as a symbol of scorn and ridicule. They both revered the animal and feared it. They heard her call as a laugh and saw the way she bobs her head as a sign of mockery. To be mocked by Gecko was a bad omen indeed for it denoted foolish decisions and stupidity. In the Philippines, Gecko is a symbol of good luck. To have Gecko living in your bedroom is a sign of good fortune; to have two is to know you are truly blessed no matter how difficult you perceive your life to be. The way Geckos will chase one another was once considered a dance, a sacred ballet that spoke of life and the challenges we might face along the way. The way Gecko is able to release her tail when threatened gave rise to the belief that she was able to assist people through times of trial and tribulation, offering self-preservation and the skills to rebuild and regenerate after hardship. Live Gecko was said to warn of the presence of venomous Snakes. When drawn in a circle, they are symbols of life and the cycles we go through as we grow and develop, while Gecko carvings were used to preserve eyesight, to protect unborn children and to ensure their safe and healthy delivery into the world. Gecko helps not only the physical child, but also the inner child. The Gecko is the protector of the innocent heart, the inner child and the dreams we promised ourselves we would bring to fruition as adults.

• Gila Monster – *Darkness and light*

Gila Monster, or *Eemuukwee* as she is known to the Huichol people of Mexico, inhabits the crevices found under rocks, warrens and dens of other animals and burrows she has excavated herself. Gila Monster hunts at night, feeding on Rats, Mice, insects, birds and eggs. Fat is accumulated in the tail; a resource that carries the reptile through the dormant winter period. Gila Monsters have a nasty bite and along with the Mexican Beaded Lizard, are the only species of venomous Lizard. Grooves in her teeth direct the flow of poison into the open wound caused by her bite. Gila Monster is said to have breath so foul that it is potent enough to immobilise prey with legend stating her breath can kill a human in their sleep.

Apart from the fact that 'Gila' is a female name of the Hebrew tradition that means 'joy', Gila Monster is believed to carry potent healing medicine and Shamans often include portions of the reptile's tail in their medicine baskets. Gila Monster transforms the soul, reawakens self-worth and returns us to a state of beauty. Gila Monster people are often those who find themselves shunned, pushed into the shadows and generally overlooked by family and friends. They often feel compelled to withdraw from society, for one reason or another. Gila Monster people become people we love to hate. Gila Monster supports these people who privately enjoy the mystery and excitement their presence invokes. It makes them feel special, different and needed. Gila Monster people are wise, generous and innovative, but victims of their own fears, insecurities and inherent darkness. They are often scarred emotionally or physically; individuals who feel safer in their own company because of past experiences that have hampered their ability to trust and see beauty in the world around them. Their solitary existence is often self-initiated and enjoyed for the protection it affords, until one day they wake up and suddenly realise they are dreadfully lonely and sad and that they don't have to be. Gila Monster offers powerful insight into the darker facets of the magical realms; knowledge that is both ancient and sinister. Gila Monster helps us see through the illusion that marks darkness as being malevolent and evil. She transforms darkness into light, illness into wholeness, despair into gladness and grief into joy. Gila Monster explains that not all 'monsters' are evil and that not all negative experiences are dark in nature. The battle between light and dark and good and evil is usually an internal one. It rarely has anything to do with forces outside our control, even though all the signs being offered at the time may indicate the contrary. Sometimes we have to face our worse fears and spend time trapped in darkness before we can be healed and made aware of the light and beauty that surrounds us. Gila Monster helps us realise the gift of awareness that comes from being trapped in darkness and helps us to step out of the shadows and to present ourselves to the world as authentic and valued members of the community. Gila Monster transmutes feelings of self-loathing into unconditional self-love, negativity into creativity and venomous thoughts, feelings and perceptions into the ability to heal and fortify.

• Goanna – *Protector of the people*

Goanna is the common name for a number of Australian Monitor Lizards, 25 of which are found in Australia. Carnivorous and varying greatly in size, Goanna appears prominently in Aboriginal mythology. Goanna has sharp teeth and claws and is an adept climber. Goanna combines predatory and scavenging behaviours, feeding on any animal he can catch and eat whole as well as carrion. Like most Lizards, Goanna lays eggs, but unlike some Lizards does not regrow lost limbs or tails. To the Aboriginal People of the Bundjalung Nation, Dirawong the Goanna is an Ancestor, Creator Spirit and protector of the people that taught them everything from astronomy and cultural lore, to traditional dance, games, beliefs, values, rules, practices and relationship to their country.

Goanna invites you to connect to the Ancestors and Creator Spirits that, according to legend, taught the people and shaped the land on which you currently reside. He invites you to acknowledge the traditional keepers of the land and to explore the customs and beliefs of the Aboriginal People who lived where you do now before European settlement. As teachers and protectors of the original people, the Ancestors and Creator Spirits will work with you to re-establish your connection to your land and to heal any unease or disease. You will find that your land will begin to work with you, affording you peace and calm, good health and fruitful relationships. Other areas of your life; your finances, for example, will also begin to improve, as will academic achievement, career prospects and the realisation of dreams and aspirations, not to mention the viability of any crops you may produce on your land, or the health and productivity of the livestock you may keep. By connecting to the Ancestral Spirits of your land, you will begin to remember the teachings, beliefs, values, rules and practices of not just the traditional keepers of the land, but also the relationship your family shared with their ancestral homeland, no matter where in the world it may be.

• Iguana – *Inner demons*

 Iguana is an arboreal reptile with stout, powerful limbs, sharp claws and a long tail. Iguana has a prominent fold of skin that hangs from the throat and regulates the animal's body temperature and also sports a crest of soft spines that extend from base of the skull to the tip of the tail. Basilisk, or Jesus Lizard, is a member of the Iguana family and is arboreal inhabiting areas near water. Adept swimmers, Basilisk can 'walk on water' for short, quick bursts; traversing in bipedal fashion, his tail offering counterbalance with specialised scales on the bottoms of the rear feet preventing the water's surface tension breaking. Basilisk has a long, whip-like tail, raised dorsal and caudal fins and overlapping scales, which afford him a magical, dragon-like appearance.

Like all Lizards, Iguana is essentially a dreamer; a potent creature capable of willing his thoughts to fruition. He lies in the sun, soaking up the sun's energy-giving rays, daydreaming and manifesting his potential future. Iguana is a gentle, peaceable creature, with a fiery side when provoked. Despite his inspiring wisdom and strength he has a dark side; a shadow aspect that emerges when he forgets to honour his true self and innate gifts of power. Basilisk was a fabulous creature said to turn anyone unfortunate enough to lock eyes with him instantly to stone. His breath was considered venomous and even withered the plants that stood in close proximity. The only way to destroy a Basilisk, it was said, was to walk backwards toward it, holding a mirror over your shoulder. If Basilisk caught his own reflection in the mirror, he would turn himself to stone. Iguana nurtures the fact that miracles can and do happen when we face our demons head on, look them dead in the eye and send them love. By turning our backs on them, we starve their ego, thus weakening their hold over us. Iguana explains that when we are faced with people, places or things that annoy or frighten us, we are inherently recognising aspects of ourselves that we are not ready to acknowledge. When we admit the fact, and integrate the suppressed aspects, we are able to see others for what and who they are, and not as taunting reflections of our dormant selves. The longer we reject self-healing as an option, the more power we offer our shadow side. Anger, jealousy and vengeance emerge in favour of inner beauty, thus preventing the realisation of our dreams. When we fail to honour our dreams, we grow resentful toward those who haven't until, due to self-loathing and frustration, we create a monster that is almost impossible to slay. Iguana shakes us and brings us to our senses before this happens, so that we may realise with clarity the world of opportunity that has always surrounded us; a world unhindered by limitation and fear. When we breathe life into our magickal (deserving) nature, and shun our demons (fear and self-doubt), we eventually realise our potential and our dreams. When we take control of our lives, we symbolically 'walk on water' in the belief that nothing is impossible.

• Komodo Dragon – *Puberty*

 Komodo Dragon is the world's largest contemporary Lizard and has an acute sense of smell that can locate carrion up to 8.5 kilometres away. He is surprisingly agile, an adept climber and a powerful swimmer. Komodo's mouth is riddled with potent micro-organisms that will see prey eventually die of infection even when they are lucky enough to escape an attack. Komodo Dragon is carnivorous (and cannibalistic), taking Pigs, Deer, Goats and Water Buffalo. Habitat shifts, poaching, excessive culling of prey and tourism have largely affected wild populations, with volcanic activity and fire posing the greatest threat. When we picture Dragons in our mind, we automatically see the scary beasts of faerie tales but Dragon's power actually lays in his ability to shed his skin and emerge as a new, transformed being.

Dragon demonstrates for us the 'will to dare' by teaching courage, strength and self-knowledge. He encourages us to face our fears, to combat them and transform them into personal gifts of inner strength and self-power. Many traditions give specific qualities to the Dragon as protectors of the elements of Earth, Water, Air and Fire. The Earth Dragon guards the treasures of the Earth and speaks of abundance and the wisdom obtained as we reach the maturity of old age. Water Dragon guides us as we meditate and contemplate. The winged Dragon of the air brings clarity of mind while sharing the gifts of intuition and heightened intellect, while the flame-breathing Dragon reminds us to honour the fire in our belly, the passion that drives our creative force, while teaching the lessons of enthusiasm and innocence. Komodo Dragon embraces the energies and corresponding qualities of fire. He brings to mind the passion and enthusiasm needed to bring any project to fruition by encouraging us to retrieve and reactivate our inherent (and mostly overlooked) skills of manifestation. Komodo Dragon guides us back to our teenage years when we held clear and untainted belief in what our future held in store for us and inspires us to reclaim the unlimited potential and untapped power that was at our disposal at that time. Komodo Dragon celebrates the potency and potential that comes with truly believing in yourself, your worth and your abilities.

Loon
Normality

 Loon is famous for her haunting song with four distinct calls described as the tremolo, wail, yodel, and hoot. The tremolo resembles foolish laughter; the wail is more like a beautiful chorus; the yodel is offered only by the male (each with their own specific version) to defend territory, whereas the hoot, or 'whoo', is used to check on the safety of family. Loon has become synonymous with wilderness and solitude and spends extended periods sitting motionless on the water, checking constantly for food. Although capable of flight, her heavy body, solid bones and awkward legs make take-off cumbersome. She occasionally drags herself onto land to nest by hobbling with her chest close to the ground.

According to legend, 'Luna', the primordial moon-goddess, first drifted alone on the primeval oceans, until she tired of loneliness and decided to create a world. Christians declared the worshippers of Luna insane and created the words 'lunatic' and 'loony' to describe a person 'touched' or 'struck by the moon'. It is still thought that irrational behaviour and mental deficiency is somehow influenced by the moon, with an increase in crime or public disturbance reportedly centred on the time of each full moon. Loon's crazy laughter-like call and the fact that she sits alone, motionless on the water, haunts lonely places and hobbles and limps and has difficulty flying like a 'normal' bird, offers a convincing link to the goddess Luna and the supposed 'moon-struck' ways of her followers. This is not to say that Loon is by any means 'crazy' or that Loon people are inherently 'different' from anyone else. It is simply meant to describe the similarities between the bird and the energy that seemingly inspires her wisdom. Loon people are often disabled in some way, but always in a way that enhances their other abilities. With her harlequin patterned plumage, Loon could be said to carry aspects of Heyokah Medicine: the wisdom to teach in a contrary manner, by mirroring weaknesses and fears back at those who demonstrate them, forcing them to acknowledge and integrate them into their lives. Loon forces us to ask ourselves why we see certain people as being different and asks 'What's normal, anyway?' Loon marks everyone as sacred. She allows us to embrace the unusual or unique aspect of ourselves by helping us recognise 'normality' in everyone around us. Loon people stand apart and are lucky in that they are in touch with their sacred selves and never feel inclined to explain themselves to anyone. They trust their inner silence, listen to their inner voice and know their Inner Landscape as readily as they know the quickest route to their local supermarket. Loon invites peaceful contemplation, silence, stillness and balance. She nurtures our ability to understand our dreams, visions and the messages we receive from Spirit, but most importantly, she teaches us to find the sacredness in all people and to celebrate everyone as 'normal'.

Loris
Caution

A nocturnal creature, Loris spends his day sleeping, curled in a tight ball high among the forest canopy and seldom ventures down to the forest floor. A slow and cautious creature, Loris is an accomplished climber with opposable thumbs and big toes, and hands and feet that are capable of grasping tightly for extended periods of time. Special blood storage areas prevent him from experiencing muscle fatigue. Potto, an African strain of Loris, will remain motionless for hours, if necessary. When threatened, Potto will adopt a defensive stance by tucking his head down and presenting his neck, which is shielded by a row of spiny protrusions covered in bumpy skin. If all else fails, Potto will ward off his aggressor by biting it.

As we grow and develop as people, we are encouraged to try new things; to experiment, explore and spread our wings. We are told to try before we buy, taste all the flavours and to never settle for second best. Although this advice is usually offered to help us break through years of indoctrination and personal limitation, it is not always sound counsel that encourages us to totally throw caution to the wind. Remain vigilant and check that what you are doing is safe. When we reach sexual maturity, we are reminded that 'if it's not on, it's not on' in regards to contraception and sexual health and every time we light up a cigarette, we are reminded of the risks and the affects our habit may have on others. Loris does not suggest we never take gambles or reject the opportunity to test and trial, but he does offer warning to be careful and to avoid the taking of unnecessary risks. Loris espouses sound judgment, good advice and purposeful opportunities for questions, open discussion and honest explanation. According to the Loris prevention is better than cure and foresight outshines consequence.

Lynx
Observation

As a species, Lynx enjoys the largest range of any wild Cat and includes the Canadian Lynx, the Eurasian or Northern Lynx and the Spanish Lynx. Diurnal by nature, Lynx preys on Hares, Rabbits, Mice, young Deer and birds, but will eat carrion when food is scarce. Lynx is now a protected species, but she was once heavily hunted for her soft, luxurious pelt and is still occasionally shot as a predator of livestock.

According to Celtic mythology, Cat was often referred to as 'the wingless Owl' and both have carried similarly powerful mysticism for centuries, with the night vision of Owl affording her a sense of privileged wisdom, ancient knowledge and law. Such affirmation eventually led to Owl being associated with scholarly achievement and degrees of higher learning. Ancient teachings, however, remember the long-forgotten acquaintance once held by Owl and Cat, with Lynx still personifying all that Owl alone has now come to represent. Lynx inspires respectful silence and encourages us to cease the chatter (internal and out) and to honour the sacred stillness. She endorses observation and the art of listening. It is said that the moment you stop pushing for something, the sooner it will be made available to you. The moment we stop asking questions, verbally seeking authentication or consulting our cards, psychic mediums or other forms of divination regarding an issue we have previously sought confirmation on, is usually *the same* moment when the window of opportunity presents the answers we seek. Lynx is willing to listen to us complain about our lives, express resentment and jealous thoughts about another or promise that, if we 'get what we want' we will *try* to do better. Lynx is more than happy to listen but don't expect a straightforward reply. Lynx is only concerned with how you look at yourself, how willing you are to identify where your weaknesses lie and what you are prepared to do to initiate changes *yourself*. Lynx asks that we take a step outside ourselves to observe our behaviour and to watch how we handle all that life throws at us. Lynx answers questions with questions seldom offering a candid answer. Lynx knows that unless you are prepared to work hard and offer some form of return for sacred knowledge, it will be lost on you; acknowledged, perhaps, but rarely integrated. So unless you are prepared to stop, listen and hear the advice being offered, and do what needs to be done to honour it, you would be wise not to consult the acumen of Lynx in the first place.

• Bobcat – *Recompense*

Bobcat is closely related to Lynx and is active both during the day and night, preferring to hunt at dawn and dusk. Bobcat is known to reproduce all year round, with gestation lasting almost 60 days resulting in the birth of up to six kittens. Despite strict restrictions, Bobcat is still extensively hunted but the species is classified as stable. Bobcat is occasionally referred to as the Red Lynx and demonstrates some of Lynx's symbolic qualities.

Like Lynx, Bobcat supports the attainment of wisdom through observation and silence, but gently enforces the necessity of acknowledgement and recompense. It is an unwritten law that advocates the offering of thanks as payment for knowledge sought and gained. Lynx observes, for example, that unless you are prepared to expel personal energy (mental, spiritual and physical) in your search for sacred knowledge, it will be lost on you; accepted, perhaps, but rarely integrated. Humans tend to take things for granted when they are unconditionally showered upon them; they tend not to appreciate things fully unless they are forced to sacrifice something personal in exchange. Being afforded the opportunity to sit in silence with an elder, for example, is one that should be graciously received, even if it appears that little or no wisdom is verbally or consciously shared. Such an experience offers humility, and when embraced in silence, usually means further instruction via your dreams later that night. Such instruction only presents itself, however, when you have enjoyed the experience free of resentment or annoyance at seemingly getting 'nothing for your money'.

• Caracal – *Disruption*

Caracal was once caught as a kitten, hand-tamed and trained to hunt birds in Iran and India. Strong, agile and capable of leaping high into the air, Caracal would be released into large public arenas containing great flocks of Pigeons and bets were laid as to the greatest number downed by any one single animal. These arenas were the birthplace of the idiom 'to put a Cat among the Pigeons'.

Caracal people have a wicked sense of humour and love performing practical jokes. They enjoy causing jocular disorder by removing essential 'ingredients' including some that should not be there in all areas of life. Although they always take full responsibility for their actions after the event, Caracal people receive satisfaction from watching people scratch their heads in confusion or squirm with discomfort as a result of their pranks. Sometimes, however, the mischief performed by Caracal people can go wrong, causing huge problems. In which case, Caracal can be seen as a warning of impending conflict, the possible negative outcome of a hoax, or, on a more serious note, trouble brewing in areas that superficially appear calm. If your world is running smoothly, with everything and everyone functioning productively as a team, then enjoy the moment because the appearance of Caracal often heralds a figurative spanner about to be thrown into the works. Caracal poses the possibility of disharmony among friends, colleagues or family members due to (usually unintentional) impertinent behaviour, while warning of consequent reprisal. A harbinger of disruption, Caracal also indicates anticipated plans being altered or cancelled, contracts being dishonoured and verbal agreements being broken, among other things. Caracal warns of impending legal matters, arguments and dishonesty. To have one's world temporarily turned upside down is usually presaged by Caracal, but even with his rather disruptive reputation and his habit of inviting chaos into our lives, Caracal's presence should be regarded as positive. Caracal's antics cleanse our space of stagnant energy and his wisdom keeps us on our toes, in a state of anticipation and readiness for change. Caracal shakes things up when we least expect it, with the intention of showing others in their true light by revealing hidden agendas and falsities, while banishing all that which has become unproductive, overly familiar and mundane.

Lyrebird

Genetic memory

 Lyrebird is known for his ability to mimic sound and has been known to incorporate the sounds of chainsaws, horns, alarms and even human speech. He vocally marks his territory, defending it from other Lyrebirds and passes his learned sounds on from one generation to the next, (with sounds heard today echoing those created by the early settlers). When Lyrebird spreads out his tail during elaborate courting display, he strongly resembles a lyre, a traditional musical instrument of ancient Greece.

According to the wisdom of the Aboriginal People of Australia, the Earth Mother holds memories and recollections of every act of creation and desecration that has ever taken place since The Dreamtime. As the children of the Earth Mother, we also hold such memories. Within every individual cell that collectively makes us whole, resides the keys to the unlocking of memories of past experiences passed from one generation to the next. They are inherited and genetic in nature. Genetic memory represents all that we have ever been or seen before and embodies all that our Ancestors have ever experienced and understood. It represents all that our body inherently understands without explanation; knowledge that cannot be justified or rationalised. The wisdom of Lyrebird supports this concept of genetic memory through his ability to remember the forest sounds of hundreds of years ago. Capable of flawlessly mimicking any repetitious noise, it is believed that Lyrebird passes on sounds he has learned to his young like we would sacred lineal knowledge. Many speak of recalling their past lives, remembering first-hand their lives as famous people in recognisable historical settings. Lyrebird invites us to ponder the option that instead of these being personal memories, they may be the memories of our Ancestors, experiences passed on genetically for us to access and to learn from in our current lifetime. Lyrebird can also display more negative indications, warning that we may be the target of another's jealousy or obsessive nature. An instinctively fine-tuned imitator that has almost lost track of its own true voice, Lyrebird's appearance may be warning us to protect our identity and persona, which are ours alone to flaunt. As an individual who blatantly purloins the qualities of others with the intention of shifting attention from who he really is, Lyrebird insinuates that others may be modelling themselves on our character, while strategically attempting to adopt our unique view of the world. Lyrebird primes us for a time of 'great remembering' and suggests that the Ancestors may be encouraging you to reclaim and reconnect to your past, or that of your family. They may be calling to you from the Void to remember an ancient connection shared or a lifetime enjoyed in a time-frame long gone. Lyrebird provides a deeper understanding of the relationships and responsibilities you enjoy today, enabling you to put them into context while affording you greater clarity and personal direction.

Magpie
Balance

 A common sight in most Australian backyards, Magpie readily takes food scraps from human hands, pet food bowls, picnic baskets and bird-feed tables and tames easily. Magpie (also known as Flute Bird in recognition of his melodious song), rises early in the morning and carols to affirm territory and herald the new day. During the breeding season Magpie becomes very aggressive: swooping and attacking passers-by launching their attack from behind. An intelligent and determined bird, Magpie will persevere until he figures a problem that, once surpassed, will afford a ready food source, freedom or adventure. Wilfulness, therefore, is the gift of power offered by Magpie.

Emissaries of balance (the yin and yang of the animal world) Magpie is the agent of awareness, the embodiment of the relationship between the opposites that are equal and the forces that champion the attainment and correct use of spiritual (or occult) knowledge. Everyone wants to feel better and to live richer lives, but few people want to put in the time or effort to achieve these benefits. Such systems ignore the balance that must be acknowledged within all things, the harmony that sits as a fine line between confusion and awareness, the obvious and the obscure, the obtainable and the unavailable; the natural yin and yang within all things. It is fairly obvious that all of Creation is unknown until it is investigated, and we should remember that the majority of Creation is essentially incomprehensible and must remain that way. We defiantly insist on forcing the few known pieces of the Universal jigsaw puzzle together, while conceitedly assuming that it is our birth right, as 'civilised' beings, to do so. Magpie demonstrates that knowledge, and the power that usually comes with it, cannot be attained overnight or bought off the Internet. True knowledge must be earned and must become a path of the heart, explored with a sense of deep sacredness. Those who seek true knowledge realise that we must become a whole person before we can truly appreciate any spiritual learning, and that the process must involve the shedding of the old self in order to reveal the authentic self hidden deep within. Such learning becomes a voyage of discovery, through which we not only obtain the Universal Wisdom initially sought, but also fundamental information about why we are the people we have become. When we acknowledge the duality within all things, we begin to realise the essential balance that must exist within our own lives – the harmony between our assets and faults, our loves and hates and our joys and sorrows. Only when we recognise the significance of the constancy needed between all things can we truly begin to appreciate the network that makes up the values and beliefs that form the foundations from which we perceive the world. Only when we are able to walk the inherent truth that we carry in our hearts, can we comprehend that we all individually form vital strands in the Great Web of Life.

Only then can we see that we are being inspired to unite in awareness with the Spirit that surrounds us, the Earth that cradles us and Creation that formed us. We are bound with the responsibility to incorporate this potential into our lives. Only then will we realise that all the knowledge we seek is right in front of us, waiting for us to literally reach out and claim it. Magpie offers a doorway to new and other realms. He offers a wealth of knowledge charged with great responsibility, permitting only those willing to honour the balance found within all things to reap its rewards.

Mara
Virtues

Mara, or Patagonian Cavy, is one of the largest members of the rodent family and her ears resemble those of a Rabbit while her body and legs are similar to those of a Deer, with a head that resembles a female Red Kangaroo. Mara is a monogamous creature and while feeding her young, the female Mara is vulnerable to predators, so the male acts as a sentry. Captive breeding is becoming increasingly important as wild populations are diminished due to habitat destruction and competition with the introduced European Hare.

Intrinsic worth is what holds us together. It's what holds our head up and affords the strength to get out of bed in the morning. Our qualities are what make us stand apart from everyone else: they are what make us unique. Mara superficially resembles a potpourri of other creatures; an amalgamation of the strongest features and qualities of several species of animal. She is an animal that isolates her gifts and potentials and displays them like trophies. 'Hare-like' features harness the cycles of life: the essential phases of life, death and rebirth that run intrinsically through all aspects of Creation. 'Deer-like' attributes reminds her to 'walk gently' upon the Earth and to show compassion for all things of Nature. 'Rabbit-like' ears allow her to remain vigilant for those things that mean her harm, tempering her fear so that she's never blinded by 'What ifs?' Her Goat-like 'pronking' suggests excitement, determination and an eagerness to venture outside her comfort zone in order to reach ever greater heights, while her resemblance to Red Kangaroo reminds her to never look back with regret, to show accountability for her actions and to welcome abundance with each leap of faith she takes. Those who embrace the wisdom of Mara also inherently carry these virtues, but in order to fully tap into their fullest potential, must first be willing to breathe life into them and honour them as 'gifts of power'. Mara nurtures us as we step out of the shadows with the intention of honouring our intrinsic worth and shuns compromise, fear and resentment. She offers purpose and direction by guiding us to the realisation of the qualities we carry and the gifts of power they represent. Only when we lose sight of our intrinsic worth and we nurture the confusion in our lives do we remain ignorant to the potential of our intrinsic worth. We feel disconnected, lost and in conflict with the world around us. When we feel in conflict, we lash out and retaliate. Mara welcomes us home by returning us to our fundamental centre. She reminds us of who we are by celebrating and presenting our virtues for all to see, while empowering us to 'get out there' and make a difference.

Marabou Stork
Emancipation

 The only Stork that feeds on carrion, Marabou Stork will congregate with Vultures and other scavenger birds when not hunting and defecates on his legs and feet to help control body temperature. Stork invokes similar symbolism to Crane. When Crane and Stork are seen in flight, they are said to generically represent the released souls of the recently departed and are therefore considered emissaries of change, death and obsolete modes of thinking.

Marabou Stork demonstrates how the gifts of change and release may be harnessed and integrated effectively into one's life. The word *death* is often taken literally, forming confronting images in the mind of emotional upheaval, funerals and cemeteries. When the word death is used in a spiritual context, however, it usually refers to a necessary ending: a transition from an outworn aspect of life into a new phase or the closing of one door so that another may open. Death and rebirth are interrelated and one cannot exist without the other. 'Death' offers freedom. It is a stage we *must* go through in order to emancipate ourselves from subjugation, melancholy and adversity. In order to experience change of any kind, we must prepare for it and 'call it in'. Marabou Stork, being that he kills other animals for food, while alternatively feasting on the discarded carcases of those killed by other predators, is a bird that has forged a strong alliance with death. Embodying the goddess in her crone phase, Marabou Stork primes us for a release of built-up emotional garbage, the dumping of 'soul rubbish' and the expulsion of 'crap' that weighs us down and binds our path so that we have difficulty moving forward in a productive way. To surrender your past to Spirit is to denounce dis-ease, acknowledge your baggage and to shed that which no longer serves you. Memory of past experience is sacred. Memories form the foundation of experience and experience leads to wisdom. It is the negative emotions associated with these memories that cloud our vision and create obstacles. Marabou Stork encourages us to release these emotions and emancipate ourselves by cutting out the dead wood in our lives. Marabou Stork welcomes death on our behalf, invoking necessary change while making the necessary changes that will ensure a high level of productivity. Remember, Marabou Stork only ever visits or makes himself available to those who intentionally put out a conscious call for change.

Marmot

Knock on wood

Marmot, Groundhog or Woodchuck is the largest member of the Ground Squirrel family. Marmot digs his burrow deep under rocks and boulders because a shallow den could result in him freezing to death in his 'sleep'. Marmot hibernates during winter, with up to half of his body weight being lost during this time. Marmot often congregates in family groups, with a single male patrolling a territory containing several females and their young.

Ancient association depicts wood as being sacred with green wood particularly representing the beginning of new life. Trees have long been linked to the mysteries of being, with whole belief systems centred on the principles of the 'Tree of Life'. As the 'Standing People' or 'Ancient Ones', trees dig their roots deep into the soil as a way of instilling resolve and fortitude in our hearts by anchoring us firmly against the pressures of life; their trunks afford symbolic stability, direction and purpose to those who seek their support and, their branches, as they reach up to the heavens, offer spiritual choice and opportunity for us to grow and develop on all levels. Marmot encourages us to plan ahead, to dream and watch for the signs offered by Nature. He reminds us to see life as being rich with potential and to take advantage of every opportunity that life may present. Marmot instils the sacredness of always giving thanks for our prosperity and knows that if he doesn't prepare adequately for the winter, the results can prove devastating. He knows that if he doesn't show gratitude for his survival, he can lose the support and endurance afforded by Nature next time around. Perhaps the ground around the rocks and boulders will be too hard to dig into, resulting in a shallow den unprotected by extra insulation. He warns us to follow suit, and to always give thanks when our efforts are rewarded. It is a relatively modern custom to 'knock on wood', for example: a simple act believed to avert ill destiny and offer thanks for bountiful good luck. It is said that when you 'knock on wood', you are invoking the spirit of the tree from which the wood was sourced while offering thanks to Spirit for initiating its growth, assuring that the root of your good fortune will never be forgotten.

Marten

Repute

Marten or Tree Cat is a member of the Weasel family with the American Marten classified as endangered in some areas. Long hair grows between Marten's toes during winter, keeping him warm so that he may trek across snow in search of food. Solitary by nature, Marten is active at night and is an excellent climber. He relies heavily on course woody debris: fallen logs and dead or hollow trees that provide den sites, prey and protection. Deforestation and land clearing has destroyed much of Marten's natural habitat, resulting in a dramatic drop in numbers. Marten is ruthlessly territorial and although a male will share his region with several females, he will not consent to the presence of another male. Since the early 1800s reports and documented sightings of 'Winged Cats' have abounded: a phenomenon that espouses the existence of Cats capable of true flight due to the physical presence of 'wings'. Because of superstition, 'Winged Cats' are usually shot or drowned as 'envoys of the devil'. In a vain attempt to explain the phenomenon of Winged Cats, an unlikely hybridisation was theorised that imagined the crossbreeding of Marten with domestic Cat.

Due to inaccurate historical accounts of Squirrel-hunting wild 'Cats', Marten/Cat hybrid is an animal whose origins are deeply rooted in misinterpretation. As a result, Marten nurtures the understanding that a freak break can lead to powerful and fortunate reputation if harnessed quickly and manipulated to maximum potential. Reputation, like Chinees whispers has a tendency to spread and grow when left to their own devices, with one person's account fuelling the augmentation of the next. Having an advantageous 'mistake', unexpected success or unlikely encounter witnessed by another could easily initiate a reputation for unusual (even superhuman) ability, gift or talent capable of instantly elevating one to an echelon unattainable by 'normal' folk. Although feared to the point of ridiculousness, Marten people find themselves climbing the ladder of success with very little effort – a ladder fashioned by fraudulent hands. Fame, fortune and social standing are qualities desired by Marten people. Marten, while guaranteeing a window of opportunity charged with potential to offer overnight success, simultaneously warns that such success is usually short-lived when not honoured for what it is. Marten encourages us to embrace opportunity when it presents, and to ride on the back of that opportunity until it is exhausted. Marten asks us to be honest and truthful at all times, however, when it comes to the retelling of how our opportunities were realised. Marten warns against believing our own lies, for lies and deceit are always exposed with any hint of success or second chance being pulled out from under us and our wings being permanently clipped. Honesty is celebrated, on the other hand, with people willing to forgive and support those who take risks in an attempt to better the quality of their lives.

Meerkat

Dependability

A very inquisitive animal, Meerkat has excellent vision and can spot a bird of prey long before most other animals can. Feeding on insects, eggs and carrion, he has a distinct odour which he discharges to discourage enemies. Each family group grades its members with specific roles of responsibility and an individual is chosen to maintain strict surveillance, climbing to the highest point of their territory to keep a protective eye over the others.

Another is typically charged with the responsibility of babysitter who organises her day around nursing the offspring of the others in her clan as they venture out in search of food.

Meerkat represents those of us who see the wellbeing of others as a priority with the knowing that in doing so, we ultimately benefit ourselves. We all have ambition and yearn to find our purpose and to achieve wondrous things. Most people believe they have a purpose and look forward to the day when they can work for themselves or follow a path unaided: a path that nourishes them and their family. Meerkat promises that when we allow ourselves to be of service to others, our efforts are always noticed and ultimately rewarded. Sometimes that reward comes in the form of a healthy wage, while other times it is verbal praise and recognition. When we willingly assist others in the reaching of their goals by offering our time or labour, we are opening ourselves up to the possibility of the favour being reciprocated. Meerkat speaks of unconditional support, assistance and generosity, and the understanding that to offer these things freely is to create space to welcome them back some day. When we yearn to be somewhere or achieve something grand and we know we cannot achieve it alone, to offer support to others and to temporarily put our goals on hold will often see our dreams coming to fruition sooner than expected. Meerkat understands that when we are dependable and work as a team, encouraging the strongest, most agile climber among us to reach the top of the Termite mound, everyone benefits. The others are either offered a hand up themselves, or the bounty is filtered down to be enjoyed by all. Meerkat believes that it ultimately doesn't matter who reaches the top first, as long as someone does. In doing so, everyone else gets the chance to step up and view the world from a wider perspective.

Mink

Acquisitiveness

Mink resembles Weasel in general appearance and is semi-aquatic. Mink is active all year round and may journey several kilometres in search of food. Mink is a ferocious and indiscriminate hunter, and in times of hardship will cache her kill; stockpiling corpses to be consumed at leisure. Mink is known to raid poultry sheds and Rabbit hutches killing all the inhabitants and stacking them in a corner. Mink builds her den among the roots of trees growing close to the edge of streams and waterholes and will also take advantage of vacant Muskrat burrows (killing and eating the original occupants first). Mink sits at the hub of the American fur industry as the primary fur-bearing animal bred on fur farms, alongside the Fox and the Sable. Mink raised on farms in a tiny cage tends to display typical signs of stress: tail sucking and biting, self-mutilation and even cannibalism. At seven months of age, the Minks are placed in large boxes where they are either gassed, have their necks broken (by hand) or are killed by lethal injection.

Acquisitiveness is described as the 'strong desire to acquire and possess'. It suggests avarice and materialistic insatiability. Mink suggests a tendency to focus on what we 'want' rather than what we 'need'. Mink instinctively caches his food because he *needs* to, not because he *wants* to. People, however, *want* Mink coats. Mink represents the fine balance that is often crossed when it comes to the accumulation of material possessions. Mink distinguishes what is justified in its acquisition and what is not. Greed feeds greed. We farm certain animals with little or no consideration for their needs. Animals are sentient beings. They experience emotions just like we do, but they deal with them and express them in different ways. Animals experience happiness, excitement, fear and grief. Animals learn from experience and fully understand what is happening to them. Despite numerous laws and global conferences convened with the intention of outlawing human slavery, millions of people around the world are still kept as slaves today. We hear this and the majority of us cringe or hang our head in shame. Mink reminds us of the sacredness found in all things. Mink reminds us of the simple philosophy endorsed by Earth Medicine – that we are all related and that the animals, birds, plants and stones (and all other things of Nature) are our brothers, sisters and equals. Mink asks us to unite against the urge to exercise power and control over others, to see living things as more than just possessions and to channel our need to own things into more productive, harmless ways. Acquisitiveness is fine. There is nothing wrong with wanting to surround yourself with beautiful things, but sometimes much has happened leading up to their point of sale that you may want to consider before you lay claim. Mink just asks that you take all the relevant consequences into consideration before claiming anything as 'yours' and that you take the necessary steps to raise awareness to the injustices currently being exacted against the weak, the voiceless and the poor – whether they be human or not.

Mole

Plant

 Mole is an insectivorous mammal that lives underground in complex tunnel networks and feeds primarily on insects and worms that fall through holes and fissures in the tunnel walls. Some are aquatic or semi-aquatic in nature. She has small eyes that may or may not be visible and ears that are generally hidden. Mole is a common garden animals often targeted as a pest because of her subterranean antics, particularly in areas famous for well-manicured lawns. Due to her underground existence, Mole was once thought to be a messenger of the Underworld and an emissary of death. In the West, Mole refers to someone who is blind to the obvious and dim-witted in character. In the general sense though, the word 'Mole' has

come to mean a double agent, Stool Pigeon, informant or someone prepared to sell covert information in order to line their own pocket.

And so Mole has earned herself a reputation as being a creature of the dark, not to be trusted. Mole Dreaming, however, does not mean that you (as the carrier of its wisdom) are untrustworthy or acting in a clandestine manner. It simply suggests that you may have unintentionally overheard or accidentally become privy to some very private or secret information that you may not realise the significance of. She asks that you consider the conversations you may have been exposed to recently (personally or not) and to label it all as sacred, while urging you to introspectively ponder the higher reasons for your being involuntarily confided in. Not known for being gossips, Mole people generally do not seek out confidential information intentionally. They are usually simply in the 'right' place at the right time. Intentional or not, though, Mole people are chosen to act as 'plants' for reasons unbeknownst to them at the time. Despite the inadvertency of their attainment of secret knowledge, however, Mole people must remain ever vigilant to what befalls their ears or crosses their desk and what their intentions are when it comes to knowing what to do with it. Sadly, many fall victims to the shadow side of opportunity, unable to avoid temptation when a peripheral opportunity exists to make a lot of money by selling their story, blackmailing the people involved or getting in on the action themselves.

• Star-nosed Mole – *Modification*

 Star-nosed Mole patrols her intricate burrows searching for Earthworms that may have entered through the walls. When she has access to a body of water however, she quite enjoys hunting aquatic creatures. Star-nosed Mole is equipped with a 22-point star-shaped appendage on the tip of her snout that acts as a super-sensitive touch organ and flexible fingers that allow her to touch and feel objects at a rate of 13 times per second. She is also equipped with tiny incisor teeth shaped like tweezers to handle prey more quickly and efficiently than any other predatory animal, which provides her with a real competitive edge. By reducing handling time to a fraction of a second, Star-nosed Mole gains energy by devouring small prey animal.

Star-nosed Mole encourages us to look to the future with a sense of anticipation; a wisdom that offers hope and the chance to manifest our heart's desire. Star-nosed Mole inspires clarity of vision and spiritual insight. She offers a guiding light that promises a fruitful future. Star-nosed Mole instils a deep conviction that paves the way for new opportunity and literally sheds light at the end of the tunnel. Star-nosed Mole people are driven by instinct and follow their nose and trust their senses. Even when a situation appears to offer nothing but dead-ends, Star-nosed Mole people are able to seize even the smallest opportunity, no matter how vague, and run with it. They make powerful guides, mentors and tutors, offering skill and knowledge with ease, due largely to their ability to read their student and impart the wisdom in a way most meaningful to their charge. Star-nosed Mole people are optimistic, outgoing, farsighted, direction-driven, and are innately benevolent, motivated and creative by nature. They make powerful problem solvers, effective advocates and fruitful entrepreneurs, because they can follow a line of thought with little or no comprehension of how or where it might lead them. They trust that it will offer reward, but trust does not always pay out. Star-nosed Mole people don't care – they trust and they follow, it's as simple as that. Star-nosed Mole acts as a reminder that hope actually exists, with hope leading to possibility. It doesn't matter how things pan out, the fact that there is hope instils a sense of calm. It inspires greater peace than knowing what is actually 'out there'. It offers a sense of anticipation and excitement. Star-nosed Mole promises that things will work out. It simply asks that we trust and know that it 'just will'. Star-nosed Mole reminds us that it is not the destination that counts, but rather the journey itself – and the sense of hope the journey rouses.

Mongoose
Heroism

 Famous for his ability to stalk, confront and kill deadly Snakes such as Cobras, Mongoose is an intrepid little animal. Giving little thought to his own safety or wellbeing, Mongoose will form a gang to collectively ward off predators much bigger than themselves, and will come to the aid of a companion in danger. After a gestation period of two months, four young are born deep underground and the male helps to protect the young after they are born. Banding together in family groups of between six to 35 individuals, Mongoose is often seen following Baboon troops; a relationship that should be studied by those who carry Mongoose energy.

True heroism is rare. It takes a very special person to put another's life before their own, especially in a setting that almost promises failure. Mongoose is the totem of those individuals who willingly risk their own lives to assist other people. Those who think little of rushing into a burning house, scaling a cliff face or diving into a frozen lake or swollen river to rescue another (usually unrelated) person, radiate the true spirit of Mongoose. On a less dramatic level, Mongoose encourages us to take risks and to delve into the unknown, or to simply find out what is there. He creates a safety net for those who are willing to take risks that outwardly seem promising and abundant, with the flipside threatening complete failure and the loss of everything held dear. Mongoose promotes risk taking, exploration and the unequivocal justification of the things that we hold sacred. Mongoose helps us to seek support when we feel overwhelmed and to acknowledge when we need rescuing. He does not, however, carry people who embrace the 'victim mentality' or who constantly dump responsibility for their actions on other people.

Monkey
The primal self

The word 'Monkey' refers to primates of both the Old World and New World, but excludes Apes. Among the 260 known living species of Monkey, many are arboreal while some prefer to live on the ground. Monkey is known for his intelligence and unlike Apes, is famous for his tail. Some Monkeys are tail-less and are erroneously referred to as Apes.

• Black-and-white Colobus Monkey – *Conduct*

The blatant dissimilarity between the black and the white of Black-and-white Colobus Monkey's fur against the green foliage of the forest creates a powerful form of camouflage known as 'disruptive colouration': the illusion that the animal is not there despite its obvious presence. There is also a plain black variety of Colobus Monkey (*Colobus Satanas*), and a form known as Red Colobus (*Piliocolobus Pennanti*). Led by a dominant male in a clearly defined territory, Colobus Monkey travels in troops made up of several family groups, but totalling anything up to 200 individuals.

Generically, all Monkeys and Apes call to us to return to our essence. They invite us, in a manner prescribed by their particular species and their specialised Dreaming, to consider our roots and the original teachings that inspired our current path. Colobus Monkey is that of the mediator, the one who offers suggestion from afar, ensuring that what we do at any given time is done in accordance with our original plan, the blueprint we were born into this life with and the 'map' that was intended to guide us to a place of greatness within ourselves. Colobus Monkey acts as an enforcer of spiritual law and the one who ensures we do not stray from the right and true path that we agreed to follow before commencing our Earth Walk. With a gentle nudge, Colobus Monkey helps us regain direction, maintain clarity and to resist the temptation to wander off our path to explore 'more exciting' but possibly less rewarding aspects of life. How we conduct ourselves early in life will offer suggestion as to the fruitfulness of the path we will ultimately follow later in life. Black-and-white Colobus, with his handsome mantle, is an authority on balance, offering a path of integrity while espousing wisdom in the areas of discernment, prudent behaviour and personal protection. Black-and-white Colobus Monkey people can appear negative on first meeting and will self-punish when they feel they are failing, are threatened or overlooked. They intentionally do things they know they shouldn't, 'skate on thin ice' and tempt fate with their health, relationships and other responsibilities. Black-and-white Colobus Monkey people can appear arrogant, vague and, at times, unapproachable. They often suffer from selective hearing and can be morose, needy and, at times, selfish. Tantrums are not out of the question. They like to get their own way and will readily display childish behaviour to gain control or make a point. They are, however, meticulous in everything they do. When displaying their more positive qualities, Black-and-White Colobus Monkey people are hardworking and loyal. Intense and overly solemn at times, Black and White Colobus Monkey people are sympathetic of others and are capable of achieving levels of personal greatness because they are complimentary and helpful. They are romantics at heart; helpful, encouraging and systematic. When encouraged, they are organised, economical and cautious with money. Their empathy makes them effective problem solvers and mediators, despite being overly emotional. Red Colobus warns of deviation from one's path and Black Colobus indicates someone haunted by disillusionment, despair and erratic thoughts and emotions. Both Red and Black Colobus Monkeys work in conjunction with Black-and-white Colobus, helping to hold those currently exploring its together until suitable professional, emotional or spiritual support can be found; help armed with the knowledge required to safely guide them back to their initial path of truth. It is never too late to return to the centre of the Web of Life and start again.

• Bush Baby – *The child*

Otherwise known as the Galago or Nagapie, which means 'little night Monkey', arboreal Bush Baby is one of the world's smallest primates. But despite his diminutive size, he produces shrill, eerie cries surprisingly like those of a human baby. Equipped with large, round innocent 'night-vision' eyes and Bat-like ears, Bush Baby is well adapted to his nocturnal lifestyle, expertly tracking insect prey in total darkness. Fast, nimble and precise, Bush Baby jumps from tree to tree, tucking his delicate ears flat against his head with his arms and legs close to his body to prevent them from being snared by branches and thorns.

With infant-like features, Bush Baby is an animal of complete trust and unconditional love. He radiates innocence while demonstrating total acceptance and an enduring sense of peace. He cries a pitiful howl in response to the realisation that someone somewhere believes themselves to be forsaken by Spirit; in recognition and pity for those who are alone, confused and trapped in darkness and illusion. Bush Baby cradles that inherent trait found within each of us that longs to be optimistic, innocent and spontaneous regardless of our age. Bush Baby instils a sense of playfulness that appreciates and supports the essential balance that must subsist between the ability to be light-hearted and child-like when desired, but serious and mature when needed. The balanced Bush Baby person is a pleasure to know and their joy and love of life invites others to follow suit. The unbalanced Bush Baby person however, may come across as 'wounded' in some way and are often described as being 'spoilt brats'. People who demonstrate the more negative aspects of Bush Baby often feel abandoned, forsaken or unlovable. They often act in a way that is socially unacceptable, often throwing tantrums or demonstrating depression, neediness, jealousy or resentment. Bush Baby encourages us to trust the relationship we have with ourselves, prompting us to take that leap of faith, to *intuitively feel* our path and see it clear of obstacles. Bush Baby demonstrates how to listen to our subtle senses instead relying on what we see, feel and hear as 'real'. He teaches us to return to the innocence of a child, to listen to 'the child within' and to once again become 'the fool' – the pure, wide-eyed one, the one free of guilt and blame, so that we may once again step out into the world with eagerness in our heart and a bounce in our step. Bush Baby supports those willing to take educated guesses and calculated risks. He warns us to be aware of the obstacles that we may come across, but not to live in fear of them. Obstacles must not be anticipated, for they are easily manifested through fear and misguided intention. Instead, they must be considered valuable lessons, bridges to be crossed when you come to them, to be questioned and investigated and integrated into your consciousness as experience-based wisdom.

• Capuchin Monkey – *The indigo/warrior child*

 Made famous as the 'organ-grinder's Monkey', Capuchin is an incredibly intelligent animal and is often kept as a pet and trained as a therapy animal. *Capuce* is French for 'skullcap' and he got his name from the fact that his fur resembles the cowl or *capuche* worn by Franciscan Monks. Capuchin Monkey has adapted well to living in close proximity to man.

The Capuchin Monkey is the totem or Power Aspect of the indigo children or, as I like to call them, warrior children. The indigo child can appear impatient, domineering and quick-tempered. They often display impatient, impetuous and disagreeable qualities because they are inherently angry. Indigo children cannot relax. They are argumentative, pushy and resentful. They hate losing and can be inflexible and stubborn. Indigo children do not suffer fools lightly, offering derogatory remarks, unemotional displays and unsympathetic observations. Indigo children question everything and can be hostile and even violent when cornered. Indigos appear suspicious of everyone and are typically overly emotional and volatile. When questioned, indigo children will tell you they feel frustrated, restless and angry. They have no logical reason for their defiance. They don't mean to be challenging or disrespectful but are easily confused and distracted. Indigo children seem to approach the world in a half-hearted, reckless manner and protect themselves emotionally by detaching themselves from family, being indiscreet and vulgar. Indigo children are often medicated due to being misdiagnosed as having ADD and ADHD. They can be manipulative, demanding and controlling at times. They display addictive personality traits, are demanding of loyalty and are often accused of being 'users'. Indigo children are loners, independent and bossy. When fully demonstrating their positive aspects, however, indigo children are awe-inspiring. They are born leaders, are energetic, dynamic and optimistic. They display the 'pioneer' archetype, while being undemonstrative in their approach. Indigos represent the initiators, the rescuers and the explorers among us. They are determined, independent and self-reliant. Indigo children are confident, capable and are goal-oriented. Motivational and wise, they are usually worldly, street-wise and experienced in life. Their knowledge comes from both a higher level of awareness and a lifetime of (often negative or abusive) experience. Indigo children are profoundly aware, intuitive and sensitive to the subtleties of life. They are grounded and practical in their beliefs, love Nature, have green thumbs, are attentive toward animals and children and make good listeners. Indigo children can easily identify a liar and a deceiver; they abhor hypocrisy and shun judgment. They Walk their Talk, are realistic and learn from experience. Innate survivors, indigos lead by example, while delegating affectively, inspiring and stimulating their crew with enthusiasm and praise. They are productive team members, are competitive by nature and strive to achieve. Although they prefer their own company to that of a crowd, indigos can be social, polite and patient when required. They are good in a crisis, great under pressure and are generally always proven right in an argument

• Guenon Monkey – *Relationship*

 A small omnivore, Guenon Monkey adapts easily to a variety of habitats and male Guenon is easily distinguished by turquoise-coloured testicles in some varieties, and is slightly larger than the females. A stone made popular by the philosophy of the Native American culture, the turquoise is a talisman of power that energetically assists with communication, protection and love. It is carried to build firm friendships, claim victory over antagonists, manifest abundance and promote good luck. It is a stone that offers vitality and is often carried as a love charm, especially when one wants to meet an individual who speaks truth and walks a path of integrity.

Guenon Monkey corresponds energetically with the properties of the turquoise, a relationship made evident by the animal's blue/green testicles: the aspect of the animal most potently charged with productive energy. Guenon Monkey is an animal of high awareness and a keeper of sacred wisdom. He offers the keys to interconnectedness and tuition in the wisdom of the animal, plant and mineral kingdoms and their corresponding energies. Those who carry Guenon as a totem or power ally are sure to find their investigation into the ways of Nature a 'remembering' experience rather than a 'learning' one. The ability of the Guenon Monkey person, for example, to effortlessly lead others deep within themselves on a meditative level, to a place of healing, creativity and clarity is awe-inspiring. Financially comfortable, dynamic and emotionally independent, Guenon Monkey people make friends easily: loyalty and commitment are their prime objectives in life. Their wisdom is sought by those who yearn to find peace of mind, emotional stability and a balanced perspective of life.

• Howler Monkey – *Broadcast*

Howler Monkey is so named because of his loud, rasping howls used to herald the beginning and end of each day. He howls to secure his territory and to protect his sources of food from other troops and can be heard over a distance of several kilometres.

When you have something to announce, Howler Monkey offers a viable vehicle to have your message heard. An animal that marks the rising and setting of the sun with triumphant chorus, Howler Monkey offers clarification as to when an arrangement will be contractually signed, consummated or confirmed. Alternatively, when a project or relationship has run its course, Howler Monkey will offer similar clarification regarding its definite termination or closure. Howler Monkey signals defined early stages; the confirmation of something meaningful and dear to the heart. He broadcasts all new beginnings, birth, admission and promotion. Similarly, Howler Monkey signs the final days of things that have reached fruition signifying the end of a season, a death, resignation or standstill. He can also herald change; a graduation of sorts, that brings closure to one phase of life while shining hope and potential on the next. When a Howler Monkey person says 'Yes', he means 'Yes', not 'Maybe' or 'We'll see'. Never offer a Howler Monkey person a 'Yes' if you are not able to honour it or you can expect an explosion of tirade and abuse because change of heart is generally interpreted as rejection or doubt; a smear against their name and character. Howler Monkey people are quick to anger. They can make mountains out of molehills; a lot of noise for apparently little reason. They do not like being 'left in the lurch', 'kept in the dark' or 'left dangling' regarding affairs of the heart or issues related to business. They enjoy knowing when they have been given a definite green light and when things are to come to a close because they hate loose ends and question marks. They prefer things to go their way. They rely on clarity, defined boundaries and clear, precise explanation.

• Macaque – *Reason*

Living in large, multi-male troops, Macaque is a social creature that will often share the care and responsibility for younger members of the group. A heavy-set Monkey, Macaque is known for his human-like traits, trusting disposition and high level of intelligence. Japanese Macaque, for example, is famous for his habit of bathing (to the delight of tourists) in ice-covered lakes, rolling snow balls, and for sitting, often lightly coated in snow, diligently grooming one another. Rhesus Macaque however, is better known for his domesticated role as circus and carnival animal and as unwilling substitutes for human subjects in medical and scientific research.

Emanating an aura of unconditional peace, acceptance and personal conviction, the humility of Macaque is breathtaking. Sustained by an inherent trust in karma, Macaque advocates that 'nothing ever happens without reason'. Where most animals offer acumen based on their interaction with their kin, prey and environment, the wisdom of Macaque stems from a lifetime spent observing humanity from a biased position of fringedweller, plaything and tool. Macaque demonstrates that although 'things happen' all the time, *nothing* ever happens by chance. 'Victim mentality' is like a noxious weed that silently creeps into a beautiful garden, throttling everything that resembles hope and possibility. Instead, Macaque offers a shift in consciousness capable of exposing the hidden reason behind all things, thus eradicating the 'victim gene' forever. Macaque speaks from personal experience as he reminds us that life is rarely free of obstacles for those truly fated to leave a positive mark on the world, illustrated by the peaceful lifestyle of the Japanese Macaque at one end of the comparative scale, and the not-so-peaceful one of the Rhesus Macaque at the other. Although the two lifestyles are worlds apart, the apparent good Rhesus Macaque's purpose holds far outweighs its circumstance (or so we have to believe, for why else would Spirit permit such an obvious misuse of power and control), with the karmic rewards matching dollar for dollar. Macaque nurtures those forced to endure what appears to be more than the fair share of misfortune in the formative years by explaining that some people must experience as much as possible (both good and bad) before they are considered 'qualified' to venture out into the world to serve humanity, help people and support the global changes that are afoot. Unless they have experienced all that life can throw at them, how can they offer others the wisdom to overcome it if they do not have the experience to back up their words of advice? Many of the world's greatest, most inspiring leaders, mentors, healers and teachers (Oprah Winfrey, for example) experienced poverty, hardship and pain before succeeding later in life. Many say that their childhood gave them ambition to aspire and grow, and that without their early experiences they would have had little reason to strive for more. This, too, is the acumen of Macaque.

• Spider Monkey – *Alternatives*

 Spider Monkey is closely related to Capuchin Monkey and Howler Monkey. He has an arboreal tail that that he uses as an extra hand and for climbing and grasping and from which he hangs for short periods of time, freeing his hands to collect food (and he doesn't have thumbs). He sleeps high in the canopy to avoid predators. When threatened, Spider Monkey erupts into a chorus of loud barks and retreats if all else fails. Fights are rare. According to legend, Monkeys first came into being after a huge wind storm blew up and swept the villages into the surrounding forests. Instead of grieving for what they had lost, however, the people decided to make do with what their new environment offered. They became Monkeys and lived thereafter in

accordance with what the jungle was able to provide. Initially they were frightened but they soon came to realise that the storm had happened for a higher reason, and that they were being offered an alternative to life they had previously not considered.

Spider Monkey suggests we think about the other options that are being offered to us in relation to the direction we are currently taking in life. He offers plenty of warning that things are not going according to plan, while offering endurance to leave unsupportive situations and swing to other more fruitful ones. Spider Monkey helps us vision a more viable future that nurtures us on all levels. He then supports us as we harness the energy and the courage to bring it to fruition and guides us to choose the right time, best words and ideal location to voice our requirements and the decisions we have made to honour them. Spider Monkey taps into the wisdom of his cousins to offer a voice and the leadership qualities necessary to inspire others to follow our lead (when appropriate). Spider Monkey people inherently know when and where the grass is greener and require little encouragement to take advantage of it. Although they are not always consciously aware of the options at their disposal, Spider Monkey people are very sensitive to their surroundings and are always the first to detect unease or brewing tension. They aren't afraid to speak their mind, and as a result, quickly get to the root of things, resolving issues before they get out of hand while seeking alternatives that offer choice and contentment all round.

• Squirrel Monkey – *The crystal/nature child*

 Squirrel Monkey is a very peaceful, arboreal creature whose future is threatened due to habitat destruction from logging and agricultural encroachment. She is indeed a beautiful Monkey who travels in mixed species groups, often associating with Capuchin Monkey. Squirrel Monkey initiates communication by following the Capuchins, who help her find food more efficiently. The allegiance does not appear to benefit the Capuchin Monkeys greatly.

Squirrel Monkey is the totem or Power Aspect of the crystal children or, as I like to call them, nature children. The one thing that is always noticed on meeting a crystal child is that they never shut up! They are chatterers, gossips, embellishers and story tellers. Crystal children talk incessantly. I have two of my own! They love trivia and can appear frivolous and dizzy. Crystal children are forgetful and forget names, 'important' details and dates. They can appear narcissistic and restless. They tend to complain about petty things, are often accused of being lazy and are sometimes egotistical and loud. People can find their ways off-putting. Crystal children are very naïve to the ways of the world. They are curious and ask a lot of questions, but often don't wait for or listen to the answers offered. Crystal children can be crass and shallow. They tend to externalise blame, anger easily and be negligent of responsibility. They are also messy and disorganised and are often described as being fake, unsympathetic and forced. Crystal children suffer from selective hearing, self-doubt and apprehension. They are daydreamers; undisciplined creatures that often don't listen. They can be attention seekers, procrastinators and time wasters. Crystal children often confuse their priorities, appear needy and are often unpopular to the majority. They yearn to be popular, successful and wise, but usually fail in their attempts because they interrupt, make excuses and are repetitive and boring. When demonstrating their more positive attributes, however, crystal children are charming, appealing and fluent. Crystal children are attractive, beautiful and youthful. They have large, innocent eyes that captivate and lure. They love being the centre of attention and are the teller of tales. Crystal children are funny, artistic and demonstrative. A crystal child will hug, kiss or reach out and hold hands on first meeting. They are emotional and passionate. Crystal children are communicative, animated and entertaining, or reserved, silent and watchful. Often misdiagnosed as autistic as small children, crystal children will stare at strangers, communicating with their mind. Their positive attitude and child-like personality are both inviting and pleasing. Crystal children are innocent; they look out at the world in awe and wonder. They are honest, truthful and live in the present. Unpredictable at times, crystal children can be candid and blunt. They are family-oriented, popular with all ages, supportive, helpful and see only the good in others. They make effective leaders, are inventive and creative. Crystal children are active, enthusiastic and inspiring. Crystal children are community-oriented, charitable and spontaneous. They love to be complimented, are forgiving and apologise without prompting. They appear exciting, enviable and lucky.

• Tamarin / Marmoset – *The rainbow/ golden child*

 The *Callitrichid* family contains 26 species of Marmoset and Tamarin, which are among the world's smallest monkeys, with some species only weighing 100 grams. Adept climbers, Marmoset and Tamarin cling vertically to trees. Their arms are shorter than their hind legs, and they do not have opposable thumbs. Diurnal by nature, Marmosets and Tamarins congregate in family groups with one to three young produced each year.

Tamarin is the totem or Power Aspect of the rainbow children or, as I like to call them, golden children. Rainbow children march to the beat of their own drums. They are weird, eccentric and strange. They are incongruous; appealing yet disconcerting. They may appear agitated, insensitive and dull; qualities regarded as tiresome and tactless. Rainbow children are selfish, critical and emotionally numb. They embrace the victim mentality, while outwardly appearing unmotivated, boorish and self-centred. They can be incredibly naïve, bordering on stupid. Rainbow children can seem dumb-witted, denying knowledge and feigning ignorance. Rainbow children seem to enjoy being stuck in a rut, preferring to complain about their circumstance rather than doing anything about it. Their lives are often chaotic and disorganised. Rainbow children can be critical, boring, old fashioned and morose. They can also be indifferent, intimidating and irresponsible. They repel others and are often accused of being deceitful, sincere and manipulative. Rainbow children can be demanding, close-minded and aggressive. They can be trouble makers and attention seekers, opportunists and instigators of peer-group pressure. When working in the negative, rainbow children are uncouth, controlling, forceful and offensive. They can be close-minded, destructive and common. Rainbow children display bizarre traits, frightening habits and unusual beliefs. They can be pitiless, unsympathetic and will do anything to make a point. When demonstrating their more favourable qualities, however, rainbow children make powerful leaders, healers and teachers. Rainbow children are intuitive, knowing and dreamy; their calm, gentle personas inspire peace and tranquillity. Rainbow children often display advanced spiritual knowing and powerful spiritual gifts. Rainbow children are telepathic. They are capable of telekinesis. They can communicate readily with animals. They are powerfully empathetic and sensitive to the vibrations and energies of plants, places and people. They are sensitive to change and readily champion charitable causes. They inherently carry ancient knowledge, are affective healers and are usually described as being 'old souls'. Rainbow children are dreamers. They have green thumbs, love animals and are at one with Nature. Rainbow children are worldly, politically aware, educated and make powerful motivators. Rainbow children are peaceful, tranquil and carry 'old world' charm. They are wise, sensitive, appealing and attractive. They radiate a powerful presence and easily attract a crowd. They make happy, content babies. They are known to stare, sit introspectively and hum quietly to themselves. They are honest, truthful, gentle and kind. Rainbow children are pacifiers. They make excellent teachers; being both inspiring but firm, quietly spoken and loved by all, but strong, powerful and assertive. Rainbow children are individual, independent and artistic. They are eloquent, inspiring and encouraging. Rainbow children are groundbreakers, innovators and initiators. They are strangely appealing, eerily attractive, familiar but exotic.

• Uakari – *Dishonour*

 Uakari lives for between 15 and 20 years in the wild. He is a shaggy primate with a furless, scarlet-coloured face. Uakari is both active and intelligent and enjoys playing games with others. Uakari gathers in large family groups consisting of up to 100 individuals but forages in groups of three or four. Uakari emits loud shrieks to define territory. Uakari is endangered because he is poached for food and as a source of bait. He also suffers due to habitat loss caused by logging and agricultural encroachment and is also trapped and degraded in scientific and medical research.

Marked by the red face of embarrassment, stress or high blood pressure, Uakari people carry shame, humiliation and contempt. Uakari people often hide their feelings and numb their emotions behind a veil of substance abuse, or punish themselves with excessive exercise or ill-temper. Uakari denotes a history of abuse that has not been fully integrated or consciously acknowledged. He speaks of shame, guilt and self-loathing that, if not addressed and surrendered, threaten to negatively affect their health and general wellbeing. Uakari people grow up feeling unnoticed, unloved and rated as second best. They believe themselves forsaken by those that should offer protection and unconditional love. Uakari suggests a cry for help, a yearning to be acknowledged and nurtured. He is a tell-tale sign that assistance is required and that dishonour has been imposed. Uakari offers the chance to put things right, to avenge a lifetime of wrongs and to rescue and support those who have never known stability or peace. Uakari offers safe haven to those with nowhere to go; a sanctuary or 'drop in centre' for people who need somewhere to rest and share their story. Those drawn to explore Uakari would do well to qualify as a counsellor or seek voluntary employment in a hostel or women's refuge. Uakari also suggests opening the family home up to orphaned or fostered children, abandoned pets and injured wildlife.

Moose
Durability

 Moose is the largest member of the Deer family and similar in size to Horse. Moose is solitary during the summer months, staying close to rivers and lakes. An adept swimmer, Moose will submerge herself entirely to avoid parasitic insects and to feed. Only the males grow antlers, using them to mark territory, defend their mate against rival males and to pull water weed and other edible vegetation out of the ground. The antlers are broad and flat and are discarded after the rut. Moose is an unpredictable animal, particularly when threatened and a normally shy cow with young can be irrational and dangerously protective. Rutting males have been known to charge at people.

Moose is an icon of the wild; an embodiment of the backwoods and all that she represents. She has become a symbol of wisdom, strength and stamina – an ambassador of the North. To the Indigenous People of America, the 'North' is represented by the Earth element. The Earth element offers purpose, direction, grounding and the promise of prosperity, while initiating personal growth, maturity and inner security. Those who embrace Moose are also welcoming the vibrational qualities of the North into their lives. Those who yearn for stability and emotional balance are typically looking to the Moose for reassurance. Those who live their life in a constant state of flux are people who would respond well to the wisdom of Moose who nurtures those who yearn to feel true confidence or believe the conviction they claim to have in relation to personal issues or affairs of the heart. Obtaining sustenance by permanently questing for emotional nourishment, Moose people would do well to focus on the tangible, constants in their life rather than striving for things temporarily (or permanently) out of reach because it offers emotional provision. Moose supports those who are prepared to take responsibility for their lives and to show accountability for their actions. In exchange, Moose cradles and nurtures permanence and healthy vulnerability. Moose people are often described as being dreamers or visionaries. They have a strong inner knowing that inspires their decisions and the directions they take in life. The trouble is confusion also reigns supreme, with gut feeling and practical consideration constantly locking horns. Moose navigates us through the emotional pool of life in a practical, grounded manner.

Mouse

Scrutiny

 House Mouse generally lives in close proximity to humans and builds his home under the floorboards, in woodpiles, behind cabinets, under cupboards, in the walls or roof cavities of buildings, or digs complex underground burrows and networked tunnels that include warm and dry nesting and storage chambers and multiple escape points. He lines his nest with rags and paper (which he tears up with sharp teeth) or natural material such as grasses, horse hair, feathers and leaves. House Mouse inhabits ploughed fields, orchards and market gardens, hedges and wooded areas. Nocturnal by nature, House Mouse runs swiftly, is a good climber and jumper and adept swimmer. He has excellent vision and hearing and a keen sense of smell and uses his whiskers to feel air movements, thus detecting predators long before they are physically present.

In medieval Europe it was believed that Mouse embodied the souls of the dead. It was assumed that the soul exited the corpse via the mouth in the form of a House Mouse. It was also thought that House Mouse could place reincarnated souls back into the bellies of women, inserting them into the womb to await re-conception and rebirth. White Mouse, in particular, was said to personify the souls of children. House Mouse promises new beginnings, rebirth and can be invoked to help tie up loose ends and initiate fruitful progression on all levels. With House Mouse as a mentor, even those who wield minimal influence in the world can achieve levels of prominence if they believe and hold greater expectations for themselves, and plod at a steady pace and progress little by little. House Mouse demonstrates that sometimes strength of mind prevails over strength of body, with most of the answers we seek hidden in how we perceive the problem. House Mouse warns of possible intrusions and betrayal of trust, showing us how to be ever alert to the telltale signs that things are not as they should be. House Mouse is always careful not to overlook any small detail that may eventually come back to haunt him, and remains ever aware that he may, should he ever let his guard down, feel the searing pain of Owl's talons in his back. Approaching the world with ego-laden grandiose plans can hinder progress just as effectively (if not quicker) as being too afraid to take the smallest of steps or the safest of risks. Not being afraid to admit that you need assistance when you find yourself tightly bound up in a situation honours the wisdom of House Mouse. However, simply listening to the analytical wisdom of House Mouse before initiating any project generally prevents us from finding ourselves in such a situation in the first place. House Mouse uses his keen sense of smell to test the air for danger and allows his whiskers to feel the air and to touch everything in his path, checking that all is as it should be. House Mouse encourages us to check everything, and then to check them again, before assuming that all is safe and sound. House Mouse promises that when we embrace scrutiny as a quality, we can never again overlook the obvious.

• Harvest Mouse – *Harvest*

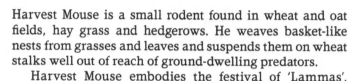

Harvest Mouse is a small rodent found in wheat and oat fields, hay grass and hedgerows. He weaves basket-like nests from grasses and leaves and suspends them on wheat stalks well out of reach of ground-dwelling predators.

Harvest Mouse embodies the festival of 'Lammas', when the gathering of the first grain harvest of the year was celebrated. Lammas means *loaf-mass day* in honour of the Christian custom that saw people place on the church altar a loaf of bread made from the first crop of wheat. Lammas originated with the Celtic Feast of Lughnasadh; a celebration of a plentiful harvest, the Earth Mother's beauty and her bounty in recognition of the fact that the grains gathered during the harvest formed the bulk of the food eaten during the winter. Lughnasadh was named after the sun god Lugh, who was thought to reside in fields of golden grain. During Lughnasadh, sports and games were played to encourage continued vitality and good health for both the people and the land. Harvest Mouse sees us reap the rewards of our hard work. He pays out for those who are prepared to work hard toward a goal, while diligently preparing, showing patience and tenaciously doing their best. The unexpected arrival of Harvest Mouse is a sign that you are about to be recompensed for your loyalty and commitment to getting the job done. Harvest Mouse reminds us, though, to never take such bounty for granted, because if we do, it will soon be spent with nothing left to carry us through 'the winter'. Harvest Mouse also suggests the realisation of dreams 'planted' earlier in the year, like seeds sown in the subconscious mind to be germinated, grown and reaped when the time is right to offer tangible opportunities.

Musk Ox
Vulnerability

Musk Ox inhabits the cold Arctic tundra and its surrounding regions and is the only hoofed mammal to live so far north. Insulated by long guard hairs and a woolly undercoat, she is robust and strong. The males produce an odour released through glands located just below the eyes and have thick horns that meet at the crown; an aspect referred to as a 'boss'. The females have smaller horns, but do not have a 'boss'. Musk Oxen gather in a defensive circle when threatened standing shoulder-to-shoulder with lowered heads, protecting their young in the centre. She also stampedes with little provocation, resulting in very young animals being left behind or lost.

Musk Ox offers stamina and protection to the vulnerable, infirm or mentally or physically immature. She shores up the weak by proffering warmth security and stamina and is particularly evident in situations where a whole neighbourhood rallies together in support of an individual or a family that has experienced loss or adversity. Musk Ox invokes a sense of community spirit; a charitable buttress that affords endurance and practical backing to start again. She provides warmth in times of coldness and calm in times of upheaval and insulates against harsh or inhospitable conditions. She physically and emotionally warms those who find themselves exposed to the elements, open to attack or susceptible to negative suggestion. Musk Ox shines through in times of difficulty and wraps herself around us like a reassuring blanket, nurturing and instilling a sense of wellness and the strength to soldier on. When we are not the ones requiring comfort though, she encourages us to reach out an empathetic hand to others. Musk Ox people are warm, gentle and mothering, trustworthy, kind and sympathetic. They are grounded and practical, approachable and all embracing. They are well equipped to deal with people who appear standoffish or 'cold' by quickly establishing a sense of safety that invites them to open up and reveal what is on their mind or burdening them psychologically. Musk Ox is the totem of people whose purpose it is to guide, inspire and facilitate healing and a sense of wellbeing and safety in others.

Muskrat
Salvation

Muskrat is a large semi-aquatic rodent and has a thick waterproof coat made up of silky underfur and coarse, glossy guard hairs. Muskrat gets his name from two anal glands located under the base of the tail, which produce a tawny-coloured, musky substance used to communicate during the mating season and mark territory. Muskrat builds his home in compact lodges crafted from dry cattails and bulrushes and relies on both plants as a source of food and as shelter against wind and strong waves that threaten the integrity of his lodge.

Because of its association with the infant Moses (the child was found in a reed basket floating among bulrushes), the bulrush has become a symbol of faithfulness, humility and salvation. A plant that similarly offers new life and devotion, the cattail was once carried by women who had difficulty conceiving, who yearned to enjoy sexual intimacy or who longed for fidelity in their relationships. As an ambassador of this wisdom, Muskrat endorses a similar understanding. Because Muskrat integrates both the bulrush and the cattail so heavily into almost every aspect of his life, he can be consulted for similar reasons. Along with obvious sexual connotations associated with the esoteric properties of Musk (it is considered an aphrodisiac with properties not unlike the human pheromone) Muskrat offers good medicine to those who need to heal and integrate sexual blocks or release anger and resentment regarding sexual abuse, rape or similar experiences in a healthy, productive way. Muskrat helps balance the emotional yin and yang aspects using a non-invasive approach. Essentially, Muskrat carries the potency to either help us conceive, carry and birth an actual baby, or to similarly (sexually and mentally) rebirth ourselves by offering clarity, peace and acceptance. Either way, he presents us with the traditional celebratory 'cigar' as an indicator of our success.

Octopus
Infidelity

Octopus inhabits many diverse areas of the ocean, particularly coral reefs. He has a soft body with no internal skeletons and no outer casing and eight 'arms', each bearing two rows of suckers with which to grab and hold prey. Octopus has a Parrot-like beak which offers him access to narrow cracks between rocks when escaping from predators. Most Octopuses eject a cloud of thick black ink when fleeing their pursuers. Most, too, have unique skin cells that allow them to change colour and reflect and refract light. Such specialised defence mechanisms allow them to blend into their environment, to communicate with other Octopuses or to ward off predators. Some Octopuses can shed their limbs, like Skink will drop its tail, as a way of distracting unwanted attention.

Eight is inherently positive; a number of great power. It speaks of authority, creativity and endeavour. Numerologically, the number eight suggests harvest and incentive, abundance, potency and growth. Astrologically, the Eighth House governs sex, death, change and those things we have little or no control over. With this in mind, eight is also the number of karma, suggesting that what we sow, we will eventually reap, and that what we do or say will someday come back to haunt us unless we maintain a sense of integrity in all that we do. Despite his obvious link to the more abundant energies of the number eight, Octopus recommends close consideration of one's credibility and the choices we make in reference to karmic accountability. Sadly, Octopus has built himself a reputation as the cheat of the animal world, who warns of infidelity and impulsive behaviour. Early myth renders Octopus as fickle and one of little faith, because he flees when under pressure, changes his colour and ejects a cloud of ink to cover his tracks. Flirtatious men and womanisers are often accused as having 'as many hands as an Octopus', thus confirming the somewhat dubious wisdom of the slippery, 'spineless' creature. Those who carry the wisdom of Octopus are advised to take a long hard look at their record of loyalty and fidelity, with those associated with an Octopus person encouraged to reassess the relationship and their sense of self-worth.

Okapi
Uncertainty

Hidden from the world until 1901 when she was first 'discovered', Okapi is possibly the only living relative of Giraffe. Like Giraffe, the male Okapi has small, naked horns on his forehead. Diurnal by nature, Okapi feeds on the thick, lush greenery that grows alongside the paths crisscrossing the forests, rather than the foliage of the dense canopied areas. Because of her limited habitat, the future of Okapi remains unstable, due also to the fact that her elusive nature makes it difficult to estimate how many remain in the wild. Enjoying restricted protection since 1932, Okapi still falls prey to illegal poachers, indigenous hunters and the effects of civil warfare.

Everything about Okapi is tentative in nature. Nothing is definite. Okapi is a fringedweller that exists in a void of uncertainty. She *sometimes* lives alone, but *may* gather in small herds at times. She is *thought* to be Giraffe's only cousin and *may or may not* be endangered. Her future is unstable, sure, but even that is questionable due to the fact that no one can penetrate the thick forests she inhabits to accurately study and record her numbers. For those who feel inspired to explore Okapi wisdom, the message is fairly obvious because Okapi is an animal ideally suited to explore the lessons of decisiveness and confidence, if only she would acknowledge the teachings of Leopard and integrate them into her life. It is exhausting to live a life of uncertainty, never knowing what is assured from one day to the next and tiresome for those who wait patiently by your side. Those who resent having to make plans more than one day in advance, or resist making decisions one way or another in even the simplest of situation, ultimately miss out on the joy found in behaving spontaneously. Leopard stalks Okapi, daring her to embrace change while taunting her to make decisions that will enhance her life, but alas, all his good intentions fall on apparently deaf ears. Instead of living one minute to the next under the assumption that we cannot make sudden decisions because we don't know what might happen, embrace the

'What if?' and throw caution to the wind. Not knowing what might happen is the whole point. It adds spice to life. Stand up and be counted and try venturing off the 'safe path' that has been diligently and blindly followed by your generations past, with little or no thought of veering off. Acknowledge your trepidation, but honour it as anticipation, and hack your way into a new, exhilarating, unchartered part of your forest. You never know what (or who) you might find.

Opossum
Denial

Opossum has ancestry that dates back 70 million years. Similar in size to domestic Cat, Opossum has a powerful prehensile tail that allows her to hang for short periods of time. Folklore suggests that Opossum hangs by her tail when she sleeps, but this is a fallacy. Nocturnal and omnivorous by nature, Opossum eats fruit, insects and small mammal. She eats carrion too, and is often struck by cars while feeding on road kill. When threatened, Opossum will belch, urinate or defecate in order to deflect attention (if fleeing is not an option), or may 'play dead', by rolling over, stiffening her body and slowing her breathing down to a point where it is almost undetectable, the whole time emitting a rancid 'death scent'.

When they feel bored, indifferent or 'pissed off' by someone, Opossum people express their contempt immediately instead of trying to figure a reason for their annoyance. Opossum people would often rather 'play dead' than face responsibilities or show accountability for their actions. They would rather pretend that the obstacles or negative influences haunting their life are the result of the words, thoughts or actions of others. They refuse to take control of their own life as it superficially appears too difficult. Instead, they would rather look with resentment upon the lives of others, choosing to recognise the hard work and sacrifice they may have had to suffer in order to achieve. Opossum people blame others for their shortcomings, preferring to vehemently deny knowledge and refuse to accept any other viewpoint. Opossum people can be short-tempered and crass. Their negative traits are most commonly witnessed during displays of jealousy and intolerance. They have difficulty encouraging or praising others in times of success; instead grumbling and criticising in a vain attempt to nullify personal feelings of inadequacy. Opossum people, often through no fault of their own, view the world from an inverted perspective. The world will often overwhelm the Opossum person, who may use words like topsy-turvy, confusing and unsettling to describe their childhood and teenage years. Opossum feeds on carrion, suggesting a symbolic connection to the Underworld. This link offers insight into how the Opossum person might shift their perception and improve their view of the world (and themselves). It clarifies those aspects of the self that need to be put to rest or allowed to die, instead of being allowed to fester and taunting the soul and creating a sense of dis-ease. By dealing with them, Opossum offers positive and immediate closure. Opossum inspires lateral thinking and skills enough to avoid stagnation and interference. She does this by instilling clarity, awareness and responsible action. Opossum primes us to turn a deaf ear to criticism, a blind eye to temptation and to avoid feelings of impatience and denial. Opossum improves our view of life too, by encouraging us to consider the lives of others when shackled by the apparent misfortune of our own. She suggests we offer support and encouragement to others, and see what mirrors back. Opossum provides the strength for us to 'to hang on' by avoiding self-pity. By offering others the very support we need, we become stronger. Instead of relying on the support others may provide us, we find the strength we seek by offering it instead. Even when the world seems turned upside down, we can reclaim a sense of stability by realising that our life is never as bad as the next person's.

Orangutan
Man of the forest

 In Malay, the word *orangutan* means 'man of the forest'. Orangutan is a large Ape that enjoys a mostly arboreal life, rarely venturing down to the forest floor and prepares sleeping platforms high in the forest canopy each night before going to sleep. He obtains adequate moisture from water trapped in forks of trees and by licking the rain off the leaves of rainforest plants. Orangutans are becoming increasingly endangered as a species, with wild populations declining almost to the point of extinction because of continued habitat destruction and the sale of infant animals into the illegal pet industry. Orangutan is a shy, solitary and highly intelligent animal and has been witnessed using found objects as tools; covering babies' heads with leaves, for example, to save them getting wet.

As the gentle 'man of the forest', Orangutan is the contemporary embodiment of the ancient Green Man of traditional folklore. Such creatures were seen as the protectors of the forests and the trees and animals that dwelt therein. Although wary of humans, they meant them no harm. As the voice and guardian of such untamed beauty, Orangutan reminds humanity of its ignorance and nearsightedness as a race. The more we plunder our forests for their resources (most of which are non-renewable in the short term), the quicker we ensure the downfall of life as we know it. According to legend, with the unnecessary death of each tree, the weaker we render the protective power of the Green Man and, with the eventual felling of the final tree, comes the annihilation of his spirit forever. When we ignore the sacredness of life on Earth, we lose sight of our own purpose and sense of belonging and with each stroke of the axe we essentially cut off our own lifeline and connection to each other. Orangutan offers a voice to the voiceless by asking us to say 'Stop. Enough's enough'. Orangutan is shared by those who fight to protect the environment and the animals currently recorded on the world's endangered species list. Orangutan inspires us to work diligently, peacefully and lawfully to bring about change on a global scale, while reminding us that one person, seemingly alone in the greater scheme of things, can help raise awareness by simply telling one friend.

Ostrich

Grounding

 The flightless Ostrich is the largest living bird on Earth. Both sexes have bare necks and thighs, long, mobile necks, small heads, large eyes, long, powerful legs, and two clawed toes on each foot capable of tearing open the stomach of a Lion. Nesting in the dry season, Ostrich prefers flat areas that receive low levels of annual rainfall and usually chooses to live alone, but will occasionally travel in loose flocks. Living for 40 years or more, Ostrich is gifted with powerful vision and agility. Equipped with extremely well-developed leg muscles, he can reach speeds of up to 50 kilometres per hour, but contrary to folklore, he does not bury his head in the sand. He does, however, swallow small pebbles to aid digestion, and for this reason, Ostrich is symbolically very grounding and nurturing of those who tend to drift aimlessly through life.

Adopting a practical, earthy approach, Ostrich promotes emotional accountability and responsibility. Being prepared to confront adversaries in order to protect what one holds sacred, to stand firmly by one's convictions and to only ever consider retreat when hopelessly backed up against a wall are indicators of someone productively working with Ostrich. Ostrich never encourages cowardice or gutless behaviour; quite the opposite. To be liable for the effect you have on others is the keynote speech of Ostrich. Maintained eye contact, relaxed body language and meaningful conversation are welcomed by Ostrich, an animal capable of detecting even the slightest whisper of insincerity. If Ostrich has appeared in your life, you are being encouraged to take a practical stance, to ground your otherwise flighty tendencies and to take responsibility for the path you are currently travelling. Do not deny anyone or anything, especially when you know in your heart of hearts you are answerable, and always Walk your Talk. This is the wisdom of Ostrich.

Otter
Playfulness

 Otter is an aquatic or marine mammal belonging to the same family as Weasels, Skunks and Badgers. She has dense, soft underfur and an outer layer of long guard-hairs that keeps her dry and warm. Some Otters (particularly Sea Otter) have become adept at opening all types of shellfish. Otter generally hunts at night.

To many, Otter is a creature of light-hearted charm; a mischievous feminine being that harnesses the energy of both Water and Earth. She helps us balance the joy found in being spontaneous and playful with the practicalities and responsibilities of living a mundane existence. She encourages us to 'loosen up' and to be less serious and anxious about life. Otter, in some traditions, is considered a trickster who, when caught, asks not be thrown into the water for fear of drowning. Of course, being an adept swimmer, the moment she is thrown in she turns and faces her aggressors, laughs tauntingly and swims away. Otter affords permission to express our emotions and to be more open with our feelings. She returns us to a state of child-like awe and delight at the world around us, nurturing us as we once again take pleasure in and appreciate the simple joy of little things. Otter quickly brings things back into perspective, when the 'important' things that previously absorbed the majority of our time and attentions suddenly fade in comparison to the sheer joy and humility of being a parent, or if not a parent, the sheer joy and humility of being alive. She helps us realise where our true power and purest sense of abundance lay, to the point where all other personal commitments take on a secondary degree of significance. Otter invites us to take time out for ourselves; some time that inspires a sense of fun and adventure and reawakens dormant memories of people, places and things that make our heart sing and things that we are inherently good at but tend to mentally shelve. Otter also helps us find pleasure in the more mundane aspects of life – the chores, jobs and responsibilities that would normally weigh us down, frustrate us or inspire resentment for those not burdened as we perceive ourselves as being. She helps us see them as essential and blessed aspects of life, duties that may not be there if not for the treasured people and opportunities in our life.

• Sea Otter – *Indulgence*

 Sea Otter feeds on abalone, crabs, clams, mussels and fish. Sea Otter is famous for being one of the few mammals to make use of tools. To open the abalone, for example, she will place a rock on her chest and smash the shell against it. Sea Otter's coat is made up of dense, tightly packed hairs that offer excellent insulation and buoyancy by trapping pockets of air. When trapped in oil slicks, she suffers greatly because her fur becomes sodden with oil, resulting in her dying of cold. Although she is now protected as an endangered species, fishermen

would like to see Otter removed from the protected list in favour of preserving the Abalone trade. An animal that dotes on her young, going to great lengths to provide adequate food and love, Sea Otter sees the sacredness in balanced fun, freedom and relaxation.

Sea Otter inspires playfulness, curiosity and joy and instils the sense of freedom only found when we are truly spontaneous and free of worry or concern for what others may think or say. Sea Otter helps us forge an agreement to reward ourselves with fun and games after dealing with our chores and other responsibilities. She offers concession for those who spend their entire time working or embroiled in monotonous, uninspiring activity that keeps them away from their family. Sea Otter lifts us out of the realms of the mundane and encourages us to learn new skills, try new things or to at least step away from activities that restrict movement or hampers vision. Although work is important because it allows us to provide for our family, it should never interfere with the quality of time we get to spend with them. Sea Otter supports us as we take tentative steps to leave our comfort zone by offering buoyancy and endurance and encourages us to let our hair down and dive head first into new arenas of life, after which she suggests we lay back, put our feet up and relax. Life should never be a case of 'work, work and more work'. Sea Otter dispels worry by reminding us that unless we step back and take the time to recharge our emotional battery every now and then, we will inevitably go under. Life will become a case of sink or swim, with all areas of our life being negatively affected, not just our work.

Owl
Deception

Owl is a silent flyer due to the velvety surface of her feathers, making the element of surprise the strength of her assault. The first that unwary Mouse knows of the presence of an Owl for example, is the pain of sharp talons felt in his sides. The Dreaming lesson here is that of deception. Today, according to her pooled spiritual teachings, Owl warns us not to assume that all is well all of the time. People and situations we trust may not be completely trustworthy, but Owl has the ability to see what others may miss. The gift of this Dreaming is to be undeceived by external appearances and to discover the truth beneath them.

• Barn Owl – *Visitation*

 Barn Owl, (Monkey-faced Owl or White Owl), is found throughout the world and feeds on rodents, reptiles, insects and small birds. She nests in tree hollows, crevices in walls and cliffs, abandoned buildings, barns, chimneys and warehouses. She has a flat, heart-shaped face, snowy white and ochre-coloured plumage and felted-edged wing feathers that afford her the gift of silent flight. If Barn Owl enters a house via its chimney, is seen sitting and calling from the roof of a house or is heard during the day or for three nights in a row, British tradition says there will be news of a death or a sudden ending.

The Indigenous people of Australia say that Owl personifies the souls of women. Therefore, according to legend, she is considered sacred. Owls are our sisters and our sisters are essentially Owls. Often the totem of mystics, shamans, spiritual healers and seers, Barn Owl, or the Ghost Owl, is the sentry that guards the passage that leads to the Underworld. It is my experience that when one is visited by Barn Owl, a loved one in Spirit is trying to make contact or is wanting to reassure those left behind of their wellbeing and happiness. Barn Owl is an emissary of change and a harbinger of the inevitabilities of life and death and is therefore also associated with people whose work centres on death. Rather than portraying death as a final destination, however, Barn Owl portrays it as the beginning of a journey rather than an ending. The word *death* is often taken literally, rousing confronting images in the mind of emotional upheaval, funerals and cemeteries. When the word death is used in a spiritual context, however, it usually refers to a necessary ending: a transition from an outworn aspect of life into a new phase or the closing of one door so that another may open. Although it *can* indicate the passing or visitation of a loved one, Barn Owl more often than not represents the death of the old familiar self – and the eventual rebirth of the new. She affords the clarity to see through the gloom, confusion and grief associated with death or change while encouraging us to reassess our life and how we live it. She primes us for a time of awakening, a period of regeneration and growing awareness. Barn Owl nurtures our dormant understanding of the bigger picture by offering insight into the darker mysteries of Creation and helps us understand or find peace with why things happen while vowing to give them purpose. Barn Owl offers death to the recognised self by daring us to ponder who, what and why we are the way we and then to seek our greater purpose and grow spiritually.

• Frogmouth – *Secret keeper*

An anomalous member of the Nightjar family, Frogmouth is not a true member of the Owl family, despite her nocturnal habits and similar hunting techniques. Frogmouth sits stock-still, her face pointed skyward like a dead branch and her grizzled tawny-grey plumage artfully camouflages her among the bark and rotting limbs of old trees. Frogmouth hunts rodents, Frogs and insects, and is commonly seen perched on powerlines, preying upon unsuspecting insectivorous Bats.

In ancient culture, the tribal elders were respected members of the community, regularly sought out for their knowledge and wisdom. Their wisdom was revered simply because it had been accumulated over many years of life experience. Although some cultures still care for their elderly at home, considering them the integral hub of the family, Western society tends to banish their elderly to aged care facilities. As a result, many of our elders do not talk about the past and instead hold their knowledge deep within themselves like a secret, to be shared only with those who seek their counsel. Frogmouth's tawny-grey plumage is reminiscent of the silver-grey hair of the elders and just as Frogmouth sits silent and still cloaked in aged-feathers waiting for wisdom seekers to come and request its guidance, our elders sit and wait wrapped in their blankets, watching for the young to return to a sacred place of remembering. As an ambassador of the elders, Frogmouth stores the secrets of our Ancestors. Frogmouth espouses that our wisdom may lack depth and encourages the seeking out elders' knowledge and to approach them with respect and ask them to share their sacred knowledge and most importantly, to ask the elders of Spirit, God, Creation and the ways of things. Ask until there is nothing more to ask, and then endeavour to incorporate the memories and wisdom of these things into your life and share them, with the blessings of your elders, as the Sacred Knowledge of your people. Frogmouth invites us to honour the elders as our mentors, teachers and counsellors now, while we still have them. If your elders are walking with Spirit, find the silence within and seek their counsel through vision. Remember them as the keepers of ancestral knowledge and your family wisdom, and know that by embracing this knowledge you will one day be approached by a younger generation who will seek the secrets you hold sacred and ask you to share with them.

• Horned Owl – *Warning*

Horned Owl gets her name from her pair of large 'ear tufts' and use them to communicate via body language. When aggravated, the tufts lie flat and when they are curious, they stand erect. Horned Owl emits a series of deep hoots, with the nesting female having a higher-pitched voice. Small prey is swallowed whole, but large prey is first torn into manageable pieces before being consumed.

Since time began it seems Owl has held great mystery for the people. She has become a symbol of prophecy, secrets and higher knowledge. As a silent flyer and a creature of the night, Owl has, on one hand, become a bird not to be trusted – as the embodiment of death, deception and negative influence, while on the other hand, is revered as a powerful teacher and ally; one who can help us navigate life with clarity, intuitive knowing and wisdom. According to superstitious folklore, when one spies Horned Owl, it is a warning of ominous misfortune. It is also said that buildings inhabited by Horned Owl are most likely haunted, because Owl is one of the few animals that can comfortably handle the unsettling energies emanated by the restless spirits of the dead. Horned Owl (or any other animal for that matter), never promises bad luck or ill fortune for those 'unlucky' enough to happen across her in the wild. I would consider it a blessing and a huge honour to have Horned Owl fly before me, especially if my experience was enhanced by the gentle light of a full moon. Instead of fearing the possibility of negative consequence however, I would ask the Owl: 'What are you trying to tell me? Do you have a message of warning for me?' I would expect the message to offer confirmation or guidance regarding some aspect of my life path that had been 'haunting' me or causing me vague concern. I would not assume bad luck because 'luck' is what we make it. Horned Owl lends her eyes so that we may see in the darkness. She helps us determine lies or dishonesty that threaten to limit our growth, dampen our potential and sway the faith we have in our personal judgment. She reveals things trying to remain hidden, camouflaged and undetectable to trusting eyes. Horned Owl is a bird of illumination and clarity, who offers rebirth and the chance to re-establish solid foundation before everything is lost or stolen by unforseen hands.

• Snowy Owl – *Weathering*

 Snowy Owl is a heavyset raptor with bright white feathers banded in black and nests on hummocks in the Arctic tundra. Like all Owls, Snowy Owl is a 'silent flyer'. Diurnal by nature, Snowy Owl also hunts at night and feeds primarily on Lemmings, Hares and other rodents. She migrates south during the winter months when her food supplies are exhausted and is often found around the lake districts, marshlands or by the sea during this time.

Snowy Owl is a creature ruled by Boreas, the North Wind. An animal that thrives equally well in both dark conditions and light, Snowy Owl is a harbinger of balance and endurance. Snowy Owl teaches us when to be powerful, aggressive, strong, and when to be humble, gentle and susceptible and helps us blend in and act appropriately to every situation. She shores us up when we feel weak and defenceless, while helping us find inner peace and tolerance when we're angry or upset. Snowy Owl encourages us to figuratively face the North Wind: to weather the storm and welcome the wisdom afforded by the elemental forces at work in our life. Snowy Owl helps us realise the hidden agendas behind every action and spoken word. With feathers of white stained with black, Snowy Owl nurtures the understanding that no one is perfect and that even those with the purest of hearts have a 'dark side' that lurks, waiting to raise its head at the first given opportunity. Snowy Owl maintains a sense of honesty and discrimination that enables us to deal with situations when they arise, with maturity and openness. Snowy Owl people are able to see both sides of the coin: to point the finger where appropriate and to show accountability for the role they may have jointly shared. Snowy Owl promises that if we tough it out, hang on and maintain resilience, honesty and truth in how we conduct ourselves and our perceptions, we will find understanding and acceptance during even the most distressing of situations. Like the pure driven snow, impeccability must be our primary motivation and focus. Armed with such a quality, Snowy Owl guarantees success, personal growth, forward motion and abundance. Snowy Owl teaches us to trust our claircognisant abilities, while instilling enlightenment, clarity and a deeper appreciation of life. She affords stamina and the strength to live in the present, instead of looking back with regret or into the future with anticipation, and to express our emotions as they present rather than suppressing them through fear.

Ox
Supremacy

 The Wild Ox family includes Yak and Gaur. Yak was once hunted for his meat and hide and few survive today in the wild. Domestic Yak has been kept as a beast of burden for centuries and is much smaller than his wild counterpart. Wild Yak congregates in groups of between 10 and 100 and finds nourishment in a sparse habitat that would never sustain other domestic stock animals. Yak provides people with a rich supply of milk, butter, meat, 'wool' and leather. Gaur, or *Seladang*, is classified as a vulnerable species, with trophy hunting, poaching and habitat loss posing the most significant threats to his survival. Gaur generally congregates in small mixed herds led by a dominant bull.

Ox reminds us of our innate strengths, abilities and gifts from Spirit. Ox reminds us that we all start life as vulnerable little calves, dependent on our parents and open to external influence. Depending on what life may throw at us, we all have the potential to become powerful and great. Unfortunately, many of us are affected by the negative influences of life, with the residue of these experiences forever tainting our view of the world and ourselves. Ox reminds us of our inherent strengths and rebuilds confidence: confidence in ourselves and our place within the world. Ox makes us feel strong, powerful and purposeful. He affords self-assurance to announce pride in our abilities, attributes and qualities, to see ourselves as strong and capable and to shun cowardice so that we may face our demons and overcome superficial weakness. Those drawn to explore Ox are being primed for new beginnings. They are being asked to follow their senses and their inner knowing, because even though they may not consciously know how or where to find answers, purpose or nourishment, Ox cultivates their ability to intuitively know. Ox balances our emotional state so that fear and doubt do not get in the way of us eventually realising our dreams. Ox creates a foundation of trust. His wisdom reminds us that we inherently know what we need and what will meaningfully nurture us, our family and our future so that we can manifest abundance and an air of supremacy. Those who embrace the wisdom of Ox have confidence in their power to create, to manifest and to bring to fruition those dreams they believe show potential. Ox reminds us to remain vigilant – watchful of possibility and ready to step into any new situation that offers opportunity. Although a master of problem solving and conflict resolution, Ox warns us, however, to guard against the insecurities and fears of others, obstacles that threaten to yoke and bind us with self-doubt.

Pangolin
Panacea

Nocturnal by nature, Pangolin is covered with large, flat, armoured scales that allow him to roll into a tight, impenetrable ball when threatened. The name *Pangolin* is a Malayan word meaning 'rolling over'. Pangolin is primarily terrestrial, but some species live in the trees. Arboreal Pangolin has a prehensile tail, used to help maintain balance. His strong claws enable him to gain access to Termite mounds and Ant nests. Pangolin has scent glands similar to those of Skunk, which he uses to spray predatory animals. Despite being declared illegal in the year 2000, the practice of using Pangolin scales has long been prized in traditional Chinese medicine as a supposed medicinal cure for many ailments. In Africa, Pangolin's head is used to impede excessive bleeding. As with all cures that rely on animal-based ingredients, it is not necessarily the animal parts themselves that offer the 'cure', but rather the spiritual 'medicine' imbued within the animal's wisdom. The client gets better because they believe they will.

Simply invoking the spirit of Pangolin would offer similar relief from the conditions listed above. By visualising Pangolin walking with an ailing person, for example, sharing his medicine on an energetic level, would afford equal benefit to physically consuming his body. To the Western mindset, the word 'medicine' automatically inspires visions of pharmaceuticals prescribed by a doctor designed to make ill people well again. When we invoke the spirit of an animal by asking it to share its wisdom, we essentially set about absorbing aspects of its strength, or 'medicine': power that can inspire change and healing on an energetic level. Pangolin explains that all things of Nature carry innate 'medicine', spiritual power capable of reinstating a sense of wholeness and wellbeing. He celebrates the vibrational potency of animals normally harvested for their medicinal worth by endorsing the invoking (rather that ingesting) of their healing potential. Pangolin offers his wisdom as the voice for all animals persecuted in the name of medicine. The fact that no animal must die in order for us to benefit from them however, sits at the core of Pangolin's message to humanity.

Parrot
Colour therapy

There are approximately 300 species of Parrot found throughout the world, with 56 indigenous to Australia. Parrot is known for his brilliant range of colours, which include every hue of the rainbow. Cockatoo is a member of the Parrot family which includes the Gang Gang, Sulphur-crested, Black Cockatoo, Galah and Corella

Cockatoo. Cockatoo has been known live to 100 years of age, often outliving his owners. Cockatoo is identified by the crest of feathers on his head that stand erect when he is excited or angry. Social birds, Cockatoo is both noisy and gregarious and is commonly kept as a pet in Australia, with many species readily mimicking human speech.

Generically, Parrot is associated with colour: the vibrant, healing energy that radiates the magic of life. Sensitivity to the vibrational properties of colour sits at the hub of colour therapy. It supposedly reinstates equilibrium to our body's internal energy centres, with each of our systems and organs resonating to their own particular colours. Colour therapy is said to stimulate our inherent ability to heal our physical and spiritual body and to repel illness and dis-ease. Parrot is a solar creature that corresponds vibrationally to the energies of the sun. Such association makes him an emissary of change: birth, death and rebirth. He heralds new growth, new ideas and the birth of the new day. Anyone inspired to explore Parrot should consider studying colour therapy in any one of its many forms. Many species of Parrot can be taught to mimic human speech. Parrot may be seen as an envoy of the animal realm, linking his world with ours through the power of communication.

• African Grey *Parrot – Intelligence*

 An unpretentious grey in colour, African Grey Parrot is an incredibly shy bird and is very difficult to find. Using his powerful bill to enlarge the cavities that naturally occur in old tree trunks, African Grey Parrot's den is large, dry and warm. Laboratory research found that African Grey Parrot can understand and perform activities requiring symbolic and conceptual skills considered fundamental in complex cognitive and communicative ability; skills typically only recognised in human subjects. More recent studies compounded evidence of human-like intelligence in the bird with observations such as cooperative alarm signalling and the recognition of other birds and individual humans as well as the ability to engage in complex conversation. African Grey is known to interact in meaningful dialogue with another, as are several other species of Parrot, but more surprising is his ability to communicate with clarity and implication with their *human* keepers, while easily mastering puzzles and other 'brain-teaser'-type activities designed specifically for primary school children.

To explore the wisdom of African Grey is to celebrate the existence of notable intelligence and the freedom it affords when explored in a productive way. To invoke African Grey is to embark on a journey of discovery, a quest that promises independence and self-assurance. When African Grey makes his presence known, ask yourself if you are wasting a chance to implement your intelligence. To carry the energy of African Grey suggests a higher than average level of intellect, acumen possibly not being taken advantage of to its fullest potential right now. Not everyone is equipped to handle

African Grey's wisdom. If you are one of the lucky few to fully appreciate his message, consider the fact that you may be wasting an innate resource capable of lifting you out of the mundane and delivering you into a world of abundance and security. To implement the true essence of African Grey is to feel the gentle shove of Spirit to develop your intelligence by returning to school and qualifying in an area that feeds your soul and offers purpose. To remain stagnant, while complaining about one's misfortunes when you are equipped with the mental aptitude to do something about it, is to dishonour the presence of African Grey Parrot. A bird of shy disposition, it takes a lot of courage for African Grey to present himself; to ignore the reason for his visit therefore, is not only considered dishonourable but also foolhardy.

• Black Cockatoo – *The Void*

Some say that in the beginning there was perpetual darkness – a gentle Void, a blanket of nothingness that tenderly swathed the Universal plains. Within this fertile emptiness the Great Mother stirred, as if waking from eternal slumber. As though trying to recall some distant memory, she began to unfold, twisting and churning, herself into fruition. She began to reach out into the darkness as a massive expanse of nurturing energy that seduced everything it encountered, willingly drawing all into her protective Womb. The dark sister of the Sulphur-crested Cockatoo, the Black Cockatoo carries Genetic Memory of this sacred time and within her Dreaming comes the lesson of surrender.

Black Cockatoo demonstrates the patience that can only come when we accept that we cannot possibly know everything at the beginning of any journey and that wisdom will present itself at the appropriate time. She helps us to take control of our life by insisting that we grow at our own pace and learn what we need to know in our own time. She encourages us to just sit in contemplation and wait for the mysteries of our life to unfold without consciously seeking answers. At the appropriate time, when our mind is still and our heart is at ease, Black Cockatoo passes the torch of illumination to her cousin, the Sulphur-crested Cockatoo. Black Cockatoo allows the mystery of inevitability to unfold within our life so that we may finally surrender to change. She teaches us to trust that whatever is meant to happen will, but only in its own time. Black Cockatoo encourages us to confront our fears, to go with the flow and to embrace all new opportunities as they present themselves, thus paving the way for Sulphur-crested Cockatoo. Red-tailed Black Cockatoo is also said to carry the energy of the Grandmothers. He is seen as a lunar-influenced bird as his red feathers represent the blood of the feminine creative force. Yellow-tailed Black Cockatoo is said to carry Grandfather energy, with yellow feathers influenced by the masculine energy of the sun, while White-tailed Black Cockatoo offers unlimited potential and the chance to embrace the wisdom channelled from one's higher self and the Angelic realms.

• Budgerigar – *Experience*

Budgerigar has evolved from the natural green hue of his wild Ancestors to a veritable rainbow of choice. The green and gold plumage of wild Budgerigar reflects the vibrational properties of our heart and solar plexus chakra centres. The heart chakra, represented in some traditions as a green spinning disk, symbolises the sincerest of human connections, acceptance and unconditional love, while the 'yellow' solar plexus chakra governs our feelings, gut reactions and innate sense of knowing. Consequently, Budgerigar represents a heightened sense of assimilation. He allows us to embrace life more richly by broadening our established knowledge, productively integrating our past experiences, deepening our view of the world, sense of love, self-worth and appreciation for those around us.

• Cockatiel – *Warmth*

Cockatiel helps us find peace in the knowing that when the skies become overcast and our day becomes gloomy, all we need do to overcome feelings of melancholy is remind ourselves that everything happens for a reason. Cockatiel helps us look out at the world with hope and promise in our hearts, and to see all negative experience as a chance to start over or as an opportunity to revaluate our motives and intent. Cockatiel's golden face is symbolic of the warmth we feel when we look toward the sun and the warmth received as we are embraced by the golden glow of promise. Cockatiel indicates that whatever life may throw at us, our future will be offered endurance, supported by the eternal love of Spirit.

• Corella – *Realisation*

Corella offers reassurance, confirmation and affirmation that things will work out for the best. The call of Corella is essentially a message from Spirit that settles the mind and heart, dispelling doubt, fear and feelings of unease. Corella offers promise that the day ahead will unfold to reveal wonderful realisations, new friendships and alliances and a healthy outlook for the future. (With sincere thanks to Erika Grimes for sharing her sacred interpretation of Corella and for giving me permission to include it in my book.)

• Galah – *Joy*

In Australian slang, to be labelled 'a Galah' means you're probably a hooligan, roustabout, practical joker or someone who is a bit silly. Galah is gregarious, raucous and socially extroverted. He is predominantly pink and grey in colour, has a superficial crest, scimitar-shaped beak and powerful claws.

Galah's pink chest is associated with the heart chakra and its energies. The heart chakra teaches trust, acceptance, self-love and love for others. Galah teaches us to love life and all that it offers and the joy that it brings. Galah brings people together because he brings the best out in everyone. Galah represents our social, interactive and outgoing side, while helping us feel happy in our own skin. He enables us to drop judgment about others and ourselves. On the other hand, the grey, which is the dominant colour of this bird's plumage, can suggest hesitancy and indecision. The wisdom of Parrot, of which Galah is a species, illustrates communication and healing. When this is cross-referenced with that of Galah, it sheds a different light. Galah can help those cynically labelled as 'Galahs' to find the inner strength to ask for help, to seek acceptance and love and to demand positive attention. Often people act like Galahs to get attention because they do not know how else to attract it. Bad attention is thought to be better than no attention at all. Young people often choose this path because it seems the only option. Galah helps us to honestly assess our actions and assists those close to us to read between the lines.

• Gang-Gang – *Return*

Gang-Gang espouses the fact that when a man is emotionally and spiritually supported by his woman, he will learn to reclaim his ability to dream and manifest through vision. When he is encouraged to communicate from the heart, show his emotions and tap into the sacred creative force that represents all that is feminine, he will begin to walk as one with his 'sisters' with his yin working in harmony with his yang. Gang-Gang supports the male so that his spirit walk and his physical walk can unite and walk as one as it did at the beginning of time.

• King Parrot – *Fondness*

King Parrot often portends feelings of love, gratitude, understanding, compassion that must be expressed in order to achieve one's greatest potential. King Parrot resonates profoundly with factors associated with the heart chakra; issues related to fondness, love, gentleness, kindness, compassion and trust. King Parrot evokes feelings of true devotion, and can suggest that we are about to meet our life partner, or that we are denying ourselves a solid friendship because we are letting personal feelings get in the way of reality. King Parrot explains that sometimes a friendship shared with someone we love is better than no relationship at all.

• Rainbow Lorikeet – *Liberalism*

Rainbow Lorikeet reminds us that we are all deserving of equal respect and acceptance, no matter what path we follow, what god we pray to or what our sexual inclination may be. Rainbow Lorikeet celebrates the Rainbow Tribe philosophy; the belief that, all people, of any colour, nation or culture are equal and of one heart. He invites us to lay down our arms and embrace all men and all women as our brothers and sisters so that we may, some day walk as one into a unified future. He celebrates diversity, personal preference and independence. Rainbow Lorikeet, for example, may be viewed as a collective totem of the gay community, because of the fact that the rainbow has long been the universal symbol of Gay Pride.

• Rosella – *Announcement*

Rosella usually portends feelings of hatred, resentment, confusion or indifference that must be expressed in order to set one's heart and soul free of torment. Crimson Rosella can indicate factors related to the base chakra, for example, aspects of self that need to be expressed, sexual issues that must be discussed and dealt with, questions associated with life path and purpose, or announcements that must be made in relation to trust, love and fidelity. Eastern Rosella announces a forced change in direction or a new phase initiated against one's will. An unexpected pregnancy, separation, redundancy, eviction or similar knock back may all be heralded by Rosella Dreaming, with a reminder that 'bad' news, when considered in hindsight, often reveals itself as a blessing in disguise.

• Sulphur-crested Cockatoo – *Illumination*

Each morning as the sun rises in the East, it symbolically promises a new beginning and a chance to start over. As the sun's golden rays stretch out across the horizon, banishing the dark mysteries of the night, it initiates opportunity. Our minds are once again made clear, our vision is exact and our sense of purpose is rampant. We intuitively know that potential is ripe and previously unrealised prospects are there for the taking. Folklore has it that when Sulphur-crested Cockatoo eats the seeds of a particular tree, a reaction takes place that enables his flame-like crest to glow in the dark. Such a legend affords Sulphur-crested Cockatoo the wisdom of the metaphoric guiding light for anyone wandering aimlessly through life. A solar-influenced creature and traditionally found sitting in the East on the Wheel of Life, Sulphur-crested Cockatoo can be seen as a messenger of light with his crest illuminating the end of the dark tunnel for individuals lost in despair.

Considered sacred by many of Australia's Indigenous elders, Cockatoo crest feathers were often carried by tribal messengers as symbols of their mission. A messenger in his own right, the Sulphur-crested Cockatoo is the purveyor of clarity and an ambassador of lucidity and offers a chance to regain control of your life. He helps us to see through the confusion that runs rampant in our lives. When stability is regained, our minds are more receptive to finding the clarity we need to productively move through life. Congregating in flocks of 50 or more, the very social Sulphur-crested Cockatoo encourages us to support those around us as they try to recoup clarity in their lives. Offering a shoulder to cry on or a willing ear often helps others regain perspective as they hear themselves speak their issues out loud, possibly for the first time. Illuminating the issues that are stagnating one's life is an effective way of banishing them forever, especially when someone external offers a productive point of view or a fresh way of looking at them. By offering assistance to others, we may find that we gain greater clarity in relation to our own issues, with awareness growing as we realise parallels and connections between each other's life experiences.

• Macaw – *Awakening*

Macaw is famous for his striking plumage, which, despite being loud and obvious, helps camouflage him among the green leaves, red and yellow fruits and flowers and the purplish-blue shadows of the tropical rainforests. Macaws bonds for life, unless one of them dies. They reinforce their bond by preening the other's feathers, sharing food and roosting side by side. Although the female is responsible for the incubation of the eggs, both parents share responsibility for the feeding and care of the chicks.

As a symbol of the sun, Macaw offers the chance to see every ending as an opportunity to start afresh because after every night, there is an inevitable dawn heralded by the rising sun and rebirthed each morning from the Twin Peaks of Earth Mother. Just as the Phoenix remerges cyclically from the residue of its own demise, Macaw offers 'rebirth' each morning and the chance to rise up and regain control of our lives. He offers a voice with which to respectfully declare our heart's desire each morning during sacred prayer to Spirit and loud enough to scream out our expectations of the world. He offers wings to attain ever greater heights so that we might achieve our personal best, and a tail to offer sound navigation and direction. Finally, he offers vibrancy and vigour audacious enough to inspire clarity and self-pride, while simultaneously warding off negative or resentful attention by helping us blend in with the crowd. Macaw nurtures us as we set about rebirthing our life and affords us endurance to sacrifice our old, worn out, tiresome selves to make way for our true and authentic selves. When we shed our tiresome selves, we release years of pent-up emotion held in check by fear, lack of self-worth and genetic patterning. We say 'good bye' to the 'us' that makes others feel strong and better about themselves. We literally die a symbolic death, to be reborn alive, revived and bold.

Peacock
Integrity

Peacock is the oldest breed of poultry known to man. Famous for his impressive upper tail feathers and dazzling colours, which are intended to attract potential mates during courtship, Peacock is an incredibly noisy bird that maintains large territories. Peacock eats insects worms, maize and wheat, and in his native land of India is welcomed into the villages where he hunts for venomous serpents such as Cobra.

According to mythology, Peacock is a symbol of the goddess's vigilance and her all-seeing eye. In keeping with Roman legend, Peacock was sacred to the Mother goddess, Juno, who weighed his tail feathers against the hearts of men to determine their integrity and their worthiness to travel to the Underworld. It is thought that to hear the mournful cry of Peacock is an indicator of one's fear of being forsaken by God. A bird that is sacred not only due to religious sentiment but because of parliamentary statute that labels him as India's national emblem. In Hindu belief Peacock is a soul-bird and a heraldic bird of good fortune, protection and watchfulness and regarded as an oracle of truth and purity. Christian superstition endows Peacock with bad luck however, claiming him to be the only creature so arrogant as to show the devil the way into Paradise. However, another legend speaks of Peacock's watchfulness that enabled him to spot Satan as he tried to infiltrate Paradise. Another story depicts Peacock as being superficial and frivolous and only concerned with the grandeur of his own appearance. The legend says that Peacock screams indignantly in reaction to his unattractive legs. To feel the need to explore the wisdom of Peacock is a warning that quite possibly your integrity may be in doubt. To guard against this, make the effort to hold beauty (as opposed to vanity) as your guide and make every effort to ensure that your heart always weighs pure by vowing to speak only the truth, to never judge and to keep a watchful eye open for iniquity in its many forms. Peacock advocates that we never sell ourselves short, while teaching us to hold our head up, to be proud of who and what we are and to believe ourselves to be (inclusive of all perceived weaknesses and flaws) 'perfect'. Peacock claims that your honour and integrity will remain intact if you do.

Penguin
Acuity

Penguin is a seagoing, flightless bird found mainly in the Southern Hemisphere, particularly in Antarctica. With flippers instead of wings, Penguin is adapted perfectly to a life spent largely in the water. Feeding mainly on krill, fish, squid and other sea creatures, Penguin hunts while swimming.

All Penguins are masters of harnessing the power found within our dreams. They teach us to find our inner power and, over time, to bring our dreams to fruition. Dreams are Spirit's way of allowing us to intuitively check in and consult with our higher selves. Many of us live our lives innocent to the presence of Spirit and assume that what we have within our physical existence is all that life has to offer. It is very difficult for Spirit to inspire us when we are ignorant to the presence of the other realms. Spirit can send out all the signs and omens in the world, but if we are blind to their presence we are not going to notice them.

Penguin encourages us to explore the significance of our dreams so that we may begin to understand our potential in a non-threatening manner. By allowing us to awaken to the power of our dreams, and by helping us realise the potential they hold as portents and signs, Penguin allows us to embrace Spirit in ways that many may take for granted. Our dreams offer the opportunity to overcome hesitation and fear that hampers spiritual growth. Penguin reminds us that when we dream, our astral body leaves its physical confines, allowing us to journey to the other realms. But, at the slightest hint of disturbance, Penguin is there to pull the astral body back to the physical body by means of a golden thread. While some believe that when we dream, the Spirit of Eagle, as the emissary of Spirit, protects the energetic thread and ensures that it remains intact. But for those who work with the energy of Penguin, the Eagle steps aside and protectively keeps watch. As we journey through the dreamscape, we simultaneously bridge the worlds; walking in both the ordinary world and the non-ordinary world of Spirit. And this is the domain of the Spirit of Penguin.

• Blue Penguin – *Willpower*

Blue Penguin grows to 40 centimetres in height and weighs approximately 1 kilogram when fully grown. The smallest Penguin in the world, Blue Penguin can be found along the southern coastline of Australia. Blue Penguin hunts during the day in the ocean. A flightless bird, Blue Penguin flaps her wings as she swims, reaching great speeds in simulated flight. Catching small fish and crustaceans, she returns to shore at dusk, scampering onto the beach in droves and quickly making her way back to her burrow and the hungry mouths of waiting hatchlings. Rather than sleep for any extended period of time like other creatures, Blue Penguin is said to snooze in short bursts – allegedly for a maximum of four minutes and repeated countless times over the course of the day.

Also known as Fairy Penguin and Little Penguin, Blue Penguin is spiritually celebrated as being capable of walking with equal clarity and intent in both the physical landscape of ordinary reality and the obscurity of the intuitive mind. Blue Penguin teaches us to picture our desired future in our mind's eye and through calling on willpower alone to bring it to fruition in the most abundant ways. Having adapted her body to suit an oceangoing lifestyle over thousands of evolutionary years, she now lacks the necessary requirements to become airborne. Instead of accepting her lot in life as a flightless bird (as Kiwi, Emu, Rhea and Ostrich have done), strong-willed Blue Penguin searches for alternative ways and has instead taken to the white foam of Grandmother Ocean.

Blue Penguin's sense of resolve will never see her restricted by tangible limitation or physical inadequacy without presenting a solid argument for her rejection. As a child you possibly dreamed of being some central member of the community, but after being distracted by the romance of life and other job opportunities that required little or no further study, you now fear you may have missed your chance. But what if you could make slight adjustments to your dream? For example, instead of becoming a veterinarian, you train as a wildlife carer instead? Your dream may have altered slightly to suit your present circumstance, but under Blue Penguin's guidance, the power within the dream is restored to full capacity. Blue Penguin prepares us for a second chance; an opportunity to recapture the dream of childhood, when we first looked to the future. She offers willpower and resolve to reclaim our potential and to never be restricted by limitation or obstruction again.

Blue Penguin reminds us that only the limitations we choose to accept and welcome into our lives have the power to truly hinder our progress. She says that the time has come to harness and focus our willpower to fulfil our dreams and to realise our potential. We are as self-reliant as the next person but we need to remember how to use our inherent talents to their fullest capacity to find solutions to all of the challenges that Spirit can throw at us.

• Emperor Penguin – *Lucid dreaming*

Emperor Penguin is the largest Penguin in the world. Emperor Penguin never sets foot on dry land. He remains in Antarctica permanently, breeding and raising his young on the icy terrain. Emperor Penguin does not build nests nor does he patrol a set territory. Emperors Penguin has tightly packed, waterproof feathers that keep his skin dry while swimming and webbed feet which offer powerful propulsion through the water. Emperor Penguin hunts fish, squids and crustaceans. Female Emperor Penguin lays a single egg, and the male tends to it while she goes off to feed. The male incubates the egg by standing with it perched on his feet, covering it with thick rolls of feathered skin and huddling together in tight groups to keep warm. They will have lost over a third of their body weight by the time the females return.

Consciously bridging the worlds via our dreams is a skill afforded by Emperor Penguin. He instructs us in the art of lucid dreaming. There are several forms of dreams: the regular 'sleeping' dreams that may or may not contain pertinent information from our subconscious or Higher Self; the 'waking' dreams, or daydreams; and lucid dreaming – a technique that is somewhat different from regular dreaming. Lucid dreaming occurs when we are asleep, but allows us to be awake within our dream. It is when we are conscious that we are in a dream and, with practice, are able to manipulate, shape, fashion or create the dream while in it As spiritual beings, we know that one half of our awareness lives in what we call the 'real world'; the tangible, logical, mundane world of the physical or masculine, while the other half lives in what is referred to as the 'dream world'; the subtle, unexplainable, mysterious world of the non-physical or feminine. The aspect of self that resides in the 'real world' is called the Familiar Self, while the aspect of self that occupies the 'dream world' is known as the Unknown Self.

Emperor Penguin allows both the familiar and the unfamiliar aspects of Self to consciously unite and work as one; to team up and deliberately bring the two worlds together, thereby validating our potential and intensifying our ability to succeed. He enables both aspects of the Self to consult and determine the best course of action that will see our wants, needs and desires birthed in the world of dreams realised in the world of reality. Emperor Penguin invites the Familiar Self to seek advice from the Unfamiliar Self. As we sleep, he offers training that will see us knowingly wake in our dream state and consciously seek out our Self to find answers to things that are troubling us in our waking life. Instead of having to metaphorise our sleeping dreams upon waking, Emperor Penguin affords us the facility to wake with an instant knowing – with a recognition of what needs to be done and how.

• Jackass Penguin – *Inanity*

Found in pockets on the mainland, breeding colonies of Jackass Penguins are found primarily on the islands that dot the South African shoreline. Standing up to 1 metre in height, Jackass Penguin is typically 'Penguin-toned' – black-backed, black footed and black-billed, white-faced and white-bellied with black stripes across his upper chest and down each side of his body. Jackass Penguin chicks are cared for by both parents in deep burrows. Incubation of the eggs takes five weeks and after hatching, the chicks are fed on food regurgitated by the parents. Hunting in groups of approximately 100, Jackass Penguin may venture as far as 50 kilometres from his nesting grounds in search of food.

Named after his unfortunate call, a bray that resembles a distressed Donkey, and after the hoof-shaped stripe that marks his chest, Jackass Penguin seems to have been burdened with the shadow aspect of the little equine as his Dreaming. According to legend, the bray of the ass is said to bring misfortune to those who hear it, with the animal considered by some to be full of ill omen as a harbinger of desolation and a welcoming call to the devil. To refer to someone as 'a jackass' is to infer stupidity, stubbornness and arrogance, while to act 'like a jackass' is to behave with disrespect, imprudence and rudeness. It is to demonstrate extreme inanity while embracing the 'village idiot' archetype, qualities guaranteed to limit one's chances of ever being taken seriously in the future. A clan charged with the gifts of willpower and realisation, Penguins encourage us to honour our dreams, to listen to the messages hidden within them and to realise their potential in the tangible world. The wisdom of Jackass Penguin, however, is that of the complete opposite, and offers a warning to avoid falling victim to his ways. Everyone has experienced a time when receiving negative attention seems better than attracting no attention at all, and although this is usually a short-lived phase for most, those who walk with Jackass Penguin often experience difficulty making the transition from being foolhardy to being wise. Jackass Penguin warns that, although superficially entertaining to us, our inane antics may be inviting others to laugh at us rather than with us. Instead of portraying ourselves as blustering fools, Jackass Penguin encourages us to have faith in our potential, believe in our self-worth and to discard the asinine stance forever.

Petrel
Belief

Several species of Petrel, including Prion and Fulmar, inhabit the Antarctic and surrounding areas. Most Petrels practise a low-flying form of flight that sees them skim the surface of the water, rousing small marine organisms with their feet. Petrel was named after Peter the Apostle and his name literally means 'little Peter'. Petrel breeds in huge colonies on cliff faces and steep rocky slopes, often many kilometres inland. Populations have been greatly influenced by the introduction of domestic Cats and Rats either intentionally or accidentally released.

Peter was a fisherman who gave up his life to follow Jesus and was the Apostle who asked Jesus to let him walk on water. A little way across, on realising what he was doing, Peter lost confidence and began to sink. Jesus fished him out of the water, saying 'You of little faith, why did you doubt me?' Petrel nurtures a sense of faith; faith in a higher level of understanding, wisdom or source of power. Petrel encourages us to consider the existence of God or Spirit and Great Mystery. Petrel acts as a witness, an ambassador of higher existence and teaches us to believe in things that we cannot see or that are out of the realms of normality. Petrel reminds us that Spirit resides within all things of Nature. Spirit is neither feminine nor masculine. It is both. It is all-encompassing and is the essence of *all life*. Spirit is both tangible and non-tangible. Spirit must be approached with a deep, innate respect, but treated with a sense of calm expectation that one usually reserves for lovers, best friends and soul mates. Spirit is the Creator; an embodiment of the Void, a resident of the Great Mystery. Spirit demands that we trust, remember and know. Petrel explains that when we find faith in a higher realm of existence, we will learn to have faith in ourselves and when we have attained that, we can find faith in humanity and the world around us. Belief in God or Spirit does not have to be a religious thing involving regular visits to church, the denial of simple pleasures or the reading of the Bible. Petrel simply asks that we show faith in the existence of God or Spirit and that we view the world and all of nature as representing a celebration or proof of their presence. All we need do is show faith in that belief. If we can do that, the peace and guidance Petrel offers is breathtaking.

Pheasant

The lovers

 India, the 'Land of the Pheasants', is home to most of the 48 breeds of Pheasant known today. Commercially bred in Europe for his meat, Pheasant is commonly kept by bird enthusiasts as an exotic addition to garden aviaries, while the stunning tail and chest feathers are favoured by hat designers and fly fishermen the world over. A solar-influenced creature, Pheasant is revered as a symbol of light in China; the quintessence of integrity and opulence and a force said to promote fortuity and achievement. In Japanese tradition Pheasant is the embodiment of thunder, which suggests great ability to harness and focus passion, energy and desire for change.

Pheasant knows commitment and devotion and symbolises the unconditional and protective love a mother feels for her children and the gentle affection one may feel for a friend. He also affords the strength and endurance needed by those determined to better themselves through study and scholarly accomplishment. Pheasant is a bird that mates for life. He demonstrates devotion to others while teaching respect for the self. Pheasant's sudden or unexpected appearance usually heralds positive harmonious connection with another person or other people. To explore Pheasant is to realise a karmic bond with another; a soul connection that must be addressed and integrated into your life even if one or both of you already have respective partners. To ignore the call of Pheasant is to risk spending the rest of your life wondering 'What if?' The appearance of Pheasant, however, does not necessarily mean a new *sexual* relationship or a partnership driven by sexual attraction. Instead, it may signify spiritual or inspirational power birthing itself within the Self, implying the harmonious blending of one's yin and yang aspects and a uniting of the two opposites of self; the two opposites that are equal, so that creation may take place on a tangible level. In other words, illumination in the form of a new relationship with one's Self that will lead to the manifestation of things yearned for on a daily basis. In order to attract the devoted love of another, for example, one must first develop a healthy, honest relationship with the Self. The exciting thing is, if we can initiate healing in our personal lives by invoking the wisdom of Pheasant, we can ask for his support in other arenas as well, by simply giving ourselves permission to lay claim to them *within ourselves* first.

Pheasant Coucal
Shift

Pheasant Coucal belongs to the Cuckoo family, but is unusual among Cuckoos in that she incubates and raises her own chicks rather than laying her eggs in the nests of birds of a different species and tricking them into raising her young as their own. Found in Australia, Timor and New Guinea and preferring both tropical and subtropical low-lying forests and mangroves, Pheasant Coucal has adapted well to the cane-field regions of northern Australia.

Pheasant Coucal shows herself after a shift, enlightenment or personal change has taken place. Her appearance comes as confirmation that all is as it should be, that all will be well and a promising sign that we have successfully taken some sort of step up, the whole time reminding us to acknowledge the things we have said, decided, actioned or intimated. Pheasant Coucal ensures we never overlook or ignore efforts to improve our lives and to that of others by manifesting as herself as a physical sign that indicates an old pattern has been broken and a new understanding will soon be realised.

Pig
Underworld

The term Boar is traditionally the name given to a mature male Hog. A Sow is a female that has had young, while Gilt refers to a female that hasn't. The term Pig refers to an unweaned baby; a Piglet is a very young animal, while Shoat refers to the same animal after it has been weaned. Collectively, they are known as Hogs when domesticated, and Boars or Razorbacks when in their wild or 'feral' state respectively. All 23 subspecies of Hog originated from the Eurasian Wild Boar. With ancestry dating back to the Ice Age, Boars were first domesticated about 7,000 years ago. Boar has prominent, outward jutting blade-sharp tusks that effectively act as weapons capable of fatally slicing open an opponent's stomach. The females form cooperative groups with other Sows, and together ferociously protect their Piglets. Although the females may travel in 'drifts' or 'sounders', the males remain largely solitary in nature.

Black Sow holds long association with the goddess in her crone aspect and the phase of life that constitutes wisdom and maturity of 'old age'. According to Celtic myth, Black Sow guards the path that leads to the Underworld and embodies a mystical journey that culminates in the divine death of the familiar sacred self. Put simply, Sow suggests the ending of a cycle. Piglet often represents the beginning of a new cycle. Just as Sow represents the cycles of Nature and the acumen and power of the goddess, so too does Boar. Boar symbolises the warrior, leader and chief and embodies the uncultivated, raw power that lies within each of us; energy that can be awakened in times of need and offered life as the hero archetype. Boar enhances our strength of character, offering endurance and power to move forward in life. Boar offers a sense of integrity and truth to our words, inspiring others to heed our advice or point of view. Boar is volatile, though, and often unpredictable. Boar people must remember to keep a lid on their emotions, and not let their feelings of frustration or anger boil over. To hunt Boar is symbolic of the journey we all eventually take to the Underworld. To follow Boar into the Underworld is to stalk our limitations and to overcome our inherent obstacles and fears. Boar offers knowledge and transformation to those brave enough to face their inner demons and slay them with the determination befitting a true warrior.

• Peccary – *Many paths*

 Peccary is a Pig-like mammal that congregates in large social groups. Although she doesn't appear to follow a particular leader, when foraging for food or fleeing from danger, the whole group will instinctively tag along behind the animal in front and when threatened will defend themselves as a herd, noisily grinding their teeth. Peccary scent-marks her territory (and other Peccaries) and has a powerful sense of smell. The term 'peccary' comes from the Brazilian *pecari*, meaning 'many paths through the woods'. She is referred to by the Spanish as *Javelina*, derived from the word 'javelin' in response to the sharpness of her tusks.

Peccary offers choice and the opportunity to explore all that life has to offer. Peccary people are never ones to stay put for too long, usually boasting long lists of life experiences and career-based qualifications in later years. They are nimble-minded, fast-talking, sharp-tongued individuals, who do not suffer fools lightly. Peccary inspires creativity, investigation and exploration. She demands a great deal of emotional stability and physical endurance to maintain the energy expelled by Peccary people; with every opportunity explored revealing further leads and experiences, with each of these fanning out in similar fashion. Peccary embodies the javelin in flight; a weapon that offers clear direction and obvious outcome. Peccary endorses throwing the figurative javelin and marking where it lands as your next port of call. In doing so, life will never be planned or restricted by responsibility, thus offering a wealth of experience and a tapestry of knowledge that will provide many a campfire story shared with grandchildren.

• Warthog – *Transition*

Warthog has a large head, a wide snout, wart-like bumps on his cheeks and a pair of formidable tusks with a Horse-like mane running from the base of his head down the middle of his back. Largely diurnal, Warthog enjoys wallowing in pools of water or mud holes and although he will retreat to a self-dug burrow (which he shares with other individuals) to escape the weather, he displays a great tolerance to extreme climatic heat – an ability uncommon in other species of Pig.

A Pig not known for his good looks, Warthog represents those who find themselves resisting necessary transition. Warthog is the totem of those who, although embracing of transition when young, have grown to distrust the process completely. Suddenly short-tempered, reclusive and vague, those walking with Warthog have generally always felt ugly and angry at themselves, possibly due to unresolved baggage or issues stemming from early childhood experiences, and have endeavoured to disguise the sorrow from the world. After years of suppression, however, the ugliness may unexpectedly begin to erupt and spew out, both physically and psychologically, and will emotionally continue to do so (at the surprise of unsuspecting family and friends), unless addressed and released by re-integrating the wisdom of Pig into their awareness. The ending of any sort that paves the way for a new beginning is heralded by Pig, with Piglet representing the 'buds' of new growth: the hint of potential or promotion or the beginning of the next cycle. If you find yourself exploring Warthog's Dreaming, be aware that you may be resisting a necessary conclusion, final step or a new phase of life. It may be time to say goodbye, move or shift perception. Your determination not to embrace the transition may be causing you to behave differently, or may be bringing to the fore years of suppressed emotion. Warthog urges us not to resist transition, but rather to embrace it and journey with it to see where it takes us. If Warthog's feelings are true, the transition in store will unfold as a tapestry of opportunity, new life and excitement, so long as you succumb and trust the process.

Pigeon
Homecoming

There are many different breeds of domestic Pigeon; the most popular being Homer Pigeon. Many cities have resident Pigeons; domesticated descendants of Rock Dove that have returned to a semi-wild or 'feral' state. Pigeon feeds on the ground individually or in flocks and roosts with others in abandoned buildings and attics, under eaves, on walls, roofs and powerlines. When drinking, she dips her bill into the water and drinks continuously. When startled, her wings make a loud, clapping sound until she is fully airborne, thus warning other Pigeons of approaching danger. Pigeon has a remarkable ability to find her way home, no matter how far afield she travels.

Pigeon enables us to feel close to those we love, even when there is a great distance separating us. She carries our prayers and messages of love to those we miss, delivering them into their dreams as they sleep. She offers endurance to do what needs to be done, so that we may remain strong and focused on the task at hand until we can legitimately return home. Pigeon can be invoked when it is our heart's desire to get in touch with someone we have lost contact with or someone we miss. Pigeon reminds loved ones who have developed the wander-bug to not wander too far and to keep in communication with those back home. Pigeon invites us to return home on an innately personal level, too. She returns us home to values once deemed old-fashioned or outmoded; to the traditional teachings of our family and the sacred wisdom of our elders. She helps us reclaim our soul essence and remember our potential helping us return home to a loving, non-judgmental heart so that we may acknowledge the sacredness found in all paths and belief systems, even when it seems that they differ or conflict with our own. Pigeon delivers us back to a state of wellbeing, stability, clarity and inner peace, topped off by the simple joy of feeling happy and loved.

Piranha
Intent

Piranha is a flesh-eating fish but poses little threat to humans and is sometimes kept as a 'pet'. The danger with allowing people to keep exotic and potentially dangerous animals/fish is realised when their owners tire of keeping them or they become too large or expensive to keep and release their 'pets' into the wild. 'Feral' Piranha has been found in rivers and streams far from his native land.

Piranha helps us harness our personal power, wisdom and inner strength by encouraging us to be mindful of the words we use in everyday speech. One of the syntactic peculiarities in the English language is that we often speak in the negative rather than the positive. We say things like 'Don't touch', or 'You haven't eaten your dinner' and use sentences that negate the positive. Interestingly, our unconscious doesn't process single negatives. In order to understand a single negative, we need to understand first what it is we are *not* to do. We store memories by attaching words to sounds and pictures connected to events experienced during the course of our lives. So, accessing the 'right' word is crucial, and is made difficult though by the fact that we are all, in our own way, linguistically specific. Language is one of the major filter systems that we define our world by, and within any language there are unique differences associated with dialect and slang (though syntax generally remains the same). The basic nature of a filter is to narrow down and separate 'some' from the 'all'. In language, we are taking an emotion or feeling and narrowing down that experience to a single word or phrase. In doing so, we are eliminating most of the experience. Have you ever noticed how many words are used to explain the meaning or intent behind a single word? A word, therefore, *forms* intent. Because a single word has so much potential information contained within it, words create power. Piranha helps us identify our compulsion to use negative language patterns and offers insight into what we can do to rid ourselves of them. Phrases like 'I hope', I'll try' or 'I wish' may seem harmless, and even inspiring, but they are in fact extremely limiting and pessimistic. We can hope, try or wish until the cows come home, but in doing so, we will never achieve because we are binding our potential with inadequacy and justification. By being mindful of the language we use, we may say a similar sounding thing, but the way in which it is worded makes all the difference to us achieving our goals. Words such as deserve, demand and expect instead of hope, wish and try compound the faith we have in our abilities and the conviction we show toward our goals and aspirations. They offer endurance and better reason for people to view us as capable and worthy of their support. Piranha reinstates the power to bring our dreams to fruition by helping us choose the most productive, fruitful and powerful words, while championing their correct and most appropriate use. He offers suggestions on how to eradicate negative self-talk so that we might surround ourselves with positive words to help create an abundant life.

Platypus

Feminine wisdom

Platypus is an unusual-looking creature with a bill like a Duck, a tail like a Beaver and lays eggs. Platypus is a playful marsupial known as a monotreme and can remain under water for up to five minutes. She swims with her eyes closed and detects any slight disturbance in the water with her sensitive bill.

Platypus resonates to the feminine energy of the element Water and the nurturing energies of the Earth Mother. Platypus characterises the true essence of feminine wisdom; the ability to trust absolutely in our inner direction and to live in concert with the rhythmic ebbs and flows of Nature's creative cycles. Both sexes are born with a venomous spur protruding from each of their hind legs. The males keep their spurs until death, while the female sheds hers at approximately three months of age. It could be said that the female Platypus loses her armaments because she trusts completely in the defensive power of her own Spirit. Platypus' self-worth and commitment to Spirit are unwavering as is her pledge to see her people reunite and walk as one. Platypus strives to remind all women of their sacred gift of wisdom; the ancient role of the mystic and dreamer who held within her hand the power to shape the future. She works tirelessly to heal her sisters of guilt and oppression and to reawaken their spiritual legacy, while simultaneously helping all men to remember their intrinsic feminine side. She strives to awaken them to their inborn, but still largely dormant, intuitive capabilities: their ability to trust, feel and heal. Platypus helps us all find harmony and equilibrium between our masculine and feminine selves, while offering us the wisdom to integrate the two into all of our attitudes and beliefs. Platypus was created under a blanket of dishonesty, judgment and betrayal. (According to legend, the Platypus was birthed from the forbidden coupling of two souls joined in unlawful union. They were cursed after eloping with her being transformed into a Duck and he, into a Water Rat. She produced offspring that were strange furry, duck-billed creatures, equipped with four powerful webbed feet.) Platypus was brought into this world as a result of true and honest love, but the consequences proved devastating. She trusts in her innate ability to support, love and comfort herself, for she has grown up never knowing the acceptance of others. Platypus awakens the sacredness of being able to have faith in your intuition. She listens to the heartbeat of the Earth Mother for direction and looks to her inner yin and yang for navigation, thus finding the strength needed to make her own decisions. She honours her inherent masculine and feminine qualities, knowing that she is more than capable of guiding herself through life without the support of others. This is the wisdom afforded all women – the ability to trust in their wisdom and intuition, and also to consciously act with purpose. Women are natural dreamers, visionaries and mystics, but they must embrace their masculine aspects in order to realise the full potential of their gifts. Platypus believes that when people take responsibility for their own healing, their relationships and their own lives, they will finally come together and walk side by side, instead of being forever separated, forsaken and alone.

Polecat / Ferret

Instinct

Wild Polecat was heavily persecuted by gamekeepers and nearly entirely wiped out as a species. Over the subsequent years, wild Polecat numbers have gradually recovered. Perfectly designed for invading and 'flushing out' Rabbits from the deepest of burrows, Polecats, like Ferret, was originally domesticated as an effective hunting aide. Today Ferret is kept as a pet, despite his offensive odour that he emits when threatened, exited or during the mating season. Shakespeare used the word 'Polecat' to describe people of disagreeable nature. The French referred to them as the *poule chat*, which means 'Chicken Cat'. Despite the fact that he is infamous for killing chickens, however, Polecat is not even distantly related to Cats.

Polecat people have an uncontrollable propensity to delve, probe, explore and hunt for information. They are naturally inquisitive and love to ask questions, find answers, solve problems and gossip. They have difficulty leaving well alone however, and dislike leaving any stone unturned in their search for perceived truth. To search for information or to 'ferret' something out with a sense of earnest and blind conviction, will sometimes see us perplexed, with our efforts affording modest reward or our missing the mark entirely. The tendency to push toward something or to strive to achieve something prematurely resulting in it being push further away is called an away-toward. Polecat asks that we resist searching for the truth, oppose asking probing questions and avoid seeking the counsel of friends or relatives when we sense that something awry is afoot. Polecat teaches us to avoid 'away-toward' by encouraging us to embrace aloofness, silence and watchfulness as an effective alternative. Polecat espouses that when we sit still, watch and wait with patience and clarity, all things hidden will eventually be revealed at the most appropriate and beneficial time, often too with things we seek with the purest of intent being presented earlier than expected.

Porcupine

Appreciation

 Porcupine is a rodent famous for her quills; thick hairs with barbed tips (as many as 30,000) that become embedded in the skin of animals that would otherwise prey on her. Despite popular belief, Porcupine does not shoot her quills at her aggressors but animals have been known to die of infection when stuck with her quill. Porcupine only ever attacks when threatened. Porcupine is mostly nocturnal and solitary by nature and eats barks when food is scarce.

Porcupine demands that we appreciate the beauty in our life; that we take time to smell the roses and to give thanks for the things we might take for granted. Porcupine asks that we give credit where credit is due, polish up our priorities and turn our attentions to things that truly matter. Porcupine reminds us that if we were to die tomorrow, for example, the company that employed us would quickly and easily replace us in a matter of days. Our family however, and those we leave behind, would feel the loss for the rest of their lives. Porcupine asks, 'Why do we absorb ourselves so much more in our work than we do our own families?' Where is the balance in that? Porcupine is inherently gentle and loves to play and interact with other animals. She is not naturally aggressive and will only ever employ force as defence. Porcupine prompts us to watch our language, to be more empathetic and to show tolerance, patience and understanding at all times. Friends are gold and family is for life, with our children personifying the very extension of our soul. We should reserve our gentle words, consideration and concern for our friends and family, and expel our frustrations, displeasure and resentment on things of little consequence. When we flare up or anger, we should do so when we are defending ourselves, our family or things that are sacred to us only, and not aim it at the very things that carry our pain *with* us and cry real tears *for* us.

Possum

Opportunity

 Australian Possum is a nocturnal marsupial mammal with some species having prehensile tails and powerful claws. They range dramatically in size, from the tiny adult thumb-sized Mountain Pygmy Possum to the domestic Cat-sized Brushtail Possum. The more common of species (namely the Brushtail and the Ringtail) are famous for their habit of taking up residence in the roofs of houses.

The best way to enhance your quality of life is to march to the beat of your own drum. Finding inspiration in others that have followed their own feelings and have reached greatness by setting their own example is admirable and constructive, but to pursue precisely their ways is mundane and predictable. To take opportunity by the horns when it is offered is to believe 100% in one's worth and purpose. To act on every thought and to honour every possibility as potential for growth is what separates successful people from ordinary folk. Possum primes you to follow your dreams. Possum urges us to see our life as being a foundation on which great things can be initiated. Without disdainfully judging our previous lack of achievement and without taking any aspect of our present life for granted, Possum encourages us to continue to seek and attempt new things. Possum teaches us to see opportunity in any condition and how to productively harness all opportunities to our best advantage. Possum encourages us to gently benefit from any circumstantial generosities afforded us and to ride unnoticed on their back until we are comfortably established, after which time retreat should be executed in an honourable and discreet manner. Possum encourages us to see the potential in any opportunity that may be presented to us, innocently or purposefully, by individuals or by circumstances. It is an inherent trait of Possum to take full advantage of all available generosities and to literally hunker down in the first abundant space on offer. Possum can also portent an obvious warning, with the caution weighing up the fine line between prostituting another's generous nature and taking gentle advantage of an opportunity afforded you by another's good will. From personal experience, Possum fully comprehends the fact that people tire quickly of those who blatantly think that the world owes them a living, or those who use others with little consideration of the consequences of their actions. With this warning in mind, ask yourself if you have a freeloader or user who seems to have taken up residence within your personal space.

Prairie Dog
Withdrawal

Prairie Dog is closely related to Marmot and most species hibernate during winter. He digs burrows (called 'towns'), incorporating food storage cavities, nesting chambers and several escape routes. When threatened by a predator, this predetermined sentry offers a quick, warning bark. He waits in anticipation and then offers a second bark before diving for cover underground. Other strategically placed sentinels continue the surveillance until the danger passes. The early European settlers referred to him as a 'sod poodle' because of his shrill bark.

Offering a powerful sense of self-preservation, Prairie Dog offers wise council to those who need help deciding when to stand their ground or when to gracefully withdraw. Prairie Dog backs away to avoid the harshness of winter and quickly goes to ground when he observes an approaching predator. He doesn't just dash off with his tail between his legs, though. He waits and watches, barking to the others to let them know what the predatory animal is doing. He stands his ground, has his say and then backs down when he knows he has said enough. Prairie Dog provides the inner strength and sense of self-worth to speak our mind and build an aura of power and endurance. Prairie Dog is a nervous animal; always scanning the horizon for danger. Prairie Dog people experience inner turmoil whenever they are faced with tension or unrest, although they endeavour not to show it. They don't cope with raised voices or overwhelming energy and when threats are regular, they lose personal power and control over their own lives. Exhaustion sets in and they surrender themselves to the dominant parties in their life, becoming easy prey. In such cases, Prairie Dog only ever endorses withdrawal when it is better (or safer) to agree to disagree. Prairie Dog also says that if you find yourself in a position where you are permanently in retreat mode, then you must pack up and leave completely. In a Prairie Dog town everyone has a role to play, but ultimately everyone is considered equal. There is no one animal more important than another. And it should be the same in our home or community. Prairie Dog primes us to express our opinion, have our say and proudly offer our expectations and set personal boundaries. Only when we are confident of where we stand in life should we bite our tongue and surrender our power. Only then will we feel confident to express judgment and be strong enough stand our ground while letting others blow steam or boastfully waste energy. Petty tyrants are always eventually exposed for the oafs they are, after all, while spiritual warriors inherently know when to stand strong and when to respectfully withdraw.

Pronghorn
Endowment

Pronghorn is a unique animal with ancestry dating back 20 million years. He is equipped with a pair of branched horns that aren't antlers. Pronghorn is capable of great speed and can maintain a good pace for hours at a time. Farm fencing has limited Pronghorn's natural movements and because he is unable to leap over it, his migration and consequent endurance has been greatly marred over the past century. There are five Pronghorn subspecies, with three considered seriously endangered. According to ancient teachings worldwide, the people have always relied upon this 'Antelope' for his resources: skin for clothing and shelter, meat for nourishment and bones and horns for weapons and tools. The generic medicine for Antelope, therefore, is 'provider'. Pronghorn, although not a true Antelope, is no exception. He has provided for the people since the world was new, and even to this day he continues to provide, if not with his meat and skin (he is still hunted in some parts), with knowledge, insight and good medicine.

Pronghorn inspires the people to move to action with haste and integrity and affords a sense of direction and purpose, grounding and balance. Pronghorn nurtures those who are strong-willed, headstrong and driven by ambition. As with all animals that sport horns or antlers, Pronghorn suggests heightened spiritual awareness, higher understanding and connection to Spirit due to an association between the horns/antlers and the crown and third-eye chakra centres. Pronghorn people, for example, are usually very tuned in to their feelings, are empathetic toward others and are generally profoundly intuitive. Pronghorn people are inspired by the signs offered by Spirit. They listen to their inner voice and seek guidance from Nature. Pronghorn people will often make decisions based on dreams, visions or symbolic messages, such as those offered by synchronicities and 'coincidences'. Although Pronghorn people are always alert to opportunities to better themselves and enhance the quality of their lives, and are generally more than equipped to provide stability, direction and purpose to others, the awareness often comes at a cost. Pronghorn is an animal that gives of himself so that others may prosper. He is an animal blessed by Spirit because he willingly makes personal sacrifices so that others may benefit. Pronghorn knows that reward is always promised to those who make personal sacrifice – particularly when it is offered freely, devoid of resentment or negativity. Although Pronghorn nurtures those who are strong-willed and driven by ambition, he also affirms that personal gain, as wonderful as it may be, hardly ever comes without consequence. Pronghorn says that if something is worth fighting for, worth facing the trials and tribulations for and is worth the consequences and potential pain, then it is probably worth its weight in gold, especially when we surrender feelings of frustration, impatience and resentment in our endeavour to embrace it. Pronghorn provides for those prepared to take control of their lives and show accountability for their actions – no matter what the cost. As such, Pronghorn offers endowment that will provide for generations to come, even if we personally do not get to reap the rewards ourselves.

Ptarmigan
Rumblings

Ptarmigan is also known as Arctic Grouse, Barren Ground Bird, Rocker, Snow Grouse and White Grouse. Because of her propensity to inhabit mountainous territory where there are regular storms and an abundance of mist, she is also called Thunderbird. Her feet are heavily feathered, which offers insulation enough to walk through snow. Ptarmigan moults and changes the colour of her feathers in accordance with the seasons.

Ptarmigan helps reinstate a sense of peace, particularly after a tumultuous period of anger, frustration or raised voices. She has a cleansing quality that not only banishes negativity but also paves the way for new beginnings and clarity. When invoked, Ptarmigan helps bring potentially volatile issues peacefully to a head, while encouraging the venting of emotions and the airing of grudges, disharmony and confusion in a fruitful, productive way. She helps us to tread carefully, particularly when the atmosphere is tense or a situation is unpredictable, and guides us as we endeavour to gently manipulate things in our favour. She helps us choose our words with care, effectively instructing us how to 'skate on thin ice' with little threat of falling through. Ptarmigan helps reduce anxiety and fear and provides for a solid foundation on which to civilly base a ceasefire, a line of reasoning or negotiation of a fair compromise. Incidentally, it is a Japanese custom to place a pine branch above a doorway to ensure continual joy is experienced by those who dwell therein. Such a custom celebrates the fact that pine trees are evergreen, a sign of ongoing positive and life-nurturing energy.

Pūkeko
The throat chakra

Also known as Swamphen or Moorhen in Australia, Pūkeko – found mainly along rivers and waterways, in swampy marshlands and sodden farmland – is the most common of the six species of rail found in New Zealand, which include Takahē, Weka, Banded Rail, Spotless Crake and Marsh Crake.

With her striking blue chest and throat feathers, Pūkeko's plumage is reminiscent of the throat chakra and the colour blue the chakra resonates with. As such, Pūkeko suggests the need to get things off our chests, to speak up and express ourselves so we feel more connected to the world around us. The energy of Pūkeko is inherently nurturing in nature, and she softly encourages us to be gentler on ourselves by sharing our worries and self-doubts with those we love thereby allowing them to become more aware of our needs. In doing so, our loved ones are offered a chance to know us better in ways that are more rewarding and sustaining for us.

Puma
Headship

Puma is also known as Cougar, Catamount (or Cat-of-the-Mount) or Mountain Lion, and is largely solitary. She is active during both the day and night and has a negative reputation with farmers, who see her as a threat to domestic stock. With the strength and power to bring down a Horse, Puma is more likely to choose wild Deer, Rabbits and Hare. Although Pumas as a whole have experienced a noticeable drop in numbers due to hunting and poaching, most wild populations remain stable. Florida Panther, a subspecies of Puma, is now seriously endangered with only about 50 animals known to exist in the wild.

Only those who remain true to themselves and who hold integrity as their highest priority make genuine leaders. A leader must be elected by the people and never self-appointed. A leader must not be afraid to direct, delegate or take responsibility when no one else is willing to step up to the mark. They cannot be swayed by the resentment or uncertainty of others, nor can they allow ego or self-importance to influence their decision making. A leader must immediately see what needs to be done in any circumstance, and be strong enough to act with little or no confirmation or support. They must appear unbiased, composed and in control, even when they are inwardly feeling overwhelmed, afraid or confused. To honour Puma, you must demonstrate unwavering faith and display great inner-strength, maturity and wholeness. To follow Puma's path of headship is too often fraught with trial and tribulation; obstacles that will test your resolve, commitment and personal belief. It will undermine your sense of security, personal protection and the authenticity of your past healing. Puma demands that, as a leader, you must first earn the respect of others before demanding it for yourself; to always show respect for others even when they do not reciprocate the honour and that you must demonstrate respect for all things of Nature, the ways of the Universe and the wants, needs and teachings of your people before your own. Because of their position, therefore, Puma people have few friends and are rarely blessed with confidants. People are loyal toward Puma people because they have to be, are paid to be or are afraid not to be. Those who walk the path of Puma have usually known great sacrifice, but have integrated such loss into their consciousness as a means to an end. Puma embodies the following of one's purpose, a spiritual directive that marks you a leader and one whose job it is to inspire others to reach a unified goal.

Quetzal
Liberty

 Quetzal was sacred to the Aztecs and the Mayans and Quetzalcoatl the 'Feathered Serpent', a solar deity was said to wear Quetzal feathers in his headdress. The word *Quetzalcoatl* translates to Quetzal-Bird Snake or Serpent with Feathers. The word 'quetzal' was often used to describe something precious. It actually means 'tail feather', and was typically associated with royalty and all things sacred. Quetzal has brilliant green plumage, with crimson feathers on his belly and under his tail. He also has a striking yellow bill. The long, green tail feathers are highlighted with blues and purples, making him an absolutely stunning bird. Quetzal is threatened with extinction because of habitat destruction and poaching. Quetzal is so sacred to the South American people that he has become the national symbol of Guatemala and is even represented on their flag. The quetzal is also the name of Guatemala's monetary unit.

Quetzal's song is believed to inspire feelings of freedom and joy, while the bird in flight resembles a flash of lightning. There is an ancient and romantic belief that says Quetzal would not survive if captured, that he would rather die than be confined to a cage. So, instead of killing him for his feathers, the Mayans would pluck out his tail feathers and then release him. When we carry guilt associated with something we have done that society deems 'bad', or we believe we may have contributed to, we essentially place ourselves in a cage and separate ourselves from the rest of society. As the guilt festers, we retreat further and further until eventually, we get so lost in despair that we no longer feel the sun on our face. We lose faith and hope. When we carry guilt, we simultaneously carry blame which feeds the guilt, and vice versa. When we carry guilt, we sacrifice our freedom. We agree to experience everything that happens to us (as well as those things we exact upon others) before entering the Earth plane. When we breathe life into the belief that we have failed, we not only fail ourselves but everyone associated with us. We fail the quest. We fail to learn, grow and better ourselves, and we fail to honour the 'contracts' and the sacrifices others may have made so that we could experience the event in the first place. Quetzal shuns failure, blame and guilt. Quetzal welcomes the sun back into our life. He lifts the clouds of doubt and softens the rains of grief. He heralds the blue sky of hope and the rainbows of choice and offers clarity, peace and forgiveness to those who have grown to believe themselves unworthy of such things. He opens the cage of guilt and blame, and sets us free. He offers liberty by inviting us to forgive ourselves and others for blaming us but most importantly, he offers the chance for us to receive forgiveness and for all parties to heal. Quetzal offers liberty by reminding us that all things happen for a reason and that every decision, action, thought or response is perfect and imbued with wisdom.

Rabbit

Cycles of change

European Rabbit is an animal preyed upon by most, if not all, predatory species. Nature has compensated European Rabbit by gifting her with rampant fertility: a single female can produce as many as 30 offspring a year, with each of them sexually maturing at 10 months of age. European Rabbit has been introduced into many other countries, usually with devastating consequences for the environment. Myxomatosis and the Calici Virus (RCV), also known as Viral Hemorrhagic Disease of Rabbits (VHD), have been intentionally released into many areas to help control the spread of European Rabbit. Although the decline in Rabbit numbers may have proven beneficial for the environment itself, the same could not always be said for the native predators that had adapted and profited from the abundant new choice of prey. Australia, for example, saw many of its Eagles suffer when the diseases were first released into their habitat.

Rabbit embodies Mother Nature's ever-changing cycles: growth; life, death and rebirth. Symbolic of seasonal change: new life in the spring, energy and vitality in summer; the inward contemplation of autumn and the wisdom and maturity of winter; to yet again return to the rebirth of spring, Rabbit keeps us in touch with the great circle of life and the natural harmony found between everything in Nature. When we acknowledge our relationship to all things, the Web of Life is honoured and balance is re-established. When we honour the ebbs and flows of the Earth Mother, we find that we are often rewarded with her fertility and her desire to see us live abundant, loving lives. To give to the Earth Mother by walking *with* her (instead of simply *on* her), the quality of our lives deepens, with all ventures embarked on prospering beyond our wildest dreams. To walk gently on the Earth, with reverence of heart and in honour of all other things, will see our wants and needs supported by Spirit and our life become more fertile, abundant and free of obstacles. When we begin to walk in harmony with the world around us, we become one with it. The greater the love and encouragement we afford the natural world, the more we will be rewarded with the same. Rabbit helps us notice Nature's portents and the cycles of change within ourselves, too, on a physical, spiritual and emotional level. She helps us notice the subtle internal changes that take place when we start to view our body as a sacred thing; a temple, a representation of Spirit and a way of acknowledging the miracle of life. Taken to heart, Rabbit ensures that our lives become more aware, fertile and abundant with minimal time and effort. All that is required is dedication, empathy, passion and a sense of sacredness.

• Cottontail Rabbit – *Fertility*

The term 'cottontail' describes a conspicuous tail that, when raised, resembles a cotton ball. Cottontail is a medium-sized Rabbit which thrives in open or lightly wooded areas that offer protection from predators and throughout the year she shelters in crude forms concealed by thick grass, brambles or thickets. The female gives birth to her young in nest cavities dug into well-drained ground. She lines the nest with fur plucked from her own belly, and conceals the young by covering them with grass. Cottontail maintains regular paths, forming barren runways in the grass or snow. During winter when the Earth is laden with snow, Cottontail sustains herself by eating buds, twigs, bark, sprouts and other woody foods. Cottontail speaks of Nature's ever-widening cycle of life, death and rebirth.

Symbolic of the changing seasons, Cottontail celebrates the life-giving energies of spring, the passion and energy of summer; the inward contemplation of autumn and the dormancy and ritualistic death acted out during winter; only to return again as if reborn in the spring. She reminds us that when we acknowledge our relationship to all things, the Web of Life is honoured and balance is maintained and we find ourselves rewarded with a level of fertility enjoyed by Cottontail and her kin. When we live in balance within ourselves, we live in balance with the world around us. When we live in balance with the world around us, we become one with all things. We realise that we are protected, whole and surrender fear. We release arrogance, jealousy and greed, and in doing so, we shun *lack*. The moment we drop 'lack' from our belief system, we realise fertility. Fertility means being able to manifest what we deserve, want or yearn for with honesty and true intent. Just like Cottontail, we harness what it means to live abundant, loving lives. And like Cottontail, who lives her minimalist life close to the Earth Mother's heart, we realise that abundance does not mean money. It means family, friends, laughter and beauty found within all things. To give to the Earth Mother by walking *with* her (instead of treading expectantly *upon* her), the quality of our lives quickly becomes richer and imbued with meaning and reward, with all ventures we embark on prospering beyond our wildest dreams. Cottontail helps us notice Nature's portents and the cycles of change within ourselves, on all levels. Taken to heart, our own lives may become more aware, fertile and abundant.

Raccoon
Guilt

Raccoon is an intelligent mammal with a reputation for slyness and mischief. The word 'Raccoon' comes from the Algonquian word *aroughcoune*, which means 'he scratches with his hands'. His scientific name *Procyon Lotor* is Latin for (procyon) 'pre-dog'

and (lotor) 'washer'. Raccoon is well known for his washing habits and washes his food thoroughly before eating it. Of the seven species of Raccoon, all are omnivorous and although he typically lives in forests and marshland, he also does well in areas of heavy human population. He raids garbage cans and bird-feed tables and because his dexterous fingers allow him to open latches and doors with ease, he is also known to enter houses (at night) to raid pantries and larders.

Macbeth tells the story of a man who commits a murderous crime which leads to his destruction and the loss of everything he holds dear including his wife, Lady Macbeth. Both Macbeth and his wife suffer extreme bouts of guilt after their felony, but it is Lady Macbeth who reveals the true level of their guilt and their fear of being exposed while sleepwalking. Lady Macbeth initially boasts by saying 'A little bit of water shall clear us of this deed', but is observed muttering anxiously, 'Out damn spot, out', while wringing her dry hands in an attempt to wash them clean. Affectionately referred to as 'the little bandit' because of his black face mask and his habit of raiding and stealing, Raccoon offers relief from guilt or shame manifested by wrongs we have committed in the past, damaging secrets we have kept and habits we keep private for fear of being judged or persecuted. Racoon is easily tamed and makes a wonderful pet, remaining faithful to his human family. Raccoon people are inherently 'good' and are not 'bad' people. They are often followers however, or people easily led by more dominant parties or who quickly find themselves caught up in the excitement of the moment. They are people who form alliances with questionable folk, or who confuse friendship with association. Raccoon people (like Lady Macbeth) appear outwardly strong, confident and trouble-free. They are usually loud, funny individuals who easily draw a crowd but what they present externally is often contradictory to how they feel internally. Raccoon people unintentionally divulge their true emotions however, by submitting a nervous twitch or repetitive habit such as wringing their hands. Although they demand others look them in the eye when they talk, they have difficulty doing it themselves. Raccoon people usually carry a secret or have something locked within them that they know they should reveal and often live double lives, usually against their better judgment. Raccoon offers the strength to step out of the shadows, to remove the disguising mask and wash our hands (finally) of the guilt or shame we carry. He also affords those who live with a Raccoon person the tact and inner strength to ask the necessary leading and probing questions that will inevitably reveal the truth so that all parties may heal and get on with their lives.

Rat
Restlessness

 Rat has long been feared and loathed as a spreader of disease, a symbol of death and an indicator of filth and decay. Brown Rat, or House Rat, is found in most human populated areas and breeds rapidly, producing up to a dozen offspring four or five times a year. Brown Rat was originally transported unintentionally to foreign lands aboard ships containing European explorers and settlers. Black Rat, also known as Ship Rat, can produce as many litters as Brown Rat but his offspring don't reach sexual maturity until the age of four months. Nocturnal by nature, Rat is an opportunist feeder and eats almost anything. In 1347 AD a great plague swept over Europe bringing death to millions. Although Black Rat was targeted as the primary perpetrator in the transmitting the disease, the true culprit was the Oriental Rat Flea that had hitched a ride upon the Rat. It is said that when a ship is about to sink, any Rats that may have stowed aboard prior to departure will make their way to the highest point before leaping overboard long before the ship shows obvious signs of going down.

Rat seems to have an instinctive ability to know when things are going wrong and will evacuate a threatened area long before they are proven right. It has been predicted, for example, that Rat will be one of the few creatures to survive a nuclear holocaust due to his ability to foresee danger and take necessary and precautionary action to avoid negative effects. In the case of the disastrous sinking of the *Titanic*, the ship could be seen as a metaphorical symbol of security while the ocean represented the emotional pool of life that surrounds us each and every day. In their bid to escape, Rats would have been seen running up the passageways, thus affording the passengers forewarning of, and insight into, their impending fate if only they had heeded their presence in a sensitive manner. Rat is a survivor and will do whatever it takes to ensure his endurance. In times of upheaval, confusion or breakdown, Rat offers warning of what evasive action should be taken, and when and how. In regards to relationships, for example, Rat suggests we act upon feelings of trouble the moment we suspect turbulence or approaching unrest by airing our concerns or making decisions that serve and protect our wellbeing. Instead of suppressing our feelings or freezing up on those around us in the hope that things will miraculously sort themselves out, Rat helps us determine if our interests would be better served by staying aboard in an attempt to work things out, or by devising an escape route, packing up our stuff and jumping ship.

Raven

Magick

Raven is a highly intelligent, blue/black feathered bird of the Corvis family. Some say that Raven communicates with other Ravens (and other species of animal) using a primitive and fundamental 'language' and has been observed, for example, 'calling' to larger predatory animals when she stumbles across fresh road kill. Her call attracts the attentions of Fox or some other carnivore strong enough to penetrate the road kill's hide, she then wait for it to eat its fill and then swoops down to feast on the exposed intestines and smaller portions of overlooked meat. Sadly, Raven has long been labelled as evil and considered a 'bad' omen with associations to witchcraft and the devil. As a result, she is often shot and killed out of fear, or as an assumed predator of newborn lambs.

Raven is a messenger of Spirit and the bringer of wisdom from deep within the Void. The colour black has always symbolised Mystery, the unknown, the non-physical realms and the road travelled by Spirit. As a guardian of the West Gate on the Wheel of Life and an emissary of the Water element, Raven provides the strength to explore the Void and the creative darkness of all that is yet to be. According to Celtic mythology, Raven is a sacred bird and is a symbol of death and war, which is not surprising considering she is a carrion eater. The Celts did not fear death and celebrated it as an inevitable aspect of the cycle of life. Raven nurtures within us the power to create something from nothing and to breathe life into a new venture or idea that has been pushed to the back of our mind. She affords the courage to identify seemingly intangible concepts, to view them as having viable potential and to manifest them into the physical from subtle realms of our dreams and aspirations. Raven shows us how to shape-shift our perceptions so that we may adapt accordingly to each new phase of life and blend into any new environment or situation. She prepares us to receive messages via our dreams and meditations; messages that, if acknowledged in a constructive manner, may result in healing and spiritual awakening. Raven puts us on notice that Spirit intends to support us as we go through the process of change and reminds us that the essence of all life is Spirit. She is the bringer of Magick and deepens our connection to Spirit by helping us remember the sacredness of prayer. Prayer sustains and enriches us. Magick is the practice of intentionally projecting the natural energy channelled from three main sources of power: Personal Power, Earth Power and Divine Power. Magick is the focusing of this collective energy with the intention of stimulating necessary change. It is a way of realising our connection to Spirit and of remembering our integrity. It is to sit within the inner silence, to cease the chatter and to reunite with the Universe. Prayer offers us the chance to talk to Spirit, and as the whisperer of Magick, Raven institutes the legacy of Magick within the soul by endorsing the sacredness of prayer; a simple act that welcomes greater transformation, new life, clearer perception and deeper healing. Our prayers must be made in honour of the Earth Mother and in recognition of all living creatures that share this land with us, and they must be made with the firm belief that all people shall someday look to Spirit and find the courage to walk as one. When we pray, we should ask for the best way to personally honour the ways of Spirit and to seek blessings for those close to our heart. When we finish we must spend a little time in silence to honour the Void, for the silence is sacred and no words are necessary when one is fixed on embracing the wisdom of Great Mystery. When we accept the wisdom of the Raven we begin to understand our innate knowledge, the deep wisdom that comes with living our purpose and the Magick harnessed when we learn how to administer it. Raven offers inner peace that will eventually lead to a deepening of the essence of the soul and a balancing of the Self. Our perception of who we truly are and what we are destined to become will begin to strengthen when we open our hearts to the wisdom of Raven.

Red Panda
Compassion

Red Panda, of which there are two species, (also called Fire-coloured Cat, Lesser Panda or Fire Fox) is the Giant Panda's only recognised 'cousin'. Growing to about 60 centimetres in length, Red Panda looks like a cross between a Cat and a Racoon. Like Giant Panda, Red Panda must eat large quantities of bamboo. Although more suited to a carnivorous diet, Red Panda cannot digest cellulose, so she must rely on the digestive properties found in bamboo in order to survive. Red Panda is an efficient climber and spends the majority of her time sleeping among the branches of the forest canopy. She has semi-retractable claws and, like Giant Panda, has a 'false thumb'. Red Panda is a solitary creature that is mainly active at night.

Sharing the humble, modest and empathetic energy of Giant Panda, Red Panda is said to resonate to the energy of Quan Yin, the goddess of compassion and mercy. Quan Yin is also known as *Kuan Yin, Quan'Am* (in Vietnam), *Kannon* (in Japan) and *Kanin* (in Bali). Like Quan Yin, Red Panda is the personification of compassion, unconditional love and kindness. Red Panda hears and answers the cries of all beings, hence some people calling her the 'Wah' due to her mournful cry. Her kind-hearted response echoes the pain and suffering felt by people and animals the world over. Red Panda, imbued with the passion and dynamic energy of fire, strengthens courage, enhances creativity and offers a keen and rapid force that brings light into one's life and illumination to one's path. Red Panda animates, quickens and transforms all who are drawn to explore it. She offers enlightened spirituality, wisdom, strength and the divine power of personal transformation. Quan Yin is said to have promised the people that she would not return to heaven until all living things had discovered and honoured their purpose. Red Panda sits close to the heavens, perched high in the trees, looking down protectively on the people. Like Quan Yin, Red Panda is so free of pride and vengefulness that it makes it hard for those who embrace her wisdom to punish, blame or accuse. Although ever watchful, Red Panda guides and inspires us to grow and heal by filling us with an overwhelming sense of empathy whenever we lose sight of our own divinity and connection to Spirit. She reminds us of the sacredness found in all life and the inherent relationship we share with all things of Nature and all people. Red Panda delivers us into a state of humility and gratitude when it is observed that we may be taking things for granted or when we are working from a place of pure ego. Red Panda nurtures the refined qualities of Quan Yin within all people; virtues said to inherently reside within those who yearn to see the world become a better place.

Rhea
Maintenance

Rhea lacks the large tail plumes of his African cousin, Ostrich, and has three toes on each foot instead of two. Once his territory is established, the male Rhea attracts females by running at them with outstretched wings. After gathering several females, he dances to impress and invites them to mate. After mating he leads them, one at a time, to a previously prepared nest site and encourages them to lay an egg. He will gather around 20 eggs in the nest before incubating them alone. The male will then protectively raise the chicks, with no help at all from the female. Abandoned or lost chicks will sometimes by adopted by other males.

In Greek mythology, Rhea was celebrated as the mother of the gods. She is also known as *Rhea Cybele* and *Magna Mater*, meaning 'Great Mother'. According to legend, Rhea married her brother Cronus and, to him, bore six children. Cronus became increasingly threatened by their future power and so, to protect his sovereignty, he devoured all but one: Zeus. As if in memory of the error of Cronus' ways, the male Rhea is now forced to eternally offer maintenance to the female of his species by tending solely to the care and protection of his children, thus offering her a life of leisure. By honouring what it means to be a 'great mother', Rhea dedicates his life to repaying his debts while willingly sacrificing his own freedom in favour of providing others with theirs. Rhea speaks of 'putting things right' and showing accountability for our actions. Rhea offers resolve to see us take responsibility for the things we have done in our lives; the things that impact on the lives of others and the things that only we can fix or maintain. Rhea inspires apologies, recompense and reward. He may also refer to repaying the 'sins of the fathers' and of past-life or karmic debts that need to be honoured this time around. Rhea clarifies questions we may have regarding certain people that cyclically appear in our life or who constantly rub us up the wrong way. He helps explain reasons for the love/hate relationships that we neither want in our life, nor do anything about ridding ourselves of, by sponsoring the idea of karmic history and issues that need to be addressed from lifetimes ago.

Rhinoceros
Staying power

 Rhinoceros has very poor vision and is unable to detect a stationary person or animal standing at a distance of more than 30 metres away. The name 'Rhinoceros' derives from the distinctive horn protruding from the animal's snout. Unlike those found on Cows, Goats and Sheep, the Rhinoceros' horn has no bony core and consists entirely of keratin anchored firmly to his skull. Of the five species of Rhinoceros found in the world today, only two are indigenous to Africa: the Black and the White. Sumatran, Indian and Javan Rhinoceros are found sparingly in pockets of tropical Asia, with both of the African species and Sumatran Rhino armed with two horns. The Indian and Javan species however, have only one horn, which obtrudes just above and between the animal's nostril cavities.

According to medieval tradition, the mysterious Unicorn ('uni' meaning one, and 'corn' meaning horn) was a symbol of virtue, entitlement and splendour. It was said that only the pure of heart could approach, domesticate and yoke Unicorn, with the honour usually passing to the youngest ('most virginal') females of the time. Unicorn and the Rhinoceros were often confused because an animal described as being of 'one horn' in early Christian times was supposed to be of a species either of, or directly related to, the legendary Unicorn. As a result, the horn of the Rhinoceros became much sought after for supernatural and therapeutic purposes; a fascination that unfortunately still lingers to this day. Rhino horn, for example, was believed to hold properties that, when consumed internally as a powder, offered aphrodisiacal outcomes while simultaneously curing impotence, worms, epilepsy, vertigo, symptoms of fever, stomach ache, convulsions and even smallpox. If you find yourself suffering from these 'dis-eases', to call upon the wisdom of the Rhinoceros as a support or an aide is one way of honouring this ancient misunderstanding that, although erroneous on a physical level, helped build respect for the mystical qualities of the animal. It is said that the spiritually sensitive, antenna-like horns of both the Unicorn and the Rhinoceros are helpful in the detection of all poisons, negative vibrations and dark-side entities (a belief that still holds true in the Middle East and far East). Being clearly phallic in form, the horn of the Rhinoceros when invoked as part of the animal's wisdom, is useful for manifesting new beginnings, fertility and advancement. It is also a powerful tool in the banishment of obstacles, unwanted interferences, fear, illness and grief. When assistance is required in the moving forwards or upwards in the world, appeal to the Spirit of the Rhinoceros and ask him to walk ahead of you, with his powerful horn pushing forward, clearing all the obstructions and limiting beliefs (yours and those sustained by others) out of the way. Offering determination and staying power, the strength of the Rhinoceros will ensure a fertile, productive life full of the things you innately know you deserve, despite what others may say or think.

Ringtail
Prospect

Ringtail is also known as *Cacomistle*; an Aztec word, which in Spanish means 'nimble thief'. Her Latin name *Bassariscus Astutus* means 'cunning little Fox'. Ringtail is a carnivorous mammal about the size of a domestic Cat. She has a 40-centimetres-long black-and-white striped tail, strongly resembling that of Madagascan Ringtail Lemur. Ringtail is affectionately called the 'Miner's Cat' and during the early 1900s, prospectors domesticated her and kept her as a 'mouser' in their mines and camps. To this day Ringtail can be tamed if hand-raised from an early enough age. Ringtail is widely distributed because it is thought she likes to explore railway cargo carriages that criss-cross the country.

Ringtail encourages us to see every new experience as an opportunity to expand on all levels in a balanced way. Like the 'Miner's Cat', Ringtail accompanies us as we dig for advantageous opportunity and promises to exercise the 'Midas Touch' when appropriate, turning all that we unearth to gold. Ringtail does not always promise to bring all our wants and desires to fruition however, and helps us find the balance between honouring an advantage and abusing an opportunity. Ringtail helps us review our prospects and make the most beneficial moves. As the 'mouser', Ringtail is the one who helps us secure a deal and turn the 'gentleman's handshake' into a contract, a deal or partnership that will both protect and ensure a golden future. Ringtail helps us ethically realise our potential and do what needs to be done to honour it. Ringtail encourages us to ride on the back of opportunity, remain on track and see where life takes us. Ringtail people work best as a team. They are fully aware of their strengths and abilities but are also willing to encourage and enhance those of their team mates. Ringtail people support the notion of 'a team is only as good as its members'. Ringtail people understand that if you treat your team members with equality and respect, their yield will prove more productive. Ringtail people know that by knuckling down and not being afraid to step out of your comfort zone, you literally climb the ladder of success and rise to higher levels of awareness by achieving greater appreciation for what is and what can be.

Road Runner

Aptitude

Roadrunner is so named because of his tendency to walk or run instead of taking to the air like other birds. Roadrunner is a swift and efficient hunter, skilled in taking Hummingbirds and Dragonflies while on the wing, and in stalking Rattlesnakes. Distracting the venomous Snake with an outstretched wing, he grabs her by the tail, cracks her like a whip and snaps her spine before bringing herhead down on a rock. To tackle the aridity of his territory, Roadrunner reabsorbs water from his body waste before excreting it. During the mating season, the male will gather food for himself, but offers titbits to his mate to induce mating. He will dance around her as she 'begs' to be fed, but will only surrender it to her after mating.

An animal that depends on his ability to think and move with speed and accuracy, Roadrunner is heavily associated with mental power, clarity and creative thinking. Roadrunner inspires hurried (but educated) decisions, speedy (but planned) changes of mind or direction, fast (but not flippant) talk and the immediate manifestation of viable ideas, plans and concepts. Roadrunner people are enhanced with nimble brains and powerful ideas. They are the groundbreakers, pioneers and explorers in their field. They can efficiently handle more than one task at a time, often completing them simultaneously and with equal merit. Roadrunner people rarely fit into the mainstream setting, quickly breaking away from the mundane order of things, instead preferring to test theories considered way before their time. Roadrunner nurtures the quick learner, the academic and the potential genius. Because of their mental aptitude, however, Roadrunner people are often loners, social outcasts or those considered 'nerds'. Roadrunner people dash ahead, leaving others in their wake fumbling to make sense of the instructions given making it hard for others to follow their chain of thought. Roadrunner people therefore need to remain vigilant against becoming blinkered in their endeavours and oblivious to the practicalities of life. Roadrunner in a nutshell nurtures academic advancement, mental enhancement and diligent study. He allows for productive time management and the successful juggling of more than one responsibility at a time. Roadrunner reminds us to remain attentive to peripheral demands, but to maintain focus on the task at hand so that our growth and development may be swift but grounded, free of obstacles and fruitful.

Robin

Aspiration

Robin is a common songbird (related to Flycatchers and Chats) known for his aggressive character. He is best admired for his song during the winter when he often sings well into the evening. Robins nests in cracks in walls and chimneys, flowerpots and discarded nests of other songbirds and is fairly fearless of humans and will venture close to a busy gardener especially when digging is being done to search for Worms and insects. A bird of the 'greenwoods', Robin is said to be the personification of Robin Hood, the hero who stole from the rich to give to the poor. The return of Robin in the New Year announces the arrival of spring – the season of new growth, rebirth and new beginnings. According to legend, any wish you make when you spy the first Robin for the New Year will surely come true. If all else fails though, the legend proffers you will be granted good fortune for the next 12 months.

Robin is the totem of those who 'wear their heart on their sleeve'. Robin people convey their emotions without restraint and are not afraid to do so publicly. They cry for the people and the state of the world, and are not afraid to voice their sadness. Robin people are easy to read because they make no effort to hide how they feel. They know what is right and what needs to be done and they are not afraid to express their opinions or to act on their feelings. You can always tell what a Robin person is thinking by observing their body language and facial expression. Robin people are inherently positive, optimistic and resilient, but are often taken advantage of when it comes to issues of the heart. They are accidental martyrs, particularly vulnerable to the 'bleeding heart' syndrome. They are people who will happily sacrifice their own wellbeing to help others, unaware that they are probably being taken advantage of. When invoked in a healthy, productive way, however, Robin is potent enough to ensure that all our aspirations are realised. He is the harbinger of new life and the birthing of dreams. He affords fruitful opportunity to start afresh and, as such, efficiently repairs the wounded or broken hearted. He heralds miraculous change, promise, strength, wisdom, ambition and personal healing. The appearance of a Robin may suggest that we are feeling over-sensitive, acting irrationally or feeling emotionally pressured to remove burdens from others. He nurtures us as we 'toughen up' and to focus our ability to bring about positive personal change and frees us up to bring our own dreams to fruition so that we are no longer a slave to others demands or our own innate sense of liability. On the other hand, Robin rebirths those who, due to emotional abuse or sudden overload of responsibility, have cut themselves off from others or the world as a whole to prevent continued heartache. The Robin perched on the shovel left standing in the snow symbolically encourages us to dig deep within our heart of hearts and thaw any 'frozen' or suspended emotion so that it may be surrendered, released and allowed to flow in a manner that is both healthy and productive. Robin restores faith in our feelings and supports us as we learn to reveal them openly once again. He shores us up to take risks, dare to dream and believe that the wish we make on the first Robin for the year will in fact come true, with our 'bleeding heart' eventually healed and true love felt both inward and out.

Salamander
Fire

Salamander is a tailed amphibian meaning he can venture onto land but must remain close to water for survival. Salamander, although prolific as a species, is unobtrusive and shy, and remains hidden from prying eyes found sheltering under rotting logs or damp leaf litter. Most Salamanders have a biphasic life cycle, involving aquatic eggs and larvae that metamorphose into terrestrial adults. Other species do not have a free-living larval stage, instead fully transmuting within the egg capsule. Others have abandoned metamorphosis altogether and remain 'larval' for the duration of their lives, but reproduce like other standard Salamanders.

When we sit and contemplate the movement of the flames leaping from the wood fuelling our campfires, especially when the wood is driftwood permeated with salt, it is not hard to fancy small Lizard-like creatures dancing among the hot coals. The association between the preferred sites for camping (with fire) and the small amphibious creatures spied at night taking advantage of the water led to the belief that Salamander was able to exist in fire, controlling its habits and harnessing its force. Over time, Salamander became known as the Elemental Spirit of Fire and the embodiment of its energy. From the moment man 'discovered' fire and first harnessed its potency, he learned that fire shows little mercy for those who abuse or neglect it. He learned quickly that if he was to integrate fire into his life, he had to restrict its movements within a circle of rocks or some other fire-retarding vessel. To assume otherwise would see everything surrounding it swallowed up and enveloped in its wrathful flames. He also learned that the only way to quash its advancement was with water, an element both quiet and contemplative. Salamander, it was decided, although living near water but seemingly 'active' *within* fire, embraced both elements equally, and like the Chinese yin yang symbol, created balance between all that is deemed creative and destructive; good and bad; dark and light; nurturing and revengeful. Salamander can be invoked to breathe life into and dampen the ferocity of fire in its tangible form, in the wilderness or the comfort of our own home. When we ignite a candle, light a wood stove or build a campfire, we essentially invoke the wisdom of Salamander. Fire symbolically governs our attitudes and how we conduct our personal lives. It governs issues related to the heart, the small intestine and pericardium, the cardiovascular and nervous system, digestive function and circulation. Whenever we set personal boundaries, partake in sexual activity or commence a relationship of any sort, we acknowledge the fire element represented by Salamander. Salamander people are passionate about most things, but not always in a productive way. They are inherently forceful, obstinate, opinionated and boastful and as with fire itself, Salamander people must be careful to maintain control and not let their fiery disposition and forceful nature get away from them because when it does the rewards gleaned from years of hard work and dedicated effort can quickly go up in smoke. Issues of the heart quickly become issues affecting the heart. For example, love and joy quickly turn to pain and despair. Salamander people need to be themselves (or they appear false and shallow), but they must (more so than others, it seems), endeavour to walk the fine line between being true to themselves and being respectful and tolerant of the opinions, beliefs and values of those around them – especially when they differ from their own.

Salmon
Reflection

Salmon is a fish that lives in both the ocean and land-locked bodies of water. Some species of Salmon are referred to as Trout. She is anadromous, which means she is born in fresh water, migrates to the ocean and then returns to fresh water to reproduce. It is said that Salmon returns to the very same river in which she was born when she is ready to spawn. Many cultures once revered Salmon with some performing sacred ceremonies to honour the first return of the season. Salmon is revered for her health-boosting oil and is considered one of the richest sources of Omega-3, which is said to be a major player in the prevention of heart disease and the battle against inflammatory problems such as arthritis.

According to Celtic mythology, Salmon that inhabits deep pools or wells surrounded by hazel trees was particularly revered because it was believed that she held great wisdom. Apparently, when Salmon fed on the hazelnuts that fell into the water, the fish's wisdom increased. It was believed therefore, that anyone who caught and ate this 'Salmon of Wisdom' would attain her wisdom. Fintan, the 'Salmon of Wisdom', was believed to have been the first mortal man to appear in Ireland before the Great Flood. He had many wives and many children but they were all drowned when the flood came. He managed to survive however, by taking the form of a Salmon. As a Salmon, Fintan gathered all the wisdom of Ireland over many centuries. He became the object of desire for the Druid Finegas, who hunted Fintan for many years with the intention of eating his flesh and gaining the knowledge for himself. The silvery, reflective skin of Salmon invites reflection: a deeper consideration of the experiences life presents and the lessons hidden within each. When we consider our life experiences in hindsight, we can usually see the reason for why things happen. Armed with this understanding, we begin to see that there are no such things as accidents and that nothing happens by chance.

Scorpion
Honour

 A member of the *Arachnid* family, Scorpion is easily distinguished by his pincer-like forelimbs designed for grasping and self-defence. The abdomen tapers into a tail equipped with a venomous stinger and poison gland. Scorpion holds his tail over his body protectively. Some smaller species are often found in urban backyards, gardens and under household objects and in the wild Scorpion seeks shelter under bark, leaf litter, rocks or fallen logs.

A sword suspended over the head signified certain execution for the doomed medieval warrior; a stance echoed by the agitated Scorpion. These ritualistic executions eventually became symbolic in nature as an act of endorsement, a mark of maturity and the affording of sacred wisdom. The wielding of the sword became a symbol of recognition, a rite of passage that saw the warrior become a noble knight. The watery correlation of the zodiacal sign of Scorpio seems to add credence to stories of heroes and their sacred swords. Magically rising from misty bodies of water or trapped within enchanted stones, many stories recount legendary tales of swords fashioned by Faerie hands and gifted to chivalrous men who honoured truth and honour above all else, only to be reclaimed by their mystical crafters on the hero's demise. Scorpion encourages us to flaunt the sting in our tail in much the same way as traditional Buddhist disciples were expected to brandish the sword of knowledge. Scorpion demands that we exert our power in subtle ways; that we remain noble and honourable in our quest for knowledge. Scorpion reminds us that although we are capable of wielding some degree of control over others, we may never be the leader. Scorpion people are forever the knight, never the king, for example. They are usually very attractive (sexually alluring, in fact), gallant, captivating, intelligent and charming. They tend to take silent pleasure in observing others style themselves on their ways, too, and although it may be tempting to take advantage of this power for reasons of self-gain, Scorpion steers us away from dishonourable attitude, channelling our potential into those areas we naturally excel in rather than encouraging us to wreak superficial control over everyone and everything. Scorpion nurtures a sense of pride, spiritual enlightenment, wisdom and nobility of heart, promise, prophecy, bravery and growth. He represents our quest for spiritual truth, while helping us face fears and prioritise honour above all else.

Seal

Inner voice

All Seals belong to the pinniped family, which is Latin for 'feather or fin foot'. Pinniped refers to her fin-like flippers. All pinnipeds venture ashore to breed, give birth and raise their young. The pinniped family is split into three groups: 'Earless' Seal or 'true' Seal, 'eared' Seal or Fur Seal and Sea Lion, and Walrus. Elephant Seal, Monk Seal and Harbour Seal are all classified as 'Earless Seals'. Earless Seal has rear flippers that point backwards, making movement on land difficult and she lacks external ear flaps. She also has a layer of blubber that offers insulation. Fur Seals and Sea Lions, however, have external ear flaps and are able to rotate their hind feet forward enabling them to move with considerable speed on land. Instead of blubber, Eared Seal has dense fur that traps air bubbles and affords insulation.

Selkies are gentle Faerie-folk that inhabit the waters of Orkney and Shetland where 'Selkie' is a local word meaning 'Seal'. Also known as Silkie, Selchie or Roane, she appears in the form of Grey Seal, but assumes human form by casting off her sealskin. She requires the sealskin to return to the sea however, so if her skin is stolen or lost she becomes trapped in human form until the skin is retrieved. Whilst in human form, she is incredibly beautiful; almost irresistible to humans. Selkies will often gather on outlying rocks in large groups to bask in the sun. A young Selkie is known for her curiosity, often travelling great distances to explore new waters and human settlements established close to the shore. Selkie is amorous, romantic and sentimental and will often come ashore to court humans, particularly women disillusioned with their lives or those wanting to be rescued from their current relationships. The male will seldom stay with his female conquest for long however, returning to the sea almost immediately. Male Selkie is responsible for the conjuring of fierce storms and the sinking of ships; his way of avenging Seal hunting. Female Selkie, though rarely intentionally seeking human lovers, will also venture ashore to explore. Occasionally a human male will find a discarded sealskin, trapping Selkie in human form. Legend has it that the beautiful maiden must marry her captor and bear him children. Selkie inevitably finds the hidden skin however, allowing her to return to the sea. Seal invokes a sense of playfulness, magic and romance in human relationships, especially those forged between lovers and dreamers. Seal emphasises the supremacy of the inner voice, reminding us of the power found within our personal rhythms, emotions and intuition. Seal helps us 'sing' from the heart for our soul mate, while simultaneously helping us find a healthy balance between love and lust and sensitivity and sensuality within ourselves and all our other relationships. She explains that how we perceive ourselves will ultimately influence the type of energy we will attract. To exude unconditional love will eventually attract the same. Seal supports us as we bask in the glow of our inner knowing. She shuns superficiality and compromise, drawing to us the partner (and the other rewards we feel we deserve) best suited to fulfil our heartfelt requirements. Seal augurs a time of peace and balance and rejects force. She calls for us to be clear in our expectations and to surrender jealousy, resentment and discontent. Seal encourages us to acknowledge and listen to our inner voice, the only counsel we need in our search for unconditional love, acceptance and loyalty.

• Walrus – *Know-how*

Walrus belongs to the pinniped family, along with Sea Lion and Fur Seal. He is best known for his long whiskers and powerful tusks. Walrus lacks external ears and is able to swim at great speeds using both his front and rear flippers to propel him through the water. He maintains body warmth by insulating himself with a thin layer of blubber.

Walrus is an animal often personified as a wise individual; broad thinking and resolved in his attitude. Walrus people are the wise ones, the old men of the sea, the ones 'long in the tooth' and full of proven know-how. Walrus people are generally well experienced in life with information on pretty much everything filed away in their wealth of worldly knowledge. Walrus people are the best to approach when in need of a mentor, advisor or testimonial. Although they may initially appear gruff, intolerant and impatient, such traits are usually unintended. They are grounded, authentic and sound, easily excited by new ideas and prepared to take risks to help get new projects off the ground; particularly those that others steer clear of because they do not fit the fashion or desired criteria. Walrus people make excellent life partners, business partners and teachers. Walrus encourages us to seek the wisdom of someone more experienced that us, someone who knows the ropes, has the contacts and who is willing to share. He promises success by reaching people, places and levels of achievement typically unattainable to 'normal' folk. Walrus offers endurance. He supports us by supporting our dreams and allows us to believe in ourselves, our worth and our abilities, so much so that those around us are forced to follow a similar belief. He offers a leg-up; a boost in power that promises to make the world stop and listen.

Secretary Bird
Stalking perceptions

Secretary Bird is a large raptor of the open, arid regions of Africa and although an accomplished flyer, will typically be seen wandering the plains on foot in search of rodents, reptiles and large insects. Secretary Bird is famous for her penchant for Snakes and she has a surprisingly powerful kick, which she uses to stamp on her prey. In the event of bush and grass fire, which are common occurrences in Africa, Secretary Bird will be found close by feeding on the charred bodies of the small animals caught in the blaze.

Secretary Bird is a powerful teacher and is brutally blunt in her methods, insisting we find our own answers. She never offers immediate assistance to those who look to her for guidance. Not ever. Secretary Bird says that all the wisdom we need to live abundant lives is stored within the self and reflected in the way we perceive and interact with the world. Secretary Bird is the keeper of our sacred blueprint and the file of our personal records. She is the pact keeper, the one charged with forcing us to take responsibility for our thoughts and actions. She is the one who reminds us of the sacred agreements we forged with Spirit before commencing our Earth Walk, and kicks us passionately when we stray from our designated path or refuse to embrace necessary healing. Secretary Bird says that there are four fundamental steps to remembering and embracing one's authentic self; the self we were meant to be and the life we were meant to live. These four steps involve the stalking of the sacred self, judgment of the familiar self, the review of one's personal history and the ultimate surrendering of all judgment. The beauty of the four steps is that, although they are separate and precise, they form a distinct and absolute whole. They work as a team; a journey, operating simultaneously, but in regimented order. When we decide that something is true, we inherently trust that no further information is required. We form a belief. This belief becomes our truth. It becomes 'carved in stone'. To review one's personal history is to give permission to remember one's past. But, instead of recounting our story as a list of day-by-day accounts, Secretary Bird encourages us to explore the narration of our life in linear form; to remember explicit events rather than every minute detail from the time we were born. By doing this, we can look at our life as a list of experiences; as Stepping Stones to Power. Our experience represents our wisdom and symbolises 'training' and our list of qualifications. Armed with this knowledge, whenever we have an experience in the future that triggers a 'familiar' emotion, we are encouraged to simply relate what we are feeling to the memory of an experience from the past. By developing a healthy, working relationship with our past, we set ourselves free from judgment. We release it and give it back. We set our judgments free by simply 're-deciding' them; beliefs that where once 'carved in stone' as personal truths become 'fluid'. We make them relevant to the way we want to live our life. When we release judgment, we are free to learn new things and create a whole list of new beliefs: beliefs that serve us instead of binding us to judgment. Secretary Bird encourages us to ground ourselves, to purposefully explore the tangible world and to take ownership of the part we consciously play in the mundane world instead of laying blame and dumping responsibility on others.

Shark

Authority

Shark breathes through his gills by extracting oxygen from the water, like all species of fish. Primarily oceanic by nature (preferring tropical to temperate zones), some Sharks have adapted to life in fresh water. The largest species of Shark is Whale Shark, which can grow to over 12 metres in length, while some deepwater Sharks only reach 25 centimetres in length. Mostly predatory in nature, Shark is generally nocturnal and hunts after dark. Although it is thought he does not intentionally target man as prey, both Great White Shark and Tiger Shark are known to be dangerous to humans. All Sharks are protected by law in Australia.

Shark endorses having respect for authority and encourages us to see the merit in respecting the need for and the maintenance of 'control' within our family and broader community. Shark is the totem of people whose job it is to protect, maintain order and dispense discipline. Just as a Shark's fin can pop up unexpectedly behind an unsuspecting surfer for example, the flashing blue light of a police car can pop up unexpectedly in the rear-view mirror of a motorist. Shark is the totem of people who have roles of authority within the community such as police, justices of the peace, school teachers and principals, prison wardens, parking officers, judges and magistrates, bank managers and members of the council. People fear Shark because they believe he attacks and kills without mercy. Not only is this not true, it's also a superficial excuse that camouflages a deeper, more personal reason. On a subconscious level, people fear Shark because they inherently relate him to authority. Those who are wary or untrusting of authority will feel similarly about Shark. Those abused, oppressed or neglected at the hands of primary people in their lives, will also feel vulnerable around Shark. Shark agrees that respect must be earned and those who distrust authority need to be shown respect themselves, or taught how to feel respect for themselves. It is obvious that people who do not feel respected by authority will feel hesitant to trust what authority supposedly represents. Wider education, an 'open door' policy and perceived genuine concern might contribute to a more positive community presence, especially when fuelled by mutual trust and sense of service. For those who have no reason to fear Shark however, just remember: never splash about in waters not intended for your use and you will be fine.

Sheathbill

Promotion

 Sheathbill lacks webbed feet and therefore is unable to swim so she cannot catch fish or other marine creatures and must scavenge for carrion and scraps of food left behind by other birds. Opportunistic by nature, Sheathbill was revered by early sealers for her thieving skills and belligerent attitude. Sheathbill often migrates to South America or the Falklands to avoid the deep cold and malevolent weather of the Antarctic winter. Sheathbill nests in rocky fissures and usually remains close to Penguin rookeries because of the greater availability of food. She disturbs Penguin during the regurgitation process, forcing her to drop food intended for her chick onto the ground where it is quickly eaten by the marauding Sheathbill.

Sheathbill is the totem of people who seem to climb to the top of the pile with little apparent effort, despite being grossly underqualified or lacking in experience. Sheathbill people are fast-talking, charming and inoffensive. They believe in themselves and are confident, unflinching and persuasive. They know what to say and when to say it, taking full advantage of any situation – even those only faintly hinting of opportunity. Sheathbill people are best described as 'street smart' and often portray themselves as being educated at the 'school of hard knocks'. They never admit to failure, and are never satisfied with busying themselves in areas perceived by their superiors as best suited to their level of training or skill. They view themselves as being better; never lowly and more than worthy of the things they see other people enjoying. What they lack in experience they make up for in charisma. Sheathbill people are so confident in their abilities to succeed that even seemingly insurmountable obstacles do not hold them back. Sheathbill offers stamina to break free of limitation. She shuns fear and trepidation and supports those, for example, who wish to return to the workforce after years of raising children or tending to the home or advancing themselves academically. She allows us the inner strength to step out of our comfort zone and to strive for greener pastures. Sheathbill instils a sense of profound self-worth that declares publicly, 'I can do anything'. Sheathbill was evident when women first won the right to vote, when the first Paraolympian won a gold medal and when man first stepped foot on the moon. Sheathbill inspires promise and a window of opportunity to lift you out of the mundane, customary realms of existence into a world of miracles, prospect and attainment.

Sheep
Conformity

Contemporary domestic Sheep are descendants of an ancient breed of wild Sheep – Moufflon, which was indigenous to the mountains of Turkey and southern Iran. European Moufflon however, is probably a descendant of an early breed of domestic Sheep that escaped and turned feral. Sheep is a grazing mammal bred commercially for his fleece and meat that are today found in nearly every country of the world. Sheep is famous for following the others in his flock without question. Birds will fly in formation, changing direction as a single entity. Sheep however, simply follows the individual who happens to be in front. The whole flock is lead by a dominant individual but even this leadership is haphazard. Males are referred to as Rams, females as Ewes, while the young are called Lambs.

Sheep people, when drawing on their positive traits, are connected to their purpose and are stable, grounded and driven and emanate a sense of endurance and steadfastness. Sheep people are ground-breakers. They are the ones with the determination and wilful mindset to make breakthrough discoveries, overcome obstacles and achieve on the grandest of levels. They are practical, sensible and reliable. They espouse the danger of blindly following others though, particularly when their example is poor or questionable. Sheep explains that when we follow someone driven by ego, confusion, anger, fear, malice or greed, we will ultimately be delivered into a similar mindset. When we feel inspired to follow in the footsteps of another, we should first seek testimonials or endorsements from people who have experienced their work or who have witnessed their acumen as a leader. Conforming to peer-group pressure, or being fooled by a 'Wolf in Sheep's clothing', generally ends in deception, downfall and entrapment. To follow those who work with an honest, altruistic, team-based spirit, though, will see us succeed, reach ever greater heights and surpass our previous best. In order for us to grow and prosper in any arena of life, we, of course, must conform to some degree of expectation. Conformity in the guise of teamwork has its advantages. Sycophants and those who cannot make their own decisions or think in an innovative way will always be followers and never true leaders. Sheep warns us of the risks involved in shunning our personal path and of losing our sense of individuality. Sheep offers legitimacy to those beliefs and values deemed untraditional or too 'out there' by our family and friends, and reawakens personal wisdom sacred to our heart of hearts. He helps us embrace a non-judgmental mind-set so that we might acknowledge the sacredness found in all paths and belief systems, even when they seem to differ or conflict with our own. Sheep leads us back to a state of wellbeing and stability, clarity and inner peace, while helping us reclaim the certainty that once supported our personal view of the world and ourselves as individuals.

• Bighorn Sheep – *Cornucopia*

 Bighorn Sheep's habitat is arid and almost devoid of green vegetation. He survives by sheltering in caves or under rocky overhangs during the hottest parts of the day and during the summer he must visit a waterhole at least every three days due to lack of vegetation. Male Bighorn Sheep partakes in head-to-head combat in order to win a mate. The length and integrity of this animal's horns helps him maintain his position within the herd and determines his level of dominance. Bighorn Sheep is well suited to living on rocky terrain with rubbery soles that provide traction as he traverses steep cliff faces.

According to legend, the infant Zeus was suckled with Goat's milk by Tyche, daughter to the King of Crete. In gratitude, he took one of the Goat's horns and offered it to her, promising that whoever possessed it would enjoy eternal abundance and material wealth. The 'horn of plenty' (which later became known as the cornucopia) became a tribute to the masculine fecundity of the gods. The word 'cornucopia' literally means *overflowing*, indicating a bounty of treasure waiting to be spilled. Although Bighorn Sheep is not a Goat, his wisdom is heavily imbued with symbolism focused on the power of his horns. Bighorn Sheep Dreaming, when invoked with integrity, can determine the degree of luck and good fortune that surrounds us in life. Instead of living life 'stuck between a rock and a hard place', or forever banging our head against a wall in frustration, he nurtures the understanding that when we share our abundance, or help others improve theirs, prosperity flows freely in our favour. Bighorn Sheep inspires us to reach ever greater heights, to personally achieve and to dream big. In doing so, he helps us break through limiting beliefs associated with money and personal gain. Bighorn Sheep endorses that it is okay to know wealth; that money can lead to happiness, but that it is what we do with our money that ensures the longevity of that happiness. An animal that knowingly takes leaps of faith, Bighorn Sheep explains that with effort comes reward. When we acknowledge the wealth that already exists in our life and we willingly share our wealth with others, we experience equal benefit; we enrich not only our lives but, simultaneously, the lives around us. When we share our wealth, Spirit rewards us by ensuring that life becomes a cornucopia of opportunity and joy – for all. Spirit supports our efforts, by matching us dollar for dollar. Bighorn Sheep espouses the fact that abundance means more than material gain. Abundance is deeply affected by the level of fate we acknowledge in our life and the degree of luck we create for ourselves every day, our determination to grow on all levels and the commitment of our friends and family to follow suit. Only when we prove our worth (to ourselves and Spirit) and we appreciate the abundance that already exists in our life, will life become a veritable 'horn of plenty'.

Shrew
Autonomy

Shrew is a small, voracious Mouse-like mammal that is neither related to Mouse or rodents in general. Some species climb trees, while others live underground or enjoy a semi-aquatic lifestyle. A few are said to secrete a toxin used to immobilise prey that targets the central nervous system. A successful bite from this animal can be quite painful, producing inflammation and reddening that may last for several days. Another strange feature of Shrew is that she has such a high metabolic rate she must eat constantly for fear of starving to death. She often consumes twice or three times her own body weight every day.

Shrew Dreaming, no matter from which angle it is perceived, speaks primarily of the strength needed to overcome adversity and tyranny and the sacredness found in being self-governing and independent. When we lack the self-esteem and assurance to question the authority that keeps us downtrodden, Shrew infuses us with the stamina and vitality to proudly stand our ground and rebel. She instils the confidence to have our voice heard and provides a forum to pronounce our rights and opinions. She charges us with the power to fight for our rights and to rise above hardship, take stock of our life and make self-governing decisions.

• Elephant Shrew – *Dissuasion*

An insectivorous mammal, Shrew belongs to a family group of approximately 275 independent species. Four types of Elephant Shrew are found in East Africa alone, and are distinguished by their distinct colour patterns. Famous for her short, bristly fur of contrasting patches of colour, bold white spots or handsome black stripes, Elephant Shrew takes her name from her elongated head and trunk-like nose. Elephant Shrew marks her territory using scent discharged from an anal gland located at the base of the tail. The gland produces such a strong odour that it deters most predators, except the animal's most prominent ones: Snakes and raptorial birds.

An animal famous for her ability to discourage her predators, Elephant Shrew effectively demonstrates that you cannot deter that which is inevitable. We can live a life of denial and pretend that all is as it could be, or that things that require attention are not as pressing we would like to admit (even when they are), but when deadlines aren't met or when responsibilities are not honoured, Spirit steps in and forces the issue. Elephant Shrew explains that we cannot dissuade that which has been predestined or agreed upon. Contracts that have been signed or verbally granted must be honoured: a law enforced by Elephant Shrew, who can smell deception a mile off and hidden truths camouflaged by lies and false promises. If you owe money, but the deadline mutually agreed to repay it has passed, then it would be wise to clear up the debt immediately or seek an extension if possible. If you have agreed to provide a service, and you have not honoured the deal, then it would be wise to do something about it today. If you have sold something under the assumption that it was of excellent condition or in full working order, and you know in your heart of hearts that you have hoodwinked the other party, then you must amend the scam this instance. If not, Elephant Shrew will be forced to reveal the error of your ways. Elephant Shrew is a creature that knows too well that dissuasion may serve the moment well, but will not remove the problem for good. You may very well discourage one problem by living a life fuelled by denial, but in doing so, you effectively pave the way for the appearance of a complete set of new ones.

Skunk

Compromise

 Related distantly to the Weasel family, Skunk is infamous for her foul-smelling spray which is ejected as a defence from two anal glands located at the base of her tail. The odour is strong enough to deflect the attention of even the most formidable predator and is very difficult to remove from human clothing. Horned Owl, like most birds, has a poor-to-nonexistent sense of smell and is therefore Skunk's only natural threat. Skunk is striped from birth, with colour and pattern varying noticeably from species to species. Nocturnal and largely solitary (except during the breeding season), she is carnivorous and will even raid rubbish bins and compost heaps when such resources are available. Although equipped with sensitive smell and hearing, Skunk has poor vision and experiences difficulty seeing objects more than 3 metres away. Because of this Skunk often falls victim to cars. Naturally short-lived (few live longer than three years), Skunk also falls prey to hunters who shoot, trap or poison her for her pelt.

Skunk traditionally speaks of character and how our attitude, self-respect and the way in which we live our life contributes to a favourable reputation. Skunk people are laid back and relaxed in their disposition. They are easygoing and casual, living uncluttered, balanced lives. The black-and-white colouring suggests harmony between the inherent yin and yang facets, with both the spiritual and physical aspects of existence being honoured both simultaneously and independently of each other. Because of their relaxed demeanour though, Skunk people are often taken advantage of; their good nature finding itself used and abused by even the closest of friends. They give unconditionally, receiving all the thanks they need from the joy revealed on the faces of those receiving their assistance, support and benefit. When someone gives of themselves on a regular basis, however, others often grow to expect it, literally taking their good will for granted. Skunk people are very patient and take a lot of provocation before angering or 'flaring up' emotionally. Skunk people dislike confrontation, but when all their buttons are unduly pushed they will retaliate in a forceful and aggressive way. Those who find themselves on the receiving end of a Skunk person's wrath will ultimately require time to rehabilitate, with apologies and explanation doing little to lessen the level of contempt. Skunk demands that we do not figuratively paint ourselves into a corner and that when we give from the heart, we do so intermittently to avoid others taking it for granted. Skunk offers the choice to either remain in a situation that demands walking on eggshells or to take control of your life in a way that reinstates personal power and self-esteem. Skunk restores strength, endurance and balance, thus guaranteeing an honourable reputation.

Sloth

Carefree

 Sloth is a slow-moving, arboreal mammal that spends much of his time suspended inverted high up in the forest canopy. Sloth eats, sleeps, mates and gives birth in this inverted position, holding on with strong, hook-like claws. Male Sloths are solitary, whereas the females may congregate in small groups. Nocturnal by nature, Sloth sleeps for up to 18 hours a day. Sloth is known for the green algae that grow in his damp fur. Sloth got his name from his slow movement.

Sloth was so named after the fifth of the Seven Deadly Sins. The Seven Deadly Sins were originally drawn up in response to the seven most serious human passions, or vices, observed by the Greek monastic theologian, Evagrius of Pontus: gluttony, lust, avarice, anger, acedia, envy and pride. Pride was considered the most sinister. The term *acedia* (Greek for 'not to care') denotes 'spiritual Sloth': a 'carefree' attitude that defines someone as 'not loving God with all their heart'. It symbolises fear, lack of thought, self-indulgent gratification and carelessness. Sloth was thought to manifest as severe idleness despite the fact he is not lazy, simply slow-moving. Sloth is considered negative because he personifies both lack of consideration and selfishness. When someone chooses to sit idle, for example, others are forced to work harder to compensate, causing dissension and frustration. Sloth is considered detrimental for the self too, as he describes the tendency to put off until tomorrow what could be done today. It was thought that Sloth could 'seduce' people by promising them 'get rich quick' schemes and seemingly risk-free conspiracies that take very little effort but guarantee plentiful returns. Demonstrating a 'carefree' attitude is admirable, so long as it doesn't interfere with or compromise one's other responsibilities, values or beliefs, which Sloth seems to imply. In contrast to the Seven Deadly Sins, humility, meekness, charity, chastity, moderation, zeal and generosity are listed as the seven favourable qualities, or virtues, humanity must strive to embrace.

Snake
Transmutation

Australia has possibly the widest variety of Snakes than anywhere else in the world. Of the 170-plus species of Snake native to Australia, 32 are aquatic in nature, 100 are venomous and 12 are potent enough to kill with a single bite. The most dangerous Snakes in Australia are those classified as 'front-fanged', which include the Copperhead, Dugite, Taipan, Black, Tiger and Brown, the Death Adder, King Brown and a few species of Sea Snake. Australia also has a healthy collection of non-venomous, 'solid-toothed' Snakes and some venomous rear-fanged varieties. Snake sheds her skin up to four times a year and does this by rubbing her head on a rough surface until the skin splits. She then slowly slips out of the old skin, discarding it to reveal the 'new' brightly coloured (but same patterned) skin underneath.

Snake can be viewed as being both feminine and masculine in nature, both solar and lunar-influenced, and as an emissary of life and death, healing and dis-ease. She embodies all possibilities, being masculine in form and phallic in nature, while traditionally accompanying the ancient Mother deities as symbols of intuition and wisdom. Snake has arbitrated the three worlds since the Dreamtime, as lightning and the solar rays of the Sky Realm, the primal waters of Earth Mother and the Underworld in which she dwells. Snake represents both conception and pregnancy to the Indigenous People of Australia, with the belief that the Rainbow Serpent shaped babies inside the wombs of women. The Celts saw Snake as a powerful symbol of fertility, often depicting serpents in their artwork with eggs lodged firmly in her mouth – an emblematic depiction of Creation, with the masculine seed meeting and joining with the female egg. Embracing the promise of new life, Snake can presage necessary healing that we must welcome if we intend to move into the next phase of our life in a complete and fertile way. As a symbol now employed by the medical fraternity, the *caduceus* is a stylised emblem incorporating a pair of Snakes entwined together in the sacred act of copulation taking a symbolic journey to the higher, mystical realms of Creation. Snake gently points out that we need to look deep within ourselves and to honour those aspects that pose the threat of making us ill. We have to surrender them so that we may see clearly again, allowing us to move forward with confidence and a renewed sense of purpose. Snake Dreaming, however, still allows us to glance back occasionally and even feel a pang of lament when we feel the need. No matter what people try to tell us, time *does not* heal all. It just makes the pain more bearable. We grieve because we love, and to stop grieving suggests that our love has gone.

Grief however, can be turned into power, because to have lived with grief is to know how to teach others to deal with it and to see beyond it. Snake suggests that we look at our baggage, our burdens and our pain and transmute them into new opportunity, new life and the chance to start our journey over again. Snake offers the chance to physically rebirth by strengthening us emotionally and deepening our relationship with Spirit. Snake encourages us to discard all outworn values and belief systems that currently hinder our growth. She supports us as we clear out the deadwood and make way for new beginnings, new life and new opportunity. Just as she sheds her old skin, Snake suggests that we cast off all fear and work through our grief, looking hard with pure loving intent for the lessons held within. We must reject the desire to dump responsibility onto others when we feel life has treated us wrong, and learn to transmute our pain into gain so that we can move forward in life. It is essential that we always take personal responsibility for our own healing, the reshaping of our reality and the recreation of our world.

• Cobra – *Fascination*

 Snake charmers are paid to thrill an audience by 'hypnotising' Cobras. As Cobra emerges from the Snake charmer's basket, he flares his hood in response to the swaying flute, from which he never averts his gaze. Cobra is almost completely deaf, so the reaction to the swaying flute is triggered solely by the assumption that the flute poses a threat. If the charmer was to stop swaying the flute Cobra would relax and probably return to the relative safety of his basket. Cobra is best known for his hood, displayed primarily when angered or threatened and he extends his ribs to either side of its head, flattening his body and fanning it out in an attempt to make him appear intimidating. King Cobra builds a nest for his eggs and remains close until they hatch. Despite the fact that he is responsible for killing thousands of people a year, Spectacled Cobra is spiritually revered and, as a result, is rarely slain by the people. Spitting or Black-Necked Cobra is notorious for his ability to accurately aim and spit his venom (over a distance of up to 2.5 metres), usually targeting his victim's face.

A somewhat reticent creature, Cobra seldom responds to people unless provoked but can prove to be a powerful force to be reckoned with when agitated. Those emanating the more positive qualities of Cobra tend to be rather curious individuals who are eager to explore new territory but are frightfully suspicious of others. Although laid back while in their comfort zone, Cobra people are quick to react to intrusion, interference and negative criticism, especially when such interaction is uninvited. With the desire to fundamentally explore the wisdom of Cobra, therefore, comes a warning not to be beguiled by the charming words or handsome appearance of another (person, place or thing), especially when others are counselling you with once bitten, twice shy-type stories – pleas that may have defiantly befallen 'deaf ears' until now. The medicine of Cobra encourages us to remove the rose-coloured spectacles that romantically taint all that we hold dear; embracing our world with a simulated air of beauty and perfection. In doing so, Cobra enables us to see truths that have been staring us in the face all along: truths available to others but concealed from us behind a veil of charisma and finery. Cobra exposes those who would otherwise disguise who and what they really are: those who are hooded, masked and distracting. Cobra also champions another train of thought: no one should have to suffer spiteful gossip, biting remarks or unjustified criticism that incapacitates as effectively as any well-aimed spit in the face or blow to the stomach. To believe in your own lack of self-worth while defending the excuses that justify such abuse is to espouse the less favourable qualities of Cobra. To bring clarity to the frequently deluded impressions that ensnare us, Cobra prompts us to listen to our gut responses, emotions and intuitional knowing that determines how we *truly* perceive others. To avoid the more negative qualities of Cobra therefore, under no circumstance second guess your instant reaction to the outwardly charming appeal of another and do not doubt your instinct by labelling your thoughts or actions as 'judgmental'. Feelings of 'too good to be true' usually prove correct, but are often only heeded in hindsight or at a time deemed 'too late'.

• Mamba – *Character*

Both Green and Black Mambas are notorious throughout Africa for their speed, agility and toxic venom. In spite of her name, Black Mamba is actually dark greyish-brown in colour. Mamba is a long, venomous Snake, which despite her reputation is quite timid. Arboreal in nature, Mamba moves swiftly through thick undergrowth and over open ground. Responsive when agitated, Mamba is capable of striking accurately (and repeatedly) at her aggressors, even when on the move.

Mamba, although deserving respect as a highly venomous Snake, carries energy that is both healing and destructive. In Africa, Snakes are thought to be either the embodiment of Spirits, to be inhabited by Spirits or to share a relationship with them. It is the belief in Zulu tradition, for example, that on his death a king will return to his people in the form of Mamba. Mamba is a Snake of high moral, strong character and keen eye: fitting traits for a rightful sovereign. A creature who is neither overly gentle nor intentionally aggressive, Mamba is a teacher of balance. She says that in order for us to reach our fullest potential, we must first honour ourselves on all levels at all times. Mamba acknowledges her strengths and weaknesses simultaneously while treating others as it would be treated herself. If she is handled with derision, she rewards her antagonist with the same. Alternatively, if she is shown compassion and gentleness, she remains calm and non-responsive. To productively embrace the wisdom of Mamba is to demonstrate unconditional loyalty to one's innate character. She insists that we 'Walk our Talk' and stand strong in our commitments. She supports us as we remember who we were meant to be as compared to the way family, friends and society expect us to act. Mamba does not advocate that we reject or ignore the occasional need to compromise, but she does suggest we look at how we go about offering it. Mamba says that before we can expect others to treat us with respect, we must shower ourselves with it first. This means saying 'No' occasionally – not to be disagreeable or difficult to get along with, but as a way of saying 'Yes' to ourselves and our higher good. To say 'Yes' when we really mean 'No' is to defeat the purpose of 'choice'. It confuses everyone, while hindering personal growth and our chance to heal.

• Python – *Restriction*

Python overwhelms her prey by constriction, is non-venomous, and lays eggs. Naturally placid and compliant, there are several smaller species of Python that are regularly kept as pets. Although lacking venom ducts, Python does have a powerful and rapid bite. Python relies on fangs to seize prey, after which she loops her body once or twice around the intended victim, tightening her grip until it suffocates. Anaconda takes the prize as the heaviest Snake, while Reticulated Python holds the record as the longest – with some documented at well over 8 metres in length (well and truly large enough to overpower and devour an adult human). The Tamil word for Anaconda is *Anaikolra*, which means 'Elephant killer', while the early Spanish settlers referred to it as *Matatoro* or 'Bull killer'. Python does not *strangle* their prey as such, but instead waits for her victim to breathe in whereupon she tightens her grip so that it has little room to breathe out. As the victim breathes in again, Python follows suit and constricts its coils leaving no room for the victim to breathe at all.

Those leaning toward the wisdom of Python therefore, would do well to consider its implication from two very different perspectives: the stance of Python and the viewpoint of her victim. Oftentimes however, those carrying Python have experienced both, thus integrating her full wisdom into their lives. Python, as the restrictor, threatens to smother those she wants to get close to. Python people must consider their approach therefore, when embarking on new relationships, friendships or ventures requiring familiar interaction with other people for fear of appearing pushy, intense or needy. Python people are often accused of being 'high maintenance' or 'in your face' in terms of their interaction with others and how they expect others to respond to them. Python people often limit the possibility of full and lasting relationships by unconsciously suggesting the notion of hidden agendas, dubious intent and unclear objectives. Those who find themselves suspicious of a Python person's motives should consider first the possibility of misinterpretation. Python people are eager, passionate, excitable and often naïve, while erroneously assuming that others share their fervent dedication. Python people are often misunderstood by people who robotically 'do what needs to be done' or who feel indifferent toward their work, hobbies or achievements. Python people are sometimes guilty of being 'close talking', loud individuals who appear ignorant to the concept of personal space. As the one experiencing Python's powerful grip, one should realise that they are being encouraged to look at what is restricting their potential from a heartfelt point of view. Python people are often slowed down by restrictive people, places or things, limiting beliefs and behaviour. Python people would do well therefore, to look at what they perceive as confining their heart, hampering their ability to breathe or curbing their ability to live a full, healthy, interrelated life. In this instance, Python people must look at their self-worth and see themselves as being equal to everyone else. To live a restricted life is to live only half a life. To always compromise one's life is to deny true happiness and to always settle for second best is to constantly wonder 'What if?' By blaming the things we believe are limiting our potential, we are effectively strengthening their control over us. We are essentially adding fuel to the fire. The moment we see ourselves worthy of more, however, we weaken the power of the grip and essentially release ourselves from such restriction. Victims remain victims for only as long as they are happy to play the part. The moment they decide to breathe life back into their self-worth, they turn the tables on their 'aggressors' and step into the more dominant position, consequently freeing themselves by demanding respect and positive attention.

• Rattlesnake – *The sistrum*

Of the four venomous Snakes indigenous to the United States, none are as infamous as Rattlesnake. Rattlesnake congregates in 'Snake dens' to hibernate during the winter months and returns to the same site year after year. Rattlesnake gives birth to live young; retaining the eggs internally until they hatch and are born. Sometimes a female Rattlesnake is killed before she is able to give birth: in the past this lead to the assumption that Rattlesnake eats her young to protect them from predators. Rattlesnake strikes out at her prey but does not hold on. Instead, the victim is allowed to run a short distance before the venom overpowers it and it dies. Rattlesnake simply follows the animal's scent, finds its corpse and swallows it whole. Rattlesnake is so named after the 'rattle' located at the tip of her tail. The rattle offers an unmistakable warning for predators to retreat, thus offering it a chance to slither away unmolested.

The sistrum was a sacred ancient Egyptian rattle used in the worship of Hathor. It created a sound that was believed to attract the favour of the gods and drive out evil spirits. The rattles were believed to harness the power of the four elements and when used with pure intent, could support the very process of creation. Rattlesnake embraces the sacredness of the sistrum, integrating its potent symbology into her Dreaming. Rattlesnake wards off negativity while driving out dark forces that threaten to influence our view of the world. She protects us by warning us, alarm-style, of possible intrusion or invasion and also warns us of psychic attack, gossip or ill-wishing brought about by another's jealousy or resentment. Rattlesnake creates a sanctuary by invoking calm, clarity and greater awareness. Rattlesnake people are powerfully intuitive, aware enough to read another's intentions long before they are consciously revealed. They are sensitive to change and instinctively know when something is wrong. They are capable of diverting negativity, reshaping its potential and so channelling it into a more positive outcome. Rattlesnake people make profound healers; gifted enough to get to the root of impending illness and to fruitfully redirect it long before it manifests physically. They are directed by Spirit to turn painful experiences into gifts of power. Trauma and illness brought about by grief, anger and confusion can be rebirthed as knowledge and wisdom, under the guiding hand of Rattlesnake Dreaming. People haunted by death, abuse, oppression and ridicule can turn their bad experiences into new beginnings, offering people of similar background the chance to rebirth themselves and start their life over by working with Rattlesnake Dreaming.

Sparrow
Self-reliance

Sparrow, (English Sparrow or House Sparrow), exists wherever people gather. She is a common sight in suburban gardens, shopping centres, picnic grounds and parks. She is more common, however, in major cities where she is supported by a plethora of nesting sites and plentiful food. She is not so common in the country and avoids mountainous areas and woodlands. Male Sparrows have grey heads, charcoal cheeks and dark grey underparts and black throats, chests and brows. The females have predominantly brown plumage, as do the young. Sparrow is gregarious and loud, nesting in crevices in walls and chimneys, ivy covered fences, under eaves and in abandoned buildings and attics.

The embodiment of a deity and once thought to protect households in medieval Europe, Sparrow was the protective totem of the peasants who lived under the oppressive feudal rule of rich and powerful landowners. Sparrow often appears in folktales as being victorious in battle, deposing other animals such as Bears, Wolves, Boars and Eagles – all of which symbolised the nobility of the time and forces considered both fearful and strong. Sparrow affords the willpower to defiantly shun the negative qualities of 'Fehu' so that we might welcome its more positive aspects into our life and realise self-protection and self-reliance. Sparrow guides us to find our Power Place, a place we might visit for contemplation and meditation purposes; a safe place in which we may consider our lot and plan our future; a place of spiritual or magical significance; a place imbued with strong power and an uncanny sense of Spirit. We visit our Power Place to gain a sense of peace, wellbeing and profound clarity. Sparrow offers us a voice and the strength to express it. She empowers us to stand on our own two feet and to see the world as a blank canvas waiting for us to paint it. She offers the tools to lift ourselves out of the mundane world, to realise our potential and to see ourselves worthy of bigger and better things. Sparrow builds inner strength and resolve to seek a home of our own, free of landlords or controlling forces that hinder our movement, and from there to establish a foundation on which to create our own personal empire.

Spider
The weaver

 Spider is an ancient creature and belongs to the arachnid family, which means she is not a true insect. Some Spiders spin silk snares to capture their prey. These webs easily trap walking, jumping and flying prey. The majority of Spider's diet is made up of insects and many of the web-weaving Spiders use silk to wrap, subdue and hold their prey before consumption. Some Spiders however, do not build webs and are known as 'ambush hunters'. This particular type of Spider has quite good eyesight and sits in the open, hidden among foliage, flowers or bark, camouflaged beautifully by her background. Ambush hunter has strong, spiny front legs that allow her to grasp and hold her prey while it is eaten.

According to Native American folklore, it was Grandmother Spider who sang the Universe into being by weaving the Web of Life. Grandmother Spider wove the first dream catcher, a beautiful and protective web woven within a ring of willow wood. In the centre she placed a single turquoise stone, a symbol of connection to the Creative Force, clarity, peace, communication and protection. It is said that with the aid of a dream catcher, our dreams can be harnessed and fruitfully brought to fruition. Spider is the weaver of visions and helps us to remember that we are the creators of our own lives, solely responsible for the directions we choose. Spider reassures us that if we do not like what we choose in life, we can return to the centre and choose again. Just as Spider reweaves her damaged web each morning, we, too, can redirect our chosen life path. As long as the web is strong enough to harness our dreams, we have the power to change direction. We each form a vital strand in the Web of Life. Without our productive input, the Web's integrity is breached, weakened and deemed incomplete, thus causing confusion and stagnation. Spider's web is symbolic of life. We are encouraged by Spider to explore life, to investigate all the strands on offer and to make the most of them. Some strands offer reward and others do not. As we journey the positive strands, all is well and life is good. We are nourished and our path seems abundant. A wrong turn however, leads us along a strand that offers nothing. Life becomes difficult with all attempts to free ourselves initially proving fruitless. The Web of Life is riddled with pitfalls, but it also promises greatness to those prepared to take risks and to work hard. As the weaver of dreams, Spider helps us to explore life and to reweave our web when our path becomes barren. She helps us reclaim our power and to bring our dreams to fruition. She warns however, that in order to open new doors we must first close old ones. Spider reminds us of the sacred role we play as a vital strand in the Web of Life. While the web-weavers draw to us the energies and inspirations to help bring our dreams to reality, the Hunter Spiders encourage us to get up off our backsides and to consciously bring about desired change instead of waiting for something to happen or for someone else to do it for us. We all yearn to take control of our lives and to make a difference to the world. We all yearn to believe in ourselves, to have faith in our ability to heal and realise our true potential. The realisation that Spider can nurture within us the wisdom to make our healing possible opens a pathway to power for those who seek her counsel. Spider encourages us to interact on a more productive and fruitful level with friends and family and to harness that support to initiate powerful change.

• Huntsman Spider – *The huntsman*

 Huntsman Spider, so called because of his speed and the way in which he hunts, is common throughout Australia but, thanks to his habit of climbing aboard ships, he's also found in other warm parts of the world including Florida, Guam, Puerto Rico, Texas, Tennessee and Hawaii (where he is commonly referred to as Cane Spider), Pakistan, India, China, Japan, Indonesia and the Philippines. Huntsman Spider does not build webs. Instead, he wanders about, hunting and foraging for food, preying mainly on insects and other invertebrates, skinks and geckos. And as such, Huntsman Spider encourages us to follow his lead.

Huntsman Spider suggests that instead of sitting at home waiting for opportunities to land on our doorsteps or for our dreams to miraculously come to fruition, we make an effort to go out and seek our own fortunes. Like a knight mounted on his horse, or a traveller carrying his possessions in a polka-dotted kerchief tied to the end of a stick borne across his shoulder, Huntsman Spider dares us to formulate a plan in our mind and to venture out, often on our own, to realise that vision and to make it real. He reminds us that no one is going to rescue us, improve our lives or bring our dreams to reality because it's no one else's responsibility but our own. Unless we are prepared to leave our comfort zone, to take calculated risks and perhaps take a few leaps of faith, then we cannot expect anything to change for the better.

• Redback Spider – *Grandmother Energy*

Nocturnal by nature, Redback Spider is highly venomous and is native to the desert regions of South Australia and Western Australia. Now found throughout Australia, Redback Spider is also found in other regions including Southeast Asia and New Zealand. A member of the Widow Spider family (meaning, she eats her mate during copulation), only the female has the famous red stripe on the top of her abdomen and the distinctive orange mark on her belly. The male, who is black all over, is much smaller than the female (she can measure up to 10 millimetres in length) and typically measures a mere 3–4 millimetres.

As she mainly hunts at night, the black shiny exoskeleton of female Redback Spider reflects her symbolic connection to the Void and all that is known to be unknowable. As such, she reminds us of the power found in dreams, visions and our inherent ability to create and manifest our dreams into reality. Redback Spider proudly advertises her association with the goddess in her Grandmother or Crone phase by displaying her vibrant red marking across her back; the red mark being symbolic of the sacred Blood of Creation and the power generated by the sacred feminine force. Redback Spider allows us to remember and harness the creative force we all energetically hold deep within our base chakra, while showing us how to marry that with the ability to dream of our future and at the same time weaving and cyclically reweaving our life whenever the need arises.

• St Andrew's *Spider – The four directions*

St Andrew's Spider, also known as Wasp Spider and Cross Spider, is so named for his habit of creating a distinct white zig-zagged cross in the centre of his web formation, and for hanging at the heart of his web with legs outstretched in the shape of a cross – reminiscent of the x-shaped cross, or saltire, St Andrew was said to have been crucified upon.

St Andrew's Spider embodies the energies and wisdom of service, growth, development, realisation and higher purpose. With this in mind, he also embodies the energies of the four directions represented by the Cross Circle or Wheel of Life, which offer deep and personal insight into the four fundamental stages of human development, from child through to youth, parent and elder. The Cross Circle also acknowledges the corresponding energies of the four directions, the four seasons and the elements that influence each in turn, and how these energies influence us collectively and individually as human beings.

• Tarantula – *Solution*

Tarantula is a huge, hairy Spider found throughout the world that eats insects, other arachnids, small birds and reptiles. Tarantula is solitary and profoundly territorial. She does not weave snaring webs like other Spiders, but instead produces silk used to line her burrow.

The male Tarantula does not reach sexual maturity until the last few months of his life. He usually lives for 10 years and the female often reaches the ripe old age of 20. She carries her egg sack (woven from silk) attached to her abdomen usually containing up to 1,000 eggs, which can take up to three months to hatch. A hunting Tarantula will overpower her prey and inject it with venom. She will then introduce a powerful digestive enzyme that quickly dissolves the insect's internal organs. Tarantula then sucks the insect dry and discards the empty shell.

Tarantula suggests offering bizarre solutions to problems that would typically cause dismay and melancholy. The Tarantella, or 'The dance of the Spider', is a rhythmic spectacular that dates back to the Middles Ages. It combines lively song with a dance that demands quick steps and ardent gesture. Legend states that during the seventeenth century, an outbreak of 'tarantism' inflicted the women of Taranto, Italy; an illness stimulated by the bite of Tarantula Spider. The victim, or *tarantata*, would fall into a trance that could only be cured by partaking in the turbulent dance. She would be surrounded by musicians playing mandolins, guitars and tambourines. They would play until she fell into rhythm and danced in time with the music, with each note triggering different gestures and movements. Once perfect rhythm was accomplished, the *tarantata* was cured. Tarantula offers 'anti-venom' to counteract situations that would normally see a family or community crumble under the pressure of its own weight. She lifts restriction, thus allowing radical free reign, resulting in the opposite of the issue at hand being realised. In the case of marriage breakdown or separation for example, custody of the offspring can become an emotional tug of war, not only between the disillusioned parents, but sometimes between the parents and the children themselves. For the parent fearful of losing custody of their child to allow unlimited access to the other parent may result in the child choosing them over the other. The more access is denied, the more the child will want to move to the other parent's new home. By offering access, they soon discover the grass is not always greener, thus ensuring sole or reciprocal custody in their favour. By enthusiastically giving someone what they want (in excess), sometimes against better judgment, is to honour the acumen of Tarantula; a creature that offers her wisdom in a seemingly incongruous way.

Springhare
Understanding

In spite of her name, Springhare is a rodent and not a Hare at all. She rarely drinks water, getting her sustenance from rain, dew and the moisture found in the vegetation she feeds on. Nocturnal by nature, Springhare digs burrows with more than one exit, forming tunnels that link to nearby setts. Discarded Springhare warrens are often used and adapted by other burrowing animals. Sanskrit describes the moon as *cacin*, which means 'marked with the Hare', from the opinion that the spots on the moon form the perfect shape of a Hare. A companion to the goddess Oestra, Hare has traditionally held sacred association with the moon, its phases and corresponding energies. Typically feminine in nature, the first quarter of the moon relates to the maiden (or youth) aspect, or the phase that represents new beginnings and the birthing of all new projects and embodies the beginning of life. The full moon represents the mother (or father) aspect; the phase that promises reward and acknowledgment and symbolises us as adults, rich with ideas and 'pregnant' with ambition and promise, when we are soon to bring our dreams and ideas to fruition. The last quarter of the moon introduces the crone (or sage) aspect; the phase that helps us to release, banish and shed outworn modes of thinking, values and beliefs.

Springhare offers potential by combining lunar and seasonal strength to pave a path of efficiency and security. Primed with fertile energy and tenderness, she imparts opportunity with little or no defined instruction or suggested course of action other than the consideration of where you presently find yourself in life. Springhare harnesses the potency of spring, with the promise of new beginnings, new life and fecundity, and helps us understand that life still offers opportunity and reminds us that we are only ever as limited as our fears and beliefs and as old as we feel. As long as you understand and trust your inherent ability to create and learn to rely on the wealth of insight collected over many lifetimes now compiled as your wisdom and find comfort in the knowing that you can always start over should you fail, you will be provided for, supported and nurtured, no matter what you choose to do.

Squid
Monsters

Squid is a part of the diverse family group known as marine molluscs and belongs to the order *Decapodiformes*, which is Greek for '10 legs'. Squid has a distinct head and 10 arms, with two tentacles longer than the other eight. Each arm has a double row of suckers used to catch and hold prey. He is a fast-swimming animal with a torpedo-shaped body equipped with a pair of fins at the tip of his 'tail'. Squid swims by jet-propulsion, sucking water into the mantle cavity near the mouth and spurting it out through a specialised tube by contracting the mantle's muscular wall. His soft body is strengthened by an internal skeletal shaft made of flexible material similar to cartilage. Most Squids eject a cloud of thick black ink when fleeing their pursuers and also have unique skin cells that allow them to change colour and reflect and refract light. Such specialised defence mechanisms allow them to blend into their environment, to communicate with other Squids or to ward off predators. Squid has a sharp horny beak fitted at the mouth, which he uses to kill and tear prey into manageable pieces. Giant Squid is said to reach a mammoth 20 metres in length, making him the largest invertebrate in the world.

Squid helps us embrace the unknown and to explore aspects of life previously considered frightening, dark or beyond our realm of understanding. He proves that there are no such things as monsters and that when we explore life with integrity and truth lighting our way, we have nothing to fear except fear itself. Squid therefore, helps us meet our fears and turn them into strengths. Squid provides for logical thinking. He quietens the heart and instils a sense of calm. He numbs the desire to panic and run, while maintaining a sense of alert caution. Squid people are able to assess their emotional reactions to situations very quickly. They are able to determine, almost immediately, whether a situation is indeed dangerous, or if it is only perceived that way because of nervous apprehension and doubt. Squid people are able to maintain a similar mental clarity in all areas of life; their mental acumen sizing up every situation, thus gauging the likelihood of impending danger or threat. Squid offers warning and provides ample opportunity for rapid retreat. Squid dissipates barriers, breaks through limiting beliefs and removes 'I can't' from our vocabulary. He protects us as we explore new realms. He promises to slay our monster and vanquish our demon, but offers a cloak of invisibility if things become too overwhelming or confronting; a smoke screen that affords the chance to step into the shadows and disappear until we are ready to re-emerge and try again.

Squirrel
Garnering

Squirrels belong to a large family of small or medium-sized rodents that includes Tree Squirrels, Ground Squirrels, Chipmunks, Marmots and Woodchucks, Flying Squirrels and Prairie Dogs. Native to the Americas, Eurasia and Africa, some species of Squirrel have been introduced into Australia. A small colony of Palm Squirrels were introduced into Western Australia and put on display at Perth Zoo (then called the Acclimatisation Committee), after which they were released in 1898. The Department of Agriculture has since proclaimed Palm Squirrel a vertebrate pest, making it illegal to catch and keep her as a pet. The earliest known Squirrels date from the Eocene and are closely related to Mountain Beaver and Dormouse.

• Flying Squirrel – *Faith*

Flying Squirrel is a gregarious rodent competent at gliding from tree to tree by means of a flap of loose skin located between the font and hind legs. Capable of travelling distances of 45 metres and over, she uses her rudder-like tail to navigate each leap. Flying Squirrel is not capable of true flight and is in fact a 'glider'. The only mammal capable of true flight are Bats. As Flying Squirrel takes to the air, she flexes the flap of skin that fuses her forelegs with her rear. As it flexes, she relies on the fact that her weight will be less than the density of the air holding her up, thus allowing her to ride on the balanced pressure long enough to reach the safety of the nearest tree. Flying Squirrel is nocturnal and an endangered species. Baby Flying Squirrels are born hairless and blind.

Faith is the keyword when looking to the wisdom of Flying Squirrel, for she knows that without it, we may never take an educated risk again. Flying Squirrel nurtures the understanding that sometimes decisions must be made without the safety net of guarantee or foresight. Sometimes we must trust that our judgment alone will be prudent enough to ensure the avoidance of obstacles or failure during our resolution making and direction changing moments (especially those which are spontaneous and totally unplanned in nature). Like a performing trapeze artist, Flying Squirrel validates the blind faith needed to release our grip on all that is definite and assured in our bid to nurture change, to sail unaided for a spell before being caught and carried to a vantage point of safety from where we may consider our progress and either 'fly blind' again or sit and contemplate our position. Flying Squirrel represents those moments when we know we must close an old door before opening a new one, but when we are afraid to do so before having some idea of what the 'new door' will look like. Flying Squirrel helps us to 'bridge the gap' by coaching how to 'fly by the seat of our pants' so that we may find the courage to temporarily face the unknown and trust that all will work out fine. Flying Squirrel only asks that we follow a path that is right for us and demonstrate integrity in all that we do.

• Grey Squirrel – *Benefactor*

Grey Squirrel has become one of Britain's most recognised mammal, more so than native Red Squirrel. Most active at dawn and dusk, Grey Squirrel is classified as diurnal and spends a lot of time foraging and feeding on the ground despite being a very agile climber. Grey Squirrel is often seen running up and down tree trunks and running (sometimes upside down) along slender branches. Grey Squirrel builds a nest (known as a *drey*) made of twigs and lined with dry grass, shredded bark, moss and feathers. He does not hibernate and must cache food stores in order to survive winter. He curls up in his drey during the coldest bouts, occasionally venturing out to collect the single nuts and seeds buried randomly during autumn. 'Lost' seeds, acorns and nuts often germinate and grow, helping to regenerate the forests and woodlands that sustain Grey Squirrel. Grey Squirrel gives thanks to the forest by leaving it offerings of nuts and seeds. Although Grey Squirrel relies on those nuts and seeds for his own survival, he leaves them willingly for the forest for he knows that without the forest's support, he would have no reason to survive. Rather than constantly taking, Grey Squirrel always offers something as recompense. The forest offers support because Squirrel is deserving of its support and knows that Squirrel will compensate the forest when he can. Because of the unquestionable faith demonstrated by the forest, Squirrel repays the forest by living a determined, disciplined and respectful life. It is almost as if Squirrel made a pact with the forest, vowing never to prove himself unworthy of the forest's support.

Grey Squirrel heralds a time of reward and the promise of support that will be offered from an unexpected source. Grey Squirrel lives his life in a constant state of preparation. He is always on the go, always on edge frantically worrying that he has not done enough to ready himself for those inevitable times of dormancy and hardship. Grey Squirrel people tend to live their life in a similar way. They scurry through life, with their heads down and tails up. Although they constantly appear busy, they always make time for other people, tending to their needs with apparent ease. They rarely physically ask for help themselves, however, preferring to pray humbly for divine intervention. When Grey Squirrel makes a medicine call, prepare yourself for a shift, a leg up and a chance to enhance your life on all levels. When the time is right (and not a moment before), Grey Squirrel people (and those who invoke his wisdom in a sacred way), are always offered support. They are promised support because they spend their life constantly giving back, ensuring that what they take is repaid with interest. The thought of taking for the sake of taking never enters their head, and because of this they (ultimately) rarely go unrewarded. The full impact of Grey Squirrel may present itself, therefore, in the unexpected form of a benefactor or may materialise in the form of a windfall, gift or inheritance, recovery of lost funds, sudden business increase or the repayment of loaned monies. It may reveal itself as a confirming handshake, forgiving nod or warming smile. When Grey Squirrel reveals the abundance that has lain dormant or hidden from you for so long, remember to give thanks by offering some portion or aspect of it back to someone less fortunate than yourself. In doing so, the cycle will be continued and the process honoured.

• Red Squirrel – *Relay*

 Red Squirrel is a gentle, arboreal rodent and famous for his long ear tufts and graceful, brushy tail that helps him balance, manoeuvre and stay warm as he sleeps. During the summer Red Squirrel's coat is thin and bright, while in the winter it is thick and dark. He inhabits open woodlands, parks and

gardens, especially those equipped with picnic tables or regularly maintained bird-feed tables.

In Scandinavian mythology, *Ratatosk*, whose name means 'drill tooth', was a Squirrel that scurried up and down the trunk of the Tree of Life, passing messages between the Eagle that lived at the top of the tree and the serpent that dwelt deep among its roots. In this context, Squirrel is a messenger: a bridge or 'walker between the worlds' that maintains balance between the positive and negative aspects of Creation. In Buddhist belief, Squirrel's wisdom is invoked to ward off psychic attack because it is thought that his tail acts as a spiritual baton against improper thoughts and spiritual challenges. In Christian faith, the Squirrel represents loyalty and unconditional love because he used his tail to cover his eyes when he spied Adam and Eve eating the forbidden fruit. In some traditions it is considered bad luck to kill or maim a Squirrel and even more ill-omened to walk under a branch on which a Squirrel is sitting. His habit of caching food was once considered a sign of avarice and greed, but it is now celebrated as preparedness and caution. Squirrel is a grounding force that relieves stress and anxiety caused by an unsubstantiated fear that what we are doing to find and honour our Purpose is not enough, or that we are not listening to or hearing clearly enough the messages being sent to us by Spirit, our Ancestors or guides. He reassures us that what we are doing is exactly what we are supposed to be doing and that we are being watched, protected and inspired the whole time. He explains that as long as we keep our intentions pure and make every effort to Walk our Talk, we will be rewarded richly for our dedication and endurance in a way that best serves our Purpose. Squirrel acts as a balancing force between the tangible, practical aspects of life and those governed by spiritual belief, as well as being a guiding force that is quick to point out when we have wandered off the path or strayed into unfavourable territory. Squirrel's only demand is that we surrender our fear and trepidation and do what needs to be done to the very best of our abilities and that we avoid pushing for things not intended for us, intentionally causing trouble or mischievously ruffling feathers. In doing so, we will find peace in the knowing that all things happen when Spirit intends them to and, if nurtured with self-respect and loyalty to our spiritual path, will bring clarity, abundance and wisdom when the time is right.

Starling
Adaptation

 There are more than 100 different species of Starling. Starling is a squat, medium-sized bird that has a distinct triangular shape when in flight. European Starling is omnivorous by nature and is highly adaptive. Preferring to nest in tree hollows, Starling will often invade the nests of other birds, driving away the adult birds and killing their hatchlings. An urban resident, Starling will also nest in buildings, entering through a hole in a wall or eave.

Introduced into Australia during the nineteenth century, common European Starling is now found in large numbers throughout the country. One of the hardest things about moving house is having to start from scratch. Starling knows firsthand the importance of being able to adapt quickly and develop new skills to fit into a new environment. When he finds himself in a foreign land for example, he wastes no time in infiltrating the countryside, establishing his own social infrastructure and forcing other creatures to comply.

Often accused of being ruthless, cruel and threatening toward indigenous bird species, Starling does what he deems necessary to ensure his health and wellbeing. Starling is the totem of migrants, gypsies and travellers, as well as those who move from house to house because of work or personal reasons. He affords the strength of character required to make it in a new kingdom. Starling people adapt quickly to new settings. They are observant, opportunistic and nimble-minded. They waste no time in building a fundamental support-base of people that will inevitably grow to become a complex and secure network of friends, colleagues and associates. Starling people are quick to learn the customs, language and traditional ways of the locals so that their arrival creates the most minimal of ripples and their presence feels comfortable and familiar. As such, Starling helps established community members adapt to the potential disturbance a new member can create. He nurtures acceptance, tolerance and a community spirit that will see everyone be more willing to integrate new concepts, people and traditions into their ways. Starling nurtures the ability for us to productively cope with, adapt to and mutually benefit from any form of change.

Swallows/Martins
Soul connections

Swallow/Martin is a perching bird known for her swift flight, her slender, streamlined body, her long pointed wings, forked tails, short bills and her ability to take prey while on the wing. She is a small migratory bird and breeds in open farmland areas and nests under the eaves of buildings, on the rafters of barns and garages and over the doorways of sheds in areas heavily populated by small insects and in close proximity to Horses and Cattle. Her call is pure and sweet; a gentle, twittering 'tweet-e-weet'.

As the harbinger of new beginnings and love, Swallow was so revered as a symbol of the goddess that it was considered as sacrilegious to kill a Swallow (or to rob her nest) as it was to steal from a church. She was celebrated as a symbol of rebirth, resurrection and new life, because her return was a portent of spring's arrival. To the men of the church, however, Swallow's forked tail was a reminder of the barbed tail of the devil and because of this, she became known to them as the 'Witch's Chick'. Believed to represent a lost soul made of flesh, Swallow was once considered a bird of Heaven sent to Earth as an 'Angelic' comfort. As Swallow darts through the air, swooping here and flitting there, she symbolically stirs up and agitates negativity, stagnation and any trace of heavy energy hiding in the shadows, her anchor-like tail harnessing, grounding and surrendering it to the Universe. Swallow works in much the same way as a spiritual guide. She brings people together who have karmic lessons to address or soul connections that need to be healed, strengthened or realised and guides us to realise our potential and to see ourselves worthy of bigger and better things. In my experience Swallow is espoused as an indicator of change that suggests either a soul-connection has been forged between you and a new friend or associate that will see your life and theirs blossom into full and wondrous magnificence, or that an unresolved soul-related issue that offers emotional growth has returned on a cyclic level that must be honoured and finally put to rest. Follow Swallow. Her wisdom promises new beginnings and the chance to heal and grow, while daring us to believe that our dreams and aspirations will someday come to joyous fruition.

Swan
The ugly duckling

'Swan' is the common name given to waterbirds that belong to the *Anatidae* family (*Cygnus* genus). Swan is closely related to Goose and Duck. Of the six or seven species of Swan, most will mate for life. On occasion, pairs will break up, especially after nesting failure.

Everyone knows the Hans Christian Anderson tale of *The Ugly Duckling;* a child's fable about an abandoned hatchling, raised by a foster family and forced to endure ridicule and rejection, but who ultimately overcame adversity to become a beautiful Swan. The parable demonstrates that until we can look inside ourselves and find the innate beauty that resides there, we cannot expect to notice the beauty that surrounds us every day. When we look in the mirror and see infinite beauty looking back, others will see true beauty, too. However, looking beautiful and radiating beauty from the heart are two very different things. All the beautiful dresses, makeup, expensive jewellery or cosmetic surgery cannot make someone who feels ugly on the inside look beautiful on the outside. Such people may look physically stunning at first glance, but physical beauty is empty unless it is complemented by beauty radiated from within. Mute Swan helps us return to a place of inner beauty by showing us how to reclaim grace and dignity within ourselves.

• Black Swan – *Mystery*

Black Swan resembles White Swan in shape but is almost completely black, save for a splash of white on her wings, a red bill and striking red legs. She is a relatively large breed of waterfowl with a wingspan of almost 2 metres. Black Swans has a long neck with up to 20 vertebrae, enabling her to reach deeper into the water than most other waterfowl in order to feed on aquatic vegetation. Black Swan is the faunal state emblem of Western Australia.

As symbols of the mysterious and magical realm of fantasy, Black Swan's feathers represent the feminine creative force; the nurturing energies of the womb and the Universal Mother. She is a messenger of the eternally dark Void and a gatekeeper to the world of Spirit. Black Swan is a doorkeeper to the other worlds and a messenger of the gods. She is a symbol of the unknown, the rare and the imaginary. Her wisdom reminds us that no matter what life dishes out, we are protected by Spirit and cradled in the arms of Earth Mother. Black Swan instils, too, the knowledge that nothing happens without reason. Individually we each represent a vital strand in the eternal Web of Life, a fact that must be integrated into every aspect of our being in order for us to reach our potential. Black Swan helps us shape our perception of the world in a productive, supportive way while radiating our true essence into the Universe for others to welcome. Black Swan gives us the strength to wait for the mysteries of life to unfold in their own time while helping us to temper impatience, resentment and anger. She instils in our subconscious the knowing that everything will work out for the best, and that all the wrongs that have previously been aimed at us will someday reveal their purpose. Black Swan helps us to realise that with every wish we make, our chance to grow, heal and prosper is enhanced. Black Swan removes the masks of illusion that hide what and who we really are from the world and most importantly, she breaks down self-imposed illusion so that we may finally see ourselves in our true light and realise our richest potential. Black Swan prepares us to realise the golden potential in those around us as we learn to love ourselves unconditionally and to radiate the inner beauty that is yearning to be heard. Black Swan awakens the grace that lies dormant and allows us to access Spirit's gifts of self-empowerment so that we may finally learn to believe in ourselves on all levels. Black Swan transforms our sense of abandonment into Mystery so that others may be drawn to us in awe and wonderment instead of being turned away by fear and confusion. Black Swan nurtures our inner beauty and encourages it to emerge. When this happens, the world applauds and showers us with reward.

• Mute Swan – *Grace*

 Mute Swan is not traditionally a migratory breed, except in areas where the lakes freeze over in winter. A favourite addition to ornamental park lakes and garden ponds the world over, she is considered a pest in some parts because she has bred profusely and competes with native birds for nest sites and food. Mute Swan builds her nest in a mound formation, usually in the middle of a shallow lake and is monogamous in nature. She is less vocal than most other breeds of Swan, hence her name. As Swan mates for life, she is considered sacred to Aphrodite, the Greek goddess of love. For similar reasons, Swan was entrusted with the pulling of Apollo's chariot and may be invoked to ensure safe passage while navigating one's return to a state of grace.

Mute Swan recognises those moments when we feel less than perfect, when the expectations and opinions of others, intended or not, begin to weigh us down. She takes the emotions raised within these experiences, processes them, and enables us to move past them to a place of personal power and grace. Mute Swan acknowledges our innate beauty, in both the physical and spiritual sense, while showing us how to empower ourselves on all levels. Grace cannot be learned. It cannot be bought or given; it can only be found within, to be remembered and embraced. People who have looked deep within themselves, who have healed their past and reclaimed their inner child, know grace. Grace is the ability to walk through life with head held high with humility, pride and a balanced ego and keeps us in touch with those less fortunate than ourselves and those who have not yet reclaimed such sacred knowledge. Mute Swan remembers what it feels like to be the Ugly Duckling but she also remembers the power she felt when she eventually realised she was, and always had been, beautiful. She remembers her beginnings and the uncertainty felt as she timidly and blindly navigated her way through life, struggling to discover who she was. To walk with Mute Swan is to embrace the unknown. Like the Ugly Duckling, Swan was oblivious to what life had in store. She had to trust that her life had a purpose and that she would someday discover it. She had to believe in herself and, although often sorely tempted, she never gave up. Swan harnessed her inner power and made a pact to strive for a better life. Imagine her surprise when she finally met people who did not know her past and who saw her as an equal. Not until she was viewed without the judgment and criticism she had grown accustomed to, did she see her true self for the first time. It was at this moment that Swan returned to a state of grace, a place of beauty untainted by the world around her. Her innate magnificence, her true essence, that she had always been too afraid to claim, finally revealed to the world who and what she truly was: a creature of perfection, love and beauty.

• Trumpeter Swan – *Readiness*

Trumpeter Swan is the rarest and largest breed of Swan in the world and is often mistaken for Tundra or Whistling Swan. By the early 1900s, Trumpeter Swan was classified as endangered due to poaching. Trumpeter Swan mates for life. She builds her nest mound from reeds, rushes, roots and grasses, lining them with her own feathers and down. The main problems facing Trumpeter Swan's future are those associated with human encroachment and habitat destruction. Trumpeter Swan is protected by law. According to the traditional symbolic meaning of the heraldic images regularly observed on ancestral coats of arms, family crests, blazons and armoury, the trumpet signified a constant readiness for war. It was a symbol of the warrior and the protector and suggested willingness for action and a desire to see peace reign across the land, no matter what the cost.

Trumpeter Swan embraces her heraldic roots, instilling watchfulness, gallantry and campaign. Trumpeter Swan does not endorse war, tyranny or fighting for the point of fighting, however. An animal of peace, grace, beauty and harmony, Trumpeter Swan speaks of preparedness, obedience and bravery. She promises a time of peace after periods of darkness, confusion and encumbrance and welcomes a time of calm, while preparing us constantly for further upheaval. To embrace Trumpeter Swan as our truth, however, does not mean that we should expect further disturbance or seek out battles or quarrel, but rather to prepare ourselves 'just in case'. We can never be taken by surprise, caught offguard or called upon unannounced when we are protected by the watchful wisdom of Trumpeter Swan. Trumpeter Swan, like a good and loyal Watchdog, will trumpet a warning the moment our borders are breached or our territories invaded. Trumpeter Swan people are punctual, precise and ready to do business at the shortest of notice. They are also bringers of good news; heraldic emissaries of certain peace.

• Tundra Swan – *Whistling*

 Tundra Swan, or Whistling Swan as she was once known, is completely white, save for her black, webbed feet, black bill and a yellow patch just under the eye. When she spends time feeding in iron-rich waters however, her feathers tend to take on a reddish tone. The call of Tundra Swan is high-pitched and quavering, resembling the sound of a pack of yelping Fox Hounds. Tundra Swans are a common species and their numbers are continually increasing.

Tundra Swan instigates the flow of positive energy through our body. She aids in the healthy circulation of life force by supporting our breathing, keeping it vigorous and strong and, in doing so, keeps us vigorous and strong. She also invites the positive flow of energy in other arenas of life such as the home and work place. She removes stagnation, resentment and blockage. A good medicine to call upon when feeling depressed, disappointed or blocked by the actions or views of loved ones or those we look up to, Tundra Swan helps us see the positive in all setbacks, obstacles or disappointing situations. She instils the belief that 'all things happen for a reason'. She also instils a sense of composure, confidence and inner beauty. Tundra Swan warns against harbouring resentment, keeping secret agendas or seeking revenge for the assumed wrongs inflicted against us. Tundra Swan asks that if we are going to whistle, to make sure we whistle to advertise the joy in our hearts or to pass the time, rather than whistling to disguise ulterior motives or clandestine intentions. When we set about eliciting negative influence, Tundra Swan will point the finger and see us come under scrutiny and, eventually, found guilty as charged. Tundra Swan invites positive energy into our life, in the form of hope, potential and peace. Just as effectively however, she is said to banish that which is destructive or negative and checks the motives for inviting certain energies into our life, filtering out those that threaten to be potentially harmful or disturbing. Tundra Swan is an animal blessed by the gods for her clear and pure song, a sound said to rouse and maintain positive energy and inspire a sense of calm, peace and balance within those who hear it.

Tapir
Suspicion

Tapir follows well-worn paths as she forages for food. Hunters use the very same paths to track her. Tapir enjoys wallowing in shallow bodies of water and in mud pools during the heat of the day and is thought that this also helps control the presence of parasitic insects. Living a largely solitary existence, Tapir will congregate in small groups during the mating season. Males urinate in regular spots as a way of scent-marking territory. Tapir will dive into available water or undergrowth to avoid danger and is able to run and swim at a steady pace. Tapir's most obvious feature is her muzzle, which is trunk-like; adaptable, prehensile and covered with sensory whiskers.

With her prominent and sensitive nose, Tapir asks that we pay heed to what our other senses may be trying to tell us, instead of relying solely on what we choose to see, trust and believe to be true. Tapir invites us to harness our other senses and to employ them when we can't put our finger on, or rationally offer explanation for, a nagging doubt that haunts the back of our mind. Tapir teaches us to listen to our feelings, instead of running from them. She provides the inner strength to trust what our senses are telling us, and to act on them by asking appropriate and meaningful questions. When we have an unsettling or surprising feeling about a particular person, place or thing, we are usually closer to the truth than we would like to admit. From the Greek *Pheran*: 'to transfer' and *Horman*: 'to excite', pheromones are a naturally occurring chemical compound which, when secreted, influence our behaviour and response to other people. Pheromones reveal our disposition, rank, desire and wellbeing, 'secrets' which are fed subconsciously as 'feelings' to the subtle awareness of other parties. We trust other people when we feel comfortable with their smell, and when their smell resonates well with ours. A change in our wellbeing, disposition, rank or level of desire will automatically affect our smell, which will, in turn, affect how others treat us. Tapir encourages us to 'listen' to these subtle messages, and to act upon all feelings of suspicion by asking appropriate and meaningful questions. To ignore them could result in you losing someone or something to mental or physical illness, infidelity, work, or some other reason. To listen, on the other hand, will see you 'sniff out' the source of hindrance before it has time to establish itself.

Tarsier

Mischievousness

 Tarsier is a small primate with long limbs that spends the majority of his time in the forest canopy. The name 'Tarsier' comes from the fact that the animal's tibia and fibula bones are fused in the lower portions, which cushion impact as Tarsier leaps from tree to tree spanning huge distances, often up 3 metres. Tarsier has pad-like suction cups on the end of each finger and toe enabling him to easily negotiate vertical surfaces, including window panes. When on the ground, he hops erect with his forelimbs tucked against his chest. Coupled with his ability to pull expressive faces, Tarsier resembles what one would expect a cheeky goblin or mischievous pixie to look like. Tarsier relies on his long tail for balance, using it as a third leg when standing erect. His eyes are huge with bony eye sockets easily exceeding the capacity of his brain case and stomach (making him an animal guilty of having 'eyes bigger than his stomach'!). Sharing the famous trait of Owl, Tarsier has a joint between the skull base and spine that allows him to turn his head in an arc of 180 degrees. Ironically, as Tarsier is nocturnal, he often falls prey to Owl.

Asian folklore often depicts Tarsier as a cheeky trickster spirit that loves to play practical jokes and perform impish pranks. Tarsier therefore involves the performance of pranks, preferably those of good nature. Tarsier people delight in making people they do not respect look like fools. Usually people of dry wit and convincing character, they relish in seizing any opportunity to cause confusion and chaos in their workplace and home. Those who carry Tarsier find it incredibly amusing for example, love sending jokes by cell phone or email and should never be entrusted with the purchasing of lunch or the making of coffee. At home they get into all sorts of mischief by breaking or spilling objects to avoid washing or stacking dishes, causing chores to take twice as long and destroying or stealing items from neighbours' backyards. Although not normally malicious by nature, Tarsier people often frighten or confound others with their jokes, so much so that their sense of humour sometimes borders on the kind of drollness that just isn't funny. If you are a fun-loving individual who enjoys performing pranks, you are most likely a Tarsier person. The key issue, though, is to ensure your sense of humour does not hurt or insult those around you or impinge on the privacy of others, for if it does and it happens enough, your desire to make others look foolish could very well backfire on you, landing you with egg on your face.

Tasmanian Devil
Purification

Tasmanian Devil will kill and eat small prey animals, but prefers to feed on carrion (usually in the form of road kill). Tasmanian Devil is Australia's only *true* carnivorous mammal (the Dingo was introduced by the Aboriginal People from Asia some 40,000 years ago). A stocky little marsupial with a backward-facing pouch, Tasmanian Devil was once common throughout mainland Australia, but is now isolated to the island state of Tasmania. Earning his somewhat dubious name by way of his black fur and blood-curdling call, Tasmanian Devil is a loner who will occasionally gather in small huddles to feed on a large carcass. Such meetings usually result in squabbles and fights, with many adult animals carrying deep scars from years of confrontation. Although there are still occasions where individual Tasmanian Devils are sighted or found as road kill on the mainland, these cases are extremely rare. A humble but cantankerous recluse, Tasmanian Devil is a shy, unobtrusive creature that prefers to feed on carrion and road kill and as a carrion feeder is seen as the cleaner, the one whose responsibility it is to ensure that the deceased are returned to the Earth Mother as quickly and efficiently as possible, minimising the risk of putrefaction and contamination to her lands and waterways.

In a similar manner, Tasmanian Devil teaches us to purify our lives, to honour our bodies and to exorcise all that is corrupted from our systems. Eating all that is wholesome, drinking all that is pure and honouring our bodies by regularly exercising and getting adequate rest, are the lessons offered by the wisdom of Tasmanian Devil. Tasmanian Devil's Latin name, *Sarcophilus* (derived from *sarcophagus*), means 'flesh lover', suggesting potent Underworld correspondences and an obvious link to the dead and dying. Meat is what nourishes Tasmanian Devil and he instinctively knows that it is the only fare that will supply him with the strength and endurance needed to fulfil his duties to the Earth Mother. Tasmanian Devil demonstrates the importance of nourishing our body with what it needs. Everyone's body is different and needs different things. Find the foods that nurture your body and spirit and stick to them. You will find your body working with you rather than against you, as you purify it of things that impede its natural cycles. Tasmanian Devil is famous for his powerful jaws and ferocious bite and must often completely bite through his catch in order to release his own death grip. Tasmanian Devil teaches us to honour ourselves and purify our life on a communicative level, offering the vice-like power of his jaws to teach us how to speak with vice-like force or, when appropriate, with gentle humility. Tasmanian Devil validates the need to cut through pretence and to get directly to the heart of things when required, thus purifying our relationships of dishonesty and misunderstanding. Tasmanian Devil supports us as we cull the 'dead' relationships from our life and the other aspects that no longer serve us. Tasmanian Devil invites us to gently set ourselves free from aspects that, because of their emotional connotations, hang like weights around our neck. Alternatively, you may choose to detach yourself from detrimental relationships that are largely one-sided or selfish in nature, or simply cleanse pessimistic opinions and feelings from your persona.

Tenrec
Distinction

Despite the fact that Tenrec gives birth to up to 25 young at once, generally only as few as 16 survive. The mother feeds her offspring from 12 pairs of nipples; the most recorded on any mammal. Solitary by nature, nocturnal Tenrec hibernates during the dry season and when threatened, raises the ridge of spine-like hairs along her back and bares her teeth.

An irritable and nervy creature, Tenrec keeps herself isolated from the people. She represents those of us who have difficulty trusting others and at times, ourselves. Resentment, frustration and fear are often the triggers that inspire Tenrec people to react to new ideas, people and environments in an apparently unenthusiastic manner. Tenrec people tend to roll their eyes, curl their lip or grunt disapprovingly when presented with alternatives to the way they would see things done. Those drawn to explore Tenrec are often unhappy or discontented with their lot and usually feel alone or forsaken by God, but have difficulty admitting it. Although they are not afraid to physically hide their unrest, they respond defensively when suggestions are made because they don't know how to internally change their beliefs. An animal recognised as the only mammal to have 12 pairs of nipples, Tenrec is an animal that knows great acumen and fecundity. She holds this sacred abundance deep within her essence, but exists in a space that chooses to ignore it as wealth. Those carrying Tenrec would do well to spend some time in quiet contemplation, introspectively acknowledging the abilities, interests and qualities that separate them from the rest of the people in a unique, positive way, instead of feeling isolated as a result of negative or limiting beliefs. Tenrec guides us to a place of illumination and realisation. We are each exceptional beings, matchless in personal and sacred ways. We each hold magical keys that afford us recognition of our purpose and Personal Power, sacred and individual gifts given to us by Spirit before our birth. We can all live abundant and whole lives when we discover and embrace our purpose; our bequest to the people. Instead of wasting energy feeling resentful or being driven by fear, look to what it is that annoys you about other people or the suggestions they make, and ask if you are guilty of doing the same. Look at the annoyance and see why and how it limits your view of the world. Ask why it bothers you so. Look to where this annoyance first appeared in your life, address it and release it.

Turn the resentment into awareness and move on, knowing that you have grown instead of allowing yourself to remain stagnant and angry. Do this with every belief or memory that holds you back until you are able to see that which was considered baggage has now become medicine, wisdom to be shared among the people, acumen that may nourish the soul and inspire positive change in others. This is the sacred and distinctive wisdom of Tenrec.

Tern

Outburst

Tern is a gregarious, noisy seabird that is closely related to Gull and enjoys a worldwide distribution. Most Terns hunt fish by hovering and diving, while some take insects off the surface of fresh water. She rarely swims, despite her webbed feet. Tern often gathers in mixed flocks including Gulls, on lakes, inland pools and beaches.

Merrows are the mythical Merpeople of Ireland. They are easily distinguished from other members of the sea-dwelling Faerie realm in that, like Tern, they are adorned with a feathery cap. The cap is said to aid in their propulsion through the nadir of the deepest oceans. Should they lose their cap, they are prevented from returning to the ocean, finding themselves instead, marooned in the shallows forever. The shy and gentle female Merrows are said to be visually striking and, like other mermaids, feel compelled to warn fishermen and sailors of approaching storms. Male Merrows are quite ugly, with green teeth, green hair and red noses. Both sexes are extremely cheerful. Tern, like the appearance of a female Merrow, heralds approaching trouble, emotional strife, 'storms', upheaval or angry outbursts. Being warned of impending turbulence however, is no reason to play down or avoid encounters with people with whom we have unresolved 'issues'. In fact, Tern endorses the complete opposite. She suggests that all communication should be encouraged and allowed to flow smoothly, with interaction kept cheerful and enchanting. That way, forecasted 'storms' will disperse and give way to blue skies and celebration. Tern warns against compromising morals or of making excuses in order to maintain forced peace and harmony. She encourages correct behaviour, respectful dealings and mutually beneficial negotiations. To keep the flow of communication lighthearted will ensure that your environment remains welcoming, open-minded and emotionally balanced. Lose your cap, though, and you may lose more than you bargained for.

Thrush
Love

There are over 300 species of Thrush, of which European Blackbird is one. She is a common garden songbird native to pretty much every continent, except Australia (although we do have several introduced species). In fact, Thrush is affectionately referred to as 'the friend of the gardener' in Britain. Thrush is an omnivorous ground forager that feeds upon worms, insects and fruit in the early morning or early evening. She is monogamous, with many species keeping the same mate throughout the year. The Thrush is the totem of 'word weavers': writers, poets, singers and songwriters (Homer was apparently gifted a caged Thrush after reciting a beautiful poem). In medieval Europe, a 'bard' was a professional poet and singer employed to compose tributes to the feudal lord, charming him and winning favours from the common folk with his flowery words.

Thrush helps us remember the ancient language of love, trust and empathy. She opens our heart to possibilities of love and romantic potentials that lay in wait for us, chiefly those hindered by fear, anxiety and doubt. Thrush coaches us as we shun limitation and hesitation, to speak from the heart and to shoot Cupid's arrow or the arrow of truth (whichever is needed at the time) with dexterity and precision. She promises a content, charmed, happy and abundant life for those who embrace her wisdom. Legend has it that Thrush prefers to build her nest among the branches of the Myrtle tree, to weave her nest from its twigs and to line her nest with its leaves. Traditionally, the Myrtle inspires long-term love and good luck, particularly for those who have one or more growing in their garden. Its wood is sacred to the goddess Venus and, when carried as an amulet, is said to attract romantic fascination and unconditional love. Thrush is the emissary of devotion, fertility, peace, abundance and eternal youth. Her wisdom has long been considered the harbinger of love.

Thylacine or 'Tasmanian Tiger'
Wisdom

Thylacine, Tasmanian Tiger or Tasmanian Wolf is an elusive creature that once roamed the forests of Tasmania. Now thought extinct, the last-known surviving Thylacine died in captivity in 1936 at the Hobart Zoo. Dog-like in appearance and classified as the largest of all carnivorous marsupials, Thylacine has a long whip-like tail and thick stripes on her back. As most of Tasmania is still unexplored, it is believed that Thylacine may still exist; living in exile, deep within the Tasmanian forest. Thylacine's elusive nature and ability to camouflage her appearance may have allowed her to flourish unnoticed, but until the day comes when the animal's existence is verified, Thylacine will remain a creature of deep mystery and speculation. If the myths are true and Thylacine still stalks the forests of Tasmania, her wisdom has kept her unseen for almost 70 years.

Thylacine encourages us to withdraw and walk alone, perhaps spending time journeying the inner landscape. Thylacine invokes a time of calm and time spent alone when we should rely on our own judgment rather than seeking the counsel of others. Thylacine raises the questions, 'What is my purpose?' and 'Why am I here?' Thylacine people find themselves craving the sacred knowledge of their elders, their Ancestral Spirits and the Earth Mother. When we begin to work with Thylacine, we quickly evolve to a point where we no longer worry about mundane issues anymore. Money for example, always materialises when we stop stressing about not having enough. When we begin working with Thylacine, the desire to seek answers is no longer birthed from idle curiosity. We find our desire to know has deepened to a far more sacred level and we yearn to understand the wisdom of Creation and the mysterious ways of Spirit. Our quest for answers becomes meaningful, rewarding and ruled by our interrelation with the world around us. Thylacine helps us identify what is important so that we might regain direction in our life. She helps us recoup control over our life and how we live it, instead of being controlled and manipulated by the trivial aspects of existence. Thylacine helps us to form judgments from which we may assess our emotions and the lessons we have experienced. As we become familiar with Thylacine, mundane realities begin to hold less appeal for us. We find ourselves seeking time alone, in solitude, as far away as possible from the anxious bustle of the tangible world. In time, we may look to Thylacine as a teacher in the hope that she may offer advice and a better sense of direction as we quest for personal truth. Thylacine supports us as we begin to question our beliefs, by encouraging us to listen with intent to our inner wisdom, the mutual connection we share with others as well as our personal feelings and emotions regarding life in general. Thylacine pioneers spiritual paths for us to follow. Thylacine is the one who walks alone seeking a broader awareness of Spirit and the Universe. She weighs up the worthiness of what she experiences before revealing it as knowledge, thus impeccably enhancing the sacred truths we already carry close to our hearts.

Tiger
Cowardice

A novelty among Cats is Tiger's love of water. Tiger enjoys bathing in ponds, lakes and rivers – a pastime adopted to help combat the oppressive midday heat of the jungle. Tiger's stripes afford her perfect camouflage in the tall grass and abundant brushwood where she stalks her prey. The use of Tiger parts in traditional medicine can be traced back to more than 1,000 years ago in Chinese culture. The practice has, in a word, *sanctioned* illegal poaching in an attempt to fill demand, pushing the three remaining species of Tiger close to extinction. Of the eight sub-species of Tiger, two stand out as the most famous: Bengal and Sumatran. Unfortunately, due to rustling and habitat destruction, there are only about 5,000 Bengal Tigers and between 300 and 500 Sumatran Tigers in the wild today. Indochinese Tiger is limited to only 2,000 wild individuals, South Chinese (or *Amoy*) Tiger to about 100, while the Siberian population is barely worth mentioning with approximately 450 animals left in the wild today. Sadly, Javan, Balinese and Caspian Tigers have all been lost to extinction over the past 50 years.

Tiger is revered throughout Asia as symbols of potency and authority. She was once employed as an executioner by the imperial courts possibly due to the Hindu principle that the god Shiva travels upon a Tiger while draped in a Tiger's skin symbolising his role as destroyer. Followers of the Buddhist religion believe Tiger to be endowed with a mystical power to defeat evil, while the ancient forest-dwellers of India once built ornate temples and sacred shrines in honour of the animal because they believed her to be deity made of flesh. Even to this day, there are stories that tell of mysterious, supernatural creatures that, although Tiger in form, are able to mimic human behaviour to such a degree that they even live in villages. Despite these legends and stories, however, the animal remains labelled as a potential killer of men by the people. Tiger is an animal that, though imbued with immense physical power and great beauty, is a clumsy hunter. When tracking, Tiger takes great care in her approach, but rumour has it that about 80% of all her strikes go unrewarded. This caution can be perhaps misconstrued as 'lack of confidence' or fear. Tiger's apprehension forces her to lie still, anticipating her quarry's every move before pouncing and overpowering the poor unfortunate animal and breaking its neck. Thus, in spite of the seemingly unfortunate keynote that encapsulates her Dreaming, Tiger proves she is no coward. An animal that knows exactly what she wants; she simply displays awkwardness when it comes to acknowledgement and confrontation, with those who embrace her wisdom usually recognising this trait as one of their own. Those drawn to Tiger's wisdom are told to face their issues front on, instead of looking for the easy way out. They are encouraged to look that which they fear the most dead in the eye and defiantly take it on. Instead of 'beating around the bush', or ignoring our problems in the vain hope that they will go away, Tiger reminds us of our inherent beauty, Personal Power and inner strength. She teaches us to harness our potential as truth, and to see ourselves worthy of greatness. Reject the shadow aspect of Tiger, which labels you a coward. Instead, be like Tiger who favours Peacock as her ideal prey and seek to integrate the path of the impeccable warrior into your way of life by vowing to always Walk your Talk and face your demons head on.

- White Tiger – *Submissiveness*

Until 1951, the legend of a sinister forest phantom troubled the jungle villages of India. It spoke of a supernatural Tiger that, instead of being the traditional golden colour, was completely white. The story invoked such interest that the animal was stalked and eventually captured and presented to the world. Instead of displaying the familiar characteristics of an albino (pink eyes and white skin), White Tiger proved to be a genetic mutant exhibiting a recessive gene that barred the animal's trademark golden colour from forming. Only 100 or so White Tigers have naturally appeared in the forests of India since the discovery of the original animal. Consecutive breeding of White Tiger in captivity shows direct lineage to the (male) 'forest phantom' captured in 1951. Despite her fabulous physical strength, the mysterious history and elusive nature of White Tiger has earned her great esteem.

White Tiger has become a revered font of submissive, protective, feminine power in Asian culture. According to the ancient art of Feng Shui, for example, White Tiger typifies the contemplative and introspective energies of the West on the Wheel of Life, as well as the reflective and romantic qualities of autumn. During autumn we begin to slow down and prepare for a time of rest. The leaves turn golden in colour, and eventually fall off the tree leaving it unprotected and exposed to the harshness of winter. In some parts of the world, winter means snow when the soil goes dormant and the animals sleep. The appearance of White Tiger proclaims a personal although brief time of winter-like dormancy. She prepares us for a time of quiet by stripping us of any desire to stand out or speak up. Those who find themselves drawn to the wisdom of White Tiger may be wondering why they feel the need to comply, compromise or bow down to expectation, particularly when these traits are typically out of character for them. The docile, dutiful energies of White Tiger are temporary however, and will eventually fade when the need for respite, a time of selflessness or contemplation passes, delivering the individual back into the clutches of her inherently powerful nature.

Toad
Hidden beauty

Toad is an amphibious creature that starts life in water as a Tadpole, but spends the majority of his adult life on land. Nocturnal by nature, Toad spends the daylight hours hiding in a cool, damp spot and lays eggs in the water. Toad has poison glands located behind his eyes and is famous for his 'warty' skin. Toad Tadpole breathes through gills but as he grows, his tail diminishes in size and he develops lungs for life on land. Toad has been associated with both positive and negative forms of mysticism since the beginning of time. To the Chinese for example, Toad is an emissary of good fortune and long life, while in Mexico he is a symbol of illumination and enlightenment. Typically viewed as a symbol of darkness and deceit, muddy pools and quagmires, however, Toad has long been considered a favourite witch's familiar and a fabled ingredient in charm work. In Celtic legend, Toad understands his lack of appeal caused by his ugliness and the horror felt by those who stumble across him by chance. He attempts to soften his reputation, though, by – according to legend - carrying a precious stone in his forehead that's said to hold the power to reverse the effect of any poison and the ill-effects of criticism, judgement and ridicule.

Despite his external ugliness, on a spiritual level Toad holds within himself the antidote to his own toxin and a release from his self-loathing. With his superficial stare and hollow eyes, Toad calls to us to look beyond the physical body and all perceived limitations so that we may unearth our true inner-beauty and self-worth. When we see ourselves as ugly, worthless or stupid, we emanate an equally toxic aura or personality. People fail to see us for what we are inside, instead they base their decisions on what they superficially see and feel. Toad suggests that we reach deep down inside ourselves in order to find and retrieve our hidden potential, because once discovered and nurtured, dormant beauty can transform our life and ultimately set us free. To embrace Toad in a productive way, therefore, may see us retrieve our 'sacred stone' and shed our 'warty' exterior to reveal true beauty that honours our emotions and creates a foundation for a happy, fertile new beginning.

Toucan
Bad luck

 Toucan is a sociable bird that raucously follows others from tree to tree. Toucan spends much of his time high in the canopy, only venturing to the forest floor to forage for food. Toucan is gregarious and fun-loving and has been spied throwing fruit to other Toucans. His long, curved bill provides opportunity to reach precarious or low-hanging fruits and nuts. Toucan uses the sharp edge of his bill to cut the fruit loose, hold it and toss it into the air to be caught again and swallowed. Sometimes mated pairs will defend a fruit tree from other Toucans by offering threat displays and bill jousts. When Toucan eats fruit, the seeds pass through his digestive tracts or regurgitated if they are too large, thus assisting in the even dispersal of seed and, in time, tree species throughout the forest.

Toucan offers hope to anyone who feels they have little or no control over the things that happen in their life and offers a beacon of faith to those who view themselves forsaken by God or cursed in some way. In some regions, Toucan is referred to as *Dios te de*, which means 'God gives to you'. It is said that the call of Toucan resembles someone chanting the decree over and over. Toucan is supposedly employed by some South American medicine men as a vehicle to the Spirit World, with another tribe sponsoring a superstition that curses the newborn child of any father who eats or touches his flesh. When someone believes in curses, they give credence to the manmade notion of 'good' and 'evil' while falling into the trap of assuming that 'bad luck' happens to them. When someone superstitiously believes that something 'bad' will happen (as a result of doing a certain thing), the subconscious mind brings it to fruition. We unconsciously look for an opportunity to make it real. We believe it will happen, and so it does. Therefore, technically we can only really blame ourselves for the misfortune in our lives and not necessarily 'forces' outside our control. Toucan nurtures the understanding that when we blame God, the area in which we live, our financial situation, a disability, illness or addiction, the government, our parents, or anything else for that matter, for the hardships that life imposes upon us, we give our power away. We essentially curse ourselves and give 'bad luck' the green light to run rampant. The only way to remove a 'curse' is to take full responsibility for our own fate and do what needs to be done to turn bad 'luck' into good fortune. By admitting that we have contributed to the occurrence of our own misfortune is to reclaim our power and shun denial. Toucan encourages us to retrace our steps, isolate the events considered significant low points and to analyse the role we wilfully played in them being realised. In doing so, we quickly discover no option but to reject 'bad luck' as a contributing factor, with poor judgment, gullibility, arrogance, assumption and ignorance offering realistic foundation for a so-called 'cursed' life. Toucan espouses that when we are prepared to go out on a limb in order to embrace self-nourishment, we are more likely to achieve than when we sit motionless, choosing to blame fate for our inability to achieve, grow, heal or prosper.

Tuatara
Evidence

 Tuatara is a Lizard-like reptile, but is not a Lizard. She is the last living remnant of the ancient *Sphenodontia*, a group of reptiles that died out some 60 million years ago. The word *tuatara* is Maori for 'peaks on the back'. Tuatara has a hidden gland on her forehead containing a rudimentary 'third eye' which absorbs essential vitamin D from the sun's ultraviolet rays during her initial months of life. She lacks visible ear openings, but is able to regrow her tail should she lose it when distracting predators. Tuatara reaches sexual maturity at approximately 20 years of age and mates every two to five years thereafter. Tuatara is only found in New Zealand and although is commonly kept as a pet, is endangered as a wild species. Ancient Tuatara exists as proof of her kind, the last in a line of sacred creatures. She reignites the Light of Spirit, past-life memory and ancestral knowledge in the hearts of those who embrace her wisdom.

Tuatara shifts our attention from the mundane aspects of life, where physical pleasure and material gain rule, to a realm of heightened awareness and elevated understanding. She teaches us to trust the validity of our previously dormant 'third eye' chakra and to once again see with the clarity and integrity that Spirit intended us to. Tuatara does not dwell in the past or look expectantly to the future. She exists solely in the present, while offering us the clarity and understanding to perceive all there is, all there ever was and all there ever will be at the same time. She opens a portal to a higher level of consciousness once delegated to only the wisest of men and women, affording unmistakable evidence of the existence of Spirit. The third eye sits at the forehead, just slightly above and between the eyes. Ruled by the pituitary gland and the subcortical areas of the brain, which are responsible for our ability to reason, will and think, the 'third eye' nurtures our inherent clairvoyant abilities – our ability to intuitively 'see', astral travel and understand concepts not bound by ordinary reality. The crown chakra sits at the top of the head and is ruled by the pineal gland and the cerebral cortex. The pineal gland lies directly behind the eyes at the centre of the brain. According to esoteric belief, the pineal gland supports our spiritual connection to the higher realms. When we meditate, the crown chakra (Sanskrit for 'wheel' or 'disk') is said to energetically reach out for support from the pineal gland. The two unite, working as one, allowing us to perceive higher dimensions with profound understanding. When the crown and third eye chakras work in harmony, however, illumination is said to take place with blinding clarity, to the point where the Light of Spirit is said to enter the head and instantly reawaken our latent ability to perceive the non-ordinary realms, our inner self and the subconscious self simultaneously. I believe this to be the wisdom of Tuatara.

Turkey
Shared blessings

 Synonymous with Thanksgiving, Turkey has become the emissary of autumn and the harvest. Once abundant throughout North America, European settlement during the 1800s saw him removed from the landscape. Moves by conservationists saw the bird reintroduced into his natural environment and has resulted in numbers rising to very healthy levels. Male Turkeys are often known as Toms, or Gobblers, and can be distinguished from the females by iridescent feathers and a beard. The females are generally an earthy brown, which camouflages them as they sit on their nests. The Aztecs so revered Turkey they cast solid-gold ornaments of the bird to use as offerings to the gods.

Although capable of flight, Turkey is a bird of the Earth. Also known as the Ground Eagle, Turkey is an emblem of the spiritual wisdom radiated by the Earth Mother and the shared blessings she offers. Her blessings come in the form of her gifts: plentiful crops, healing herbs, minerals, timber, water and animals. Turkey encourages us to use these blessings well and to give thanks by acknowledging and giving back to the Earth Mother. With an abundance of beautiful feathers and rich meat, Turkey honours the 'giveaway' and gives of himself to exchange life for death. He sacrifices himself to feed others, honour their lives and strengthen their bond with Spirit and the Earth Mother. To give something away because you know it will make someone smile or feel good is the way of Turkey. A friendly smile can mean a lot to someone who feels alone. Always remember that the more you give of yourself, the more the world will want to share with you. This is the wisdom of Turkey.

Turtle
Earth Mother

Freshwater Turtle is an aquatic reptile that relies on water to aid in the swallowing of food and mating. She has webbed feet and sharp claws, which she uses to pull herself onto rocks and half-submerged logs. Freshwater Turtle deprived of water will eventually dehydrate and starve to death. Marine Turtle has flippers; paddle-like appendages that affords her efficient underwater locomotion, but make movement on land clumsy and slow. Marine Turtle sustains a solely aquatic lifestyle, only coming ashore to lay eggs. She has been swimming the Earth's oceans for more than 150 million years and has barely changed since the reign of the Dinosaur. Six of the world's seven species of Marine Turtle occur within Australia's Great Barrier Reef.

Most of us have found ourselves wandering aimlessly through life at some time or other, unsure of what course of action we should take or the best decision we should make. Despite those who love and respect us, we find ourselves feeling alone and isolated from everyone and everything. We forget our connection to Spirit and the relationship we have with the Earth Mother and Creation and feel apart from rather than a part of Nature. Due to the fact that she has walked the Earth since time was new, Turtle has become a symbol of the Great Mother and of the Earth herself. Turtle has a protective shell that safeguards her vulnerabilities, just as the Earth Mother has a defensive sheath that shields it from the inhospitable forces of space. Turtle instils within us the awareness of the unconditional love and nurturing the Earth Mother provides and reminds us that we are never alone and that no matter where we go, we are constantly cradled in the protective arms of the Earth Mother. Turtle promises that if we learn to ground ourselves in her nurturing energy and continue to move through life at a steady pace, we will be assured completion of all set tasks. Based on her ability to retreat into the safety and darkness of her protective shell, and to emerge when any threat has passed, symbolic links have been forged between Turtle and the Sweat Lodge. Despite the figurative rebirth experienced by Turtle each time her head materialises, Turtle's form strongly resembles the customary dome-like structure of the Sweat Lodge and the path that leads from the Lodge to the sacred fire is often referred to as the 'Neck of the Turtle', with the fire pit itself representing Turtle's head. Sweat Lodge is a tangible way for us to return to Spirit and to reconcile our relationship with Creation so that we may reconnect to the place we have and the role we play within it. It is a cleansing ceremony for all aspects of being on the physical, mental, emotional and the spiritual levels. As we exit the Lodge, we fall exhausted upon the Earth like newborn babies crying with joy, limp, wet and covered with mud, the blood of our Earth Mother. We are reborn and so deeply humbled by the magnitude of the experience that life is never the same again. Turtle reminds us of the wisdom offered to those who have a deep love and respect for the Earth Mother; those who walk gently on the Earth, who honour all things of Nature as equals and who understand that to degrade the Earth in any way is to defile the name and honour of one's own mother. *Mi taku oyasin* is a phrase used in ceremony that means, 'we are all related' and is embodied by the wisdom of Turtle. It reminds us that we are all part of the whole as children of the Earth Mother.

Vulture

Benevolence

Vulture is usually found in areas that support large populations of grazing animals, such as Wildebeest, Zebra and Gazelle. All Vultures are scavengers, meaning she 'preys' on leftover scraps of kill. Vulture was once thought to be a raptor, but DNA testing has revealed that Vulture is in fact a member of the Stork family. The more common species of Vulture found in Africa are suited to feeding primarily on soft tissue (muscles and intestines, etc) because their bills are not strong enough to rip open large carcasses unaided. Instead, she waits until half-eaten remains of a kill are abandoned before moving in to have her fill. Without scavengers like Vulture to 'clean up' after the predators, the African landscape would be littered with putrid, decomposing carcasses.

The understandable connection between Vulture and the dead was observed and celebrated by many cultures. It was worshipped as a carrier of the dead by the people of Persia, who believed that a corpse had to be opened by Vulture before being committed to the grave to confirm safe passage of the soul. To this day, the dead are still placed in sacred towers to be worried by Vulture as an assurance of rebirth. It was also once said that all Vultures were female and that they immaculately conceived their offspring; a belief supported by the early Christian church as an explanation for the virgin birth. In Africa, the Vulture is called *tumbuzi*, 'the one who disembowels' and people hold Vulture in high esteem, classifying her as a 'soul bird' and as a carrier of the dead. Vulture clearly states that before any new beginning can be endorsed, a ritualistic death or notable ending must first be celebrated. Vulture heralds a time in which one must begin eliminating old habits and jaded approaches so that new ventures may be initiated. Cut out everything that may be described as petty, broken or tired and look, once again, to the fundamentals of life. Vulture's caring, loving energy supports those prepared to welcome endings as a chance to put outgrown aspects of life behind them. She helps suppress fear and anxiety by holding you close to her heart. She wants you to grow and reach your intended potential. She wants you to reject your inhibitions, limitations and indoctrinated beliefs and values. Such a process is seen as 'ritualistic death' because it represents the death of the familiar or programmed self in preparation for the sacred rebirth of the new. At times change may seem overwhelming and something to be feared and avoided, but when instigated in a safe, nurturing environment, one soon discovers that (both ritualistic and actual) death is inevitable, necessary and temporary. Vulture is benevolent and not something to be feared. She represents transition and the opportunity to lead a new, more fulfilling way of life.

Weasel
Remote viewing

 A ferocious and merciless hunter, Weasel is known to occupy the dens of animals he has killed, raising his young in nests lined with his victim's fur. Weasel is also known as Ermine, and has brown fur in the summer and snow-white fur in the winter. In either phase, a black tip is evident on the tail. Nocturnal by nature, Weasel is infamous for raiding chicken coops. Driven into a frenzy by the panicked birds, Weasel is known to kill randomly and then leave in a hurry without eating any. Weasel is a tiny but deadly hunter; stalking his prey with stealth and accuracy, rushing in for the kill without a sound. Weasel is hunted by Owl, Hawk and Snake, and by man for his thick, soft pelt. Weasel is also known for his keen eyesight, craftiness, inner stillness, control and profound tracking ability.

The people held his wisdom in high esteem as a quality that empowers the scout or warrior with stealth, silence and cunning. Those who carried Weasel were traditionally revered as spies. They were entrusted with the retrieval of information that afforded their people the upper hand. They would infiltrate enemy camps, sometimes in secret and sometimes under the guise of someone wanting to join their clan permanently. As if protected by a 'veil of invisibility', Weasel would quickly gain trust while gleaning vital information and once obtained, would then disappear into the shadows and return to his people with knowledge that would offer them great advantage. To this day, Weasel nurtures the ability to 'see' things not readily seen. Weasel people typically make competent psychics and mediums, for example, because they are able to gain access to the 'other worlds' and return with sacred wisdom unobtainable by any other means. Weasel people are also usually empowered by the gift of 'remote viewing'. Remote viewing enables one to see people, places or things without having to be physically present at the target sight. Weasel people have high integrity, are very loyal and radiate purity of heart. Weasel is a symbol of high standing and royalty. Weasel people are privy to secret information. They know things that they cannot explain. They are gifted with the ability to 'just know'. They will often say things in a manner that suggests they have been told or entrusted with personal information, when in fact they have tapped into the subconscious mind or Akashic Records of those with whom they are speaking. Weasel people are neither nosey nor gossipy. They gain their knowledge because they exude a deep sense of empathy and respect for people. They are very sensitive to the subtle realms and the energy of people. It is very difficult to keep anything hidden from a Weasel person, and is virtually impossible to lie to one.

Whale
Ground signatures

The Whale family, which includes Dolphin, Orca and Porpoise, represent some of the largest and most intelligent mammal that have ever lived on Earth. Whale has a streamlined body, dorsal fins and a pair of horizontal flukes on the end of the tail. She has nostrils located on the top of the head, affectionately known as 'blowholes'. Whales are typically divided into two subgroups: 'Toothed' and 'Baleen'. Toothed Whale preys on other marine creatures (Seal, Penguin and fish), while Baleen Whales strain tiny organisms, such as krill, through sheets of hair-like filamentation known as baleen. Whale plots her course using echolocation, a process by which low-frequency sound waves are emitted. Navigation is ensured by the messages received via the consequent echoes. Excessive hunting and human ignorance have led to many species of Whale being listed as endangered. Earth Mother has been trying to warn humanity for ages of the changes she has in store for us. She has been causing mudslides, earthquakes, floods, droughts and strong winds for centuries, but in recent years there have been an increased number of occurrences, with each major event proving more devastating than the one prior. The people who survived the Asian tsunami in 2004 for example, say the wave came out of nowhere and as it rushed the beach, hit with such force that it crushed everything in its path. Leading up to the tsunami, a large pod of Whales and Dolphins beached themselves in Tasmania, and I took it as a warning of the Earth Mother's unrest. Whale beaches herself 'all the time', but it was the unusual presence of Dolphin that truly rung the warning bell for me. It may surprise some and afford others a sense of comfort to know that despite the ferocity of the tsunami, not a single wild animal carcass was found by rescuers or aid workers. Many animals rely on atmospheric pressure to navigate their path using infrasound and, unlike us, have never lost their ability to communicate directly with the Earth Mother, nor have they forgotten their inherent relationship with the forces of Nature. Able to read the ground signatures sent by the Earth Mother as vibrational warnings, the animals would have begun to move inland at the first given indicator, following signs undetectable by humans. So why did the Whales and Dolphins beach themselves in Tasmania – not once, but twice? Sure, it may have been that their ability to read the ground signatures were confused by the tremors thus leading to the death of the entire pod, but I believe the animals acted on behalf of Earth Mother with an innate desire to see humanity heal and walk as one. I believe there will be more events. Maybe not tomorrow, but they will happen and we need to prepare *as a people*. We need to stop, take notice and begin to heal what we have done to our planet and see ourselves as accountable.

Whale stores Earth Mother's sacred records and pays witness to the proceedings that collectively authenticate the spiritual makeup of the Earth; the memories of each and every event that has ever contributed to her shaping and stores them deep within her being. Whale channels this information so that we might remember the spiritual history of those areas sacred to our personal journey. She offers ways to work with the land, to enhance our medicine, our lives and the planet as a whole. It is said that those who work with Whale hold within their DNA the ability to hear the secret language encoded in the audible rhythms and vibrations generated by the Earth Mother. The throbbing, metrical song of Whale offers us the chance to reconnect with the heartbeat of Earth Mother. It reminds us of the double heartbeat we heard as we grew in the womb of our mother, the sound of our heart beating in unison with hers. The more we fight amongst ourselves and allow chaos to rule, the more unsettled the planet will become. The more we judge and repress others, lie, manipulate, cheat and steal; the more we rape the planet and take that which is not rightfully ours, the greater the gap we build between our healing and that of Earth Mother. The more we refuse to acknowledge what is taking place in our own backyards and endeavour to right all our wrongs, the more Earth Mother will be compelled to eventually punish all her children by forcing them to take full responsibility for their actions, leaving them to face the consequences of their selfish, materialistic motivations alone. I believe this is why the Whales beached themselves. They were trying to wake us up before the Earth Mother gave up. Whale people are very sensitive to their environment and have a strong psychic connection to the Earth Mother. Whale people require stable surroundings and reliable relationships to maintain an overall sense of wellbeing. Whale inspires sensitivity to the vibrations emitted by the Earth Mother. This is why Whale people react so strongly to them. Whale forewarns us of the rumbles occurring within the Earth Mother's belly long before any resulting event can occur. Whale prepares us for inevitable geographical change in a balanced, practical way.

• Beluga Whale – *Appeasement*

Beluga Whale, also known as White Whale, White Porpoise, Sea Canary and Squid Hound, is a small member of the Toothed Whale family. Beluga means 'white one' in Russian. The Beluga's neck vertebrae are unfused, affording her great flexibility and she has no dorsal fin. She congregates in family pods of up to 10 individuals and is a relatively slow swimmer. Beluga is also known as a 'Sea Canary' because her song, which includes clicks, squeals and whistles, is so loud it is audible above the water. Her song is used to communicate with other Belugas, to calm her offspring and to warn other Belugas of approaching predators. She relies on echolocation to locate prey, breathing holes in the ice and to aide in general navigation. Orca and Polar Bear prey on Beluga and have hunted her for centuries.

An Inuit legend tells of Sedna, a young, wilful girl who accepted the advances of a mysterious young man from a far off place. He promised her a good life but returning to his land he revealed himself in his true form: a huge Seabird. She was forced to endure a rank-smelling nest covered in excrement and nothing but rotting fish to eat. Sedna and her father stole away in his boat and the Seabird conjured up a huge storm that threatened to capsize the boat and drown them. Fearing for his life, the father threw his daughter into the sea, but Sedna clutched at the side of the boat. Afraid that she would tip the boat over, he cut off her fingers with his fishing knife and she sank into the depths, her amputated fingers becoming Seals, Orcas, Belugas, Walruses, Polar Bears and fish; her fingernails transforming into whalebone. Sedna is revered as a 'food dish', the protector of all life in the sea and as 'she who sustains the people'. The animals of the ocean are happy to be hunted by the Inuit people because they know the people love Sedna, grieve her death and revere her power and generosity. As a representation of Sedna's power, Beluga Whale speaks of *appeasement* and the realisation of forgiveness. Beluga Whale alleviates the natural propensity to yearn, particularly when it is in vain, and helps us find peace in the knowing 'what's done is done'. Beluga Whale supports us as we come to terms with things no longer in our control. She helps us resist the futile temptation to panic or fruitlessly offer apologies and beg for forgiveness. Beluga Whale does not offer endurance to whingers, finger pointers or those not willing to take ownership for their behaviour. Beluga Whale teaches us to remain calm, admit fault and show accountability for our actions. She nurtures acceptance for the outcome of our conduct and, over time, reinstates pure intent, a reformed heart and a willingness to learn from our mistakes. Beluga Whale people are those who have made major blunders in life. They tend to be people who seemingly put their own wants and needs before those of others and who then must pay for their actions with a loss of freedom, trust or respect. They seem to need to experience the very worst in life before they find peace within themselves. Beluga Whale people always come through okay (they are survivors), but not before risking everything and nearly losing the lot in their struggle to maintain stability and reason.

Beluga Whale is beautiful. She is gentle, reassuring and full of promise and encourages us to slow down, to look around and appreciate the beauty we have in our life. She helps us sing from the heart in celebration of the gifts we have and the treasures that surround us and for those yet to be found. When we are touched by the acumen of Beluga Whale, we can rest assured that things will resolve in a manner befitting the circumstances and that everything will turn out okay.

• Narwhal Whale – *Detoxification*

Narwhal Whale has only two teeth, both of which are found in the upper jaw. The female's teeth usually remain hidden from view, but the male Narwhal is famous for his spiralled tusk, which can grow up to 3 metres long. The tusk is simply one of his teeth which has broken free and grown. The integrity and length of the tusk announces his potency to the females, with the males often sparring for the right to mate using his tusks as weapons. Narwhal Whale's single, corkscrewed 'horn' was harvested for centuries as the 'alicorn', the one tangible alternative to the mysterious horn of Unicorn. In medieval times, the ivory tusks were literally worth their weight in gold and were believed to purify water of pollutants and to clear the cloudiest of pools when submerged and said to offer instant cure for any illness.

Narwhal encourages us to cleanse our life of toxins; to purify our mind, body and spirit of negative influence. He encourages us to rid our lives of poisons and impurities, while affording the endurance required to vanquish all addictions. If Narwhal Whale has made his presence felt therefore, you may need to reassess your diet, your environment and the integrity of the medicines you may have begun to rely on. You may also want to totally detoxify your environment. Chemical overload in our homes and workplace will potentially affect our vitality, creativity and general happiness. Instead of relying on commercially produced pharmaceutical drugs or chemical-based treatments consider more 'user friendly' alternatives: vitamins, homeopathic, naturopathic and herbal remedies; vibrational remedies like essences or aromatherapy; relaxation massage, meditation, exercise and meaningful, reciprocal conversation.

• Orca – *Bounty*

Orca, or Killer Whale is the largest member of the Dolphin family. Orca is found in all the ocean's of the world and is commonly referred to as the 'Wolf of the sea'. She travels in family-oriented pods of 50 or more and is considered stable as a species. Despite no longer being a target by commercial whalers, Orca is still occasionally trapped for display in marine parks. Orca is perhaps most famous for her impressive dorsal fins. Orca is a powerful swimmer, often seen leaping clear of the water and falling back with a splash. Orca is an expert hunter who teams up and herds her prey. She has been observed upending floating bodies of ice, dislodging Seals basking in the sun. As the Seals tumble into the water Orca is waiting, circling ready to catch them. She will also swim with great speed into the shallows (often nearly beaching herself in the process) to snatch Penguin and Seal as they rest on the shore, and will even smash up through thin ice, taking Seal and Penguin from below as they go about their business on the ice above.

Orca helps us gather what we need to ensure a bountiful life. Orca ensures that we always have enough to eat and that we never go without by instilling a sense of resourcefulness and endurance. Orca attracts abundance and providence by encouraging us to take responsibility for our future while reminding us of the inherent skills, strengths and wisdom we have garnered over a lifetime of experience. Orca encourages us to think creatively, to look for different and new ways of tackling problems that may have once baffled or overwhelmed us. Orca offers a chance for us to rebirth on all levels. It was not uncommon in early stories for the hero of a story to be swallowed by a Whale, with their journey into the creature's belly being symbolic of our descent into the Underworld on our 'death' and their eventual re-emergence representing our inevitable rebirth. Orca offers the chance to start over, to transmute negative experiences into gifts of power. Orca people are able to see a situation for what it is and to think outside the box in order to benefit from it. They surrender all feelings of anxiety and fear and breathe their way through their moments of self-doubt. In doing so, they remove the obstacles created by limiting belief and easily find the clarity and awareness that may have previously eluded them. Orca reminds us that when we ask for something, we must be prepared to offer something in exchange – even if it is only two words, 'Thank you'. Thankfulness and humility are the keys to receiving true abundance. Call upon Orca to help find peace in the circumstances that have befallen you and use the wisdom found to benefit your life and those around you. Invoke Orca to harness the wisdom of the ocean and to better understand the wealth of life and knowledge that she holds.

Wildebeest
The victim

 Also known as the Gnu, Wildebeest is a member of the bovine family. She has downward curving horns with ends that point up and inward. Wildebeest grazes on open grasslands in breeding herds of up to 150 females, their calves and approximately three males. During the dry season many groups will unite to form a great herd that may contain tens of thousands of animals and, as such, will travel up to 1,600 kilometres in

search of water. After a gestation period of eight and a half months, each female will produce a single calf, many of which fall prey to Lion and Hunting Dog.

In her purest form, Wildebeest offers a strength and perception that protects against being wronged by others. She helps us become more conscious of situations that may lead to us to being taken advantage of, while instilling a depth of insight that allows us to realise and celebrate the inherent victim trait that is alive and well within all of us. In her positive role, Wildebeest effectively guides us in and out of these moments of apprehension and misunderstanding until we say 'No more', and put our foot down. Wildebeest affords the skills and strategies needed to embrace life's challenges, face our fears and integrate the gift of inner strength. Wildebeest assumes the 'flock approach'. Wildebeest warns of the risk of being propelled by mass hysteria or of being brainwashed by trendy or offbeat beliefs. When you wholeheartedly give your power over to someone or something else, you run the risk of losing your sacred individuality and you become 'one of a mob'. You sell yourself out and lose your voice. You may begin acting irrationally or become blind to perils that would normally be recognised and avoided, hazards detected by sound thinking, personal judgment and acumen. Congregating as a means of offering support, celebration or ceremony is to come together in a productive way. It benefits the whole party, with such a gathering usually the result of individual consent. Putting excessive trust or relying too heavily on the recognition or authentication obtained from dominant or manipulative sources external to one's self, however, suggests a lack of trust in one's self-worth and personal judgment. Such a tendency hampers vision, restricts movement and limits choice. Wildebeest, therefore, stimulates the need to take stock of our own life, to take responsibility for our actions and to begin productively nurturing ourselves on all levels. Wildebeest banishes forever the 'victim mentality' that endorses the 'it wasn't my fault' attitude or the belief that we cannot succeed unsupported or on our own steam.

Wolf

The pack

The Wolf family includes Dingo, Coyote, Jackal, African Hunting Dog, Dhole (or Red Dog), Racoon Dog, domestic Dog and Fox.

• Arctic Wolf – *Robustness*

Arctic Wolf occupies some of the most unwelcoming environments in the world; a land bombarded by mercilessly cold weather and extended periods of darkness. He travels in tight family groups led by a dominant breeding pair, with all adults responsible for the feeding and care of the young. Patrolling huge territories, Arctic Wolf eats every part of his kill, including the skin, fur and bones because he never knows when he will be fortunate enough to eat again. Arctic Wolf is a cooperative hunter, stalking prey together in packs. Wolf has been persecuted by man throughout history as a perceived threat to domestic stock or for superstitious reasons.

Arctic Wolf backs us up and supports us as we consider the process of change and offers resilience to those who have spent a lifetime battling the system: a system that would otherwise see them surrender and succumb to demand. People who refuse to yield to pressure are those who carry the wisdom of Arctic Wolf in their heart of hearts. He offers a voice loud enough to be heard, so that we might fight our case and defend our rights to live how we see fit, so long as our actions do not impinge on the lives of those around us. Arctic Wolf endorses tradition and the ancestral ways of the people. He says, 'If it was good enough for my family, then it is good enough for me'. Arctic Wolf people rarely move house, for example, and they drive old cars and have difficulty keeping up with modern tastes, expressions, fashions and technological advancements. They are not so much 'old fashioned' as they are 'stuck in their ways'. They dig in their heels and display determination and resolve in all that they do. They rarely give in and never surrender without first putting up a good fight. Arctic Wolf people are savers, hoarders and survivors and know how to make do. They have known a life of hardship and have become resourceful and robust as a result. They hold onto things 'just in case' and hate letting go. Once they make up their mind, little or nothing can be done to sway their decision. They see yielding to pressure as being a sign of weakness and as giving away their power and of selling their soul to the devil. They are difficult to take care of in their later years therefore, because they do not appreciate decisions being made for them or to have their daily routine changed or altered without their consent. Arctic Wolf offers great wisdom; wisdom gleaned from tried and true methods, tradition and the teachings of the Ancestors. He offers endurance to battle on regardless, to turn our face to the wind and to soldier on.

• Black Wolf – *The shadow self*

Black Wolf displays a melanistic colour variation; a mutation commonly seen in domestic dogs and cats. But apart from coat colour variation, Black Wolf is the same species as Grey Wolf.

Every one of us has a shadow side; an aspect of our personality that could – depending on the level of freedom and voice we choose to afford it – be described as opportunistic, lustful and predatory. As an archetype, Black Wolf can reference the licentious quality of some people, in particular the darker, lascivious, sexually driven side of human nature. Red Riding Hood, for example, is best known for the wolf that hungrily stalked her through the forest as she journeyed to her grandmother's house. Some may assume it was because he, as a carnivorous beast, wanted to eat the girl. But, in truth, the famous red hooded cape was symbolic of her virginal state (being that she was not yet a woman), while his wolf-form was representational of his desire – as a predatory male – to couple with her. As such, Black Wolf teaches us to learn from the lessons offered to us by our 'shadow self'; that dark aspect of self that we tend to keep private...

• Grey Wolf – *The pathfinder*

 Grey, or Timber Wolf, is now endangered. Grey Wolf is not always grey and can also be black, brown, white or a combination of colours. Mexican Wolf is a subspecies of Grey Wolf but due to over-hunting is now almost extinct in the wild. Efforts to save the species have led to a captive breeding program aimed at some day reintroducing the animal into pockets of his original habitat. Grey Wolf is a social animal, living in family groups of between six to 10 individuals. Each pack contains a dominant breeding pair: an 'alpha' male and female, their current pups and usually the previous year's pups as well. In order for a subordinate animal to attain breeding status, he can either remain with the natal pack and work his way up the hierarchy or leave the clan entirely, find a mate and start his own pack. Remaining with the family group often means running the risk of never achieving dominance, and leaving makes him vulnerable to attack from rival packs and humans. Despite being profoundly loyal to the family group, individualism is also held high in esteem by Grey Wolf. It is said that although he is happy to remain within the family setting, it is not uncommon for an individual to get it into their head to venture out into the world and 'seek their fortune' – with little or no warning.

The sharing of knowledge is deemed a sacred act for Grey Wolf. He plays with and protects pups belonging to other members of the clan, contributing his 'wisdom' like a tutor or guide. Enhancing or building upon the knowledge however, is considered even more significant and it is with this intention that Grey Wolf will break away from his pack and go in search (as the 'lone Wolf') for new and greater wisdom. Traditionally, Grey Wolf is the totem of the teacher, pioneer and guide. Grey Wolf encourages us to break away from traditional belief, organised religion, family settings, jobs that demand regular work hours, and any other conventional, structured system that limits or shuns creative thinking and free-spirited ideals. Grey Wolf instils a strong sense of self, purpose and direction. He invites us to respectfully put all our indoctrinated beliefs, conventional thought patterns and traditional values aside, with the intention of developing a whole new set that will nurture us as individuals. Grey Wolf will never lead you astray or leave you stranded in an unknown forest. Rather, he is imbued with integrity and purpose designed to inspire and augment self-esteem, personal power and direction. Those drawn to follow the path of Grey Wolf usually find themselves breaking away from the structure and order of mundane existence to explore the broader, subtler realms of life. Armed with wisdom and sacred knowledge previously unknown to their people, they revisit what was familiar and share what they have learned, thus enhancing and deepening the spiritual foundation of their clan. According to tradition, Wolf people impart knowledge easily and effectively because they work from a place of pure intent. They appreciate the value of dynamic languaging, stimulating voice inflection and non-threatening body language. They make efficient problem solvers while quickly instituting a nurturing environment and support network for their students reminiscent of a responsive family setting.

• Maned Wolf – *Perspective*

Maned Wolf, or 'The Fox on Stilts', is largely solitary. A pair will share a territory but will rarely come together – except to mate. Omnivorous by nature, Maned Wolf feeds on small mammal, birds, fruit and insects and occasionally domestic animals but chooses to avoid carrion. Maned Wolf relies on the height advantage offered by his legs to spy prey animals hiding in tall grass. Because of his long, graceful legs, the 'Fox on Stilts' can offer wider perspective to those who seek its wisdom.

Maned Wolf lifts us out of the mundane and offers us the wisdom necessary to seize opportunity and run with it. Never satisfied to be described as plain, normal or ordinary, Maned Wolf represents those who dare to think big, dress big and act big, and who view themselves as different or special in some unique way. Maned Wolf people love bright clothes and gaudy accessories. They are often described as 'go getters' or 'head hunters' and are people who sniff out and stalk potential rather than waiting for it to come to them. They are always noticed as the centre of attention and, because of their cheerful, captivating personalities, they are always first on the list of prospects when it comes to promotion in the workplace or advancement in general. Maned Wolf offers 'height advantage', either physically or symbolically to those who carry his acumen. For those who are tall or 'big', Maned Wolf enhances the psychological advantages of being tall by including integrity and balance. For those who lack physical stature, confidence or experience but yearn to be seen as 'big', Maned Wolf promotes hope and foresight that will motivate others to share their vision. Maned Wolf people are lucid dreamers, creative thinkers and leaders. Many of today's successful entrepreneurs are Maned Wolf people because they view themselves as rising up in the world, offering them a greater advantage than those who are afraid to rise from their seat let alone any level of repute. Maned Wolf espouses the belief that when you view yourself as successful and abundant (in a practical, honest way), you raise others to your level of consciousness. In raising them up, you offer them hope and a wider perspective. They enjoy the feeling and vow to maintain it, thus instilling a mentality of abundance instead of lack. An illusion of sorts, Maned Wolf creates an air of accomplishment that inspires others to view you as established, popular and successful in your field; a role model and mentor to those following in your footsteps.

• Red Wolf – *Call of the wild*

Red Wolf is a small relation of Grey Wolf. His coat ranges in colour from cinnamon to red, and from grey to black. Red Wolf congregates in small family packs, usually consisting of a monogamous adult pair and their two or three pups. Before being classified as extinct in the wild, Red Wolf roamed the temperate deciduous forests, coastal prairies and marshes of North America. Habitat loss due to agriculture, logging and human encroachment, excessive hunting and crossbreeding with Coyote have contributed largely to the decline in pure Red Wolf numbers. Red Wolf was one persecuted as a killer of livestock, but with his eradication came an increase in Coyote populations. Although extinct in the wild, Red Wolf has not been entirely lost to us. Captive breeding programs have been established, with intentions of someday reintroducing Red Wolf back into his natural habitat. Howling is an important and effective means of communication for all species of Wolf. Wolf howls to define territory, advertise or defend a kill and to bring the pack together. The howl of Wolf is captivating. It inspires mixed emotions, from those of fear and dread to that of celebration and freedom. To many, the howl of Wolf is reminiscent of shape-shifters, Were Wolves and impending change. Shape-shifting forms the hub of many cultures, religions and traditional belief systems. For centuries, rituals have integrated shape-shifting practices into their arrangement.

Red Wolf embodies the raw essence and sacredness of shape-shifting. Shape-shifting fuses the spirit of an animal with that of an individual seeking its wisdom. By studying the movements and behavioural patterns of this animal in the tangible sense and deepening our understanding by watching him with our mind's eye during vision and meditation, we can learn the symbolic and magickal language of his ways: his wisdom and sacred powers. Once we become familiar with these workings we can, with Red Wolf's guidance, imitate and then integrate them into our everyday lives via dance and dramatic movement. Red Wolf changes our mental perception of our body, enabling us to translate an animal's message or power into reality, thus confirming the intent for performing a ritual in the first place. By demonstrating our willingness to look at our physical form as a corporeal representation of an animal's spirit, Red Wolf helps us drop our inhibitions and ego and walk as one with Spirit. When we do this freely, the ordinary world stops, the Wolf listens and the wild welcomes us home.

Wolverine

Insatiability

 Wolverine, or Skunk Bear, is a rare member of the Weasel family and is the larger 'cousin' of Marten. Wolverine is known for her tenacity and determination, aggressively defending her need for freedom. She is found in high elevation forests and alpine regions, enjoying a life of solitude and isolation. Wolverine is an adept tree climber and will eat just about anything from fruit to carrion. Her Latin name is *Gulo Gulo*, which means glutton. However, she only eats what she needs and hoards and defends the rest for later. Once a Wolverine identifies a regular source of food she will visit that source again and again until it is exhausted. She must display insatiable qualities in order to survive. She protects her cache by marking it with a musky odour immediately recognised by other carnivores. With a stocky build, ferocious dog-like Wolverine powerfully protects her territory against intruders. Names like 'devil bear', 'demon of the north' and 'evil one' have helped confirm the malevolent reputation of Wolverine as an uncompromising scavenger. Wolverine is completely intolerant of humans and Wolves. She depends solely on the wilderness for her survival and anything that threatens that way of life creates chaos in her world.

Wolverine warns us to take what we need, to prepare well for the future, but to never emotionally bite off more than we can swallow before considering our motives or personal integrity. Wolverine people work hard for what they have. They strive to live good, wholesome lives, but often find themselves disillusioned by society because of repetitive or cyclic negative interaction or disappointing experiences that build and build and eventually tip them over the edge. Like a distant memory, Wolverine people know goodness exists, but have difficulty accessing it or finding in their world. Instead of trusting the joy found in family and friends, Wolverine people are typically bad tempered, intolerant and cynical. They are often loners and surround themselves with rare and beautiful material possessions and often have healthy bank accounts. Wolverine invites us to explore the wilderness, to spend time alone and to journey within the sacred self. In doing so we may find the space to address our fears and heal ourselves on a deep, personal level. Wolverine espouses the simple truth that if you do not know yourself then no one else will ever truly know you either. Wolverine endorses the taking of emotional risks by allowing others to gain access to your heart. She assures us that just because we may have had a string of bad experiences (or just one significant one) that may have threatened our emotional integrity, it is never too late to welcome love back into our life.

Wombat
Gentle aggression

Wombat walks with a slow, lumbering gait but can run at a fast pace when alarmed. Wombat lives in underground burrows up to 20 metres long and hollows it out by lying on her side and digging with front legs, pushing the dirt out with her hind feet. Largely a nocturnal, herbivorous creature, Wombat has no real predators. She can defend herself against Dingo and Wild Dog by means of powerful claws, sharp teeth and a thick hide. Females have a backward-facing pouch so that it doesn't fill with dirt as she excavates her tunnel. Wombat is an aggressive, bad-tempered animal that often falls prey to cars as she casually ambles across country roads at night. The claws of an adult Wombat are capable of ripping open the belly of a marauding canine, but this is a threat held in reserve and activated only when absolutely necessary. Equipped with cartilage plating in her rump, a female Wombat will block her burrow by sitting face first just inside the opening of her den when Dingo threatens entry. A hungry Dingo may attempt to force access by chewing on the rump of the Wombat but with no feeling to weaken its stance Wombat proves a fearless adversary. Determined to protect her young, Wombat initially waits and will crouch down if Dingo persists, apparently allowing Dingo access to her den. Eager to get to the young Dingo crawls over Wombat, wedging between the roof of the den and Wombat's strong backbone. Wombat then stands up, crushing Dingo against the roof of the tunnel. Despite being physically built for the fight, Wombat chooses to express herself assertively first, reverting to aggressive confrontation only when necessary. She relies on the virtue of her rivals, hoping that they will see her point while she preserves her energy in case raw hostility becomes necessary. She prefers to negotiate initially, expressing herself plainly and reverting to force only when all else fails.

Wombat Walks her Talk. She tells things exactly how she sees them. She will not be put down or belittled by anyone. She views her opinions, beliefs and values as sacred and definitely worthy of recognition. She insists that others take heed of her opinions and is self-assured enough to outwardly enforce her demands. If she has to, she will implement her expectations vehemently, even physically if need be, but until the need arises she expresses herself with gentle force, influence and tenacity. To 'Walk one's Talk' is vital if one wishes to live a balanced, wholesome, spiritual life. Wombat teaches us to speak up and to confront all wrongs aimed at us with confidence and self-assuredness. Although she rejects being overly forceful, violent or rude in our delivery, Wombat upholds the belief that everyone has the right to express their opinions without fear of reprisal, and understands how easy it is to feel impatient and intolerant of those who refuse to listen to advice rooted in wisdom and experience. Wombat speaks of assertion and determination and metaphorically digs for truth, revealing it as wisdom found deep within our psyche. Wombat brings us back to our centre and restores personal power, clarity and self-worth. She grounds us as we set about doing what feels right for us instead of wasting attention on the superficial demands of others. She helps us temper rage, feelings of frustration and resentment and turns aggression into assertiveness. Wombat is one of Earth Mother's keepers of herbal lore; the medicinal properties of the plants, flowers and herbs. Ask yourself if you need to visit a natural therapist, particularly a naturopath, traditional herbalist, homoeopath or practitioner of Chinese medicine. Thank Wombat for her wisdom and be sure to follow it through with resolve and tenacity. If you do you will not only discover a way to heal yourself, you will also find yourself 'walking your talk'.

Woodpecker
Heartbeat

 Woodpecker belongs to the *Picidae* family, which includes Flicker and Sapsucker. Woodpecker has a chisel-shaped beak and a long, sharp tongue suited to drilling and probing under tree bark and powerful claws that allow her to cling vertically to tree trunks. She has an extra thick skull and special sacs that cushion the brain against impact, studies of which have led to technology offering assistance and prevention of head injury in humans. Woodpecker is easily encouraged to visit household gardens using bird-feeders stocked with commercially prepared feed. Woodpecker is more often than not seen drilling into the bark of dead trees, thus curbing the spread of boring insects into healthy trees. Woodpecker also provides valuable den sites for tree-dwelling mammal, reptiles and other crevice-nesting birds.

Woodpecker is apparently named after Picus, the son of Saturn, who regularly called upon the bird to help hone his augury skills. According to another legend, Woodpecker was called the 'boat builder's bird', sent to Earth to show man how to hollow out tree trunks and make canoes. Woodpecker was also said to personify the energy of fire and lightning, a truth realised in the red flashes that stain her plumage and by her habit of pecking wood – a sound that resembles the striking of flint to spark a flame. The drum-like rhythm of Woodpecker echoes the pulse of the Earth Mother's heart. Its rhythm guides us to other dimensions, new opportunity and heightened levels of awareness. Woodpecker offers clarity and awareness and the shunning of tunnel vision. We are often so consumed by mental and spiritual activity that we tend to neglect the tangible world, our health and other responsibilities. Woodpecker reminds us to tap into our inherent rhythms and to intuitively listen to what our body may be trying to tell us about our physical wellbeing. Woodpecker reinstates a sense of emotional balance, buoyancy and stability. She helps us regain a solid foothold on life and rekindle the fire in our belly and returns us to our centre. Woodpecker stabilises our emotional body and heals physical imbalance by tapping into our DNA, retrieving our sense of identity and personal truth. The drumming sound of Woodpecker is reminiscent of the double heartbeat a child hears while in the womb. The power of Woodpecker is realised audibly and vibrationally, thus realigning all beings on a united heartfelt level. Woodpecker reawakens ancient knowledge stored in the memory of all people. She nurtures us as we seek the wisdom held in store, to be remembered when we re-embrace the heartbeat of our Earth Mother. She is the balancing force of the planet and personifies the heartbeat of the Earth Mother, thus monitoring and interpreting the ground signatures that warn of geographical change.

Wren
Ambition

 'Wren' is the common name given to members of the insectivorous songbird family. Wren constructs woven basket-like nests from twigs and grasses, often suspended from branches too delicate for larger predatory birds. Wren is a common sight in most country gardens and darts from one branch to the next among the shrubs and low-growing bushes, or hops across the lawn in search of small insects. Wren travels in small flocks of six to 12 individuals. Domestic Cat is a major predator. Wren appears in legends from all around the world, usually associated with intelligence, strength of mind, endurance, ambition and bravery.

A fable once told of a competition between members of the bird kingdom where representatives from every species participated to discover who could fly closest to the sun; closest to the Creator. Afterwards, all the birds fell back to Earth exhausted, dehydrated or burned black from the sun's heat knowing that the only one truly capable of successfully completing the task was Eagle, who regally stood back waiting for his turn to compete. Spiralling higher and higher Eagle flew, until it was quite evident that he had won the competition. Eagle was surprised to hear a frantic little voice above his head say, 'What about me?' And a Wren was worriedly flapping his wings with perspiration pouring from his brow, and his feathers were beginning to melt. Eagle smiled for he knew that the little bird could never have flown that high without assistance. 'Well done', Eagle whispered. No one had noticed, including Eagle, that Wren had hidden himself in the Eagle's feathers. Wren knew that he had taken a huge risk and had assumed that the Eagle, as an emissary of Spirit, would not betray his honourable view of the world and would eat him to hide his defeat. Eagle recognised this act of brave resolve and announced Wren as the victor, rewarding him with the title of 'bravest and most ambitious bird'. Wren heralds the coming of new challenges fuelled by unwavering faith in our ability to achieve them. Wren carries the torch of the East: the beacon of illumination, intuition and intellect. He embodies the ability 'to know' – the light that tempers the darkness within so that we might welcome change. Wren helps us to envisage our future, maintain mental lucidity and to close old doors so that we may open new ones.

Zebra
Individuality

Zebra is best known for her varied stripe patterns. Mares give birth to a single foal after a gestation period of one year. Seven to 10 days after giving birth, females will mate again, with the foal at foot being weaned at one year of age. Immediately after birth, Zebra foal sets about memorising his mother's stripe pattern so that he may identify her from the other females in the group. Family herds, maintained over a lifetime, are led by a single dominant male, typically containing six mares and their young. Occasionally, however, several family groups will merge to form a larger, stronger herd. On first glance, the natural and immediate assumption is that all Zebras look the same. The truth is however, that no two Zebras bear the same stripe pattern. Like human fingerprints, Zebras each have a clearly defined and unique stripe pattern that marks them as individuals.

Horse generically manifests the understanding of Personal Power. Personal Power was given to us by Creation in the hope that we would share it with others while teaching them how to discover their own. Personal Power must never be wasted or kept to ourselves, but shared for the benefit of humanity. Zebra (also known as Tiger Horse) follows typical equine tradition by offering those who look to her wisdom the ability to harness their own Personal Power by offering a sense of balance and direction. By breaking through the illusion that as individuals we do not have a united voice, and that we must comply with stereotypes and expectation and we are 'just numbers' within the system called 'life', Zebra reminds us that if we ever want to find out what our life purpose is, what it means to have Personal Power and why we are here, we must first realise the magic that comes from identifying our own sacred individuality. We may all look the same at first glance, but we each carry a unique genetic blueprint that disaffiliates us, in a healthy way, from everyone and everything on the planet. With the combined wisdom of Tiger and Horse, we may learn to combat cowardice and insecurity, face our fears and harness our purpose by embracing the wisdom of Zebra. Zebra encourages us to put our ears back and gallop in the first direction that takes our fancy, to explore what the journey offers and to integrate the learning as our Personal Power. It is not the destination that counts, but rather the path that takes us there. The secret is to remember that you are unique: a perfect being worthy of a perfect life tailored to your individual needs. You owe it to yourself, now, to stop the pretence that you are 'just one of a crowd', and to begin seeing yourself as unique and worthy of being heard. You *do* have something to offer. You *do* hold power. You *can* and *will* make a difference because you hold within you sacred knowledge that no one else can deliver: a beautiful and individual intended by Spirit to be shared with the people.

CONCLUSION

The inner-city shaman

Those lucky enough to live in the country tend to take the silence and solitude for granted. You almost expect to receive signs from the animals on a daily basis. Taking a stroll down the driveway to collect the mail may be met with the cry of Hawk heralding incoming messages, or the discovery of a mob of Kangaroos in the neighbouring paddock encouraging you to take that leap of faith you have been trying hard to ignore. You may even find a puddle of Tadpoles that nag you to consult your inner child in regard to some unresolved emotional issue.

Life in the city is different. She waits for no one. In the city, the paddocks you see in the country become billboards, bush tracks become bitumen roads, gardens become balconies lined with potted geraniums and great bodies of water become earthenware bowls on your windowsill. You must look to the trees in inner-city parks as spiritual support as you meditate to find answers, while many of the rituals and ceremonies normally performed outdoors are now confined to indoors. You learn to interpret the wisdom of the animals that dwell in the city instead of the wild beasts of the wood-lands and fields. The 'feral' Pigeon seeks to remind you to touch base with family and friends from time to time, Ants parading on the pavement ask for patience and teamwork, while adaptable Possum encourages you to take responsibility for your own actions and to develop strategies that will enhance your quality of life. That Starling feather being washed along the flooded gutter may be hinting at the need for emotional adaptation, while Seagull hovering over the grimy, recirculated water in the city-square fountain may be suggesting that you ride out current upheavals and to avoid unnecessary squabbles.

City life does not need to be difficult, restrictive or spiritually unrewarding. Spirit has provided more than enough signals to confirm and encourage. When you feel alone or at a loss, do as the wise ones did of centuries past, consult Nature and Spirit. Find yourself a sacred space, sit quietly, and find the inner silence. Allow your eyes to wander over the cityscape. What do you see? Look with your inner eye and your heart. Feel the city and look for its animals. Allow the animals to come to you. Do not allow the muggy, dirty, full-on rush of the city confuse you. Do not allow the heat, the panic, the 'Oh my God, I'm late' attitude of the people to sway your focus. When you see your animal teacher, ask it to share its wisdom. Let the words enter your mind intuitively and listen carefully. Do not interrupt and certainly do not try to analyse. Write your message down and forget about it. Later, read it again and meditate on it if you wish. This is your answer. It may be something as simple as Turtledove eating crumbs on the steps of Parliament House, whispering something as profound as the confirmed love of another, or Parrot on the side of the Arnott's biscuit truck that may be silently congratulating you for being spontaneous, chatty and brightly dressed in colours that contradict the dull grey of the city.

Animal signs are limitless. They are as easy to find in the city as they are in the country. Even in the city, however, one must give thanks and make offerings in return for the knowledge received. Visit a piece of Nature (she is very determined and will show up in the most unlikely places: the pond in the grounds of the city hospital, a tree in the park or the circular flower display at the front of the fast food store), give thanks and push a small offering into the soil, out of sight of other people. The cycle is now complete.

All that is left for you to do is to wait.

NOTES

NOTES

NOTES

NOTES

Titles by
Scott Alexander King

Books
- Afterworld
- Animal Dreaming
- Earth Mother Dreaming
- Indigo Children and Cheeky Monkeys
- World Animal Dreaming

Oracle Cards and Tarot:
- Animal Dreaming Oracle Cards
- Bohemian Animal Tarot
- Creature Teacher Cards
- Nature's Wisdom Message Cards
- Oracle of the Innocent Heart
- World Animal Dreaming Oracle Cards

Meditation CDs:
- Celebrating Australia's WHEEL OF LIFE
- Healing with the Animals
- Meet your Power Animal

ABOUT THE AUTHOR

Scott Alexander King was born to love animals. He spent much of his childhood observing, drawing and writing about the animals he experienced in the small, tattered journal he always carried in his pocket. He would record every animal he saw: where he saw them, what they looked like and what they were doing at the time. This was an activity he never tired of. So much so that, in essence, he's still doing it today!

Scott is the author of the best-selling, internationally recognised *Animal Dreaming* – a shamanic reference book and field guide that offers spiritual insights into over 200 native and introduced Australian animals and birds and the *Animal Dreaming Oracle Cards*. He is also a husband (he met his beautiful wife in a pet shop!) and a father of three. He and his family – along with a huge menagerie of animals – live in the breathtaking Northern Rivers where he endeavours to write every day. Scott is available for workshops, seminars, readings and interviews.

Visit his official website www.animaldreaming.com or seek him out on Facebook www.facebook.com/scottalexanderking